China and the West:
Comparative Literature Studies

中西比較文學論集

China and the West:
Comparative Literature Studies

Edited by
William Tay · Ying-hsiung Chou · Heh-hsiang Yuan

with an introduction by A. Owen Aldridge

The Chinese University Press
Hong Kong

© 1980 by The Chinese University of Hong Kong

All Rights Reserved

International Standard Book Number: 962-201-201-9

Calligraphy by Dr. Ambrose Y. C. King

Distributed by
The University of Washington Press
Seattle and London

Printed by Union Printing Company, Hong Kong

CONTENTS

	Preface	i
A. Owen Aldridge	Introduction	iii
Douwe W. Fokkema	New Strategies in the Comparative Study of Literature and Their Application to Contemporary Chinese Literature	1
André Lefevere	Some Tactical Steps Toward a Common Poetics	9
Wai-lim Yip	The Taoist Aesthetic: *Wu-yen tu-hua*, the Unspeaking, Self-generating, Self-conditioning, Self-transforming, Self-complete Nature	17
W. L. Wong	Selection of Lines in Chinese Poetry-talk Criticism—With a Comparison between the Selected Couplets and Matthew Arnold's "Touchstones"	33
Tak-wai Wong	Period Style and Periodization: A Survey of Theory and Practice in the Histories of Chinese and European Literature	45
C. H. Wang	The Bird as Messenger of Love in Allegorical Poetry	69
Dominic Cheung	Carolyn Kizer and Her Chinese Imitations	77
Ling Chung	The Reception of Cold Mountain's Poetry in the Far East and the United States	85
Ping-leung Chan	The Tragic Theme in *Li sao*	97
Ying-hsiung Chou	"Lord, Do Not Cross the River": Literature as a Mediating Process	109

William Tay	The Substantive Level Revisited: Concreteness and Nature Imagery in T'ang Poetry	127
Thomas Yuntong Luk	A Cinematic Interpretation of Wang Wei's Nature Poetry	151
Andrew H. Plaks	Full-length *Hsiao-shuo* and the Western Novel: A Generic Reappraisal	163
Francis K. H. So	Some Rhetorical Conventions of the Verse Sections of *Hsi-yu chi*	177
Han-liang Chang	The *Yang Lin* Story Series: A Structural Analysis	195
Clara Yü Cuadrado	Cross-cultural Currents in the Theatre: China and the West	217
Simon S. C. Chau	The Nature and Limitations of Shakespeare Translation	239
Ping-cheung Cheung	*Tou O yüan* as Tragedy	251
Antony Tatlow	Peasant Dialectics: Reflections on Brecht's Sketch of a Dilemma	277
John J. Deeney	Comparative Literature and China: A Bibliographical Review of Materials in English	287
	Contributors	303
	Subject Index	307
	Name and Title Index	313

PREFACE

The appearance of the book signifies a hope that our future effort will be a continuing pursuit of the goal of the Hong Kong Comparative Literature Association; namely, to bring about a better understanding between the comparatists of the East and the West through a study of the literary heritages of both worlds.

The diversity of the topics, of the approaches, and of the concepts in this volume reveals a flexible attitude characterizing the founding principles of the Hong Kong Comparative Literature Association, which are also shared by friends and colleagues at the two universities in Hong Kong (The Chinese University of Hong Kong and the University of Hong Kong) and in academic institutions elsewhere. The constitution of the advisory board shows a comprehensive geographical and academic representation. It is our belief that such sharing and such representation are symbolic of the communication of minds which, though diverse in speculation, are singular in intention: to seek understanding and enlightenment. This belief in the mind as the meeting ground for intellectuals of different backgrounds and views provides the stimulation that inspires the enthusiasm of many who have given their time and effort to bring this volume to the readers.

Enthusiasm alone is insufficient; cooperative effort is essential in materialising ideas in presentable forms. In this case, the editors of this volume are grateful for the advice of Drs. John J. Deeney, Antony Tatlow, Tak-wai Wong, W. L. Wong, and Professors Douwe Fokkema, Rikutaro Fukuda, Andrew H. Plaks, Dong-wook Shin, C. H. Wang, Yen Yuan-shu, and Wai-lim Yip. The editors are also grateful for the editing and proofreading assistance rendered by Stephen C. K. Chan and Susan B. Yuan. We are also thankful to Miss Judy Leung of the Comparative Literature Division of the Institute of Chinese Studies, The Chinese University of Hong Kong, for typing the index. A special word of thanks must be expressed to Professor A. Owen Aldridge for his willingness to write a critical introduction to this volume at short notice. The Chinese calligraphy is by Dr. Ambrose Y. C. King, Head of New Asia College.

Finally, credit should go to Drs. Ambrose Y. C. King and Phillip S. Y. Sun for their initiative help in making possible the publication of the book by the Chinese University Press. We would also like to thank Mrs. Pansy Wong of the Chinese University Press for overseeing the production work of this volume.

Ying-hsiung Chou
William Tay
Heh-hsiang Yuan

Comparative Literature & Translation Centre
The Chinese University of Hong Kong
1979

Introduction

A. Owen Aldridge

The practice of literary criticism has never been more widespread in Europe and America than in the last fifty or so years. As a result many sophisticated teachers and students seem to be as much concerned with theory and methodology as with the actual substance of the literary texts they discuss. The emphasis on criticism has accompanied the development of comparative literature as an academic discipline, both in its earlier stages when it for the most part included merely the literatures of Europe and America and in its most recent development, when it has expanded to embrace the literatures of the Orient as well as the West. The present collection of essays by outstanding western and Chinese scholars which originated through the joint efforts of the Hong Kong Comparative Literature Association and the Chinese University of Hong Kong is designed for the most part to relate Chinese literature to its western counterparts by the use of modern theoretical techniques.

While most of the essays focus upon Chinese literature, they are intended as much for a western as an eastern readership, thereby complementing James J. L. Liu's *Chinese Theories of Literature* (Chicago, 1975). The present state of scholarship on comparative literature and China is admirably summarized by John J. Deeney in the present volume.

One of the European contributors, André Lefevere argues convincingly that literature is not a scientific discipline and exposes the confusion and turmoil resulting from the number of different schools in modern criticism. The often contradictory claims of Freudianism, Marxism, anthropology, structuralism, mythography and their various combinations and aberrations have nothing to do with a scientific discipline, he maintains, but represent instead "a battle between conflicting ideologies." It is obvious that western criticism is not monolithic and that it cannot be applied indiscriminately to Chinese works of art. Much of it is out-dated, and the value of the latest vogues (The French Freudians, the "schools" of Derrida and of Foucault) has not been tested. Even that which has stood the test of time and may survive into later generations does not have universal application. Instead of going with Lefevere to the extreme of Pyrrhonism, however, it is possible both to consider critical pluralism superior to dogmatic absolutism and to admit the value of eclecticism, both as an abstract principle and as a critical approach. Despite the prevailing custom of underscoring common elements in literary works through classification (chiefly by genre, chronological period, or theme), significant writings even in a single national literature are exceedingly varied—with as many individual differences as the authors who created them. Some works can be brilliantly explained or illuminated by a particular method of criticism to which other works have no relevance whatever. The essays in the present collection certainly reveal an eclectic spread, ranging in their inspiration from Matthew Arnold's notion of "touchstones" to Lévi-Strauss's theory of sets of oppositions or polarizations in life and art.

Although Lefevere refutes the notion of literature as a science, he argues that there can be a "metascientific foundation" for a common poetics. He advocates, therefore, the making of an inventory of everything which may be said objectively about a work of literature, including its historical background and the translations it has had. Such a process involves the demotion of language from the most important element in literature to only one among many. Another contributor, Wai-lim Yip reveals that the Taoist view of language and art also denies any special privilege to the status of the word. Taoist thought has previously been compared to the nature-orientation of Romanticism, and several of Yip's illustrations from Taoist poets strongly resemble Wordsworth, even though in a preceding publication Yip has cautioned against reading Taoist notions into the English poet. ["Aesthetic Consciousness of Landscape in Chinese and Anglo-American Poetry," *Comparative Literature Studies,* XV (1978), 223-226.] The following lines from Su Tung-p'o, however, certainly suggest the English poet's concept of recollected emotion.

> If you want poetry to be miraculous
> Nothing works better than being empty and tranquil.
> In tranquillity, one perceives everything in motion.

The question of the adequacy of translations for the understanding of literary texts in a separate culture is not brought forward by any of the contributors in a formal manner, but all of them assume that communication by translation is adequate or at least legitimate. All quotations from Chinese texts throughout the book, therefore, are given in English or in both English and Chinese. Those articles which treat the method of translating from Chinese into English succeed at the same time in illuminating the nature of Chinese poetry. A classic collection of Chinese poems rendered into English by Arthur Waley is so true to the original, we are told, that a later American poet, Carolyn Kizer, by imitating these translations, that is, in producing works twice removed from the initial Chinese texts, succeeded in effectively capturing "the subtlest nuances of the Chinese works while often bringing latent connotations to full and precise imagistic expression."

The problem of artistic elements in non-esoteric poetry or in popular literature in general may be conceived in connection with some primitive nature poems attributed to a Chinese bard Han Shan or Cold Mountain. The story of the reputation of these poems exemplifies a commonly observed phenomenon in comparative literature, that an author may achieve greater success outside of his own national culture than within it. Shaftesbury, Ossian and Chatterton are examples in the English tradition. The artistic value of the poems associated with Cold Mountain has been considered as quite limited by the mainstream of Chinese scholarship, but in Japan and most recently in the United States the colloquial style and mystical philosophy of this personality have won for him extraordinary celebrity. If Cold Mountain has come "to symbolize the alter-ego of an introspective man, alone and alienated from his society," he has much in common with the protagonist of Kawabata's Nobel-prize-winning novel *The Sound of the Mountain*. Paradoxically, Cold Mountain's poems seem to be non-conceptual, but they are at the same time highly epigrammatic.

Elitist attitudes have long been a problem in literary history. The pronouncements of critics are frequently at odds with the attitudes of the reading public at large—the experts insisting on the merits of works which the generality finds without interest, and conversely disparaging works which attain great popular acclaim. Some national literatures similarly arrogate preeminence for themselves; it was seriously debated in the eighteenth century, for example, whether French literature outweighed all the others of Europe. As an antidote to national elitism, modern theory has embraced the concept of universal literature, rejecting in Lefevere's words the notion that "one literature is 'better' or 'richer' than another" or that research in one is "more 'relevant' or 'more deserving of attention' than research in another." Elitism is still widespread in modern criticism, however, easily detected by appeals to "the informed reader," "the skilled reader," or "the critical approach."

One of the oldest methods in western criticism is that of pointing out beauties and faults, which goes back at least to Longinus and attained great popularity in the eighteenth century. In the Victorian period Matthew Arnold selected eleven passages of outstanding effectiveness which he characterized as touchstones for recognizing literary greatness. Nine are from epic poetry and two from Shakesperian plays. The only non-English source is Dante's *Divine Comedy*. On the surface, the establishing of criteria such as this seems to represent elitism along both national and class lines. Arnold's touchstones may certainly be compared to Etiemble's notion of "literary invariants"—that there are elements common to all literatures which may be isolated or extrapolated as criteria of excellence. The concept of touchstones implies, moreover, esthetic and moral absolutes and fails to take into consideration differences in culture, historical periods, and emotional attitudes. Arnold's broad critical stance, on the other hand, represents a refreshing and rewarding method of approaching literature—through the personalized essay. As W. L. Wong remarks in comparing Arnold's individual reactions with Chinese "poetry-talk" criticism, "the comments of a widely-read and well-tempered critic, however terse they may be, are something to be reckoned with." Although Chinese criticism in general has been frequently disparaged as impressionistic and Arnold is often dismissed as old-fashioned, elitist and intuitional, both traditions present criticism as an art, rather than a science. The act of criticism appears as the result of personal research, personal acuity, and most important, personal involvement.

The beauties and faults method of criticism subscribes to the dictum of Ts'ao P'i that literature is "a splendid enterprise that will never perish" and to Wong's opinion that "poets are immortalized by their best known lines." It has little in common with the Marxist view that "great" literary works succeed in creating an imaginary, coherent universe embodying the world view of a particular segment of society, whereas "minor" works fail to present such a coherent or unified outlook. Equally removed from impressionistic criticism and sociological criticism are those literary technocracies which analyze presumed structural relationships and portray them by means of geometrical designs and quasimathematical formulae. These techniques are applied in the present collection to an ancient oral ballad and to three Yang Lin stories. Diagrams are added, moreover, to a treatment of the translating of Shakespeare into Chinese which is otherwise traditional.

The purpose of Ying-hsiung Chou in treating the ballad "Lord, Do Not Cross the River" is a traditional one, to compare its various oral versions with written counterparts. In carrying out his project, Chou not only analyzes the relations between singer and auditor, but also looks for polarizations or sets of oppositions which he portrays in words and in graphs. Chou's conclusion, which sees the universal conflict between man and nature as abstracted into Platonic love between the "courtier of the River God" and the "concubine of the stream," does not depend upon diagrams or binary sectioning, however, but could be derived through traditional methods. Since the diagrams which are supplied illustrate the relationship between abstract planes or surfaces rather than elements of the narrative, it is relevant to inquire, in the words of Eva Kushner, "whether structures are perennially present in a Platonic sort of sense, and impose themselves to the creator and through the work of art to the historian." ["Diachrony and Structure," in *Synthesis,* V (1978), 48.] If we assume the nominalist position in reply and ascribe structures to the mind of the beholder or critic, we may still inquire in reference to the Chinese ballad whether the creator of the "literate counterpart" of the original oral version had any inkling of these structures.

The theoretical basis of the American New Critics as well as that of the European structuralists suggests that the artistic work or its elements is hypostasized in the manner of a Platonic absolute. This approach, while seeking to place the critic on a level with the poet, actually minimizes the creative act of both the poet and the reader and, consequently, the human element which is indispensable to art. Conceiving of a literary text as a "predominantly aesthetic sign" may possibly be a means toward developing a poetic theory applicable to both East and West, but, as Douwe W. Fokkema indicates, the relationships between text and social content, and text and reader's response are essential to the concept of art. Almost a century ago, a French author defined scientific criticism as "the science of the work of art conceived as sign." [Emile Hennequin, *La Critique scientifique* (Paris, 1888), p. 22.] In elaborating his theory, this author considered artistic works as indexes or signs reflecting the soul of the artist and the soul of the people. If we interpret people as referring to readers, we have a plausible theory which places the text between the author and the reader and gives all three elements a function in the artistic process.

An essay by Han-liang Chang on the *Yang Lin* story series gives the reader primary consideration in that it first provides a traditional account and subsequently a structural analysis, allowing the reader to compare the two methods of exposition. In keeping with structuralist theory, the author goes through the process of "plot-simplification," that is, laying bare the essential structure presumed to inhere within complex literary works. Whether or not such a method provides a basic understanding of literature, there is no question that it would be valuable to the comparatist if the analysis of Chinese stories could be related to a similar analysis of western stories. Such a procedure would do much to validate the structuralist method, but unfortunately

Introduction

neither Chang nor other practitioners of the method in general have expanded their perspective beyond selected texts in a single literature. Chang's conclusion that the *Yang Lin* story series deals with *rites de passage* in a genre closely related to the Bildungsroman does not depend in any way upon his structuralist demonstration, but rather upon traditional extrinsic research. The elements of legend and dream together with a colloquial style artfully devised by a skilled man of letters provide valid points of comparison with Washington Irving's *Rip Van Winkle*. Both Chou and Han-liang Chang accept the feasibility of reducing Chinese literary works into binary pairs, but Wai-lim Yip suggests that in Taoist poetry at least the dichotomy between nature and art is subtly avoided through the merging of the two.

Han-liang Chang's conclusion that the *Yang Lin* story portrays the initiation of its protagonist in a circle from reality through illusion to reality once more represents a mimetic interpretation, that is, a recognition that one of the purposes of literature is to portray reality. Francis K. H. So in treating the verse sections of the vernacular novel, *Hsi-yu-chi,* adopts the conventional view that Chinese literature is in the main non-mimetic, apparently as a means of providing an esthetic texture for a non-elitist work. *Hsi-yu-chi* combines verse and prose in part because it was intended for a literate, but not highly educated readership. With Pigsy and Monkey as main characters, it has some resemblance to European beast epics of the Middle Ages. By using classical western terminology to analyze its rhetorical system of composition, So diverts attention from the realistic elements in the work. He compares, for example, the rhetorical design of its introductory poem, a description of the creation of the world, to that of the thirteenth century English romance *Havelock the Dane,* one of the few precise textual parallels between the western and eastern traditions indicated in the entire collection. So also notes in *Hsi-yu-chi* several examples of *ecphrasis,* the description in verse of an object of art, and points out the location of other examples in Homer. Although these poetic passages have been interpreted by So and others as slowing the narrative pace and, therefore, impeding the effect of actuality, they share with the other poetic passages in the work a highly descriptive function, which could be considered as mimetic in character. Rhetorical devices do not necessarily counteract the mimetic function of literature, but frequently complement or support it. This is true for both literature of the "broad masses" and that of the intelligentsia. As Andrew H. Plaks remarks of the fiction of the same general period as *Hsi-yu-chi,* "in both China and Europe the novel carries with it the aesthetic expectation of a 'realistic' representation of some phase of human existence."

Although realism is usually associated with narrative fiction, the mimetic function exists also in poetry. William Tay studies one important aspect, nature imagery. In a statistical analysis of two representative anthologies (the counting done manually, not by computer), he concludes that Chinese poetry is replete with "simple images" and that generic images outnumber specific ones. Tay's textual commentaries provide the western reader indirectly with a considerable amount of information concerning the general characteristics of Chinese poetry. To illustrate his point that interpretations are revealed in translations—or, in reverse, that translations depend upon interpretations—he quotes several examples by westerners belonging to the Imagist school. Compactness and density have long been accepted as fundamental qualities of Chinese poetry, and the Imagists together with some other western critics cited by Tay have been attracted to this poetry in large measure because of its concreteness. It is somewhat paradoxical, therefore, that the total impression provided by Chinese poetry should be, in Tay's words, "oriented toward generality." Perhaps compression itself imparts the illusion of concreteness to Chinese poetry (the absence of singulars and plurals, inflections, prepositions, and other grammatical elements); whereas its "referential generality" is not apparent until subjected to rigid scrutiny such as Tay's.

Han-liang Chang follows the example of structuralism by intentionally avoiding diachronic elements, and nearly all of the other essays tend to neglect historical relations, either by ignoring period denominations, by omitting reference to dates of composition or by drawing illustrations from widely separated historical periods. This neglect of chronology may be due primarily not to a conscious preference of critical analysis over literary history, but to the great difficulties inherent in tracing the development of Chinese culture. It seems incredible that the first Chinese history of Chinese literature was not published until 1909, but the statement of Tak-wei Wong to this effect is supported by a British scholar, Herbert A. Giles. The latter described his *History of Chinese Literature* (New York, 1901) in its preface as "the first attempt made in any language, including Chinese, to produce a history of Chinese literature." Apparently the first formal history of Japanese letters in Japanese was published by Sanji Mikami and Kuresabura Kazu in 1890. According to Tak-wei Wong, the problems surrounding the denomination of Chinese periods are almost insurmountable, and history without periodization is "practically unworkable." One of the simplest methods of delineating literary periods is to ascribe the names of ruling monarchs or dynasties, the method which has been used most widely in the East and to some degree in the West. Even a barely literate westerner has heard of the T'ang or Ming periods and vaguely associates them as chronological segments with such western ones as the Victorian age or *le siècle de Louis XIV*. The main difference is that the Chinese dynasties cover a span of several centuries whereas the western rulers represent a single century at the most. In order for literary periods to be meaningful, they must represent specific denominators—stylistic, social, political or philosophic—as well as a mere chronological span. Most western period terms are based upon prevalent styles and intellectual currents rather than chronology, for example, Baroque, Enlightenment, or Romantic. The brevity of western periods makes it possible to discern outstanding characteristics, but even then—as A. O. Lovejoy has pointed out—such concepts as Romanticism have a variety of different and even contradictory meanings attached to them. The difficulties inherent in the western system are vastly increased in the Chinese because of the much greater span of time involved. In one proposed system, Chinese literature is divided into four epochs covering 32 centuries. This may be contrasted with the western system which covers only 25 centuries, if the Bible and Greece and Rome are included, but merely eight centuries, if the Renaissance is taken as a starting point. It is possible to draw period parallels between East and West only when the boundaries are broad and flexible, for example, within the familiar triads of ancient-medieval-modern or of slavery-feudalism-capitalism. But even these broad designations in the two cultures do not coincide chronologically. Wong's survey of the problems of periodization in the West together with his astute analysis of one of its most elusive periods, the Baroque, provides a basis for his parallel consideration of the situation in regard to China. Although the discipline of comparative literature re-

Introduction

veals similarities in the two geographical areas, there seems to be no reason for not accepting Wong's conclusion that periodization in China must be carried out with other parameters or frames of reference than those used in the West. It may be possible, however, to make comparisons of period characteristics between East and West independent of chronology. Irving Babbitt has argued, for example, that the closest approximation to the Rousseauistic type of Romanticism is found in the early Taoist movement in China, and A. O. Lovejoy has traced the vogue for irregularity, asymmetry, variety and surprise in art and literature—a major characteristic of Romanticism—to European notions of Chinese gardening.

In the West it is possible for a single writer to achieve preeminence in two or more styles, each representing a distinct literary period, but such a broad spread is much less likely in the East. In both parts of the world, however, it is possible and even commonplace for a writer in one literary period to be influenced by a writer in a previous one. Thanks to the methodology of comparative literature, it is now possible to show similarities in a writer belonging to a remote period of eastern literature to a writer in a more recent period in the West. Allegorical literature developed many centuries B.C. in China, but it did not flourish until the Middle Ages and the Renaissance in the West. Both cultures use the turtledove as a symbol of romantic love, and C. H. Wang reveals how this bird is portrayed symbolically as an amatory messenger in an ancient Chinese poem *Li sao* and Spenser's *Faerie Queene* twenty centuries later. In an earlier study, Wang analyzed sartorial emblems in the same two poems.

A completely different perspective toward *Li sao* is offered by Ping-leung Chan who considers the poem in reference to the much-discussed question of whether the element of tragedy exists in Chinese literature. The protagonist of *Li sao* is a court official who falls into disgrace through his overzealousness. Slanderous rivals engineer his removal from the court. Disenchanted with life after his banishment, he consults a number of spiritual guides who urge him to leave the country, but he at first refuses to compromise his standards by flight. Eventually he embarks on an allegorical quest for the ideal woman. Chan succeeds in isolating in these events a number of elements considered essential to tragedy by various western critics, particularly a tragic flaw, a reversal of fortune, and the apparent supremacy of injustice over justice. Although it is undeniable that these separate elements exist, one may doubt whether the work as a whole projects the image of individual suffering which encompasses the Book of Job or the great tragedies of Sophocles or Shakespeare. The journey in the last part of the poem with its moral, allegorical overtones resembles John Bunyan's *Pilgrim's Progress* more than any western work of tragedy. Even considering the Book of Job, one may doubt that allegory and tragedy may coexist in the same work. It is difficult to conceive of a character as a tragic hero, moreover, if he has any options, and the protagonist of *Li sao* has several. The poem stems, furthermore, from a period of Chinese society in which the freedom of choice in real life hardly existed. A major theme of *Li sao* seems to be the appreciation of individual worth, and received opinion in almost any culture considers that the person whose true value is not recognized by his peers or who has for some reason lost face is not in an enviable position. Only in this sense does the protagonist of *Li sao* seem to be worthy of the serious commiseration customarily accorded to a tragic hero.

A more specific notion of the essence of tragedy is provided by Ping-cheung Cheung in his investigation of whether the concept exists in Chinese traditional drama. Most western readers would probably agree that the work which he chooses for analysis, *Tou O yüan,* a well-known Chinese play today, belongs to the genre of tragedy. The plot outline is much closer to western tradition than is that of *Li sao,* and it in addition approaches closer to the human condition than most of the classical Greek tragedies. The protagonist, Tou O, a girl, is left motherless at the age of three and abandoned by her father at seven. She then marries at seventeen the son of a woman to whom she had previously been sold, but is almost immediately widowed. Shortly thereafter two other characters, a father and a son, save Tou O's mother-in-law from being murdered, and as compensation they demand that the mother-in-law marry the father and that the young woman marry the son. Tou O refuses, however, since a marriage under any circumstances would represent a violation of her mourning. At this point she is torn between loyalty to her deceased husband and loyalty to her mother-in-law. As the action proceeds, the father dies of poisoning. Tou O is accused of murdering him and tortured in order to obtain her confession. Since she is innocent, she calls in question divine justice, but in order to save her mother-in-law from being put to the same torture, she finally confesses despite her guiltlessness.

The question of whether this sequence of events is tragic cannot be settled by reference to Aristotelian or any other formal criteria. It depends on the prevailing philosophical attitudes—chiefly ethical—in the culture in which the question is raised. In a society dominated, for example, by the stoic concept of the final victory of virtue over all suffering, there can be no tragedy at all—Seneca notwithstanding. Theoretically there can be none either in a Christian culture, which regards death as a release from suffering, but in practice nearly all Christian dramatic works consider both physical suffering and death itself as tragic. Both Christianity and Buddhism, moreover, have the notion of retribution, but this theological attitude also has little effect upon dramatic writing—and is irrelevant to tragedy.

Western notions concerning the essence of tragedy are almost as manifold as the critics who propose them. Even Aristotle sets a double standard by attributing tragedy variously to a formal element in the work itself (the fall from high place) and to the psychological reaction in the reader or beholder (catharsis through pity and fear). Cheung separates tragedy from melodrama and draws on a host of definitions of tragedy, including those of Aristotle, Schlegel, Hegel, and modern critics, to arrive at a quintessential definition: tragedy is a serious action which brings great pain to the protagonist to some degree because of external circumstances but largely through his own doing. Cheung stresses that his definition is based upon dramatic criticism, not life, and that the element of the tragic is not in itself sufficient to make a work pass as a tragedy. He, nevertheless, considers that *Tou O yüan* belongs to this category. In Shakespeare's time a play was simply a tragedy if the major characters died in the end or a comedy if all remained alive. Cheung's quintessential definition is equally arbitrary and formal, lacking any reference to reaction from the audience. A broader definition which would probably be accepted by the average westerner is that tragedy consists in the dramatic representation of individual suffering to a degree out of the ordinary brought on by any cause and which arouses sympathy in the audience. According to either the quintessential or the broad definition, *Tou O yüan* would seem to be a tragedy. It would not be so ranked, however, according to the Aristotelian principle of a fall from high place nor from the neo-classical one that the protagonist and other characters must belong to royalty. *Tou O yüan* has a number of thematic parallels to *Antigone*, a work which fits the Aristotelian mode. It is regrettable that Cheung does not explain whether considerations in the Chinese tradition would keep *Tou O yüan* from being regarded as serious tragedy. In keeping with Chinese custom, the play combines comic with serious themes, another reason why it would not meet western neo-classical standards.

Although Aristotelian concepts may have some value in the treatment of Chinese drama, they have very little relevance to Chinese narrative fiction primarily, as Andrew H. Plaks observes, because everything in Aristotle which later critics have applied to fiction was originally based upon epic poetry, but no epic tradition exists in China to which the modern novel can be considered a continuation. Instead of a single continuous tradition, therefore, Plaks emphasizes the role of historiography, tracing the roots of the Chinese novel to historical fiction and the prose essay. Extremely valuable for the direction of future research in comparative literature is his conclusion that the most striking parallels between the conventions of Chinese and European fiction are found in the relation between the novel and intellectual history. Plaks also joins the question of elitist versus popular literature (high or low styles in Auerbach's terms) with one of the major problems of the study of periods and genres, whether one may correctly ascribe to individual works, particularly major ones, the characteristics assumed to belong to a certain span of time or type of literature. Plaks observes that both in the western and eastern traditions the imitation of the rhetoric of the masses or of picaresque types is a deliberate esthetic choice with no suggestion that the author is attempting to cultivate a popular audience. He also indicates that his conclusions are derived from the great Chinese novels—as all genre study must ultimately base itself upon the major works. These conclusions, bearing on fundamental parallels between the rise and development of the novel in the West and lengthy fiction in China, are of great interest to comparatists. In both cultures, according to Plaks, the rise of the novel coincided with extensive social and economic activity, it focussed on mimetic representation while recognizing the limitations of human character (as seen in ambiguous or flawed protagonists), and it developed an ironic perspective, reflecting not only upon the internal events and figures of the narrative but also upon the broad intellectual foundations of each of the respective traditions. Plaks constantly reminds us that there existed no major contact between China and the West which could explain why similar themes and structures should have emerged from parallel historical and social conditions, and he specifically declares himself sceptical of formulae such as "an inevitable function of human culture" or "an inevitable phenomenon of human creativity." He does not justify his doubts although the tone of his article in general suggests a basic distrust of all theories of historical determinism. An ancient and extensive epic tradition exists in Japan, in contrast to China, and Plaks particularly cites the *Tale of Genji* as evidence. The disparate development of narrative molds in the parallel culture of China and Japan would seem in itself to disprove theories of economic or social causality.

Some attention to the influence of China on the West is given by Clara Yü Cuadrado in her treatment of the theatre, the first part of which concerns the "mirage" of China as presented on the eighteenth-century European stage. She raises no effective challenge, however, to Plaks' sceptical suggestion that the early impression made by Chinese literature was no more serious than that of other fashionable Chinoiseries. Most of Cuadrado's article concerns the modern period and deals more with theatrical production and dramatic techniques than with literary texts. On the question of tragedy, she observes that since the religious-philosophical background of Chinese drama requires that poetic or distributive justice be uniformly maintained, there can be no tragedy in the Greek sense—a judgment which hardly conforms to Ping-cheung Cheung's portrayal of *Tou O yüan*.

Both Cuadrado's essay and a companion one by Simon S. C. Chau on translating Shakespeare into Chinese raise the question of the distinction between literature and stage productions. Chau's exposition of the difficulties of translating Shakespeare very properly begins with a distinction between the translation of his work as literature such as poetry or fiction and the transposal of his plays as dramatic performances. One of the essential properties of literature is the communication by means of words, defined as sounds conveying meaning to which a written symbol is attached. Oral works of any kind—poetry, fiction, popular wisdom—are not literature until they are transcribed. Cinema and the dramatic arts can also not properly be classified as literature although they are closely related to it. An analysis of the translations of plays belongs to comparative literature, but a treatment of play production or dramatic techniques belongs to theatre history or the dramatic arts. The two essays in question, however, can be categorized as comparative literature under the rubric of literature and the other arts. The same is true of Thomas Yuntong Luk's likening of Wang Wei's nature poetry to a "cinematic succession of shots." Although using the vocabulary of film, Luk really demonstrates the parallel of poetry and painting. Wang Wei actually portrayed the same scenes in paintings and in words, and his poetry is pictorial rather than cinematographic, lacking as it does the element of motion, which is indispensable to cinema, indicated in its etymology from the Greek word for movement, *kinema*. Because of this pictorial element, Luk has no real need, therefore, to defend himself, as he does, against "historical anachronism" or "inter-media promiscuity."

Both Cuadrado and Chau emphasize the differences between western and Chinese culture rather than their similarities, and to some extent both authors stress the accoutrements of drama rather than such intrinsic literary qualities as plot and characterization. As one Chinese critic remarked concerning productions of western plays, "It is all right for reading, but when it comes to staging them, the difficulty is enormous." It may even be argued that differences in historical periods are greater than those in cultural traditions. William Butler Yeats has affirmed that the Japanese originators of the Nō drama are more congenial with modern Americans and Europeans than with the ancient Greeks or with Shakespeare and Corneille. Chau himself points out that Elizabethan and traditional Chinese drama have more in common than do Elizabethan and modern western works, although he labels this resemblance as almost irrelevant because nearly all Chinese theaters today have adopted the framed stage and western methods of production, scarcely a proof that cultural differences interfere drastically in Shakespeare adaptations. One might also observe that if the framed stage has been widely adopted in China, it is now being less rigidly used in the West than in the period of the realistic theatre. Because of the tremendous changes brought about by the passage of time, it is probably true that the resemblances between Chinese culture of the twentieth century and contemporary western culture are considerably greater than those between ancient and contemporary Chinese culture. The conclusions that translations of western dramas are popular in print, but not on the stage can hardly be said to reflect profound cultural disparities. Parenthetically an ode to Shakespeare by Liu Po-tuan has been translated and is known in the West.

Antony Tatlow's essay on Brecht and peasant dialectics indicates a much closer harmony between Chinese and western culture. His demonstration of the resemblances between Brecht's theatre and Taoist thought amounts almost to a critical discussion of the relations of Taoism to modern social problems. Like Plaks, Tatlow insists on the critic's duty to explore the relationship of literature to history and life. He specifically rejects, however, mechanistic theories which portrary art and literature exclusively in terms of economic and social movements, and by implication, those which, on the other hand, disregard diachronic relations. His is the only essay not drawing examples of western literature from English or American sources. Reversing the method of the other contributors, the bringing to bear of western criticism upon eastern works, Tatlow not only applies eastern concepts to western culture, but reveals the direct influence of Chinese philosophy upon Brecht and other Europeans, including Tolstoy.

Tatlow quotes a sentence from a German Sinologist which might be used as an epigraph for the entire book: "Eastern man creates the world, western man defines it." Symbolically this could represent the process of applying western methods of analysis to eastern works of art as it is practised in the present scholarly enterprise, a procedure rewarding to readers from both cultures. Although it might seem that those with a background in eastern literature and culture would have the most to gain from this book, since it is Chinese works which are in the main subjected to scrutiny herein, the average western reader on his side will be able to use his ingrained critical terminology as a means of becoming acquainted with unfamiliar texts. The reader who is approaching Chinese literature for the first time, as well as the one who has traveled only a short distance along the way, will acquire a significant insight into the art of masterpieces about which he has previously had merely a vague and confused notion.

New Strategies in the Comparative Study of Literature and Their Application to Contemporary Chinese Literature

Douwe W. Fokkema

One of the major problems in the study of Chinese literature and literary history is the relation between text and social context. The student of literature who wishes to compare Chinese and Western literature cannot take for granted that the concept of literary text in China and the West is identical, or even in a simple way comparable. This observation applies to both ancient and modern times. However, only recently methods have been found to compare the two widely varying traditions in an unbiased way.

The development of Comparative Literature is closely connected with that of the study of literature in general, which, if we restrict ourselves to modern times and allow the necessary simplifications, can be divided into three stages:

First, the age of positivism—inspired by Hippolyte Taine—focussed on the genetic causes of the literary work. This stage gave rise to Comparative Literature as a separate discipline, notably in France, with due emphasis on the examination of motifs and subject-matter, as well as on the study of the fate (French: *fortune*) of literary works. The nineteenth-century and early twentieth-century French school of Comparative Literature was positivist to the extent that it did not question the status of the facts it investigated; it overestimated the possibility of isolating elements of literary texts, and rarely asked whether these isolated elements were relevant to the explanation of the literary aspects of the texts under examination. Several trends of positivist literary scholarship, such as the predominant attention to the origins and effects of literary texts, can also be found in Marxist writings, although these usually dismiss positivism as incompatible with their own underlying materialist philosophy.

Second, due to the lack of satisfactory results of these investigations into the conditions and effects of literature, a reaction followed which directed the attention to the unity and autonomy of the literary text. Possibly the new direction was influenced by certain developments in literary history, notably the rise of Symbolism, which emphasized the uniqueness, integrity and permanent nature of the literary work. There are various schools which more or less simultaneously defended the autonomy of the literary text: New Criticism, the "immanent interpretation" of Wolfgang Kayser and Emil Staiger, further T. S. Eliot and F. R. Leavis, as well as Benedetto Croce. They all feared that genetic explanations might lead to the annihilation of the literary work and considered paraphrase sacrilegious to the "essential structure"[1] of the work of art. Their concept of literary text was that of a given fact, invariable throughout history, a monument rather than a document.[2]

The New Critics rejected paraphrase as a heresy, and this view—whether they were aware of it or not—was a symptom of an anti-rational attitude which eschewed causal explanation.[3] In principle, the concept of the uniqueness of the work of art was incompatible with its analysis in rational terms, for such analysis must rely on the generality of constituent elements and the general aspects of their arrangement. We cannot but see a contradiction between the New Critics' position that the meaning of a literary work can never be adequately phrased and their fine and convincing interpretations, which, however, at times suffer from a certain opacity. The lack of clarity in many specimens of New Criticism results from a rather exclusive reliance on procedures of "internal recoding,"[4] i.e., reliance on rephrasing the literary text by using the terms and structures of that text in a different order.[5] In short, the New Critics, like similar schools in Europe, almost completely refrained from the use of a metalanguage. If the interpretation of a literary work remains couched in terms of that work, it is hard to see how a basis can be found for the comparison with other literary works.

One might object that the New Critics invented at least a rudimental metalanguage by coining their specific understanding of terms as "irony," "paradox," "coherence," etc., but the precise definitions of these terms are hard to find and in the New Critical practice the meaning of, for instance, the term "irony" has been stretched to a point where it has come to signify any type of balancing qualification.[6] In the critical practice it appeared that irony is a necessary constituent of the particular type of coherence which is postulated for any text of the literary tradition. If the terms of a metalanguage are without distinction applicable to all texts of a given corpus, it is hard to see what purpose they are to serve. Therefore, the few technical terms which we find in the writings of the New Critics did not provide a tool for comparative studies.

---

[1] Cleanth Brooks, *The Well-Wrought Urn: Studies in the Structure of Poetry* (London: Methuen, 1968), p. 166.

[2] Cf. D. W. Fokkema and Elrud Kunne-Ibsch, *Theories of Literature in the Twentieth Century* (London: C. Hurst, and New York: St. Martin's, 1977), p. 136.

[3] Brooks, however, conceded that we may "be able to adumbrate what the poem says if we allow ourselves enough words, and if we make enough reservations and qualifications, thus attempting to come nearer to the meaning of the poem by successive approximations and refinements, gradually encompassing the meaning and pointing to the area in which it lies rather than realizing it" (Brooks, p. 168).

[4] Jurij Lotman, *The Structure of the Artistic Text,* trans. Ronald Vroon, Michigan Slavic Contributions (Ann Arbor: Department of Slavic Languages and Literatures, Univ. of Michigan, 1977), p. 35.

[5] Having stated that the interpretation of a poem will be at best a crude approximation, Cleanth Brooks admits that the interpreter "will be compelled to resort to the methods of the poem—analogy, metaphor, symbol, etc.—in order to secure even this near an approximation" (Brooks, p. 168).

[6] "Irony is the most general term that we have for the kind of qualification which the various elements in a context receive from the context," writes Brooks (p. 171).

With respect to the second stage, the position of Russian Formalism is ambiguous. On the one hand Tomaševskij warned that "one cannot paraphrase Pushkin"[7] and Viktor Šklovskij approved of Tolstoy's firm refusal to summarize *Anna Karenina*: "If I would want to say in words all that I intended to express in the novel, I would have to rewrite the very novel which I have written."[8] But on the other hand, the Russian Formalists have not hesitated to analyze literary texts in terms of constituent elements, such as meter, rhyme and other sound patterns, motifs, motivation, *fabula* (i.e., the representation of the action in its chronological order and causal relations), and *sjuzhet* (i.e., the plot or narrative structure). They also introduced a metalingual terminology by coining the concepts of device, factor, constructive principle, function, dominance, system, structure, series, deformation, automatization, de-automatization, etc.

On the one hand, they considered the literary text as a given fact whose structure can be explained with reference to the constituent elements of the text. On the other hand, from the very beginning they recognized that a text can be created as a non-literary message and be received as a literary message; and, inversely, that a text can be created as a literary message and be received as a non-literary message. For Šklovskij, who took this position already in 1916, the artistic quality of a text is "the result of the nature of our perception."[9] We may add that the nature of our perception may vary with the situation in which the text is read, with the knowledge and experience of the recipient, his psychological disposition and political inclinations. But admitting that the same text may be admired and despised by different readers or even by the same reader at different stages of his life does not necessarily mean a surrender to subjectivism. The study of literature does not dissolve into psychology. The later development of Russian Formalism and Czech structuralism have shown that, even if the postulate of the invariable literary text (the concept of the literary text as a monument) is dropped, a viable, and indeed increasingly vital study of literature is possible.

Russian Formalism and Czech structuralism gave rise to a third stage in the development of literary studies by viewing the literary work as a sign or an assembly of signs, which, as carriers of potential meaning, must be actualized in an act of communication. This led, among other things, to the distinction of artefact and aesthetic object, or the text (*signifiant*) and its interpretation (*signifié*).[10] It also enhanced research into the various actualizations or interpretations of texts and their relation to the coinciding social, historical and cultural circumstances. Contemporary Chinese literary history abounds in examples of new interpretations of both classical and modern works under the influence of changing social and political circumstances. As is well known, these changes do not occur at random but are interrelated and to a certain degree can be generalized. For instance, when Marxism had become the

---

[7] Victor Erlich, *Russian Formalism: History, Doctrine*, with a Preface by René Wellek, 3rd ed. (The Hague: Mouton, 1969), p. 53.

[8] Jurij Striedter, ed., *Texte der Russischen Formalisten*, I: *Texte zur allgemeinen Literaturtheorie und zur Theorie der Prosa* (Munich: Fink, 1969), p. 109.

[9] Ibid., p. 7.

[10] Jan Mukařovský, *Aesthetic Function, Norm and Value As Social Facts*, trans. Mark E. Suino, Michigan Slavic Contributions (Ann Arbor: Department of Slavic Languages and Literatures, Univ. of Michigan, 1970), p. 90. Originally published in Czech in 1935. See also Jan Mukařovský, *The Word and Verbal Art: Selected Essays*, trans. John Burbank and Peter Steiner, Foreword by René Wellek (New Haven and London: Yale Univ. Press, 1977).

institutionalized ideology of the People's Republic of China, the communist leaders promoted a reinterpretation of the literary legacy in Marxist terms. The criticism of Yü P'ing-po's 俞平伯 interpretation of the *Dream of the Red Chamber* (*Hung lou meng* 紅樓夢) in 1954 was a polemic between proponents of different actualizations of the novel, each group having a particular position in the world of literary scholarship and in society. In 1960 the criticism of Lin Mo-han 林默涵 and Ch'ien Chün-jui 錢俊瑞 of Tolstoy, branding him as a stupid landlord and hysterical, sentimental, religious person, originated with critics closely associated with the Central Committee and tried to annihilate the view of Tolstoy as the great humanist, which had been upheld for many years by quite another group of people. Finally, the years just before, during and after the Cultural Revolution have shown quite clearly that the fate of writers and their books to a large extent is related to social conditions and the prevailing political trend.

But the example of contemporary Chinese literary history is not unique. Also when government and party interference are negligible, as in democratic societies, social and historical developments affect the actualization of particular texts and, consequently, their place in literary history (the rise and development of Expressionism cannot be discussed without reference to World War I; the origins of Modernism are indissolubly connected with simultaneous developments in philosophy; Surrealism exploited the invention of psychoanalysis, etc.). That is why Jurij Tynjanov and Roman Jakobson in their programmatic statement "Problems in the Study of Literature and Language" (1928)[11] emphasized that the immanent study of literary history alone cannot explain the particular pace of literary evolution or the selection of one particular direction where various options are theoretically open. In their view, the problem of the direction or the dominant direction can be solved only through an analysis of the interrelationship between the literary and other historical series. Being critical of historical materialism, they rejected the dogmatic view that the developments in the socio-economic "series" at all times are to determine those in the other series.

Roman Jakobson further distanced himself from what we have called the second stage in the study of literature when, in his article "What Is Poetry?" (1933, originally in Czech),[12] he pronounced himself against the isolation of art, while defending the autonomy of the aesthetic function. He writes: "Neither Tynjanov, nor Mukařovský, neither Shklovskij nor myself—we do not proclaim the self-indulgence of art, but assert that art is a constituent element of the social system, an element which is correlated with other elements."[13] Within the framework of the third stage, the problem of the literary text as an aesthetic object of particular readers has become a social problem. In this stage the roles of researcher and reader are firmly separated: although the researcher, of course, must also read, his main interest is the interpretations and evaluations of other readers. This approach calls for a study of literary texts in relationship with their actualizations by particular readers, or rather groups of readers. As the literary text is conceived as a sign or structure of signs, the third stage would qualify for being called semiotic.

---

[11] Ladislav Matejka and Krystyna Pomorska, eds., *Readings in Russian Poetics: Formalist and Structuralist Views* (Cambridge, Mass.: MIT Press, 1971), pp. 79-82.

[12] W.-D. Stempel, ed., *Texte der Russischen Formalisten*, II: *Texte zur Theorie des Verses und der poetischen Sprache* (Munich: Fink, 1972), pp. 393-418.

[13] Ibid., p. 413.

More than thirty years ago, Felix Vodička has sketched his conception of literary history, which fully belongs to the tradition of Czech structuralism. Written in 1942, his article "Literary History, Its Problems and Tasks,"[14] has been neglected too long. For Vodička the literary work (artefact) is the central category of the study of literature. He divides the tasks of the literary historian into three parts:

(1) The first and central task is directed at the texts which at some time and by some reading public have been actualized as literature and which form a historical series. For the literary historian, not only the object but also the historical moment counts. According to Vodička literary texts should be studied as embedded in their historical order, and not as isolated phenomena. The study of the historical order of literary texts will yield insight into changes in the organization of literary form and meaning. The study of the immanent development of literary structures will always remain a central task of the literary historian.

(2) The second task is geared towards the production of the text and results from the attempt to comprehend the tension between the literary performance of the writer on the one hand and the literary and social context of his time (including the barriers of material conditions, government regulations, censorship, etc.) on the other. In studying this relationship it is of vital importance to view the literary text as a sign with a predominantly aesthetic function, directed at a more or less definite readership living in a particular cultural and social context.

(3) The third task is oriented to the reception of literary texts. Apart from the material conditions of the distribution system (publishing houses, bookshops, literary journals, the intermediary function of storyteller, radio and television), the reception of literature is regulated by literary norms, as well as the tolerated or expected deviation from these norms. Literary norms may vary among different groups of readers, but the latter do not necessarily coincide with social classes. Data for this type of research will be found in literary criticism, rather than in sociology. Literary norms are not fixed entities; they change under the influence of new literary texts and general cultural and social developments. It belongs to the task of the literary historian to analyze and explain the changes in the literary norm system of different readerships.

The three tasks of the literary historian, as expounded by Vodička, are closely connected and complement each other like the three panels of a triptych. For instance, particular changes in the immanent development of literary structures can sometimes be explained with reference to the challenge of a new historical situation or to newly formulated demands by literary critics. In Chinese literary criticism the concept of socialist realism was formulated and officially propagated from the early 1950s. But in 1958 the growing political tension between the Chinese and Soviet Communist Party was a reason for the literary officials in Peking to drop the ideal of socialist realism (which, in their view, had been betrayed by the revisionists) and to launch the slogan of "the combination of revolutionary realism and revolutionary romantic-

---

[14] Available in German translation: "Die Literaturgeschichte, ihre Probleme und Aufgaben," in Felix Vodička, *Die Struktur der literarischen Entwicklung*, ed. Jurij Striedter et al. (Munich: Fink, 1976), pp. 30-86.

ism." Thus, political developments led to new demands by propaganda officials and literary critics, which changed the orientation of those writers who subscribed to the new policy. In spite of the vagueness of socialist realism and the non-committal nature of the new slogan, it is warranted to say that in practice the latter called for a higher degree of thematic selection in the representation of society. The new literature emphasized the voluntaristic effort to change society in terms that were believed to appeal to a reading public larger than ever had been reached by socialist realist works. Or, in Maoist terminology, the ideal of popularization (*p'u-chi kung-tso* 普及工作) superseded that of elevation (*t'i-kao kung-tso* 提高工作).

The history of contemporary Chinese literature can be written only with due emphasis on the different political and cultural situations in the People's Republic, in Taiwan, in Hong Kong and elsewhere. And, if one focusses on contemporary Chinese literature in the People's Republic, it is inevitable to study the interaction between the immanent development of literary structures and the conditions of the production and reception of literature (i.e., between all three parts of the object of the literary historian). Only such an approach will yield an insight into the Chinese literary system. And only after a comparison has been made between the Chinese and, e.g., the English or American literary system may one proceed to comparing specific elements of these systems, such as particular genres, or devices, or themes.

Evidently, the structuralist approach which deals with the literary communication situation as a whole and with the function of the various elements in that communication situation, highly differs from René Etiemble's suggestion to compare specific literary genres and stylistic devices from completely different traditions. Although Etiemble has made an invaluable contribution to East-West Comparative Literature studies by criticizing the Eurocentric nature of traditional Comparative Literature and its restricted study of factual relations (*rapports de fait*), he mistakenly assumed that certain texts at all times are received as literature, and that there are "literary invariants" (*invariants littéraires*) which can be abstracted from the text. Etiemble set his hopes on the attempt to "isolate all elements which are common factors of all literature,"[15] but remained blind to the fact that the same elements may have different functions in different contexts, whereas in principle any element may be carrier of the aesthetic function he was actually looking for.

Etiemble correctly questioned the apologetic defence of the Great European Tradition, but weakened his argument by postulating a Great Asian Tradition. The very concept of literary tradition must be investigated. First, the question must be asked whether or not we wish to consider literature as an art. If the answer is affirmative, the problem arises as to how to define the aesthetic function of art.[16] The answer to that question inevitably leads to the problem of the communication situation. Research into text-functions with respect to the historical and contempor-

---

[15] "...isoler tous les éléments qui sont facteurs communs de toute littérature." Cf. René Etiemble, "Littérature comparée ou Comparaison n'est pas raison," in *Hygiène des lettres*, III, *Savoir et goût* (Paris: Gallimard, 1958), p. 167.

[16] For the early stage of Chinese literature important research was done by Yuan Heh-hsiang in his article "A Study of Some Literary Expressions in the Wei Tsin Period" (*Tamkang Review* 4, No. 2 [1973], 11-36), which focusses on the emotive function of poetry. Kenneth J. Dewoskin studied the origins of fiction in "The Six Dynasties *Chih-kuai* and the Birth of Fiction," in Andrew Plaks, ed., *Chinese Narrative: Critical and Theoretical Essays*, with a Foreword by Cyril Birch (Princeton: Princeton Univ. Press, 1977), pp. 21-53.

ary literary communication situation calls for new ways of writing literary history. The present challenge is to conceive of the literary text as a predominantly aesthetic sign, originating from a definite historical context but transcending documentary historical value.[17]

---

[17] This paper was written during the academic year 1977-78, when I was a Fellow at the Netherlands Institute for Advanced Studies in the Humanities and Social Sciences (NIAS), Wassenaar, The Netherlands.

Some Tactical Steps Toward a Common Poetics

André Lefevere

In what follows I shall try to sketch a possible metascientific foundation on which a truly common poetics for something approaching world literature could be based. The sketch given here will, of necessity, be brief. The same problem has been dealt with at greater length in my *Literary Knowledge*,[1] albeit in a way not entirely unvitiated by what I would now call "naive falsificationist tendencies."

During the last two or three decades quite a respectable number of scholars concerned with the study of literature in what we still call "the West" have tried to establish their study on a more scientific basis, mainly as a reaction against the "popular view that in literary criticism all knowledge about texts is useful and all approaches to the text contribute to the greater understanding of literature, accompanied by the tempting appeal to such virtues as many-sidedness and tolerance [which] only results in muddle and confusion, less real knowledge and a level of intellectual interest rarely above the lowest possible."[2]

It is, however, most ironic that most scholars who have set out to make the study of literature more scientific in the West have not, as a rule, seen fit to take the time to find out where the demarcation line between what can be considered "scientific" and what cannot actually happens to be running. Instead, most recent theorists have rather unthinkingly, but none the less wholeheartedly, embraced that concept of science which is connected with logical positivism, precisely at a time when philosophers of science were demonstrating that this concept, the "Received View," had rather outlived its usefulness.

The majority of literary scholars in the West who are commendably interested in the scientific foundations of a study of literature seem or prefer to be unaware of the fact that "a general consensus that the Received View is inadequate now seems to hold among most philosophers of science. This consensus is, however, quite limited: while there is general agreement that the Received View is inadequate, there is no

---

[1] André Lefevere, *Literary Knowledge* (Amsterdam: Van Gorcum, 1977).
[2] J. M. Ellis, *The Theory of Literature* (Berkeley: Univ. of California Press, 1974), p. 70.

general consensus what the source of its inadequacy is."³ Nor is there, one might add, a general consensus as to what it should be replaced by.

There does, however, appear to be a fairly general agreement on the following assumptions:

> Consider the classical philosophical theses that an absolute causal account can be given of phenomena, that ultimate laws of a deterministic sort can be gleaned from natural phenomena and that some rockbed of perceptual certainty is necessary to gain a firm knowledge of the world. All three of these theses are false and hopelessly out of date in terms of the kinds of theories now coming to dominate science. In ordinary affairs and ordinary talk, such certainty and absolutism are not necessary and are in fact deleterious to the exercise of good sense. It is from ancient antecedents in religion and philosophy, not from ordinary experience, that these fallacious doctrines have been drawn and have received sanction for so long a time.⁴

Knowledge is, in other words, neither fixed nor stable, neither firm or unchangeable. It is a challenge, not something acquired. It is something that must be made by man, not revealed to him. It is, quite simply speaking, in our hands. Knowledge is, furthermore, not unified in the sense the Received View tried to give to that word —a sense responsible for the many rather irrelevant models, formalizations and axiomatizations still with us today in many works of literary scholarship—irrelevant because they serve only to point out that the scholar in question has assimilated an outdated methodology, not to clarify the issues at hand.

Attractive though the proposition may have been, it is simply impossible to develop one methodology which would be uniformly valid for all types of scientific investigation, and then to proceed to apply that methodology across the board, with total disregard for the specific nature of what one sets out to investigate. "No abstract, formal system . . . can ever specify—still less *guarantee*—its own empirical relevance or range of application. So we must surely investigate separately, in each particular case, just what form of articulation—axiomatic, taxonomic, graphical or whatever—is appropriate to a scientific theory covering this or that subject matter, at this or that stage of historical development."⁵

The articulation of a scientific theory is, therefore, in part defined by what it is supposed to be about. The basis on which scientific theories are elaborated—the demarcation line between what is science and what is not—is, on the other hand, the same for all scientific endeavour. At this point further problems arise. At present this demarcation line appears to be Popper's requirement of the intersubjective testability

---

³ F. Suppe, "The Search for Philosophic Understanding of Scientific Theories," in *The Structure of Scientific Theories*, ed. F. Suppe (Urbana: Univ. of Illinois Press, 1974), p. 115.

⁴ P. Suppes, "The Structure of Theories and the Analysis of Data," in *The Structure of Scientific Theories*, p. 283.

⁵ S. Toulmin, "The Structure of Scientific Theories," in *The Structure of Scientific Theories*, p. 606.

or falsifiability of hypotheses that constitute a theory. Yet the very ways of testing, which were rather unproblematic in Popper's naive falsificationist view (as soon as a counter-example falsifies a theory that theory should, to put it in a slightly oversimplified manner, be abandoned) present problems of their own. Whereas naive falsificationism still appears to hold up for the testing of "single hypotheses, which do not face experience backed up by a more or less bulky body of theoretical assumptions,"[6] it has simply proved too . . . naive where the testing of theories is concerned:

> There are no . . . clear-cut text-book "truth conditions" for the systems of hypotheses occurring in real science: there are consequently no decision criteria, and no hint that there can be any. The most that can be secured is a set of numerous and nearly independent *controls,* which are singly insufficient to guarantee complete truth but which can jointly detect partial truth. What is important about these tests is not that they supply decision rules concerning our acceptance or rejection of scientific theories as if these were good or bad eggs: this they cannot do. What they do is to show the extent to which any factual theory succeeds and the extent to which it fails, and by so doing they can occasionally show new research lines likely to be rewarding.[7]

Among the theories proposed after the demise of the Received View, Stephen Toulmin's, with its emphasis on the concept of a "discipline" not as a static, but as a dynamically evolving entity, appears to me to be most promising for the elaboration of a scientific study of literature.[8] Inside a given culture many disciplines arise to deal with specific problems: how to split atoms, for example, or how to repair washing-machines. Each discipline has its specific goal and in the course of its attempts (over the years, decades, centuries) to reach that goal it evolves a repertory of procedures: it evolves its own transmit. The transmit of a discipline—any discipline—contains a collection of rules for problem-solving, *as well as* the problems that remain to be solved. This transmit is handed down by competent practitioners of the discipline, by means of teaching, or writing, or both. Inside the transmit a distinction must be made between the core and the periphery. The core consists of those rules or methods everybody more or less agrees about; the periphery contains the rules that are being elaborated in an attempt to solve current problems.

For the discipline called "literature," this state of affairs has been described by Weng Fang-kang 翁方綱 in the following terms: "when literature is formed, then rules are established. In the establishment of rules, there are those which are established at the beginning or at the center: this is the way the rules establish the correct basis (of poetry) and trace its source. Then there are those which are established about the details, about the flesh texture of the seams: this is the way the rules exhaust all forms and all possible changes."[9]

---

[6] M. Bunge, *Scientific Research II* (New York: Springer, 1967), p. 341.
[7] Ibid., p. 356.
[8] S. Toulmin, *Human Understanding* (Princeton: Princeton Univ. Press, 1972).
[9] Weng Fang-kang, quoted in James J. Y. Liu 劉若愚, *Chinese Theories of Literature* (Chicago and London: The Univ. of Chicago Press, 1975), p. 95.

Some disciplines are scientific in nature, others are not. This does, however, not imply (even though positivists have tried very hard to establish the contrary) that non-scientific can be equated with non-sensical. Many of the decisions we shape our life around, for instance, are not usually arrived at as the result of scientific procedures, but they are, as a rule, not nonsensical.

In scientific disciplines attempts at solving the problems of the periphery take the form of what we have come to call—since Popper—"conjectures and refutations": hypotheses, or theories are formulated and submitted to what are usually called "forums of competition." These forums consist of the practitioners of the discipline who decide on publication of articles in learned magazines, or the publication of books, or who gather for conferences, etc. Hypotheses and theories are, in other words, submitted to the consensus of the qualified practitioners of a discipline for approval or rejection. In fact, it is this consensus which, in practice, "tests" hypotheses and theories by means of reviews, quotations, the "academic grapevine," etc.

A discipline does, in other words, not only consist of a more or less disembodied set of rules; it also very much consists of the group of those who are generally recognized as its competent practitioners. Needless to say, this group may accept or reject theories on their scientific merits only, but it may also allow its judgement to be guided by extra-scientific motives: e.g., jealousy, or antipathy, or the struggle for power and prestige within institutions. These motives may lead to the slighting, or at best the grudgingly paternalistic acceptance of certain directions of research within the discipline.

Some disciplines boast a strong, stable transmit; others do not. I submit that a possible science of literature falls, at the present moment, under the second category rather than under the first one. If, for example, any member of our culture should have the wish to become a butcher, practitioners of his discipline will teach him how to cut joints and how to dismember animals elegantly and efficiently. If, on the other hand, he or she wants to study literature, chances are that he or she will be mainly taught Freud, or Marx, or anthopology, mythology and linguistics, or a weird hodgepodge consisting of all those elements, and various others that can, seemingly, be added or subtracted more or less at will, or whim.

One could state matters in a more radical manner and say that a science of literature does, at the present moment, definitely not display a core and a periphery, but rather a number of ostensibly peacefully co-existing yet deeply antagonistic cores, or "poetic concepts" which often contradict each other and yet "one cannot say that of two contradictory poetics, the one refutes the other. As poetic concepts are not systems of empirical hypotheses, but rather systems of normative stipulations, any refutation of one system by the other is out of the question: the different systems of norms are incommensurable."[10]

In other words, a person who holds, say, the psycho-analytic poetic concept will find it impossible to argue on a more or less rational basis with a person who holds, say, the Marxist one. Each will either have to damn the other wholesale, or else to admit that the other's "contribution is valuable as well," thus undercutting his own. This situation, in which stagnation reigns supreme in the world of the deaf and dumb, is usually referred to as "pluralism." One may wonder to what extent it has

---

[10] H. Verdaasdonk & C. J. Van Rees, "Reading a Text vs. Analysing a Text," *Poetics*, 6 (1977), 69.

been caused by the "lit biz" itself, with its ever stronger insistence on the ever growing importance of ever higher degrees. Texts simply must be written about because candidates simply must be examined, even if the number of texts to be written about is rather limited, or if it is doubtful that anything can be written about certain texts which has not already been written before. Unless one sovereignly asserts (without giving any reasons for this remarkable act) that whatever has been written before, though not entirely devoid of merit, has, unfortunately, failed to make use of the "right" methodology, inspired by the "right" poetic concept. It is easy to see how methods will proliferate like weeds if this process happens to be repeated a number of times. It is also painfully easy for all to see that this state of affairs does not exactly create a climate for more or less rational discussion about more or less solvable problems. What we witness is not the development of a scientific discipline, but a battle between conflicting ideologies.

It would appear, therefore, that a science of literature is, at this moment, rather sorely in need of a stable transmit. I shall attempt to briefly sketch the broad outlines of one such transmit in the following paragraphs. Such a transmit is a vital necessity if literary scholars are ever to be able to argue on common ground, not just in the West but, *a fortiori,* between West and East.

Let me, at the outset, propose a distinction between "literature" on the one hand, meaning the actual production of literature, of "the category of texts considered worth treating in the way that literary texts are treated,"[11] and what I propose to call "metaliterature" on the other hand. Literature is a non-scientific discipline, which has as its goal to describe experience and, in doing so, to gain and share knowledge—a knowledge not necessarily, and often emphatically not equivalent to intellectual knowledge alone. To achieve this goal literature has at its disposal a repertory of procedures, "an imaginary inventory of all possibilities of literary creation."[12] This inventory can be analyzed and argued about in an intersubjectively testable, i.e., scientific, manner. Even if, for example, your psycho-analytic critic and your Marxist critic will no doubt declare the same sonnet to be either a description of the ravages of the Oedipus complex or a bitter comment on the inevitability of the class struggle, they might agree that it is a sonnet.

The inventory includes, among other elements, genre, form, mode, style, rhetoric, prototypical characters and situations, the natural language in which the work is written with all its ties to the culture of which it is to some extent the repository, plot, symbol, motif, allusion, etc. Needless to say, this inventory cuts across both linguistic and national boundaries and it is open to modifications. Indeed, changes in literary history may be accounted for in terms of modifications of the inventory.

Metaliterature is the discipline which makes statements about literature. It aspires to be scientific, i.e., to make statements and propose hypotheses, to construct theories which are, as far as possible, intersubjectively testable. This can, at present, be most profitably done by means of a description and itemization of the inventory, or, in other words, by "dissecting the muscles and tracing the veins of literature,"[13] of the changes that take place in it and, as far as possible, of what causes these changes, and of how

---

[11] J. M. Ellis, p. 50.
[12] F. Vodicka, *Die Struktur der literarischen Entwicklung* (Munich: Fink, 1976), p. 37.
[13] Liu Hsieh 劉勰, *The Literary Mind and the Carving of Dragons* 文心雕龍, tr. Vincent Yu-chung Shih 施友忠 (New York: Columbia Univ. Press, 1959), p. 7.

these changes migrate from one literature to another. A modification of the inventory of Chinese literature is, for instance, the rise of the *san-ch'ü* 散曲 which may be traced to the abolition of the imperial examinations under the first Mongol rulers of China.

This inventory is, of course, descriptive in nature; it is not prescriptive after the manner of the "poetics" written from the Renaissance to the eighteenth century in the West, nor does it have the pretense of being able to (help) generate literary production. There is also no connection with conservatism, or archaism, as is often the case with Chinese theorists of literature who may be thought to have formulated vaguely analogous proposals. We are not concerned with following "the ancients foot by foot and inch by inch" and, in doing so, to "really follow the rules"[14] because the rules explicitated in the inventory are not there to be imitated by the reader, but to serve as a kind of blueprint, a set of guidelines for the concretization of works which make use of those rules, even if they only parody them. For literature is never created by "a player of backgammon who seeks lucky chance";[15] every writer is born into a set of models, for him to apply, to modify or to reject. Writers do, in other words, consciously or not, have a whole inventory at their disposal. They use certain elements of it, to the exclusion of others. If the reader is to be helped in his concretization (assimilation) of the literary work by literary scholars (and what else could literary scholars possibly be for, one cannot help wondering), literary scholars should be able to explain to him what a certain item of the inventory meant at a certain time, how the writer in question has modified it, with what intentions he has done so, etc. It is not the task of literary scholars to impose their own concretization of a work on the unsuspecting reader. In other words, since literature is a way of gaining and sharing knowledge, literary scholars should use their knowledge of literature in such a way that both writer and reader can most fully integrate the knowledge they share and gain into their lives.

It is obvious that we shall never empirically arrive at a moderately exhaustive inventory of this kind. But then, "it is not necessary for historical laws to be empirical in order that they be valuable, both for expressing knowledge and for generating understanding. Classical mechanics, the basic law of economics, the ideal gas laws and many others are not demonstrably empirical."[16] What matters is that we "should arrive at laws which are the simplest useful approximation" and "theoretically tractable."[17] On this basis metaliterature would be able to make accessible works of literature that are not, or no longer, accessible to the reader, by means of commentary (relating the inventory to those elements of it used in the work, and the work in turn to the inventory) or by means of translation, not by means of the kind of criticism we have grown so tiresomely familiar with at present and which so pitifully combines "fetishism of the book with shamanism of the interpreter, science and subjectivity, pedanticism and soul: modern humanistic scholarship."[18]

---

[14] Li Meng-yang 李夢陽, quoted in Liu, p. 91.

[15] Liu Hsieh, quoted in Liu, p. 91.

[16] M. Scriven, "Logical Positivism and the Behavioral Sciences," *The Legacy of Logical Positivism*, ed. P. Achinstein & S. Barker (Baltimore: Johns Hopkins Univ. Press, 1969), p. 206.

[17] M. Scriven, "The Key Property of Physical Laws: Inaccuracy," *Current Issues in the Philosophy of Science*, ed. H. Feigl & G. Maxwell (New York: Holt, Rinehart & Winston, 1959), p. 100.

[18] N. O. Brown, *Love's Body* (New York: Vintage, 1966), p. 199.

In this connection the writing of a translation can be said to be scientific to a higher degree than the writing of commentary, at least on the obviously falsifiable level. One can, in other words, check the translation with the original; subterfuges and equivocation are not possible to the extent they are possible in commentary and criticism.

To sum up: the aim of metaliterature, an essentially ancillary, not an expansionistic scientific discipline, would be to make materials for the most complete possible reception/concretization of a literary work available to the reader, not to impose a certain kind of reception on the reader, nor to study the reception of the work, since both the latter activities can hardly be pursued in an intersubjectively testable way. Metaliterature is, it should be obvious, not an "empty formalistic game." On the contrary, it treats the reader as the adult human being who is able to integrate (assimilate, receive, concretize) the knowledge offered in the work into his life, if he so desires, or to reject it if that is his wish. It does not draw up lists of books the reader has to think of as "good" or "great." It does not force interpretations on readers. Rather it holds that knowledge of forms (the inventory) is indispensable if it is to be able to help the reader gain the knowledge he wants to gain.

This way of looking at literature seems to me to remove various chips from various shoulders. For one, the theory quite simply does not allow any room for any centrism of any kind, be it Sinocentrism or Europocentrism. It tries to advocate the scientific study of literature through the study of the inventory of literary procedures. It does not claim that one literature is "better" or "richer" than another, nor does it claim that research in one literature is more "relevant" or "more deserving of attention" than research in another. All kinds of research into the inventory of literary procedures are relevant in so far as they lead to the most complete possible concretization by the reader.

For another, the theory does away with two of the most diehard legacies of European Romanticism: the primacy of language in the work of literature, and through that the rather illusory search for "the typically . . . (fill in the language)" in a work of literary art, which has, traditionally, opened all kinds of doors for all kinds of obscurantism, chauvinism and the like. The theory also puts an end to the "polyinterpretability" of the literary work of art, another essentially Romantic, and therefore historical, not absolute and timeless notion, simply by leaving the polyinterpretability where it belongs: in the mind (or even the heart) of the reader during the act of concretization, not at the center of a science of literature.

In the third place the theory does away with the opposition between "national" and "comparative" literature. What is really, testably Chinese in Chinese poetry, for example, is the system of forms, genres, that China has devised. Research into this system is also research into comparative, or even "general" literature, because it is research into the inventory, and because that inventory is, and cannot possibly not be, world-wide and therefore transcends national boundaries at the very outset.

Fourthly, this theory revalorizes the Cinderella figure of comparative literature: translation. From a peripheral phenomenon indulged in at times by tired philologists or dilettante scholars it becomes one of the two central features of a scientific study of literature, a fact which can only serve to enhance its quality as well, and which will have to lead to a rethinking of translation theory and practice in the context of an integrated theory of literature. The demotion of language from the Romantic be-all and end-all of the literary work of art to one element among many of the inventory of procedures is a necessary prerequisite to the revalorization of translation, as is the notion that intersubjective testability marks the boundary-line between the scientific and the non-scientific.

It may seem, at first sight, as if this theory rather radically severs much from the main body of literary scholarship that has traditionally been thought to belong there. This is an infantile disease of all new theories, and must be taken as such. New theories have to draw strong demarcation-lines between themselves and their predecessors, and, in doing so, they do not always fully realize, or fully see at the outset what the practical consequences of their theoretical pronouncements are. In other words, the results in the periphery of statements made in the core are not always obvious. Which is why the real work must now go on in the periphery, and its results may, of course, lead to a reformulation of the center which has no pretentions to being absolute, unchangeable or even unchallengeable. Science progresses through evolution. Only ideologies can muster enough arrogance to deny time.

The Taoist Aesthetic: *Wu-yen tu-hua*, the Unspeaking, Self-generating, Self-conditioning, Self-transforming, Self-complete Nature[1]

Wai-lim Yip

In the parable, "Inferno, I, 32," Jorge Luis Borges has God reveal to a leopard that it is to become a word in a poem which has its precise place in the scheme of the universe. I take it to mean a parabolic paraphrase of Mallarmé's famous motto: "Everything in the world exists to eventually culminate in a book." This special privilege given to the status of the word, which has, since Mallarmé, dominated the entire spectrum of modern poetry, is curiously at odds with the Chinese, in particular, with the Taoist view of language and art. To be more precise, as the leopard in Borges' parable is puzzled over such an assignment, many modern poets and aestheticians are caught between the denunciation and the promotion of the power of language. The complex morphology of this intertwined double-headed snake in modern poetics is, however, not the purpose of the present paper; it will be reserved for another occasion. We will examine here the Taoist world view and the way in which it opens up a decreative-creative dialectic with a special set of perceptual-expressive procedures that characterize much of Chinese poetry and poetics.

*

First, reflection on the fundamental facts of the external world will immediately make us see that there is totality or the totalizing process of the Great Composition of things in Phenomenon,[2] changing and ongoing, whether we want to talk about

---

[1] All quotations from Lao-tzu's *Tao-te-ching* 道德經 (abbreviated as *Lao*) will be indicated by chapter. Those from *Chuang-tzu* 莊子 and Kuo Hsiang's 郭象 annotations follow Kuo Ch'ing-fan's 郭慶藩 edition of *Chuang-tzu chi-shih* 莊子集釋 (Taipei: Ho Lo, 1974), abbreviated as *Chuang*. Translations of passages from *Chuang-tzu* in the text are primarily Fung Yu-lan's 馮友蘭 (1933; rpt. New York: Paragon, 1964) with modifications by me for stylistic cogency. When feasible, one or two phrases from Burton Watson's *Complete Works of Chuang-tzu* (New York: Columbia Univ. Press, 1964) may be adopted.

[2] That is, phenomena as a whole; the singular form is here used to avoid conceiving them as differentiated units.

it or not. From a complete awareness of this totalizing Composition comes the call for respecting and preserving things in their pristine forms as they emerge from and merge into an undifferentiated Oneness. Thus, the Taoist world view begins by rejecting the premise that the structure of Phenomenon (Nature), changing and ongoing, is the same as we conceive it. All conscious efforts to generalize, formulate, classify and order it will necessarily result in some form of restriction, reduction or even distortion. We impose these conceptions, which, by definition, must be partial and incomplete, upon Phenomenon at the peril of losing touch with the concrete, original appeal of the totality of things. All such means of rationalizations, Lao-tzu tells us, are deceptions:

> The Tao that can be told is not the constant Tao;
> The name that can be named is not the constant name.
> Lao, 1.

道可道。非常道。
名可名。非常名。

> He who knows does not speak;
> He who speaks does not know.
> Lao, 56.

知者不言。言者不知。

The "Tao (Way) told" and the "name named" belong to the realm of concepts and linguistic formulations from which things and beings are totally free. As Heidegger would put it twenty-three centuries later, "all essents are not affected by concepts."[3] Since, strictly speaking, any thought of a thing becomes itself a verbal act, the deverbalized world (*wu-yen* 無言 or *wu-yü-chieh* 無語界) is the first step toward grasping the totality of things. Ideal knowledge is no knowledge. In Chuang-tzu's words,

> The knowledge of the ancients was perfect. How perfect? At that time, they did not know that there were things. This is the most perfect; nothing can be added. Next, they were aware of things, but they did not yet make distinctions between them. Next, they made distinctions, but they did not yet judge them. When judgements were passed, Tao was destroyed (*Chuang*, 74).

古之人其知有所至矣。惡乎至。有以為未始有物者。至矣盡矣。不可
以加矣。其次以為有物矣。而未始有封也。其次以為有封焉。而未始
有是非也。是非之彰也。道之所以虧也。

Chuang-tzu is particularly protective of the wholeness of the original cosmic scheme, which classifications and conceptions tend to dissect into separate units. The restrictiveness of words and ideas is further articulated in the book of *Chuang-tzu*:

---

[3] *Introduction to Metaphysics* (New Haven: Yale Univ. Press, 1959), pp. 5, 29. In this study, I will restrict my quotations to this work. I shall refer to Heidegger's *On the Way to Language* and *Poetry, Language and Thought* in a larger comparative study, part of which will involve Taoism again.

> What the world values is books. Books contain nothing but words wherein are found values of sorts. What words value is the sense of things. The sense of things reaches into something but that something is not to be conveyed by words. . . . What can be seen by seeing is forms and colors; what can be heard by hearing is names and sounds. How sad! Men of the world think that forms, colors, names and sounds are adequate means to grasp the full feel of things. But forms, colors, names and sounds are not adequate to grasp the full feel of things. "He who knows does not speak; he who speaks does not know" (*Chuang*, 488-9).

> 世之所貴道者書也。書不過語。語有貴也。語之所貴者意也。意有所隨。意之所隨者。不可以言傳也。…視而可見者。形與色也。聽而可聞者。名與聲也。悲夫。世人以形色名聲為足以得彼之情。夫形色名聲果不足以得彼之情。則知者不言。言者不知。

Words are inadequate either to encompass the entirety or to penetrate into the invisible smallest parts:

> Viewing large things from the standpoint of the small, one cannot exhaust them. Viewing small things from that of the large, one cannot see them clearly. Fineness is the smallest of the small and the gigantic is the largest of the large; each different in its convenient way—this is natural. The idea of fineness and coarseness are restricted to things with form. Things so fine that they have no visible form cannot be demarcated by numbers. Things so large that we cannot encompass cannot be exhausted by numbers. What words can speak of is the coarseness of things. What our sense can reach is the fineness of things. That which cannot be spoken of or sensed is that which coarseness and fineness cannot restrict (*Chuang*, 572).

> 夫自細視大者不盡。自大視細者不明。夫精。小之微也。垺。大之殷也。故異便。此勢之有也。夫精粗者。期於有形者也。無形者。數之所不能分也。不可圍者。數之所不能窮也。可以言論者。物之粗也。可以意致者。物之精也。言之所不能論。意之所不能察致者。不期精粗焉。

Inherent in this recognition of the inadequacy of language is the acceptance of man as limited and the rejection of the idea of seeing man as preeminently the controller or orderer of things, the consequence of which we shall explore presently. In the meantime, let us turn to two contemporary philosophers, William James and A. N. Whitehead, who, spurred by an epistemological agony ushered in by the scientific world, have delineated a world-sense which has echoes, in some measure, of the Taoist wholistic view, but which also addresses the alienation of modern man. James says:

> The world's contents are given to each of us in an order so foreign to our subjective interests that we can hardly . . . picture to ourselves what it is like. We have to break that order altogether . . . we break it into histories . . . into arts . . . into sciences . . . we make ten thousand separate serial orders of it . . . we discover among its various parts relations that were never given to sense at all . . . and out of an infinite number of these we call certain ones essential and law-giving, and ignore the rest. . . . He [man] says impressions of sense *must* give way, *must* be reduced to the desirated form.[4]

James recognizes full well that we have no organ to apprehend what he calls the "collateral contemporaneity" of all the beings and events that exist and happen at any given moment. And yet, the Western man insists that they be represented in a way that fits his perception of a manageable sequence and order. In the words of Whitehead,

> the radically untidy, ill-adjusted character of the fields of actual experience is concealed by the influence of language, molded by science, which foists on us exact concepts as though they represented the immediate deliverance of experience. The result is that we imagine that we have immediate experience of a world of perfectly defined objects implicated in perfectly defined events. . . . My contention is, that this world [neat, trim, tidy, exact] is a world of ideas, and that its internal relations are relations between abstract concepts.[5]

To be free from the destructive breakup of our total sense of the world, Chuang-tzu gives priority to the preconscious, preconceptual, prelinguistic nonverbal world where its pristine form can come freely to us in its own way. Chuang-tzu exalts the pre-knowledge of the ancient men and Lao-tzu calls for the return to the childlike correspondence with the world ("Keeping to the constant instinctive virtue, one returns to childlikeness." *Lao*, 28). Both the "ancient men" (before any polarization took place in their consciousness) and the child (in his naive condition) respond directly to, and correspond in natural measure with, the appeal of the concrete world without traversing through or into abstract concepts. This tuned correspondence with the world of objects is described in the book of *Chuang-tzu* as the Free Flow of Nature:

> The people have their constant instinctive nature: to weave for clothing, to till the fields for food. This is their shared virtue, one, total, undivided and is called the Free Flow of Nature. Therefore, in a time of perfect virtue, people move slowly, their gaze one-minded. In such a time, mountains have no paths, lakes no boats or bridges. A million things

---

[4] *The Will to Believe and Other Essays* (London: Longmans, 1905), pp. 118-120.
[5] *The Aims of Education* (New York: Free Press, 1967), pp. 157-8.

emerge simultaneously, one region joining another in a continuum. Birds flock, animals herd; grass and trees flourish. You can tie a cord to birds and animals to lead them along or climb up and peer over the nests of crows and magpies. In this age of perfect virtue, men live co-extensively with birds and animals, group side by side with a million things. Who would try to mark off superior men from inferior men? With the same "no knowledge" (*wu-chih*) their virtue stays put. With the same "no desire" (*wu-yü*), they remain simple and unhewn. Simple and Unhewn—there we have the true nature of man (*Chuang,* 334-6).[6]

民有常性。織而衣。耕而食。是謂同德。一而不黨。命曰天放。故至德之世。其行塡塡。其視顚顚。當是時也。山無蹊隧。澤無舟梁。萬物羣生。連屬其鄉。禽獸成羣。草木遂長。是故禽獸可係羈而遊。鳥鵲之巢可攀援而闚。夫至德之世。同與禽獸居。族與萬物並。惡乎知君子小人哉。同乎無知。其德不離。同乎無欲。是謂素樸。素樸而民性得矣。

It is clear that for Lao-tzu and Chuang-tzu, *Simple* and *Unhewn* (*su p'u*) is that realm of our original total consciousness which is open and unblocked to the free flow of things and which is lost to most people through their acquisition of knowledge, one of the many forms of systematizations imposed upon our original nature. Our original nature, had it been understood from the very beginning, would have continued in close measure with what it was. Since it is no longer the case, it is important, the Taoists tell us, that we retrieve it by understanding man's original place in and relationship to the Great Composition and Free Flow of things. The greatness of Chuang-tzu lies in the special way in which he philosophizes for us this relationship, making it possible for us to allow our original condition which has never really evaporated in spite of our acquisition of knowledge, to grow once again within ourselves.

Understanding that man is but one among millions of other beings in the totalizing fabric of Phenomenon ("Sky and earth came into being with us together; the myriad things and us are one," *Chuang,* 79), we have no reason to give special privilege to man and to his mental constructs as the sole authority on a subject which is larger than himself and which he has no ability to fully encompass. The rebirth of our original condition depends, therefore, on the removal of formulated categories from our consciousness and on our affirmation of the million things in the concrete world outside concepts and language as "self-so-complete" objects, each functioning, generating, conditioning and transforming itself according to its own nature. As "the air of Nature blows on the million things in a different way so that each can be itself" (*Chuang,* 50), and, as lengthening the ducks' legs or shortening the cranes' legs means pain and is a result of working against nature (*Chuang,* 317), we must leave all forms of beings as they are by nature. Each form of being has its own nature, has its own place, just as a tree, by nature, grows upward; a river, flows downward; a stone, hard;

---

[6] This chapter, believed to be written by later Taoists, is fully in keeping with Lao-tzu and Chuang-tzu's teachings. It is a direct extension of Chuang's passage on "ancient men" and Lao's idea of *su p'u*: "Constant instinctive virtue now full, one returns to the Unhewn" (Ch. 28).

water, soft. The legendary P'eng rises ninety thousand miles (*Chuang*, 2), a little quail never gets more than ten yards (*Chuang*, 9). A certain tree lives many centuries, a mushroom only a short time (*Chuang*, 11). Each performs according to its own nature. How can we take *this* as *subject* (principal) and *that* as *object* (subordinate)? Merely one form of being among millions of others, what right do we have to classify other forms of beings? How can we impose "my viewpoint" upon others as the right viewpoint, the only right viewpoint? When we do that, are we not like the frog inside the well who claims the partial sky that he sees to be the full sky? As if to echo one of Chuang-tzu's titles, "On making everything equal" in which these germinal ideas are articulated, Heidegger says in his *Introduction to Metaphysics,* "all essents (beings) are of equal value," and we must avoid singling out any particular essent, including man.

> For what indeed is man? Consider the earth within the endless darkness of space in the universe. By way of comparison it is a tiny grain of sand; between it and the next grain of its own size there extends a mile or more of emptiness; on the surface of this grain there lives a crawling, bewildered swarm of supposedly intelligent animals, who for a moment have discovered knowledge. And what is the temporal extension of a human life amid all the million years? Scarcely a move of the second hand, a breath. Within the essents as a whole there is no legitimate ground for singling out this essent which we called mankind and to which we ourselves happen to belong.[7]

What right do we have to turn the original nature of another fellow-being into something which it is not? White clouds are white; green mountains are green. Green mountains cannot blame white clouds for being white. White clouds cannot blame green mountains for being green. The so-called possible and impossible are possible and impossible because they are said to be so.

> The "this" is also "that." The "that" is also "this." According to "that," there is a system of right and wrong. According to "this," there is also a system of right and wrong. Is there really a distinction between "this" and "that"? . . . Not to discriminate "that" and "this" as opposites is the very essence of Tao (Way). There you get the Axis of Tao. There you attain the Central Ring to respond to the endless (*Chuang*, 66).

> 是亦彼也。彼亦是也。彼亦一是非。此亦一是非。果且有彼是乎哉。
> …彼是莫得其偶。謂之道樞。樞始得其環中。以應無窮。

Thus, obliterate the distinctions and view things from both "this" and "that"—view things as things view themselves, which is the true balance of Nature (*Chuang*, 70).

---

[7] *Introduction to Metaphysics*, pp. 3-4.

In the words of Kuo Hsiang, the most important annotator of Chuang-tzu, "All things are what they are, without knowing why and how they are . . . although things are different, yet they are the same in that they exist spontaneously as they are." "Since nonbeing is nonbeing, it cannot produce being. When being is not yet produced, it cannot produce other things. Who, then, produces things? They spontaneously produce themselves. . . . Everything produces itself and is not created by others. This is the Way of Nature" (*Chuang,* 50).

When Chuang-tzu claims that "Tao is everywhere," he does not mean any sort of human-invented concept such as Logos or Creator that determines the outlines of the beings in the phenomenal world, but the self-realization of each form of being as it is, uninterfered by abstract concepts or systems. This is the context in which Chuang-tzu says, "Sky and earth came into being with us together; the myriad things and us are one."

With this awareness of man's place in the free flow of things, we are to turn our attention toward the unspeaking Other world rather than toward the speaking Self, the Other world being, of course, those absolutely lively, self-generating, self transforming (*tu-hua* 獨化) beings surrounding us. This particular mental horizon—things-oriented rather than man-oriented—entails a totally different set of attitudes, aesthetic assumptions and strategies. The main aim is to receive, perceive and disclose Nature the way Nature comes or discloses itself to us, undistorted. This has been the highest aesthetic ideal in Chinese art and literature, *tzu-jan,* i.e., be-nature-thus-natural. A brief review of the two directions of our perceptual priorities may be useful here.

Whereas in one, as the ego attempts to explain the non-ego, the perceiver constantly imposes ideas or concepts on or matches them with, images or objects in concrete Phenomenon, in the other, as the ego loses itself into the undifferentiated mode of existence, into the totalizing flux of events and changes constantly happening before us, to "think" is to respond to the appeal of the presencing of things in their original state of freedom. Whereas the former tends toward the use of analytical, discursive and even syllogistic progression coupled with linear and temporal perspective, resulting in a sort of determinate, get-there orientation, the latter tends toward a dramatic, simultaneous presencing of the multi-dimensional, multi-relational objects instead of their being coerced into some preconceived orders or structures. The Taoist aesthetic, by definition, precludes the demand for categorization and commentary, and the affirmation of things as they are also precludes any necessity of metaphor and metaphysics which have played a central role in much of Western poetry. A metaphor, on the most basic level, means that we use an object to designate an idea, a vehicle (thing named) for tenor (things meant). Metaphysics means to reach beyond *physis,* to borrow an interpretation from Heidegger, *physis* being the emergence of things which includes both their "being" in the restricted sense of inert duration and "becoming."[8] But things in Phenomenon clearly need neither metaphor nor metaphysics to be what they are. A good example of this articulation is found in a large percentage of Chinese landscape poems such as those of Wang Wei, of which I have written in great detail in my *Hiding the Universe* and my article, "Aesthetic Consciousness of Landscape in Chinese and Anglo-American Poetry." Briefly, these poems are non-metaphoric and non-symbolic: the objects presented are nothing more than the objects

---

[8] *Introduction to Metaphysics*, p. 14.

themselves. The poet does not step in, but rather, he allows the scenery to *speak* and *act* itself out. It is as if the poet has become the objects themselves.

But the complexity of the Taoist aesthetic is not fully circumscribed if we do not confront the subtle interplay of the built-in contradictions throughout the Taoist texts and if we do not try to see in what way the decreative process leads to or becomes the creative. This decreative-creative dialectic appears on the surface in the form of negation or renunciation: The Way of Nature is ineffable; language is inadequate; we should take no action (*wu-wei* 無為), have no mind (*wu-hsin* 無心), no knowledge, no self (*wu-wo* 無我); we should not speak about Tao; Tao (Way of Nature) is void and there is nothing in it. Paradoxically, in this seeming renunciation is the affirmation of the concrete total world, a world free from and unrestricted by concepts. The renunciation then is not negation, but a new way of repossessing this original concrete world by dispossessing the partial and reduced forms the process of abstract thinking has so far heaped upon us. Thus, without taking actions as those defined by a closed system of abstract thinking, everything is done in accordance with our instinctive nature. Without exercising our conscious mind, we can respond fully to things that come into the orbit of our ken. With conceptual boundaries removed, our bosom is thus open, unblocked, a center of no circumference into which and across which a million things will regain their free flow and activity. It is clear that the Taoist perceiving-receiving activity must also be viewed from this decreative-creative dialectic.

> Do not listen with ears, but with the mind. Do not listen with the mind, but with the vital force (*ch'i,* or energy flow) within us. The function of the ear ends with hearing; that of the mind, with symbols and ideas. But the vital force is an emptiness ready to receive all things. Tao abides in the emptiness; the emptiness is the fast of mind (*Chuang,* 147).

無聽之以耳而聽之以心。無聽之以心而聽之以氣。聽止於耳。心止於符。氣也者。虛而待物者也。唯道集虛。虛者。心齋也。

> Acting in the manner of man, it is easy to be artificial. Acting in the manner of nature, it is difficult to be artificial. I have heard of flying with wings, but not of flying without them. I have heard of knowing with knowledge, but not of knowing without it. Look at that which is empty. In the empty room, there is bright light, there is happiness. If you cannot stop there, your mind is galloping abroad though your body is sitting. If you can keep your ears and eyes to communicate within, and shut out consciousness and knowledge, then even the gods and ghosts will come to dwell with you, not to mention men (*Chuang,* 150).

為人使易以偽。為天使難以偽。聞以有翼飛者矣。未聞以無翼飛者也。聞以有知知者矣。未聞以無知知者也。瞻彼闋者。虛室生白。吉祥止止。夫且不止。是之謂坐馳。夫徇耳目內通而外於心知。鬼神將來舍。而況人乎。

> Crush limbs and body, drive out hearing and vision, cast off form, do away with knowledge, and become identical with the Great Road—this is called Sitting-in-forgetfulness (*Chuang*, 284).

> 墮肢體。黜聰明。離形去知。同于大通。此謂坐忘。

Whereas many other modes of apprehending Phenomenon come to it with a handful of readymade gauges, measuring and matching, the Taoist mind is blank, so to speak, upon which the original natures of beings can have their full imprint, uninterfered with, undistorted. Such a state has also been compared to still water when it is the clearest (*Chuang*, 193) in which beings can mirror themselves. This condition of the mind resembles the trance-like consciousness of the mystics; in particular, it is close to the three stages of self-annihilation, forgetfulness and the moment of lightning-like illumination or inspiration. Henri Brémond, discoursing on the war between Anima (deeper self, Intuitionism) and Animus (surface self, Intellectualism), describes the triple process this way: Since pure intelligence cannot reach the ultimate reality, it is by way of the annihilation of the surface self, the retreat of the rational power that the contact with the Soul is possible. From the retreat comes a state of forgetfulness, a state when all obstructions by the surface self are removed when Inspiration finally occurs like a spark coming from the deepest source of our soul.[9] In his "On making everything equal," Chuang-tzu describes a sage's state of mind in his communion with the Music of Nature:

> Nan Kuo Tzu Ch'i sat leaning on a table. He looked to heaven and breathed gently, seeming to be in a trance, and unconscious of his body. Yen Ch'eng Tzu Yu, who was in attendance on him, said: "What is this? Can the body become thus like dry wood, and the mind like dead ashes? The man leaning on the table is not he who was here before." "Yen," said Tzu Ch'i, "your question is very good. Just now, I lost myself, do you understand? You may have heard of the music of man, but not the music of earth; you may have heard of the music of earth, but not the Music of Nature" (*Chuang*, 43-5).

> 南郭子綦隱機而坐。仰天而噓。荅焉似喪其耦。顏成子游立侍乎前。
> 曰。何居乎。形固可使如槁木。而心固可使如死灰乎。今之隱機者。
> 非昔之隱機者也。子綦曰。偃。不亦善乎。而問之也。今者吾喪我。
> 汝知之乎。女聞人籟而未聞地籟。女聞地籟而未聞天籟夫。

Indeed, the parallels are intriguing. St. Teresa says, for instance, that in her mystical communion she neither sees nor hears. For Plotinus, "Unifying contemplation occurs when the soul closed its door on everything."[10] Blake, St. John of the Cross, Eckhart, and Pascal all have written feverishly about the retreat of the self as a precondition

---

[9] *Prayer and Poetry*, tr. Algar Thorold (London: Folcroft, 1927), pp. 108ff.
[10] Ibid., pp. 147, 116.

to merge into the Ultimate. In a wider sense, we must consider the Taoist condition of *wu-hsin* (no-mind) mystical—this is partly why Ch'an Buddhism later has wholeheartedly taken over this aspect as its central motto. It is at least mystical in William James' sense:

> It is as if there were in the human consciousness a *sense of reality, a feeling of objective presence,* a perception of what we may call *"something there,"* more deep and more general than any of the special and particular "senses" by which the current psychology suppose existent realities to be originally revealed.[11]

And yet, the Taoist trance-like consciousness is at root different from Western religious mysticism: it does not work up to a leap into the noumenal or the metaphysical world; to the Taoist, as we may now understand, the phenomenal *is* the noumenal.

This somewhat mystical state is often described as *shen* (literally, spirit), a condition of mind after it has entered into the inner mechanism and activity of a thing or things. In Chuang-tzu's "The Fundamentals for the Cultivation of Life," a prince was astounded at a cook's skill in cutting bullocks, not only because every blow was done in perfect rhythm, but because he seemed to have seen all the joints and cavities inside the body, for he knew exactly where to turn his blade before he encountered obstruction. The cook explained, "What I love is Tao, which is more than mere skill. When I first began to cut up bullocks, I saw before me whole bullocks. After three years' practice, I saw no more whole bullocks. At present, I meet it with *shen*, not with my eyes" (*Chuang,* 119). Perhaps it is because of this mystical tincture amidst a poetics of the real and the concrete that all later literary and art theorists, Taoist and Confucian alike, from Lu Chi 陸機, Liu Hsieh 劉勰 to Chang Yen-yüan 張彥遠, Ssu-k'ung T'u 司空圖, Su Tung-p'o 蘇東坡, Yen Yü 嚴羽 and post-Sung critics, have made it into the pivot of their theoretical formulations, for this decreative-creative dialectic helps to identify the ineffable and the real as one without resorting to human-invented dogmas as ways to explain beings and phenomena.

Lu Chi (261-303):

> In the beginning, suspend vision, bring back hearing, become lost in contemplation to reach out for contact—there spirit gallops into the eight limits of the cosmos, there the mind glides into million of miles of space. Reaching, the full feel of things, at first, a glimmer, gathers into luminosity when all objects are brightened and clarified, each lighting up the other onward.

> 其始也。皆收視反聽。耽思傍訊。精鶩八極。心遊萬仞。其致也。情曈曨而彌鮮。物昭晰而互進。

---

[11] *The Varieties of Religious Experience* (New York: New American Library, 1958), p. 61.

> The mind is cleared to crystallize contemplation.

罄澄心以凝思。

> Trying the Void to demand for Being; knocking upon Profound Silence for sound.[12]

課虛無以責有。叩寂寞而求音。

Liu Hsieh (cir. 465-520):

> The perceptual activity travels far in spirit (*shen*). Completely stilled, contemplation centered, it reaches out to a thousand years. . . . The principle of perceptual activity is miraculous when the spirit consorts with the external world . . . to develop one's perceptual activity, the most important thing is emptiness and quiescence when one's five viscera will be cleansed and the spirit purified.[13]

文之思也。其神遠矣。故寂然凝慮。思接千載。…故思理爲妙。神與物遊。…是以陶鈞文思。貴在虛靜。疏瀹五藏。澡雪精神。

Chang Yen-yüan (fl. 847), art critic:

> Drawings by rulers are dead. Keep to one's spirit (*shen*), concentrate on Oneness, there one finds true paintings. . . . He who moves his thought and brush but is conscious of his painting as painting misses it. He who moves his thought and brush without being conscious of his painting as painting gets it, no sticking in his hand, no stagnation in his mind; it becomes so without knowing how.

界筆是死畫也。守其神。專其一。是眞畫也。…夫運思揮毫。自以爲畫。則愈失于畫矣。運思揮毫。意不在於畫。故得於畫矣。不滯於手。不凝於心。不知然而然。

> Gather one's spirit, think freely—there is miraculous understanding of Nature. With both the external world and one's self forgotten, with form cut off, knowledge done away with, even if one's body becomes dry wood, one's mind, dead ashes, there will be no hindrance to the miraculous principle of Nature. This is the Tao of painting.[14]

---

[12] "Wen-fu" 文賦 in *Lu Shih-heng wen-chi* 陸士衡文集 (*SPTK* ed.; rpt. Taipei: Shang-wu, 1965).

[13] "Shen-ssu" 神思 in *Wen-hsin tiao-lung* 文心雕龍, annot. Huang Shu-lin 黃士琳 (1738; rpt. Taipei: Kai-ming, 1959), 6.1.

[14] *Li-tai ming-hua chi* 歷代名畫記, annot. Yu Chien-hua 俞劍華 (Hong Kong: Nan-t'ung, 1973), pp. 35-36, 40-1.

凝神遐想。妙悟自然。物我兩忘。離形去智。身固可使如槁木。心固可使如死灰。不亦臻於妙理乎。所謂畫之道也。

Ssu-k'ung T'u (837-908):

> Live plainly: wait in silence—
> It is here the Scheme is seen.[15]

素處以默。妙機其微。

Su Tung-p'o (1036-1101):

> If you want poetry to be miraculous,
> Nothing works better than being empty and tranquil.
> In tranquillity, one perceives everything in motion;
> In the state of emptiness, one takes in all the aspects.[16]

欲令詩語妙。無厭空且靜。
靜故了羣動。空故納萬境。

Yen Yü (fl. 1180-1235):

> The last attainment of poetry is entering into *shen*.

詩之極致有一。曰入神。

> The highest kind of poetry is that which does not tread on the path of reason, nor fall into the snare of words . . . the excellence is in . . . transparency and luminosity, unblurred and unblocked, like sound in air, color in form, moon in water, image in mirror.[17]

所謂不涉理路。不落言筌者。上也。…故其妙處透徹玲瓏。不可湊泊。如空中之音。相中之色。水中之月。鏡中之象。

Wang Kuo-wei 王國維 (1877-1927):

> There is a self-reflecting *world* and there is a selfless *world* . . . the selfless world is achieved in quiescence and the self-reflecting world is arrested from movement.[18]

有有我之境。有無我之境。…無我之境。人惟於靜中得之。有我之境。於動之靜時得之。

---

[15] *Shih-p'in chi-chieh* 詩品集解, annot. Kuo Shao-yü 郭紹虞 (Hong Kong: Shang-wu, 1965), p. 5.

[16] *Chi-chu fen-lei Tung-p'o hsien-sheng shih* 集註分類東坡先生詩 (*SPTK* ed.), 21 (p. 391).

[17] *Ts'ang-lang shih-hua chiao-shih* 滄浪詩話校釋, annot. Kuo Shao-yü (Peking: Jen-min wen-hsüeh, 1961), pp. 6, 24.

[18] *Jen-chien tzu-hua* 人間詞話, annot. Hsü Tiao-fu 徐調孚 (Hong Kong: Chung-hua, 1974).

The centrality and continuity of the Taoist decreative-creative dialectic is clear here and needs little comment. However, we must stop for a second and return to the initial contradictions. One can say that, within the Taoist activity of consciousness, a complete awareness of things as they originally are can be regained by this decreative-creative process, but the miraculous receptivity to the concrete world achieved by emptying out the trappings of our intellect, is a state prior to expression. The ideal Taoist poet, when pushed to the logical end, should be silent and seek no expression, for the affirmation of the nonverbal world cancels out such a possibility. Chuang-tzu himself is fully articulate on this contradiction:

> Since all things are one, is there room for speech? Since I have spoken of "one," can there be no speech? One and "speech" make two; two and one make three. Proceeding from this on, even a skilful mathematician cannot exhaust it, let alone an ordinary man! Since, from nonbeing to being, we can get three, how much further we will go, moving from being to being. Thus, move not, let be. Tao knows no boundaries. Speech has no constancy (*Chuang,* 79).

> 萬物與我爲一。旣已爲一矣。且得有言乎。旣已謂之一矣。且得無言乎。一與言爲二。二而一爲三。自此以往。巧歷不能得。而況其凡乎。故自無適有。以至於三。而況自有適有乎。無適焉。因是已。夫道未始有封。言未始有常。

Tao cannot be told and yet Lao-tzu and Chuang-tzu cannot help but use the word Tao to circumscribe it. While using it, they remind us that it should immediately be forgotten so that we can be one with Nature again. The word Tao is used as though it were merely a pointer, a spark toward the original real world. But how can language, as a form of human invention, function in this way? What kind of negotiation can we have at all between the pre-poem moment of total awareness and the act of expression?

There is an assumption in the Taoist decreative-creative dialectic that when we achieve our original condition and become one with Tao, everything else will follow its natural course. The hand and the mind will felicitously correspond, as in the case of the cook cutting the bullocks, or like the wheelwright chiseling the wheel: every blow is exactly right (*Chuang,* 491). When we achieve our original condition, we will have in us a faculty akin to Nature itself. To use Chuang-tzu's words: "To stop without knowing how it stops" (*Chuang,* 70). We all walk, and we walk without being fully conscious of our walking. (We would be in trouble if we should be conscious of it; our legs must be hurting, etc.) Walk without being aware of walking—this is one example of our natural condition. A modern example may be stick-shift driving. A good stick-shift driver should be driving the car as if it had an automatic transmission, changing gears without being conscious of it. To arrive at this readiness, Chuang-tzu tells us: "Fishes, (born in water, growing up in water) forget themselves in water. Men, (born in Tao, growing up in Tao) will forget themselves being in Tao." (*Chuang,* 242). Thus, the boatman can row a boat as if it were not there and regards the rapids as though dry land (*Chuang,* 642). And Lü Liang can dive into and emerge from water as if breathing air because, growing up by the water, he has conditioned himself to water-nature (*Chuang,* 656-8).

It is apt to recall here the idea of *tzu-jan,* i.e., be-nature-thus-natural. The Chinese poet exalts the moment when we can witness in a poem Nature working itself out: to structure and disclose Nature the way Nature structures and discloses itself. The tension between Nature (effortless emergence of things) and Art (human effort) is subtly avoided. In a stricter sense, Art, by definition, can never be Nature. What the Taoists imply from the very beginning is really restored naturalness or second nature, an activity or expressiveness akin to that of Nature.

> Bend down—and there it is:
> No need to wrest it from others.
> With the Way, in complete consort—
> The mere touch of a hand is spring:
> The way we come upon blooming flowers,
> The way we see the year renew itself.
> What comes this way will stay.
> What we get by force will drain away.
> A secluded man in an empty mountain,
> As rain drops, picks some blade of duckweeds
> Freely to feel the flash of dawn:
> Leisurely, with natural balance.[19]

> 俯拾卽是。不取諸鄰。俱道適往。著手成春。
> 如逢花開。如瞻歲新。眞與不奪。強得易貧。
> 幽人空山。過雨採蘋。薄言情悟。悠悠天鈞。

Thus echoed and expanded by a ninth century poet-aesthetician Ssu-k'ung T'u and by many many poets and critics throughout the centuries. Sometimes, readiness, spontaneity and free flow of energy are synonyms used to describe the condition of becoming Nature. In calligraphy or painting, which has to be executed in unhesitatingly quick brushstrokes because of the ink being fluid and the rice paper being fast absorbant, the energy flowing out from our body to the executing brush must not be blocked. Similarly, in the T'ai Chi exercise and movement, it is the free, natural, energy flow of our body that we want to emulate in order to achieve a reconditioning of its function. To the Taoists as well as to many calligraphers, painters and T'ai Chi masters, the unimpeded correspondence and coordination between the hand and the mind—natural action coming directly from natural condition—is an unshaken faith and, to them, there is nothing mysterious about it.

As we now see, the Taoists believe in an inseparability between consciousness and expression, as it is reflected in those arts that emphasize *ch'i* or energy flow. But in what way can we make the same claim for the creation of a poem, when the poets too, prize the energy flow as an important hallmark of their naturalness? Can we at all see language as an instinctive part of growth in us as is walking? While Lao-tzu and Chuang-tzu have never explicitly said so, Taoist poet-critics certainly imply this possible comparison. For example, when Su Tung-p'o talks about his own style, he paraphrases Chuang-tzu by saying:

---

[19] *Shih-p'in chi-chieh,* p. 19.

> [Writing should be like] moving clouds and flowing water which have no fixed form but move (literally, walk) on where they have to move on and stop where they have to stop.[20]
>
> 如行雲流水。初無定質。但常行於所當行。常止於所不可不止。
>
> My writing is like water gushing out from an ample, deep spring.... It can move on a thousand miles a day without effort and turns with mountains and rocks and shapes itself according to the objects it encounters. This is something the artist is not conscious of. What he is conscious of is this: that it moves on when it has to move on and it stops when it has to stop.[21]
>
> 吾文如萬斛泉源。不擇地而出。⋯雖一日千里無難。及其與山石曲折隨物賦形。而不可知也。所可知者。常行於所當行。常止於所當止。

The suggestion is that expression (the felicity of language) can be as natural as water, an object of Nature.

In spite of this interesting analogy, there is no way in which we can avoid seeing language as a product of culture. As such, it will always contain elements that are highly obstructive to the attainment of the cosmic measure of things. The Taoist consciousness, dispossessing to possess, decreating to create, has helped to eliminate these elements so that the poetic language is conditioned to a closest possible degree of approximation of Nature as it is. Chuang-tzu has actually commented on the function of speech that suggests this direction:

> Speech is not merely the blowing of winds. It is intending to say something. But what it is intending to say is not absolutely established. Is there really such a thing as speech? Is there really no such thing as speech? Someone considers speech as different from the chirping of young birds. But is there any distinction between them, or is there no distinction? How is Tao obscured that there should be a distinction between true and false? How is speech obscured that there should be a distinction between right or wrong? Where is Tao not present? Where is speech not appropriate? Tao is obscured by partiality. Speech is obscured by vain show. Therefore, there are contentions between the Confucianists and the Mohists. Each one of these two schools affirms what the other denies, and denies what the other affirms. If we are to affirm what they both deny and deny what they both affirm, there is nothing better than to use clarity (*Chuang*, 63).

---

[20] *Ching-chin Tung-p'o wen-chi shih-lüeh* 經進東坡文集事畧 (*SPTK* ed.), 46 (p. 279).
[21] Ibid., 57 (p. 335).

夫言非吹也。言者有言。其所言者特未定也。果有言邪。其未嘗有言
邪。其以爲有異於鷇音。亦有辨乎。其無辨乎。道惡乎隱而有眞僞。
言惡乎隱而有是非。道惡乎往而不存。言惡乎存而不可。道隱於小
成。言隱於榮華。故有儒墨之是非。以是其所非而非其所是。欲是其
所非而非其所是。則莫若以明。

And clarity means to view things as things view themselves: no judgement, no obscurity; no vain show, no obscurity. Instead of using language to infuse into objects ego-reflecting meanings, structures and systems, it is to be used to punctuate the vital rhythm of the things as they emerge from and merge into Phenomenon, innocent, free, original. By continually decreasing discursive and explanatory elements and procedures in the poetic line, by promoting the co-extensive presencing of objects, the poets who possess what the Chinese call the "bosom" of Taoist consciousness, help to bring forth a special type of non-mediating mediation, leading to an art of non-interference, akin to the workings of Nature, and a use of language as a pointer toward the finer interweaving of the unspeaking, concrete, changing Nature, like the word Tao which we are to forget once it is pronounced, like the fish trap which can be forgotten once the fish is caught (*Chuang*, 944).

Selection of Lines in Chinese Poetry-talk Criticism
—With a Comparison between the Selected Couplets and Matthew Arnold's "Touchstones"

W. L. Wong

In traditional China, since the eleventh century, many comments on poetry had appeared in the form of poetry-talk (*shih-hua tz'u-hua* 詩話詞話). Diversified are the contents of poetry-talk which include theoretical statements on poetry, practical criticism and anecdotes of poets. Such modern scholars as Kuo Shao-yü 郭紹虞 and James J. Y. Liu 劉若愚 have been diligent in expounding the theories of poetry which are seldom systematically presented in works of poetry-talk. Their studies have brought fruitful results. As regards the methodology of criticism in those works, virtually no research has been directed at it, except perhaps the frequently heard remark that the criticism in Chinese poetry-talk is impressionistic criticism in its pejorative sense. The impressionistic criticism in Chinese poetry-talk is characterized by its use of general, metaphoric and concise statements. In terms of precision and detailed treatment, the impressionistic practice is of course no match for the still influential New Criticism. Nevertheless, one should know that the comments of a widely-read and well-tempered critic, however terse they may be, are something to be reckoned with. Conciseness, moreover, can be a virtue.

Chinese critics who wrote in the form of poetry-talk were fond of, to the degree of indulging in, selecting their favorite lines as a kind of commentary, which is part of the Chinese impressionistic tradition. This article[1] analyzes the methods of selecting lines in works of poetry-talk, traces the origin of this practice, discusses the relation between this practice and certain features of Chinese poetry; it also compares the selected couplets with Matthew Arnold's "touchstones." The works of poetry-talk referred to in this study range from *Liu-i shih-hua* 六一詩話 in the Northern Sung to

---

[1] This article is based upon a chapter of my dissertation "Chinese Impressionistic Criticism: A Study of the Poetry-talk (*shih-hua tz'u-hua*) Tradition," the Ohio State University, 1976. I would like to take this opportunity to express my gratitude to Professors David Y. Ch'en, Yan-shuan Lao and William Graham, Jr., of the Ohio State University, who read and gave their thoughtful comments on this dissertation.

Jen-chien tz'u-hua 人間詞話 in the late Ch'ing. A total of twenty-one titles, they should serve ably to represent the critical tradition of poetry-talk over a period of some nine hundred years.[2]

The Critical Vision

The objects that receive critical attention in Chinese poetry-talk vary from a single character in a line, a line, a poem, a poet, a genre to the poetry of an entire historical period. There is a story in *Liu-i shih-hua* (abbreviated hereafter as *Liu-i*) about a missing character in a line of Tu Fu 杜甫 (712-70). A certain official who enjoyed reading poetry obtained an old edition of Tu Fu's poems and found that the final character in the line "The body is light—one bird . . . ." 身輕一鳥 . . . . was missing. This official and his guests tried to find a character that would best complete the line. One proposed the character *chi* 疾 (swift), one proposed *lo* 落 (falling), one proposed *ch'i* 起 (rising), and one proposed *hsia* 下 (descending), but they could not reach a consensus. Eventually the official obtained a better edition and learned that the missing character was *kuo* 過 (passing). He lauded the use of this character by Tu Fu and regretted that his guests could not figure it out; in other words, none of his guests could compose a line with such an excellent choice of words.[3] This story clearly illustrates how important a single character can be in the eyes of a critic.

Another one-character story, this one reported in *Huai-lu-t'ang shih-hua* 懷麓堂詩話, tells that a poet wrote on the wall of a temple a couplet which partly reads, "At the front peak, the moon shines over the water of a river" 前峰月照一江水. After leaving the temple, he contemplated about what he had written and decided that the character *i* (a or one) should be changed into *pan* 半 (half). Thus he hurriedly walked several dozens of *li* 里 back to the temple to change it. To his surprise, he found the character *i* had already been changed into *pan* by someone. "There

---

[2] The twenty-one works of poetry-talk being studied are: Ou-yang Hsiu 歐陽修 (1007-1072), *Liu-i shih-hua* 六一詩話; Chang Chieh 張戒 (fl. 1135), *Sui-han-t'ang shih-hua* 歲寒堂詩話; Yen Yü 嚴羽 (fl. 1180-1235), *Ts'ang-lang shih-hua* 滄浪詩話; Wang Jo-hsü 王若虛 (1174-1243), *Hu-nan shih-hua* 滹南詩話; Ch'en I-tseng 陳繹曾 (fl. 1330-1333), *Shih-p'u* 詩譜; Li Tung-yang 李東陽 (1447-1516), *Huai-lu-t'ang shih-hua* 懷麓堂詩話; Hsieh Chen 謝榛 (1495-1575), *Ssu-ming shih-hua* 四溟詩話; Wang Shih-chen 王士禎 (1634-1711), *Yü-yang shih-hua* 漁洋詩話; Shen Te-ch'ien 沈德潛 (1673-1769), *Shuo-shih tsui-yü* 說詩晬語; Yüan Mei 袁枚 (1716-1798), *Sui-yüan shih-hua* 隨園詩話; Chao I 趙翼 (1727-1814), *Ou-pei shih-hua* 甌北詩話; Weng Fang-kang 翁方綱 (1733-1818), *Ch'i-yen-shih san-mei chü-yü* 七言詩三昧舉隅; Shih Pu-hua 施補華 (19th cent.), *Hsien-yung shuo-shih* 峴傭說詩; Liang Ch'i-ch'ao 梁啟超 (1873-1929), *Yin-ping-shih shih-hua* 飲冰室詩話; Wang Cho 王灼 (12th cent.), *Pi-chi man-chih* 碧雞漫志; Chang Yen 張炎 (1248-1320?), *Tz'u-yüan* 詞源; Yang Shen 楊慎 (1488-1559), *Tz'u-p'in* 詞品; Ho Shang 賀裳 (17th cent.), *Chou-shui-hsüan tz'u-chüan* 皺水軒詞筌; Hsü Ang-hsiao 許昂霄 (18th cent.), *Tz'u-tsung ou-p'ing* 詞綜偶評; Ch'en T'ing-cho 陳廷焯 (1853-1892), *Pai-yü-chai tz'u-hua* 白雨齋詞話; Wang Kuo-wei 王國維 (1877-1927), *Jen-chien tz'u-hua* 人間詞話. Examples supporting my views in this article are drawn from the above twenty-one works, but I am aware that many more examples can be drawn from other sources.

[3] The edition of *Liu-i* consulted in this study is that of the *Li-tai shih-hua* 歷代詩話, ed. Ho Wen-huan 何文煥 (Taipei: I-wen, 1974). See *Liu-i*, 4ab in this edition for this one-character story.

is a master here," he sighed with approval.[4]

In these two stories, it is contended that the use of one character is better than others. But the reason why it is better is not disclosed. More examples like the above two stories can be cited. Hsieh Chen's remark, that the character *yung* 湧 (to bob, to surge) in Tu Fu's "Stars descend over the vast wild plain; / The moon bobs in the Great River's flow"[5] 星垂平野濶，月湧大江流 is especially *ch'i* 奇 (marvelous),[6] belongs to this type of statement that judges but does not explain.

We have just seen critical attention being directed at a single character of a particular line. We also find critical statements that refer to a huge object. The poetry of the Sung dynasty, for instance, is often judged against the poetry of the T'ang dynasty; and the *tz'u* poetry of the Southern Sung is frequently contrasted with that of the Northern Sung. The stylistic difference between *shih* and *tz'u* is another topic often discussed. As a rule, what the Chinese impressionistic critic makes are broad generalizations; he evaluates or describes or both but does not analyze. As regards the difference between the T'ang and the Sung poetry, we encounter such an analogy:

> The T'ang poetry is like a noble prince whose behavior is refined and tasteful. The Sung poetry is like the small villager turned rich overnight. He is elaborately dressed up, bowing to his guests; but his speech and his appearance are uncouth and vulgar.[7]

唐詩如貴介公子，舉止風流。宋詩如三家村乍富人，盛服揖賓，辭容鄙俗。

Elsewhere we find the following metaphoric comparison between the *tz'u* poetry of the Northern Sung and that of the Southern Sung: "The *tz'u* poetry of the Northern Sung is the *feng* in *Shih ching*, while that of the Southern Sung is the *ya* in it" 北宋詞，詩中之風也；南宋詞，詩中之雅也.[8] Here we need not worry about whether these general statements are justified. Suffice it to say that the vision of many of the Chinese impressionistic critics is vast enough to cover such huge bodies of poetry.

Though the critical vision of writers of poetry-talk can be very vast, the main objects that receive critical attention remain the individual poems and poets, the study of which is the legitimate business of practical criticism. The Chinese impressionistic critic is reputed for using extremely terse statements to express his impressions on poems and poets. In *Tz'u-tsung ou-p'ing* 詞綜偶評, where *tz'u* poems are commented upon one by one, quite a number of *tz'u* poems are each summarily described with a statement like "pure and forceful" 清勁、"Being pure, fresh, handsome and free, this poem has them all" 清新俊逸，兼有之矣, or "Clear, sparse, plain and dis-

---

[4] The edition of *Huai-lu-t'ang shih-hua* consulted in this study is that of the *Li-tai shih-hua hsü-pien* 歷代詩話續編, ed. Ting Fu-pao 丁福保 (1916; rpt. in 5 vols. Taipei: I-wen, n.d.). See the cited *shih-hua*, 8b in this edition for this story.

[5] Here I borrow the translation by James J. Y. Liu. See Liu Wu-chi 柳無忌 and Irving Y. Lo 羅郁正, eds., *Sunflower Splendor: Three Thousand Years of Chinese Poetry* (New York: Anchor, 1975), p. 143.

[6] See Hsieh Chen, *Ssu-ming shih-hua*, 1.12b, in *Li-tai shih-hua hsü-pien*.

[7] Ibid., 1.4b.

[8] See Ch'en T'ing-cho, *Pai-yü-chai tz'u-hua*, 7.5a, in T'ang Kuei-chang 唐圭璋, ed., *Tz'u-hua ts'ung-pien* 詞話叢編 (prefaced 1934; rpt. in 12 vols., Taipei: Kuang-wen, n.d.).

tant, the content of this poem matches its title very well" 蕭疏淡遠，雅與題稱.[9] As for the treatment of poets, the uniquely metaphoric section in *T'ai-ho cheng-yin p'u* 太和正音譜, for example, illustrates how economic a remark on the overall style and achievement of a writer can be.[10]

Selection of Lines

But a more common practice among the Chinese impressionistic critics is to criticize a poem or a poet by selecting lines from the poem (or poems) and making remarks on them. For instance, in Ou-yang Hsiu's *Liu-i*, a couplet is selected from a poet under discussion:

> As to his "The morning orioles outside the woods sing a thousand notes; / The fragrant grass before the flight of steps measures a foot high," it seems that these lines do not reflect his personality.[11]

又如「曉鶯林外千聲囀，芳草堦前一尺長」，殆不類其為人矣。

Elsewhere, Ou-yang commends a late T'ang poet for his craftsmanship. He quotes two couplets from this poet:

> Some of his lines read, "The breeze warm, the sound of birds is scattered; / The sun high, the shadows of flowers are manifold." Also: "At dawn, mountain birds clamour; After the rain, apricot flowers are scarce." Truly good lines![12]

其句有云：「風暖鳥聲碎，日高花影重。」又云：「曉來山鳥鬧，雨過杏花稀。」誠佳句也。

In another place, a couplet from a poem written on a special occasion is cited:

> The newly completed long bridge at Sung-chiang is unprecedented for its grand and beautiful design. The scene is what Su Tzu-mei [Su Shun-ch'in 蘇舜欽, 1008-48] depicts as "The glittering clouds open for the golden disc; / On the heavy water lies a colorful rainbow." At the time, it was generally agreed that no lines could do the bridge justice except this sublime couplet.[13]

松江新作長橋，制度宏麗，前世所未有。蘇子美「新橋對月」詩所謂「雲頭灧灧開金餅，水面沉沉臥彩虹」者是也。時謂此詩非此句雄偉不能稱也。

---

[9] See 4a, 11a, 23b respectively in this *tz'u-hua*, in the *Tz'u-hua ts'ung-pien* edition.
[10] Cf. Chapter 3 of my dissertation.
[11] *Liu-i*, 13a.
[12] *Liu-i*, 5b.
[13] *Liu-i*, 9b.

The practice of quoting a line or two to support a critical judgment is by no means extraordinary; it is a fundamental device in any critical discourse. In Chinese literary criticism, Chung Hung 鍾嶸 (fl. 483-513) is probably the first or among the first who cited lines to support a critical opinion. A passage in his *Shih-p'in* 詩品 reads:

> In expressing feelings, we do not value the use of allusions. [The line] "I think of you as water flows" simply states what is seen. [The line] "There is much sorrowful wind on the High Terrace" also merely reveals what one has witnessed. [The line] "I climb the mound in the morning" does not allude to anything. [The line] "The bright moon shines on the piled snow" does not come from the Classics or the Histories.[14]
>
> 至乎吟詠情性，亦何貴於用事？「思君如流水」，旣是即目；「高臺多悲風」，亦惟所見；「清晨登隴首」，羌無故實；「明月照積雪」，詎出經史！

However, there is something unique in the quoting of lines in Chinese impressionistic criticism. Lines are often selected not for supporting a critical opinion, but for their intrinsic attractiveness. Moreover, lines are often chosen to be appreciated in isolation, the critic being not concerned with the coordination between the selected lines and the rest of the poem from which the lines are drawn. In *Liu-i,* for instance, at least the third passage in the order of our citation is quoted not so much for its supporting function as for its intrinsic attractiveness. The couplet "The glittering clouds open for the golden disc; / On the heavy water lies a colorful rainbow" is there simply because it beautifully depicts the scene of the newly constructed bridge.

In *Yü-yang shih-hua* 漁洋詩話 (hereafter *Yü-yang*) and *Sui-yüan shih-hua* 隨園詩話 (hereafter *Sui-yüan*), the practice of quoting lines for their intrinsic beauty, not for supporting a critical opinion, is more obvious. It is the habit of Wang Shih-chen 王士禎 (1634-1711) to select lines and make comments on them, which invariably read: "These lines have the *san-mei* 三昧 of the T'ang poets";[15] "These are all *ching-chü* 警句 [epigrammatic lines]";[16] "These are all *chia-chü* 佳句 [good lines]";[17] or "These lines are not inferior to those of ancient writers."[18] These comments are expressions of a reader's impressions, synonymous with saying "These lines are good!" Each of these comments is hardly intended to support a particular critical opinion. As for Yüan Mei 袁枚 (1716-98), the author of *Sui-yüan,* he goes a step further by often quoting his favorite lines without making any comment at all. For instance, there is a short paragraph in *Sui-yüan* which simply states:

> The official T'ang Hsin, en route to assuming his duty, wrote "On the Lake," which reads: "The small bridge be-

---

[14] *Shih-p'in chu* 詩品注, annot. Ch'en Yen-chieh 陳延傑 (Hong Kong: Shang-wu, 1969), p. 7.
[15] *Yü-yang*, in *Ch'ing shih-hua* 清詩話, ed. Ting Fu-pao (Shanghai: Chung-hua, 1963), p. 177.
[16] Ibid., p. 178.
[17] Ibid., p. 179.
[18] Ibid., p. 219.

tween the shores is often crossed by horses; / The slim willows, like the mist, do not hinder the orioles." An "Impromptu" composed by Yang Tzu-tsai of Chianghsi province has the following lines: "When fisherman's lamps are about to go out, the lights on fishing boats appear. / The drizzle has no sound; the falling flowers have increased."[19]

湯中丞莘來聘,「湖上」云:「小橋隔岸時通馬,細柳如烟不碍鶯。」
江西揚子載「偶成」云:「漁燈欲滅見漁火,細雨無聲添落花。」

All the above couplets drawn from *Liu-i* and *Sui-yüan* have two things in common: to begin with, they are all *tui-ou chü* 對偶句 or antithetical couplets; secondly, what they depict is scenery. We also find that in *Liu-i*, *Yü-yang* and *Sui-yüan*, most of the couplets their authors cite are marked by these two features. In particular, virtually all the quoted couplets in *Yü-yang* are antithetical and scenery-oriented. In another work, *Ou-pei shih-hua* 甌北詩話, many special sections are devoted to listing antithetical couplets selected by its author Chao I 趙翼 (1727-1814). Under one section, approximately 329 antithetical couplets are chosen from the Regulated Verses (*lü-shih* 律詩) by Lu Yu 陸游 (1125-1210). The selected couplets are grouped under three headings: *shih shih* 使事 or "using allusions," *hsieh huai* 寫懷 or "expressing personal sentiments," and *hsieh ching* 寫景 or "depicting scenery." There are also sections for antithetical couplets selected from the works of Su Shih, Wu Wei-yeh 吳偉業 (1609-71) and Cha Shen-hsing 查慎行 (1650-1727). The selected lines of Cha Shen-hsing are almost as numerous as those in the Lu Yu section. Moreover, there is another section for couplets chosen from a variety of poets.

Antithetical Couplets vs. Matthew Arnold's Touchstones

An antithetical couplet, as the term indicates, is a pair of lines each of which contrasts the other. In order to contrast the other, each line must first have a meaning of its own. Thus, when a line of an antithetical couplet stands alone, it is a self-sufficient unit, with an independent meaning. When it joins another line to form an antithetical couplet, the two merge into a larger unit, often producing some sort of dramatic effect. In Chinese versification, it is required that there be two antithetical couplets in a Regulated Verse. Each of the two antithetical couplets in a Regulated Verse is part of the whole poem and should, of course, coordinate formally and thematically with the rest of the work. And, for that matter, the best way to understand and appreciate an antithetical couplet of a Regulated Verse is to do so in the total context of the poem. Nevertheless, due to the characteristics of the antithetical couplet just mentioned, the antithetical couplet can survive—and survive well— when it is taken out of context as an independent poetic structure. The antithetical

---

[19] *Chien-chu Sui-yüan shih-hua* 箋注隨園詩話, annot. Lei Chin 雷瑨 (Taipei: Ting-wen, 1974), 12.6. Other examples of Yüan Mei's quoting his favorite lines or poems without making any comment are seen in 2.3; 8.30; 8.40; 9.9; etc. In the original text, the first line of Yang's couplet reads 漁燈欲滅見漁火. The first *yü* 漁 in this line might be a misprint. I consulted another edition, i.e., *Sui-yüan ch'üan-chi* 隨園全集 (Taipei: Ch'i-ming, 1960), p. 211, and the reading is exactly the same.

couplet can thus be regarded as a mini-poem. In effect, the two-line *tui-lien* 對聯, which is essentially the same as the *tui-ou chü* except that the former can vary its length while the latter is limited to either five or seven characters in each line (as in the Regulated Verse), has long established itself as a kind of mini-poem, completely independent and self-sufficient.

Take the following antithetical couplets for examples:

> To live, I aspire to be Li Kuang, the Flying General;
> To die, I wish to be Liu Ling, the drunken lord.[20]

生希李廣名飛將，死慕劉伶作醉侯。

> The eve of a year coming to an end.
> A man, thousands of miles away, yet to return home.[21]

一年將盡夜，萬里未歸人。

> At dawn, mountain birds clamour;
> After the rain, apricot flowers are scarce.[22]

The first antithetical couplet is from a poem by Lu Yu, selected and classified by Chao I as one using allusions. As both Li Kuang and Liu Ling are famous historical figures, alluding to them poses no problem in our understanding the meaning of the couplet. This couplet neatly projects two views of life, one Confucian as represented by Li Kuang, and one Taoist as represented by Liu Ling. Though taken out of context, these two lines form a self-sufficient structure which produces a contrastive effect easily detectable.

The second antithetical couplet is from a poem by a minor T'ang poet, also selected by Chao I who probably would have classified it as lines that express personal sentiments. Again, we do not have to know the whole poem in order to understand and appreciate this couplet: the sadness of the lone traveler, an archetypal emotion in Chinese poetry, is powerfully conveyed through a dramatic contrast achieved in part by the pairing off of the time element "a year" and the spatial element "thousands of miles"; and in part by the ironic situations—the closeness to year's end and the separation from one's home.

The last couplet, the now familiar lines from *Liu-i*, is what Chao I would call lines that depict scenery. Couched in concrete diction, this couplet is a lively landscape painting in words and is even more immediately perceivable than the second one. Since this couplet alludes to no historical figures or events, even a less educated reader can understand it. This type of scenery couplet is certainly the most independent and self-sufficient among the three. As aforementioned, we find that most of the couplets selected in *Liu-i*, *Yü-yang* and *Sui-yüan*, especially *Yü-yang*, belong to this type.

To further illustrate the independence and self-sufficiency of the antithetical couplets, we may compare them with the touchstone passages in Matthew Arnold's criticism. In his "The Study of Poetry," Arnold advocates the use of touchstones as

---

[20] Quoted in *Ou-pei shih-hua*. See *Ch'ing shih-hua*, p. 82.
[21] Ibid., p. 172.
[22] Quoted in *Liu-i*, 5b.

a basis of a "real" estimate of poetry. His touchstones are "lines and expressions of the great masters" against which other poems are judged for "the presence or absence of high poetic quality" in them. By "high poetic quality," Arnold means "high seriousness" and the "grand style." Nine of the total eleven touchstone passages chosen by Arnold are from epic poems, the *Iliad*, the *Divine Comedy* and *Paradise Lost;* and two from Shakespeare, *Hamlet* and *Henry IV, Part II*. One of the touchstones, what Arnold describes as "that incomparable line and a half of Dante," reads:

> *Io non piangeva, si dentro impietrai;*
> *piangevan elli;*
> (I did not weep: so strong grew I within:
> they wept;)[23]

Another touchstone, from *Paradise Lost,* is as follows:

> And courage never to submit or yield;
> And what is else not to be overcome?

The first touchstone lines point out a difference: "I did not weep"; but "they wept." But who is "I" and who are "they"? Why did "I" not weep and "they" did? What is the story behind this line and a half? As to the second touchstone passage, it gives us nothing other than the emphatic "courage." After reading these two lines, we are likely to ask: Whose courage is it? Under what circumstances is this courage to be shown? We never understand—not to say appreciate—these touchstone passages until and unless we know well the contexts in which they appear. Having thoroughly studied Arnold's eleven passages and their related literature, John Shepard Eells, Jr., came to this conclusion:

> If their best imaginative values are to be felt and realized, they [i.e., the eleven touchstone passages] must be read and pondered in their contexts. . . . A comprehensive understanding of the touchstones apart from their contexts is clearly impossible.[24]

The difference between the antithetical couplets and the touchstone passages is tremendous, but it should not be too great a surprise to those who realize that the antithetical couplet is a unique feature of Chinese literature.

It has been argued that the reason why Arnold takes these passages as touchstones by which he judges other poems is that the "high poetic quality" they possess cannot be easily explained in words—we may recall his hesitation in clarifying his term "grand style" with "verbal definition." In this sense, Arnold may be regarded as an intuitionist critic, one who doubts that verbal discourse can fully interpret the beauty of a work of art.[25] Arnold is not alone as an intuitionist critic because the limitation of words had long been recognized in China and, as the foregoing has

---

[23] The translation is by J. A. Carlyle. I quote this translation from John S. Eells, Jr., *The Touchstones of Matthew Arnold* (New York: Bookman, 1955), p. 255.

[24] Ibid., p. 207.

[25] Ibid., p. 204.

shown, Chinese impressionistic critics are much more advanced than Arnold in criticizing without making any critical statement at all. It should be stressed, however, that Arnold is not really an intuitionist critic. While there is a tint of intuitionism in his touchstone doctrine, his criticism at large is marked by a profound intellectual appeal. Genuine intuitionist criticism is found in the Chinese impressionistic tradition, in such works as *Yü-yang* and *Sui-yüan,* where lines are selected and presented as they are, either with an immediate comment which is next to no comment, or with no comment at all.

The intuitionist criticism of selecting lines and selecting lines only did not originate in works of *shih-hua.* T'ang critics had already started this practice. In the Sung dynasty, Li Tung 李洞 (1088-1158) chose lines by the poet Chia Tao 賈島 (788-843) and collected them in a *chüan* 卷, entitled *Chi Chia Tao shih-chü-t'u* 集賈島詩句圖. Another similar work of selected lines is called *Huei-ch'ung chü-t'u* 惠崇句圖; Huei-ch'ung, as mentioned in *Liu-i,* was a monk-poet of the Sung dynasty. These two works are among the earliest compilations of *shih-chü-t'u* (chart of selected lines). They are both now lost but, since they are quoted or allegedly quoted in other books, we can still find out what these *shih-chü-t'u* are like. In *Yin-ch'uang tsa-lu* 吟窗雜錄, thirteen couplets are allegedly drawn from *Chi Chia Tao shih-chü-t'u*. These couplets are all antithetical and are mostly scenery-oriented, including the famous one, "Birds perch on the trees by the pond; / A monk knocks at the door under the moon" 鳥宿池邊樹，僧敲月下門.[26] The hundred couplets of Huei-ch'ung recorded in *Ch'ing-hsiang tsa-chi* 青箱雜記 reveal an identical phenomenon: they are antithetical and are mostly scenery-oriented.[27]

So far, only examples from works of *shih-hua* have been cited to demonstrate the popularity of the antithetical couplet. In works of *tz'u-hua,* to criticize by selecting lines and making or without making comments on them is also very common. Antithesis is not a requirement in every tune pattern of *tz'u* poetry and, when antithetical lines do exist, they are not as clearly visible as the antithetical couplets in the Regulated Verse. Nevertheless, antithetical lines are all the same favorite targets of the critical eye in the selection of lines. For instance, in *Tz'u-p'in* 詞品, all the eight short passages quoted from Chiang K'uei's 姜夔 (1155?-1235?) *tz'u* poems mainly consist of antithetical lines;[28] and the two short passages quoted from Lu Yu comprise lines purely antithetical.[29] Also, at one point in *Chou-shui-hsüan tz'u-ch'üan* 皺水軒詞筌, five of the six quotations from *t'zu* poems, which serve to support a critical opinion, are entirely antithetical lines.[30] Other similar examples in works of *tz'u-hua* are too many to enumerate.

---

[26] From his "T'i Li Ning yu chü" 題李凝幽居.

[27] *Ch'ing-hsiang tsa-chi* is the work of Wu Ch'u-hou 吳處厚. The edition I used is the one in Ch'i Ai-sheng 齊愛生, ed., *Pi-chi hsiao-shuo ta-kuan* 筆記小說大觀 (Taipei: Hsin-hsing, 1962). In this paragraph, I have heavily relied on Lo Ken-tse 羅根澤, *Chung-kuo wen-hsüeh p'i-p'ing shih* 中國文學批評史 (Shanghai: Ku-tien wen-hsüeh, vols. 1-2, 1958; vol. 3, 1962), pp. 495-505, for information on *shih-chü-t'u*. The interested reader is referred to this section in Lo's book for details.

[28] 4.6b-7a, in the *Tz'u-hua ts'ung-pien* edition.

[29] Ibid., 5.7b.

[30] 4a, in the *Tz'u-hua ts'ung-pien* edition.

Obsession with Selected Lines

What emerges from all the above findings is a peculiar poetic idiosyncrasy—an obsession with the antithetical couplet. In Chinese manuals for literary compositions, the structural principle of *ch'i ch'eng chuan he* 起承轉合 (beginning, development, transition and conclusion) is emphatically taught to would-be writers. Another principle, that of *hu-ying* 呼應 or coordination among the parts in a literary work, is also regarded as essential to any good writing. In Chinese poetics, a good poem should possess good selectable lines on the one hand, and be a good poem as a whole on the other. The phrase *yu chü wu p'ien* 有句無篇 (possessing good selectable lines but not a good poem as a whole) is used as a critical admonition.[31] Despite all this, it is the obsession of the Chinese impressionistic critic to select antithetical couplets and appreciate them in isolation without trying to analyze their relationship and coordination with the rest of the poem from which they are drawn. If the concept of *yin* and *yang* is applicable to Chinese poetics, we may speculate that it is the antithetical couplet as the perfect embodiment of *yin* and *yang*—the harmonious power of matching and contrasting—that enchants its lovers. We may argue on behalf of the lovers that, as *yin* and *yang* are the essence of the universe, the antithetical couplet is the essence of the poem. It is not too much to say that for those who are fond of composing *tui-lien,* participating in the literary game *shih-chung* 詩鐘 (The Poetry Bell),[32] and selecting antithetical couplets, the well-wrought and self-sufficient structure, that is, the antithetical couplet, is the real poem in its quintessential form.

Therefore, although Yüan Mei, one of the many lovers of antithetical couplets, regretted that "most of the poems he wrote when he was young are mostly *yu chü wu p'ien,*"[33] he spared no occasions to praise lines—and merely lines. He was once so impressed by an antithetical couplet that he declared the poet who wrote it would be remembered for this couplet alone.[34] The relationship between the poet and his lines can be more intimate than that: he is often identified by his best known lines. There is a story reported by Yüan Mei that the poet Wu Hsiu-ling 吳修齡 who wrote "The wild geese take the autumn scene away; / The sail brings the beautiful mountains along" 雁將秋色去，帆帶好山移 was later called Wu Hao-shan 吳好山 or Wu the Beautiful Mountains because this antithetical couplet was widely appreciated.[35] If such an additional name complicated the trouble in identifying a Chinese person, who was variously called by his courtesy name, studio name, etc., the Chinese impressionistic critic obviously enjoyed being a trouble-maker. Two poets, as *Yü-yang* tells us, were given the additional names Ts'ui the Yellow Leaves and Wang the Yellow Leaves respectively because their well-acclaimed lines contain the words *huang yeh* 黃葉 (yellow leaves).[36] Incidentally, it is Wang Shih-chen himself who initiated the first additional name. On one occasion, Wang almost ruined a friendship for his favorite hobby of name-coining:

---

[31] Critics who hold this view include Shih Pu-hua (*Hsien-yung shuo-shih*, in *Ch'ing shih-hua*, p. 990), Wang Kuo-wei (*Jen-chien tz'u-hua*, in the *Tz'u-hua ts'ung-pien* edition, 2.5b) and many others.

[32] For a discussion of the meaning and the methods of *shih-chung*, consult Wang Sung-ch'ang 王嵩昌, *Shih-chung ke-li ts'un-kao* 詩鐘格例存稿 (Taipei: n.p., 1969).

[33] *Chien-chu Sui-yüan shih-hua, pu-i* 補遺, 4.22.

[34] Ibid., 1.6.

[35] Ibid., 3.37.

[36] *Yü-yang*, pp. 168, 202.

> Ch'i Shan-chou . . . has written a poem which reads, "A night of east wind blew the rain away; / A river of fresh water raised the fish and shrimp." Deeply delighted with the lines, I jokingly called him Ch'i the Fish and Shrimp. Ch'i was angry with me. I smiled, apologizing, "Please don't be angry with me. There are antecedents." He asked about the antecedents and I said, "Haven't you heard about Mei the Globefish?"[37] Ch'i could not help laughing and quit.[38]
>
> 祁珊洲⋯有詩云：「一夜東風吹雨過，滿江新水長魚蝦。」余深喜之，戲呼爲祁魚蝦。祁作色而怒，余笑謝曰：「兄勿怒，此自有先例。」祁問何例，余曰：「兄不聞梅河豚？」祁乃失笑而罷。

Besides Mei the Globefish and Ch'i the Fish and Shrimp, we have plenty of similar epithets attached to the names of poets who have been particularly remembered by a line or two: "the Red Apricot Minister" 紅杏尙書, "Ho the Plum" 賀梅子, "Chang the Three Shadows" 張三影, "Mountains-rubbed-by-light-clouds Ch'in the Scholar" 山抹微雲秦學士, "Dawn-breeze-and-fading-moon Liu the Three Changes" 曉風殘月柳三變,[39] to cite but a few. If literature is "a splendid enterprise that will never perish," as Ts'ao P'i 曹丕 (187-226) contends,[40] those poets are immortalized by their best known lines.

Lines are also employed as critical statements. Ch'en T'ing-cho 陳廷焯 (1855-1892) believes that the beginning words "I look beyond, the autumn leveling" 望遠秋平 in one of Ch'en Yün-p'ing's 陳允平 (1205?-85?) tz'u poems reflect the "poetic mood" of Ch'en's entire works and therefore these words can be used as "an eulogy on all [Ch'en's] poems."[41] Remarks of this nature are plentiful in Wang Kuo-wei's 王國維 (1877-1927) Jen-chien tz'u-hua:

> "The golden partridges on the painted screen" are Wen T'ing-yün's words, which may well characterize his tz'u as a whole. "The chattering of orioles from the lute strings," words of Wei Chuang 韋莊 (836-910), may also well characterize his tz'u as a whole. As for the characteristic of Feng Yen-ssu's 馮延巳 (903-60) tz'u, if we want to take a line from his own tz'u to describe it, "With eyes full of tears I try on formal dress" may be more or less suitable for the purpose.[42]
>
> 「畫屏金鷓鴣」，飛卿語也，其詞品似之。「絃上黃鶯語」，端己語也，其詞品亦似之。正中詞品，若欲于其詞句中求之，則「和淚試嚴妝」，殆近之歟？

---

[37] This Mei Ho-t'un is Mei Yao-ch'en 梅堯臣 (1002-1060), who wrote a poem, quoted in Ou-yang Hsiu's Liu-i, 2a, which reads: 春洲生荻芽，春岸飛楊花；河豚當是時，貴不數魚蝦。

[38] Yü-yang, p. 179.

[39] The five tz'u poets are Sung Ch'i 宋祁 (998-1061), Ho Chu 賀鑄 (1063-1121), Chang Hsien 張先 (990-1078), Ch'in Kuan 秦觀 (1049-1100) and Liu Yung 柳永 (fl. 1034).

[40] Quoted from his famous essay "Lun wen" 論文.

[41] Pai-yü-chai tz'u-hua, 2.5a.

[42] Jen-chien tz'u-hua, 1.2a. Here I borrow T'u Ching-i's 涂經詒 translation, with minor modifications. See T'u Ching-i, tr., Poetic Remarks in the Human World: Jen-chien tz'u-hua (Taipei: Chung-hua, 1970), p. 8.

With regard to Wu Wen-ying's 吳文英 (13th cent.) *tz'u,* I can take a line from his own to characterize it: "Shadows in green disarray falling on a somnolent window." With regard to Chang Yen's 張炎 (1248-1320?) *tz'u,* I can take a line from his own to characterize it: "Jade grown old and fields lay fallow."[43]

夢窗之詞,余得取其詞中之一語以評之曰:「映夢窗凌亂碧。」玉田之詞,余得取其詞中之一語以評之曰:「玉老田荒。」

What we have encountered above are all lines: lines that are selected and appreciated apart from the context, lines that immortalize poets, and lines that are fed back to their original creators as critical statements about them. Thus we see that, in Chinese impressionistic criticism, there is an obsession with selected lines, especially with the antithetical couplet. For such critics as Wang Shih-chen, the obsession is, in the very act of selecting the lines, also a relaxation—an enjoyment in picking and playing with good lines which many a poet has worked hard, even with great pains, to create.[44]

---

[43] Ibid., 1.6a. Again I borrow T'u's translation with minor changes; see T'u's work, p. 34.

[44] For instance, Tu Fu was a hard worker, who confessed that "I am addicted to indulging in good lines; / If my words do not surprise people, I'll die still trying" (from "Chiang-shang chih shui ju hai shih liao tuan shu" 江上值水如海勢聊短述). Also, Ch'en shih-tao 陳師道 (1053-1101) has been remembered for his locking himself up in a room in search for good lines.

Period Style and Periodization: A Survey of Theory and Practice in the Histories of Chinese and European Literature

Tak-wai Wong

Seymour L. Flaxman in his paper entitled "Chronology and Literary History" stated: "The attempt to define literary movements as successive chronological developments in history has often led to misconceptions and distortions. Careful examination frequently reveals the elements of a new style in the work of writers belonging to the movement preceding it. Great writers, moreover, may transcend movements and achieve mastery of two or more styles. This raises a fundamental question in literary periodization and historiography."[1] This question has seldom been answered with adequate critical awareness. In fact, as René Wellek pointed out in his 1940 essay entitled "Periods and Movements in Literary History," although different period labels or schemes have been adopted in histories of national literatures, "very few writers . . . indicate the principles which underlie the formation of periods in literary history."[2] It was not until the late sixties when scholars began to concern themselves with the theoretical paradigm of literary historiography that the study of these principles were taken up and placed in a proper perspective, one which takes into consideration both the socio-historico and ideo-literario factors. Since the publication of Claudio Guillén's essay entitled "Second Thoughts on Currents and Periods"[3] in 1968 and of the "Symposium on Periods" issue of the *New Literary History* in 1970, scholarly surveys and discussions in English on the problem of period-style and periodization have appeared one after another, such as Klaus Weissenberger's and Fritz Martini's essays on,

---

[1] *Literary History and Literary Criticism,* Acta of the Ninth Congress International Federation for Modern Languages and Literature, 25-30 August 1963 (New York: New York Univ. Press, 1964), p. 224.

[2] *English Institute Annuals* (New York: Columbia Univ. Press, 1940-41), p. 73.

[3] *The Disciplines of Criticism, Interpretation, and History Honoring René Wellek on the Occasion of his Sixty-Fifth Birthday,* ed. Peter Demetz, Thomas Greene, and Lowry Nelson, Jr. (New Haven: Yale Univ. Press, 1968), pp. 477-510; reprinted in Guillén's *Literature as System: Essays toward the Theory of Literary History* (Princeton: Princeton Univ. Press, 1972), pp. 420-69, under the title "Second Thoughts on Literary Periods."

respectively, "The Problem of Period Style in the Theory of Recent Literary Criticism" and "Personal Style and Period Style: Perspectives on a Theme of Literary Research,"[4] as well as Ulrich Weisstein's chapter on "Epoch, Period, Generation, and Movement" and Guillén's article on "Change and Contradiction in Literary Periods."[5] These examples, though too few to constitute a trend in literary study, have brought up critical problems—such as those of terminology and of assigning dates to different periods—and have expounded various conceptions—such as the synchrony and diachrony of periodization—of period style and periodization that concern both the literary historian and the comparatist.

To start with, we have to bear in mind that the writing of a history of literature without periodization is practically unworkable, and that the problem of writing the history of a period is first a problem of description—we need to discern the decline of one convention and the rise of a new one, be it a literary genre, a stylistic trend (represented by a dominant style or a cluster of related styles), or a direction of taste and sensibility. Insofar as we consider literary history "a continuous and organic account of a development," Croce's rejection of literary history as a survey of cultural epochs on account of its "merely pedagogic and didactic junction" and his argument that the only kind of proper literary history is a collection of monographs on single artists is unjustifiable. Besides, the division of literary history into periods is, in Edward H. Carr's words, "not a fact, but a necessary hypothesis or tool of thought, valid in so far as it is illuminating, and dependent for its validity on interpretation."[6] It subsumed a process of deriving, from the common qualities of literary works by individual writers, the significant characteristics of the dominant style/style-complex (generic as well as rhetorical) and/or the prevalent world-view

---

[4] Both essays are translated from German and published in *Patterns of Literary Style*, ed. Joseph Strelka (University Park: The Pennsylvania State Univ. Press, 1971), pp. 226-64 and 90-115, respectively. The other recent contributions of importance that have not been translated into English are *Analyse de la périodisation littéraire*, Proc. of a Conference held in Bordeux, ed. Charles Bouazis (Paris: Editions universitaires, 1972), which "is rather disappointing . . . insofar as its contributors restrict themselves to a more or less dogmatic sociological point of view or, where they come to grips with the problem as an aesthetico-literary one, simply ignore the existing secondary literature in English and German, a circumstance which greatly diminishes the value of their contributions" (Ulrich Weisstein, *Comparative Literature and Literary Theory*, Bloomington: Indiana Univ. Press, 1968, pp. 66-67), and the "Courants littéraires—Époques littéraires" articles published in *Neohelicon*, 1, Nos. 1-2 (Proc. of the Budapest "Colloque méthodologique de littérature comparée" held in November 1971. Budapest: Akadémiai Kiadó, 1973), which includes Anna Balakian's "Époque, période, courant: historicité et affinités dans l'histoire comparée des littératures" (194-200), Alexandre Dima's "Périodes et courants littéraires" (223-29), Aleksandar Flaker's "Einige prinzipielle und praktische Bemerkungen zur Frage der Periodisierung" (254-62), Mihai Novicov's "Un point de vue structural dans la recherche des relations existantes entre périodes et courants littéraires" (266-73), André Stegmann's "Problémes méthodologiques et terminologiques pour une périodisation en littérature" (274-85), and other essays.

[5] *Comparative Literature and Literary Theory*, pp. 66-98 and *Neohelicon*, 1, Nos. 1-2, 210-23, respectively. The other English articles included in the same *Neohelicon* issue are Henry Remak's "The Periodization of XIXth Century German Literature in the Light of French Trends: A Reconsideration" (177-94), A. Owen Aldridge's "The Concept of Classicism as Period or Movement" (230-44), Péter Egri's "The Epoch and Trend Aspects of Baroque Art" (244-54), Mikló Szenczi's "English Renaissance Literature. Periodization by Concentric Circles" (285-90), etc. In the following issue there is Helmut Hatzfeld's long essay on "Rococo as a European Epoch-style" (*Neohelicon*, 1, Nos. 3-4, 43-75).

[6] *What is History?* (New York: Knopf, 1962), p. 76.

of their respective periods, and applying these characteristics hypothetically to other works of their coevals so as to test the validity of the criteria and to discover the additional manifestations of the *Zeitgeist*. Or as Henry Remak put it,

> A period scheme is only a scheme. From the general characterization one should always proceed to the differentiation of the individual work. . . . It is by contrasting the individual work with the presumed denominators of the period that one detects far more nuances than one would discover if the work were contemplated in isolation. . . . Further, if one analyzes enough individual works in the light of the presumed periodization concept, one will inevitably arrive at conclusions which will modify the hypothesis.[7]

The problem is how to determine the denominators of a period. For Marxist scholars, a literary period should be established by criteria indicative of social or economic changes. Although they assume that there are *courants stylistiques* (each of which has its own temporal peculiarity),[8] they reject all periodizations based solely on styles and contend that literary currents, in themselves, can hardly serve as a suitable basis for periodization. But for scholars like Mario Praz,[9] a literary period should be established by purely literary criteria, such as stylistic traditions or literary genres that have "regulative" value during the period. A position of compromise would be one similar to that assumed by Remak:

> while we should try to keep our periodization terms as literary as possible, the object (i.e., the period) must dictate the choice of the term; we must not dictate, not even literarily, to the period. . . . [Depending] upon the character of the period, we use as common denominator a term from the history of art, philosophy, religion, political or even military development.[10]

Or in Aldridge's words, "literary terms, as comprehensive as those of periods, should not exclude recognition of the interplay of forces (e.g., social, political, religious) and the complexity of life."[11]

Among the many criteria for establishing a literary period, period-style—such as Baroque, Rococo, when properly defined and used in the sense of a trend or a complex that represents writers' common preference for certain rhetorical devices, imagery

---

[7] *Neohelicon*, 1, Nos. 1-2, 178.

[8] Tibor Klaniczay: "Les éléments de base d'une périodisation convenable ne peuvent être que les grandes étapes de l'histoire de la civilisation et de l'art déterminées du point de vue économique et du point de vue l'histoire sociale, qui vont de pair dans tous les cas avec la naissance ou la disparition d'un ou de plusieurs styles nouveaux. A ces époques correspondent soit un seul grand style d'époque, soit plusieurs grands styles universels successifs (par ex. le moyen age), soit plusieurs courants stylistiques paralléles" ("Styles et histoire du Style," *Littérature Hongroise. Littérature Européenne*, ed. István Sötér and Otto Süpek. Budapest: Akadémiai Kiadó, 1964, p. 25).

[9] For Praz's views, consult his article on "Literary History," *Comparative Literature*, 2 (1950), 97-106.

[10] *Neohelicon*, 1, Nos. 1-2 (1973), 179.

[11] Ibid., 233.

patterns, and syntactical structures *and* at the same time reflects the *Zeitgeist,* the historical and social dynamics of the period—is one of the most effective denominators. As the relationship between literary process and social or economic change is intimate and crucial, the problem of period style is closely linked with that of periodization and of the typology of poets.[12] Considering that "both the principle applied in periodization and the length of the time unit have a definite bearing on any analysis of period style,"[13] and that the study of period style is "ontologically entailed, directly or indirectly, in the criticism of individual works,"[14] it will not be difficult for us to accept the above statement as a hypothetical truth. This truth, like Wellek's definitions of "a period" (a time section dominated by a system of literary norms, whose introduction, spread, diversification, integration, and disappearance can be traced[15]) and of "an individual work of art" (part of the concept of a given period and its process of definition[16]) may appear to be plain and uncomplicated. Yet to define a period style or to derive an objective principle of periodization is by no means a simple matter.

Though with Wellek's introduction of "period" as a dynamic regulative concept,[17] and Guillén's discussion of the diachronic concept of "period,"[18] the question whether the traditional groupings into periods should be renounced for their unrealistic representation of the process of historical time seems to have been settled,[19] the problems of terminology and assigning dates[20] to individual periods still remain unsolved.

Guillén's review of the difficulties raised by periodization, especially with regard to diachrony[21] and the organization of historical time, has led him to the compromising

---

[12] Weissenberger, pp. 226 & 258.

[13] Ibid., p. 226.

[14] Alastair Fowler, "Periodization and Interart Analogies," *New Literary History,* 3 (1972), 489.

[15] Wellek, p. 89.

[16] Ibid., pp. 90-91.

[17] Ibid., p. 92. This concept was later advanced by Mario Praz in his article on "Literary History" (see note 9).

[18] Guillén, *Literature as System* (see note 3), pp. 420-69.

[19] Guillén specifically cited Edward A. Freeman's view in *The Unity of History* (1872) that "the traditional separation of the past into periods should be abandoned, as being detrimental to a unified vision of man's historical achievement" (*Literature as System,* p. 424). He pointed out in one of his more recent essays that "the old notion of period as a concept wholly and fully coincident with a section of time and thus constituting a discrete unit of history is being discarded" ("Change and Contradiction in Literary Periods," *Neohelicon,* 1, Nos. 1-2, 214). By redefining "period" as a dynamic concept incorporating contradiction and change, the literary historians seem to have managed to justify themselves for periodizing literature.

[20] Generally, we find more precise dating in static and synchronic periodization, and more symbolic dating in diachronic temporal-division. As Louise F. Cazamian stated plainly in his *A History of French Literature* (Oxford: Clarendon Press, 1955), the dates he assigned to The Renaissance, 1491-1590, were "purely symbolical"—they were chosen simply because the last decades of the 15th and of the 16th centuries were both harbingers of the coming periods. Among all the solutions, Ferdinand Brunetière's opinion that one should use the date of publication of important works or important literary events in periodizing (from the preface to his *Manuel de l'histoire de littérature française* published in 1898) seems to be workable for histories of national literature, provided that the dates given are taken in their symbolic sense.

[21] His initial hypothesis is that "Currents are diachrony, and periods, synchrony (of values)" (*Literature as System,* p. 422). "While the static or synchronic conception of periods usually depends on stylistic harmonies, the dynamic or diachronic view draws upon social tensions" (Ibid., pp. 429-30). "The notion of literary currents is frankly diachronic, dynamic, open-ended, and suggestive of relations with historical and social development" (Ibid., p. 453).

position of defining "period" as a critical concept applicable to a section of historical time which should be understood as a "plural number or cluster of temporal processes, 'currents,' 'durations,' rhythms or sequences flowing simultaneously side by side—and to its dominant structures and values."[22] In other words, what he proposes is a theory of multiple-periodization, either in terms of dynamic, dialectical periods or of separate "currents," suggestive of relations with historical and social developments. Or more specifically, for example, the Baroque *period* should not be understood as a monistically defined section of time, but as a "blending of Baroque, Classical, and Mannerist 'currents' "; the Symbolist *period*, not as a single duration in literary history, but as a "strong symbolist 'process' in poetry, in aesthetics, in the novel, coincident and diachronically contemporaneous with continuing realistic or naturalistic vein in the novel . . . with the final stages of certain Romantic styles . . . [and] with the final phases of the Parnasse."[23]

Hence, a literary period should be a "conjuncture,"[24] which implies the articulation or junction of various "indicators," such as styles, genres, conventions, etc. And Guillén's final stance is that until a conjunctural terminology is developed, he prefers an "alternative" which "relies on the use of a noninterpretative chronology" and "stresses essentially the confrontation, within such chronological units, of a plurality of durations, movements, systems, schools, institutions, and other temporal processes."[25]

With Guillén's conception of period in mind, we may come to realize that a period term like *Baroque,* because of its peculiar nature of reconciling disparate elements, is potentially "conjunctural" in nature. For it may be conceived as the continuation of the classical "current" which, encountering obstacles (e.g., emergence of new ideologies and/or new sensibilities) on its course, weakens into an "undercurrent," while the diverted "body of water" becomes the "main current" (the Baroque) with the beginning, the middle, and the end of the new course represented respectively, e.g., in English literature, by the Mannerist, the Metaphysical, and the High-Baroque, which varies its manner of flowing (as exhibited in personal styles) according to the particular geographical features or landscapal structures (such as an individual writer's personality, learning, etc.).

Although Guillén does not deal specifically with the problem of period-style, he does point out that "it is not uncommon for a critic to confuse his typology of stylistic responses with the section of time to which they responded, and to conclude that a style is a period or a concept fully coincident with it."[26] It is true that a style, "even when it is normative and collective, and defines a set of verbal conventions shared by a group of writers, singles out alternatives rather than confrontations,"[27] and therefore cannot represent all the valuable artistic work of a period. Frank Warnke has also indicated that "no one literary style can conceivably give voice to the entire range of values accessible to literature"[28] (by "range of values," he un-

---

[22] Guillén, *Literature as System*, p. 464.

[23] Ibid., pp. 464-65.

[24] Ibid., p. 468. He pointed out that the term has become clearly associated, through its uses in economic history, with mutability and the flow of time, while singling out dominant moments and trends.

[25] Ibid., p. 469.

[26] Ibid., p. 427.

[27] Ibid., p. 466.

[28] "Metaphysical Poetry and the European Context," in *Metaphysical Poetry*, ed. Malcolm Bradbury and David Palmer (London: Arnold, Edward, 1970), p. 273.

derstands a concept including both technique and attitude). However, it does not follow that there is no justification for the use of a particular style label for a period. Warnke's observation applies not only to "literary style," but also, and even more aptly, to those Marxist criteria for periodization such as "historical change" and "social phenomena." And it depends how we interpret the term *period style*.

The monolithic conception—that each period has a style, that is (by extension) one style only—which is based on a simplistic historicism, presumes a fundamental interrelationship between "the style" which is supposedly historically and artistically uniform and "the philosophy" or "world-view" of a given period. It is closely linked with the static concept of period as harmony or singleness of style, so characteristic of *Geistesgeschichte* which regards period style as the expression or mirror of the predominant *Weltanschauung*.[29] Jean Rousset's attempt to define the seventeenth century in terms of the Baroque style[30] and Helmut Hatzfeld, the eighteenth century in terms of the Rococo style[31] should serve to illustrate this conception of period style as the expression-form and manifestation of a *Zeitgeist*, or as the denominator for the "spirit" of an ascribed period.

The pluralistic conception—i.e., period style as "a cluster of related styles"[32] or of various stylistic currents, or as the dominant style of all concurrent styles in a given period—clearly belongs to the same hypothetical category as Guillén's dynamic view of "period." Frank Warnke's identification of the Baroque with the Metaphysical/Mannerist and the High-Baroque styles also exemplifies this conception.[33]

The structuralist view of period style as a structure[34] can be regarded as the extension of the pluralistic conception. It primarily concerns the relational, trans-

---

[29] Weissenberger (note 3), pp. 233-39.

[30] J. Rousset, "La définition du terme 'baroque,'" *Actes du IIIe Congres de l'Association Internationale de Littérature Comparée* (The Hague: Mouton, 1962), p. 167.

[31] H. Hatzfeld, "Rococo as a European Epoch-Style," *Neohelicon*, 1, Nos. 3-4, 43-75. What he attempted to demonstrate in the article was that the "rococo syndrome" which contained the various motifs and attitudes related to elegance, eroticism, and wit produced the epoch-style of eighteenth-century European literature—"In eighteenth-century novel, drama and poetry there stand out motivistically two types, the *coquette* and the *petit-maître*. They have a pastoral-anacreontic corollary in the shepherdess and the shepherd. From the viewpoint of human attitudes, there is a propensity to elegant compliments, flirtation, an erotic view on nature and mythology as well as a brilliant critical irony culminating in the *bon mot* and the epigram" (p. 44). For further discussion, see his *Literature through Art: A New Approach to French Literature* (New York: Oxford Univ. Press, 1952) and *The Rococo: Eroticism, Wit, and Elegance in European Literature* (New York: Pegasus, 1972). Herbert Dieckmann is also a promoter of the period concept of Rococo. His position is clearly stated in the article, "Reflections on the Use of Rococo as a Period Concept," *The Disciplines of Criticism*, ed. Peter Demetz, et al. (New Haven: Yale Univ. Press, 1968), pp. 419-36.

[32] The phrase is Frank Warnke's: "As the designation of a period, Baroque refers not to a precisely definable style but to a cluster of related styles" (*European Metaphysical Poetry*, p. 3).

[33] Ibid., pp. 3 & 21-24.

[34] The general definition of structure may be rendered as "an ensemble of elements, objects, or parts, which is significant by means of the relationships between those parts." Patrick Brady defined it as "a hypothetical, heuristic model (existing at a fairly high level of generality) used for the relational investigation of phenomena" ("From Traditional Fallacies to Structural Hypotheses: Old and New Conceptions in Period Style Research," *Neophilologus*, 56, 1972, 5). David Wilson's Ph.D. dissertation, "The Language of the French Baroque: Levels of Structure in the Poetry of Jean de Sponde, Jean de La Ceppède, and Théophile de Viau" (Univ. of California, Berkeley, 1970), is an interesting example of this kind of approach.

formational, and self-adjusting aspects of the structure.[35] In other words, a period style is a relational totality,[36] both structured and structuring, "involving internal modifications tending towards genesis or replacement of the structure,[37] and towards its preservation."[38] From this standpoint, the Baroque style, for example, can be interpreted as the relational totality of the seventeenth century for its exploration and implication of the relationships between disparate objects, and co-existing stylistic currents, as well as of the interrelationships among individual works, such as that of Donne, Crashaw, Góngora, La Ceppède, Paul Fleming, etc., thus forming a "system of intelligibility" from which new perspectives can be discovered and established through the postulation of this stylistic hypothesis.

With regard to the other approaches to the problem of period style, Weissenberger has outlined the following:

> The Formal-Aesthetic: applies descriptive linguistics for detail analysis of elements of speech.
>
> The Formal-Historical: emphasizes the historicity of the respective stylistic elements, such as that of the genres.
>
> The Aesthetic: transfers concepts and categories from the domain of aesthetics to the sphere of literature on the principle of analogy.
>
> The Cultural-Sociological: defines the relationship between the period-style elements of different periods in terms of the repetition of constituent cultural-sociological components.
>
> The Literary-Sociological: interprets the phenomenon of period style as determined by socio-economic conditions, literary groups and schools, or simply by predominant tastes.
>
> The Psychological: considers period style as the articulation of psychological states or conflicts—periods are expressed in "the oscillation of literary styles as marked by the poles of a psychological field-potential, the poles of emotion and intellect, for example."
>
> The Existential: explains period style in terms of a common space-time experience.
>
> The Organological: subjects the discussion of period style to biological or organic laws of growth; periodization according to generations can be related to this approach.

---

[35] Jean Piaget's definition of structures—relational, transformational, and self-adjusting are the three characteristics of structures. See his *Le structuralism* (Paris: Presses Universitaires de France, 1968). Brady adopted Piaget's categories in his discussion of the "structural" concept of period styles (Brady, 7-9).

[36] "A period style is clearly a relational totality in precisely this sense: its very existence is postulated on the basis of observed similarities between elements, and it has the status of a relationship, it is constituted by the relationship, between these elements. These elements, moreover, have, by reason of these resemblances and relationships, a semantic function within the whole or hypothesis of the particular period style" (Brady, 7).

[37] "Une activité structurante ne peut consister qu'en un système de transformations" (Piaget, p. 11). "In the case of any given period style (e.g., the Rococo) transformation is concerned with emergence from and return to a dormant or latent status" (Brady, 7).

[38] "Once a style is given sufficient impetus (e.g., that given the Rococo by Watteau), it achieves a momentum of its own and seeks to complete itself, eliminating irrelevant or contradictory aspects concomitant in its original form of expression (e.g., elimination of Watteau's use of black, or diagonals, his idealism, etc.)" (Brady, 8).

The Statistical: utilizes the findings of descriptive linguistics for quantitative analysis of grammatical phenomena, to determine the frequency and distribution of stylistic features and catalogue period-style elements.[39]

From Weissenberger's critical survey we realize that the period-concept of Baroque has appeared in most of the major studies concerning the problem of period-style, and served as a strong example in the various approaches. It has been interpreted either as the totality of the normative stylistic features shared by major writers (descriptive linguistics and statistics have made important contributions in the area of verifying and determining the presence of the appropriate stylistic criteria in the representative works of the period),[40] as the cultural phenomenon identifiable as aesthetic categories through which all disciplines can be, in one way or another, analogically related,[41] or as the expression-form of the predominant *Weltanschauung*, such as the tension between "medieval Christian transcendentalism and modern natural realism."[42]

Martini's discussion of "the problem of the context and dialectic of period style as rooted in and conditioned by history, and of personality style as an existential phenomenon"[43] reveals another relational stratum. The interrelationships between personal and period style which are simultaneously linked with generic and group style has led him to presume that it is impossible to characterize a period style as a collective, authoritative style in terms of epoch when plurality and contradiction in styles are encountered. According to Martini, period style is basically a "common and supraindividual constant of all representative forms in any one period in which trends evolved more or less compulsorily according to socio-historical development."[44] Generally speaking, his conception is monolithic and his view primarily historical—stages of the history of literary form can be represented by the dominance of period-oriented style (until the 18th century), the liberation of personal style (18th and 19th centuries), and the emergence of group style (at the end of 19th century).

Weisstein's treatment of the historical concepts and the problem of periodization from a comparative viewpoint has demonstrated the difficulties in establishing a universal system of literary periods[45] and consequently the fallacies of the kinds of periodization based on a/the cyclical concept of history,[46] philological classification

---

[39] Weissenberger, pp. 226-58.

[40] Evelyn E. Uhrhan's "Linguistic Analysis of Góngora's Baroque Style" (*Descriptive Studies in Spanish Grammar*, ed. H.R. Kahane and A. Pietrangeli. Urbana: Univ. of Illinois Press, 1954, pp. 179-241) and Dolores M. Burton's *Shakespeare's Grammatical Style: A Computer-assisted Analysis of Richard II and Anthony and Cleopatra* (Austin: Univ. of Texas Press, 1973) would serve as appropriate examples.

[41] It has been very popular among Baroque scholars, such as Theophil Spoerri, Helmut Hatzfeld, Marcel Raymond, Jean Rousset, and many others, to translate Heinrich Wölfflin's categories (linear and painterly, plane and recession, closed and open form, multiplicity and unity, clearness and unclearness) into categories of literary style; for detail information of these categories, see Wölfflin's *Kunstgeschichtliche Grundbegriffe* (München: Bruckmann, 1915) or Hottinger's translation *Principles of Art History* (1932; rpt. New York: Dover, 1950). See also Fowler's essay on "Periodization and Interart Analogies" (*New Literary History*, 3, 487-509).

[42] Emil Ermatinger's view cited in Weissenberger, p. 234.

[43] Martini (note 3), p. 92.

[44] Ibid., p. 97.

[45] *Comparative Literature and Literary Theory*, pp. 66-98. See also Joseph Szili's "Universal Periods in Literary History," *Zagadnienia Rodzajow Literackich*, 14 (1972), 5-14.

[46] Weisstein, p. 77. This concept, in Weisstein's opinion, is based on "the conviction that an inexorable law governs the course of history" and is the basic construct of Vico's, Spengler's, and Cazamian's theories.

(which varies from one national literature to the other), annalistic grouping of events (which merely identify simultaneous events rather than to order or periodize them), and generation duration (which "mixes biological criteria with historical and stylistic ones"). His efforts in bringing the problem to the attention of the comparatist are admirable. However, not until each of the major national literatures has derived a valid system of periods based on its typological categories, evolutionary rhythms, and stylistic transitions (as affected by obvious linguistic change) will we be ready to explore the possibility of developing a valid universal system of literary periods assigned to neutral but "conjunctural" labels. Of course, it will not be an easy task. Just considering the problem of period styles and their use in constituting such a system, the differences in the development of national literatures (the phenomenon of timegap), the coexistence of styles representing subsequent phases of development, as well as the abundance of local shades and varieties, will indicate the underlying difficulties. Even if we stay within the boundaries of national literary histories, we are still confronted by the problem of temporal division and that of labeling the phases or stages with appropriate terms. Because of the complex and close relationships between literary and other cultural phenomena such as social reform or political change, histories of literature often resort to varying principles of periodization—literary, political-social, linguistic, philosophical, and so on—and thus invite criticism for lack of consistency. But such inconsistency seems to be inevitable as it is extremely difficult for literary historians to arrive at a homogeneous scheme of periods without adopting artificial and partly false categories. Any periodization, as Guillén has pointed out, "while sufficiently 'objective' or 'real,' is partial and does not preclude . . . other principles of organization of historical time."[47] In other words, uniformity of period terms may well result in the falsification of history. A survey of some representative histories of national literature[48] will reveal that periods are usually given as a century,[49] or labeled after the name of the ruling monarch (e.g., Elizabethan, Victorian; le siècle de Louis XIV; la época de Felipe II),[50] or of the major literary figure/figures (e.g., The Age of Chaucer, of Milton; l'âge de Corneille; la época de Lope de Vega),[51] or represented by a movement (e.g., *Sturm und Drang,* Romanticism, Realism, Symbolism), a cultural phenomenon, or a prominent characteristic (e.g., Renaissance, The Age of Enlightenment/Reason), or introduced as a linguistic stage (e.g., Old English, Middle English; High German).[52]

Generally speaking, most literary historians tend to adhere to a general and stationary pattern of periodization, either in terms of centuries, or historically establish-

---

[47] Guillén, *Literature as System,* p. 433.

[48] Thirty-two histories of English literature, eighteen of French literature, eight of German literature, and five of Spanish literature were included in the survey.

[49] Either subdivided according to literary genres, such as "17th century: Poetry, Drama, Prose, Prose-fiction," or according to the achievement or the chronology of writers.

[50] Belonging to this category are periods named after a historic/political event (e.g., the Restoration Period), or identified as a time-section between two historical events/accession and death of monarchs (e.g., From the Anglo-Saxon Invasion to the Norman Conquest, From Accession of the Tudors to the Death of James I).

[51] Belonging to this category are periods represented by two or more major literary figures spanning a time-section (e.g., From Donne to Marvell, From Steele and Addison to Pope and Swift).

[52] While movements (e.g., Romanticism, Realism, Symbolism, etc.) are international phenomena, linguistic stages are limited to the early periods in English and German literature.

ed divisions, such as, in the case of English literature, The Middle-Ages—The Renaissance—The Restoration and The Neo-Classical Period—The Period of Romanticism—The Victorian Age—The Modern Period, or in the case of French literature, Le Moyen Age—La Renaissance—L'Époque Classique—Le Siècle des Philosophes—Le Romanticisme—Le Réalisme—Le Symbolisme et La Littérature Contemporaine. Very few of them have taken the trouble to replace arbitrary non-literary period labels with clearly-defined literary ones. The fact that different phases of literary evolution—stylistic or generic—seldom coincide with century-transitions, monarch-successions, reigns or dynasty-changes should explain the ineffectiveness and arbitrariness of such labels as "The Seventeenth Century," "The Jacobean Period," "Le siècle de Louis XIV," or "T'ang Period." However, despite the extended historiographical work done in defining the period-concept of "Baroque," the term, though appearing almost in all the major studies on period style and periodization (either as a distinct epoch, or as a key-example of modern period concepts, or as an illustration of the problem in periodizing literary history), has still not been widely adopted in literary histories as the period denominator of the time-span between the Renaissance and the Neo-Classicism. As a period term, it has appeared more frequently in histories of German literature, among which Ernst Rose's work[53] stands out as a unique example. Jacques Roger's *Histoire de la littérature française*[54] and Juan L. Alborg's *Historia de la literatura Española*[55] are the two other examples (there is not one among English literary histories) that have demonstrated a firm use of the period concept of Baroque.

The situation in the area of Chinese literary history is, if anything, gloomier. According to a preliminary survey, the first Chinese history of Chinese literature[56] was published in 1909. Subsequent productions such as Hsieh Wu-liang's 謝无量 *Chung-kuo ta wen-hsüeh shih* 中國大文學史 are mainly evidences of historical verification of the literary materials which, as Fu Ssu-nien 傅斯年 pointed out in 1919,[57] demonstrated no critical awareness of serious concern in the problem of tem-

---

[53] *A History of German Literature* (New York: New York Univ. Press, 1960), in which the author identified eight periods in the history of German literature, and attached a style to each of the periods, e.g., the Symbolic Style of the Middle Ages, the Tense Style of the Baroque Period, the Witty Style of the Enlightenment, the Dissociative and Surrealistic Style of the Twentieth Century, except the Age of Goethe and the Nineteenth Century which shared a style—the Style of Personal Experience. Other histories include Werner P. Friederich's *History of German Literature* (New York: Barnes & Noble, 1948), J. G. Robertson's *A History of German Literature* (Edinburgh & London: Blackwood, 1959), J. M. Ritchie's (ed.) *Periods in German Literature* (London: Oswald Wolff, 1966), and Bruno Boesch's (ed.) *German Literature: A Critical Survey*, tr. Ronald Taylor (London: Methuen, 1971).

[54] (Paris: A. Collin, 1969). He included a chapter on "La poésie baroque" (by J. Céard), pp. 269-87, which deals with "La notion de baroque," "L'homme baroque," and "La stylistique baroque" in a comprehensive way in terms of French poetry between 1575 and 1630 (L'âge Baroque).

[55] (Madrid: Editorial Gredos, 1966-72). He identified the era of Góngora and Calderón as the "Época barroca" (refer to his chapters on "Góngora y la lirica barroca," "La dramática barroca," and "El estilo barroco del Calderón").

[56] According to Hu Huai-ch'en 胡懷琛 (*Chung-kuo wen-hsüeh shih kai-yao* 中國文學史概要, 1931; rpt. Hong Kong: Shang-wu, 1959, p. 11) and Liang Jung-jo 梁容若 (*Chung-kuo wen-hsüeh shih yen-chiu* 中國文學史研究, Taipei: San-min, 1967, pp. 121-23), Lin Ch'uan-chia's 林傳甲 *Chung-kuo wen-hsüeh shih* 中國文學史 (published in 1909) is the earliest "Chinese" history of Chinese literature.

[57] "Chung-kuo wen-hsüeh shih fen-ch'i chih yen-chiu" 中國文學史分期之研究, *Hsin-ch'ao* 新潮, 1 (Feb., 1919), 323.

poral division. Most of them, regarding periodization as merely a narrative convenience, adopt either the dynasty or the genre categories. The few attempts to deal with the problem of periodization in Chinese literary history, generally speaking, lack critical insights and theoretical paradigms. None of the discussions actually take into consideration the various norms, such as stylistic tendencies, generic conventions, that dominate literature in specific time-spans. Fu Ssu-nien in his short essay "Chung-kuo wen-hsüeh shih fen-ch'i chih yen-chiu"[58] proposed to divide the history of Chinese literature into four epochs: (1) The Early Ancient or the Period of Free Literary Development 文學自由發展期, from Late Shang 商 to the end of Chan-kuo 戰國 (late 12th century-mid 3rd century B.C.); (2) The Middle Ancient or the Evolution Period of the *P'ien-li* Style 駢儷文體演進期, from Ch'in 秦 to the end of Early T'ang (mid 3rd century B.C.-late 7th century); (3) The Late Ancient or the Period of the Rise of New Literary Genres 新文學代興期, from High T'ang to Mid-Ming 明 (early 8th century-mid 15th century); and (4) The Modern or the Neo-Classical[59] Period of Literature 文學復古期, from the times of Hung-chih 弘治 (1488-1505) and Chia-ching 嘉靖 (1522-1566) to the present (before the May Fourth Literary Movement 五四文學運動). The first period explains the "contemporaneity" of the six major "literary" categories:

1. Poetry—the *Kuo-fengs* 國風 after Pei 邶, with the exception of Pin 豳, and the so-called "*pien-ya*" 變雅.
2. The historian's prose—*Kuo-yü* 國語, *Chan-kuo ts'e* 戰國策, *Wu Yüeh ch'un-ch'iu* 吳越春秋.
3. The philosopher's discourse—Confucius' *I-hsi* 易繫, Tzu-ssu's 子思 *Chung-yung* 中庸, *Lao-tzu* 老子, *Mo-tzu* 墨子, *Chuang-tzu* 莊子.
4. The *fu* 賦 literature—Hsün Ch'ing's 荀卿 *fu* compositions.
5. The *Ch'u tz'u* 楚辭—works by Ch'ü P'ing 屈平, Sung Yü 宋玉, Ching Ts'o 景差.[60]
6. The folk airs and ballads 歌謠之文學.

What characterizes these different categories as parts of a whole, according to Fu, is the shared spirit of free development in form and content, and therefore the immense creativity evidenced in the many thematic as well as formal variations and extremes found in the pre-Ch'in "literary" writings. With this consideration, the period-description phrase, "tzu-yu fa-chan" (free development), would seem to be acceptable, if not for the arbitrariness of categories two and three. Certainly there are fine literary qualities in *Tso-chuan* 左傳 or *Chuang-tzu*. Nevertheless, they belong more to a history of ideas, to historical or philosophical writing than to literature.[61] In addition, category four—the *fu*—which is based upon the speculation that such a prose genre,

---

[58] Ibid., 323-28.
[59] The term "Neo-Classical" is a tentative translation for *Fu-ku* 復古.
[60] In Fu's essay, it reads as P'u Ts'o 普差 (324)—probably a typographical error.
[61] According to *Hsien-ch'in wen-hui* 先秦文彙, ed. Li Yüeh-kang 李曰剛 (Taipei: Chung-hua ts'ung-shu pien-shen wei-yüan-hui, 1963, part I of Chung-hua wen-hui series, general ed. Kao Ming 高明), *Tso-Chuan* belongs mainly to the categories of *hsü-chi* 敍記 (38 entries, II, 982-1051), *chuan-chih* 傳記 (9 entries, II, 828-915), *shu-shuo* 書說 (10 entries, II, 624-38), *tsou-i* 奏議 (8 entries, II, 527-37), and *lun-shuo* 論說 (7 entries, I, 114-20); *Chuang-tzu* belongs exclusively to the category of *lun-shuo* (26 entries, I, 566-720). Of course, this system of classification is not necessarily the most ideal one. However, the question of genres in Chinese literature is beyond the scope of this paper.

having only one extant example in Hsün Ch'ing's *Fu p'ien* 賦篇, was popular during his time, is hardly convincing. Although the writings in *Ch'u tz'u* are, stylistically speaking, different from Hsün Ch'ing's *Fu p'ien,* they belong more to the genre of *fu* for their syntactical structure than to the category of *tz'u* which is more an "anthological" style (*Ch'u tz'u* is basically an anthology) than a literary genre. In fact, categories four and five may be combined into one category (anyway, category four having only one extant example is hardly a category) as what we find in the *Hsien-ch'in wen-hui* and other anthologies—the category of *tz'u fu* 辭賦. Of course, *fu* does become an independent literary genre later on.

The second period accounts for the beginning and flourishing of the *P'ien-li* style which finds expression in Li Ssu's 李斯 prose works,[62] Ssu-ma Hsiang-ju 司馬相如 and Yang Hsiung's 揚雄 *fu* compositions,[63] and particularly the writings of Hsü Ling 徐陵, Yü Hsin 庾信, Wang Po 王勃, and Yang Chiung 楊炯.[64] According to Fu, *p'ien-wen* 駢文 and *lü-shih* 律詩 are, in terms of generic form, the culminating products of the style in question. As a whole, the principle underlying the formation of this period—that of determining a literary trend in terms of "period-style"—is well-founded. Unfortunately, the term *P'ien-li,* like *Baroque* in its early history, is used primarily in a pejorative sense, referring to an artificial style characteristic of "ungenuine" literary writings.[65] For any period-style term, if it is meaningful or sufficiently "objective" at all, should be free of extreme evaluative denotations or associations, and should be able to represent a multitude of stylistic features determined by intrinsic investigation,[66] and to "overcome the collectively felt schism of essence between subject and object" by distinguishing "the role assumed by poetic imagination, symbol, myth, and organic nature."[67] As an heuristic instrument, it should be employed as a "neutral" term so that the literature of its ascribed period would not be slighted because of derogatory meanings caused by partial and sometimes distorted studies.

The third period witnesses the successive emergence and dominance of new literary genres (e.g., *ch'i-yen shih* 七言詩, *tz'u* 詞, *ch'ü* 曲, *ch'uan-ch'i* 傳奇) which, according to Fu, can be grouped under two categories: literati and popular literature—the former represented by Tu Fu's 杜甫, Po Chü-i's 白居易 poetry, Han Yü's 韓愈, Liu Tsung-yüan's 柳宗元 prose, as well as prose-poetry 散文七言詩 of the Sung writers; the latter by the vernacular fiction, the *tz'u,* the *ch'ü,* and the *tsa-chü* 雜劇. Evidently, the formation of this period is again, like that of the first period, based upon the

---

[62] Such as his "K'e-shih" 刻石 essays and "Chien chu k'e shu" 諫逐客書.

[63] Such as Ssu-ma Hsiang-ju's "Tzu-hsü" 子虛, "Shang-lin" 上林, "Ta-jen" 大人, "Ch'ang-men" 長門, "Mei-jen" 美人 and Yang Hsiung's "Kan-ch'üan" 甘泉, "Yü-lieh" 羽獵, "Ch'ang-yang" 長揚, etc.

[64] Such as Hsü Ling's "Yü t'ai hsin yung hsü" 玉臺新詠序, Yü Hsin's "Ai Chiang-nan fu" 哀江南賦, "Hsiao-yüan fu" 小園賦, "K'u-shu fu" 枯樹賦, Wang Po's "Teng-wang ko hsü," 滕王閣序, and Yang Chiung's "Ts'ung chün hsing" 從軍行.

[65] Fu (note 57), 326: *"P'ien-wen . . .* such 'fake' literature of the entertainer-incantation type" 駢文…此俳優偶咒之偽文學.

[66] Generally speaking, the period style of shorter time-sections or phases can be accurately determined by intrinsic investigation, "while for the major style epochs inductively gained results from cultural-sociological neighboring fields should be included to prove the internal unity of a period" (Weissenberger, p. 258).

[67] See Wellek's essays on Romanticism—"The Concept of Romanticism in Literary History," and "Romanticism Re-examined"—in *Concepts of Criticism,* ed. Stephen Nichols, Jr. (New Haven: Yale Univ. Press, 1967), pp. 128-221.

principle of diversity as a literary phenomenon. In other words, it is the plurality of literary genres that characterizes the two periods; neither is there a linear unity represented, for example, by the singleness of style in a classical or a *P'ien-li* period, nor a converging unity as what we find in the multiplicity of styles in a Baroque period.

The fourth period, to which Fu refers as the "Chinese Renaissance,"[68] represents a "rebirth" of classical modes of expression, as is evidenced in "Ch'ien hou ch'i tzu's"[69] 前後七子 writings which are conscious attempts to imitate the masterpieces of Ch'in and Han prose writers and of the "High T'ang" poets 文必秦漢詩必盛唐, and to observe the decorum found in writings of the past. It is no longer a period of literary innovations. According to Fu, it exhibits a "divorce of literature from life" which, as a result, turns Chinese literature into an "inhuman literature," with exceptions only in a few works, such as those by Ts'ao Hsüeh-ch'in 曹雪芹 and Wu Ching-tzu 吳敬梓. Again, like the term *P'ien-li*, *Fu-ku* is used strictly in a pejorative sense, referring to the mechanical imitation of literary styles of the past, without any creative impulse toward the representation of contemporary reality. From such a standpoint, great works, such as *Hung-lou meng* 紅樓夢, *Ju-lin wai-shih* 儒林外史, are bound to be regarded as merely unique products unaffected by the bad taste of their times, not as distinctive voices of an age. Outstanding writers like Mao Ch'i-ling 毛奇齡, Yün Ching 惲敬, Kung Tzu-chen 龔自珍 are also found to have failed reaching the domain of "genuine" literature, and resorted to the "fantastic" or the "grotesque" 怪誕 for distinguishing themselves.[70] With such a label as *Fu-ku* used in a derogative sense, Mr. Fu has not only slighted the accomplishments of individual poets such as Wang Shih-chen 王士禎, Chu I-tsun 朱彝尊, Na-lan Hsing-te 納蘭性德, Ch'en Wei-sung 陳維崧 who, in spite of their admiration of the T'ang and Sung masters, are able to distinguish themselves with a voice and a style of their own, but also overlooked the significant roles played by the fiction genre in representing the many planes of reality of the age and in achieving a mode of expression that incorporates various generic forms (*shih, tz'u, ch'ü*) in an aesthetic structure.

In short, the primary problem of Fu Ssu-nien's tetradic periodization lies in its system of nomenclature which is based upon either the principle of diversity or that of partial value-judgement. Nevertheless, his proposal of the four temporal divisions, which he thought would represent more accurately than the triadic periods[71] the shifts of literary taste/sensibility and the transitions of styles in Chinese literature, deserves our further attention.

Lu K'an-ju 陸侃如 and Feng Yüan-chun 馮沅君 in the "Introduction" to their

---

[68] Liu Ta-chieh 劉大杰 cited in his *Chung-kuo wen-hsüeh fa-ta shih* 中國文學發達史 (1949; rpt. Taipei: Chung-hua, 1968, p. 1008) Liang Ch'i-ch'ao's 梁啓超 view in *Ch'ing-tai hsüeh-shu kai-lun* 清代學術概論 that the Ch'ing period on the whole very much resembled the European Renaissance in scholarship, except in the areas of arts and literature where the Chinese made little development.

[69] "Ch'ien ch'i tzu" led by Li Meng-yang 李夢陽 and Ho Ching-ming 何景明 started the first *Ni-ku* 擬古 (imitating the past) movement in the Ming dynasty; "Hou ch'i tzu" led by Li P'an-lung 李攀龍 and Wang Shih-chen promoted the second *Ni-ku* movement.

[70] Fu, 327.

[71] Early Ancient: from Huang-ti 黃帝 to Chien-an 建安; Medieval: from Chien-an to T'ang; and Near Ancient: from T'ang to Ch'ing 清. These are the three "instruction-stages" designed for the history of Chinese literature course by the Chinese department of Peking University during the twenties (Fu, 323).

Chung-kuo shih-shih[72] 中國詩史 published in 1931 proposed a triadic division: Ancient (1401 B.C.-A.D. 220), Medieval (220-907), and Modern (907-1911), which is based upon "the general trend of change in poetry."[73] The "Ancient" consisting of four periods—"Sprouting" 萌芽 or Early, *Shih ching, Ch'u tz'u,* and *Yüeh-fu* 樂府—is characterized by a natural and spontaneous mode of expression free of formal and metrical restrictions. The "Medieval," though much shorter in time-span, comprises also four periods, each represented by a major poet, namely Ts'ao Chih 曹植, T'ao Ch'ien 陶潛, Li Po 李白 and Tu Fu. It witnesses the emergence and development of a poetic language—a language more aesthetically restrained and programmed than the vernacular—which not only combines the quality of "natural" beauty with that of "man-made" beauty 人工美 (e.g., formal rules of versification) but also identifies the poet as a special class in society.

The "Modern," beginning in Late T'ang, also includes four periods, the first three represented by Li Yü 李煜, Su Shih 蘇軾, and Chiang K'uei 姜夔, and the last by *San-ch'ü* 散曲, a literary genre that comes to dominance during the Yüan dynasty and registers the culminative achievement of an epoch in which the evolution of Chinese poetry takes on two directions, one toward musico-forms, the other "vernacularization" of the poetic language.

Lu and Feng's tripartite division certainly reminds us of the almost archetypal pattern in historical periodization of Western culture—the triad "ancient-medieval-modern," which may be traced back to the Renaissance and to Cellarius.[74] One of the contemporary instances illustrating this tripartite concept is N. I. Konrad's adoption of the triad as "a system of general periods based on the evolution of world literature" to represent the three major stages—slavery, feudalism, and capitalism—of social evolution.[75]

> He demonstrated the analogous character of Eastern and Western literary evolution through comparable types of literary products present in both cultural spheres—histories by Polybius and Plutarch and histories by Ssu-ma Ch'ien in Antiquity; mysteries, miracle plays and farces in medieval Europe and nō-plays and "kyogen" interludes in medieval Japan; court

---

[72] "Tao lun: Chung-kuo shih-shih ti ts'ai-liao yü fen-ch'i" 導論：中國詩史的材料與分期, *Chung-kuo shih-shih* (Shanghai: Ta-chiang, 1931), pp. 3-13. This introduction together with the appendix, "Fu lun: hsien-tai ti chung-kuo shih" 附論：現代的中國詩, were not included in the 1956 edition (Peking: Tso-chia). Besides, there were some changes in the manner of dating and period-labeling in the three available editions: the 1931 edition has a precise dating system all through (e.g., The Age of Li Po, 618-755; the Age of Tu Fu, 755-970; the Age of Li Yü, 907-960, and so on), while the 1933 edition changes to a less precise one (e.g., the Age of Li Po & the Age of Tu Fu are dated between Sui Wen-ti 隋文帝 and T'ang Chao-tsung 唐昭宗; the 1931 edition (so is the 1933 ed.) uses the names of major literary figures (except the Early Ancient periods and the last Modern period) as period-labels, while the 1956 edition replaces them with dynastic names (e.g., from "the Age of Li Po" to "Early-High T'ang Poetry"; from "the Age of Tu Fu" to "Mid-Late T'ang Poetry"; from "the Age of Li Yü to T'ang-Five Dynasties *tz'u*").

[73] Lu & Feng, p. 7. Here is another strong example of the triadic periodization.

[74] Guillén, *Literature as System*, pp. 413 (note 67) & 423 (note 6).

[75] "O nekotorykh voprosakh istorii mirovoy literatury," *Zapad y Vostok* (Moscow: Academy of Sciences of USSR, 1966), pp. 446-65 (See Szili's "Universal Periods in Literary History," 8, note 4).

lyrics in medieval France and China. He pointed out that cultural periods corresponding to the phases of transition from one stage of social evolution to another, e.g., the period of Hellenism and the Renaissance period, are also detectable in the East, i.e. a Renaissance period began in China in the 8th century, in Central Asia, Iran and North-West India in the 9th century, in Italy in the 13th century, and in England and Japan in the 17th century.[76]

With regard to Konrad's primary assumption that world literature functions as a unified system and therefore is definable in terms of synchronous periods, Joseph Szili's criticism[77] has demonstrated its inadequacy, if not invalidity. The time gap between "identical" periods alone will pose a serious problem for the literary historian who attempts to represent the stages of the evolution of literatures with common temporal categories. The Medieval Period in Western history, for example, which corresponds to the Ch'i-Liang 齊梁 -Mid-Ming period (c. 6th to 15th century) in Chinese history, would be imprecise as a temporal division marking off an important change in the general trend of Chinese poetry. Furthermore, "what is called modern," as Weisstein has pointed out, "is always seen in contrast to the ancient, the familiar or the classical."[78] In other words, the shifting of historical perspective in linear time will constantly demand the relabeling of the then "modern" period with more accurate temporal indicators such as "post-medieval" or "pre-modern."[79]

Lin Keng 林庚 in his discussion of the periodization problem in Chinese literature[80] stated that the development of Chinese society does directly affect the internal rhythm of its literary evolution (implying a causal relationship between dynastic milieu and flourishing of literary genres), and therefore the division into periods may be done according to major socio-political events, such as dynastic changes or large-scale rebellions which anticipate substantial social changes. In his opinion, the traditional groupings into dynastic units are acceptable for the reasons that longer dynasties, such as Han, T'ang, Sung, Ming, Ch'ing, often reveal a definite unity because of a higher degree of "traditionality" and stability, and that the early decades of these dynasties seldom produce great works of literature, thus serving as ideal points for temporal division. His proposition of using "An Shih chih luan" 安史之亂 (The An Shih Rebellion, 755-763) in the sense of a "watershed" 分水嶺 to divide the history of Chinese literature into two "mega-periods" may appear to be a diachronic supplement to his static and synchronic view. Unfortunately, on the one hand, it upsets his own dynastic scheme of periods, and on the other, fails to convey the sense of continuity in the

---

[76] Szili, 8.

[77] Szili, 8-9. Szili proposed an alternative scheme including a tribal phase, a period of peoples, and a period of nations.

[78] Weisstein, p. 70.

[79] However, to use prefixes like "pre-" or "post-" before a well defined period, like "Pre-Romanticism," or "Pre-Classicism," merely indicates an anticipatory current or trend or an extension of the period, which does not make the so-named "period" a true literary period that has its very characteristics.

[80] "Kuan yü Chung-kuo ku-tien wen-hsüeh shih yen-chiu shang ti i hsieh wen-t'i" 關於中國古典文學史研究上的一些問題 Wen-hsüeh i-ch'an hsüan-chi 文學遺產選集 (Peking: Chung-hua, 1960), III, 59-67.

evolution of Chinese literature.[81] In fact, if we conceive periods as traceable tendencies,

> first as germs embedded and largely hidden in others which may have a different direction, then asserting themselves vigorously and dominating a span of years to which they give their name, finally after the period of their ascendancy, their transformation or submergence in, or even lingering through less vigorous life alongside, new tendencies,[82]

the early decades of the longer dynasties can be treated, in a more meaningful manner, as the subsidiary of a once dominant literary current or the final phase of a period. For instance, Early T'ang and Early Sung literature, as the historians of Chinese literature are very much aware, can be regarded respectively as the continuation of the stylistic traditions prominent during the Six Dynasties, and the Late T'ang and the Five Dynasties.[83] Moreover, although characterization of a period must take into account the history of genres, the dominance of a genre does not necessarily determine the characteristic of a period. Certainly, there is validity in Brunetière's theory of the evolution of genres, which states that each literary genre, such as epic poetry, classical tragedy or the romantic novel, reaches its perfection in one particular period, and any later writing in this genre is inevitably inferior. The literary historians will have little difficulty in identifying the appropriate genre for each period. It is possible that the rise and decline of a literary genre coincides with that of a dynasty, but historical facts have recorded no such phenomenon. Lin Keng's contention that there is a *causal* relationship between dynastic milieu and flourishing of literary genres is, at best, a hypothetical truth. The common practice of identifying a period with *generic dominance* among historians of Chinese Literature indicates an emphasis on the static aspect of the development of literary genres, and suffers from a monolithic historical perspective as well as from a limited representation of the larger unity of the period—uniformity in *formal* features and diversity in *individual* styles do not constitute a "period style." To emphasize its dynamic aspect, the literary historian has to take into consideration in periodizing literature the *emergence* of a literary genre (e.g., *tz'u* in Late T'ang), which often reflects a significant *change* of taste or sensibility. It is the result of a necessary rhythm within literary history itself, and is the manifestation of the concept of style exhaustion, which was expounded by Ku Yen-wu 顧炎武 (fl. early 17th century) in his *Jih chih lu*[84] 日知錄 and later restated

---

[81] He introduced the "watershed" image as a conclusive concept in his essay. Although he tried to relate it to the development of Chinese literature, the term itself failed to convey the sense of continuity, for currents do not go "uphill" (Lin visualized the development of Chinese literature in terms of an ascending and a descending process with "An Shih chih luan" as the highest point—the "watershed"—of the ascending stage).

[82] R. B. Farrell, "Problems of Periods and Movements," *Periods in German Literature*, ed. J. M. Ritchie, 2 vols. (London: Oswald Wolff, 1966), I, 6.

[83] "Ch'u-T'ang ssu-chieh's" 初唐四傑 style, for example, very much reminds us of the "Hsü-yü" style 徐庾體, and the "Hsi-k'un" 西崑 poets, of the style of Li Shang-yin 李商隱.

[84] "三百篇之不能不降而楚辭，楚辭之不能不降而漢魏，漢魏之不能不降而六朝，六朝之不能不降而唐，勢也。…詩文之所以代變，有不得不變者。一代之文，沿襲已久，不容人人皆道此語，今且千數百年矣，而猶取古人之陳言，一一而摹倣之，以是爲詩，可乎。" *Jih chih lu chi-shih* 日知錄集釋, 16 vols. (Canton: Shu-ku t'ang, 1869), IV, 21.14b-15a.

in Wang Kuo-wei's 王國維 *Jen-chien tz'u hua* 人間詞話.[85] Frank Warnke, in his discussion of "Metaphysical Poetry and the European Context," has given a succinct remark on this phenomenon:

> In any culture, when a certain range of artistic values has been cultivated, with an everincreasing technical proficiency, for a considerable length of time, it is only to be expected that a point of saturation will eventually be reached and that sooner or later a sense of those values lying outside the range of the established style and clamouring for expression will lead some particularly forceful and independent poet—a Donne, a Théophile, a Marino, a Góngora—to formulate a new style to give expression to the neglected values.[86]

Warnke's view may appear similar to Brunetière's theory, only the latter confines itself to single "generic style" as static representation of a period, while the former places its emphasis on multiple "period style" as dynamic interpretation of a period. This concept of generic/stylistic evolution was quite explicitly elucidated in James Liu's 劉若愚 article, "Lun T'ang-shih chih fen-ch'i" 論唐詩之分期.[87] He proposed to determine the temporal divisions according to the "natural growth and decay" of the poetic genres and style.[88] In the essay, Liu described the development of T'ang poetry in terms of three successive phases: a formative phase (c. 618-710) marked by experimentation and relative naivety, a phase of full maturity (c. 710-70) characterized by great vitality and technical perfection, and a phase of sophistication (c. 770-900) typified by tendencies toward the exuberant or the grotesque. He drew also parallels between the three phases and the Quatrocento, Cinquecento, and Baroque periods of Italian art, and the Early Renaissance, the Elizabethan, and the Baroque periods of English literature.[89] Unfortunately, he did not relate how he arrived at the chronological divisions. Except for the distinction of the last phase as a phase of "sophistication" (which is usually referred to as the declining or decadent period of T'ang poetry), his conception of the T'ang dynasty as a self-contained literary period is not much different from the traditional views—those of the "Three T'ang" and the "Four T'ang" that can be traced back respectively to Sung Ch'i 宋祁 (998-1061; Yen

---

[85] "四言敝而有楚辭，楚辭敝而有五言，五言敝而有七言，七言敝而有律絕，律絕敝而有詞，蓋文體通行既久，染指遂多，自成習套，豪傑之士，亦難於其中自出新意，故遁而作他體以自解脫，一切文體所以始盛終衰者，皆由於此。" *Wang Kuan-t'ang hsien-sheng ch'üan-chi* 王觀堂先生全集, 16 vols. (Taipei: Wen-hua, 1968), XIII, 5940.

[86] *Metaphysical Poetry,* ed. Malcolm Bradbury and David Palmer (London: E. Arnold, 1970), p. 273.

[87] *The Quill* (University of Hong Kong Arts Publication), 4 (1958-59), 18-20. "詩體之變遷，為一有機體之變化，按其內在之需要而生者" (18).

[88] "然則唐詩應如何分期？竊以為與其格於國勢興衰與政治變遷之舊例，不茲就詩體及風格本身之自然消長而劃分之" (Ibid., 18). This view had been expounded by Ch'ien Chung-shu 錢鍾書 in his *T'an-i lu* 談藝錄 (1948; rpt. Hong Kong: Lung-men, 1965) which started with an exposition of "The poetry of T'ang and Sung are distinguished by their difference in style and temperament, not by their affiliation to different dynasties" 詩分唐宋乃風格性分之殊非朝代之別 (pp. 1-5).

[89] His view was later incorporated in the chapter on "Li Shang-yin and the Modern Western Reader" of his *The Poetry of Li Shang-yin* (Chicago: Chicago Univ. Press, 1969), pp. 253-54.

Yü 嚴羽 and Wu Ching-hsien 吳景仙 of the Sung dynasty as well) and to Yang Shih-hung 楊士弘 of the Yüan dynasty.⁹⁰ A survey shows that the majority of the literary historians adopt the Ming scholar Kao Ping's 高棅 chronological divisions,⁹¹ in some cases with minor changes or new labels. Su Hsüeh-lin 蘇雪林 in her *Chung-kuo wen-hsüeh shih* 中國文學史 proposed that the division of T'ang literature should begin with the reign of Hsüan-tsung 玄宗, with the First Period ending before "T'ien-pao chih luan" 天寶之亂 (c. 713-55), the Second Period from Post-"T'ien-pao chih luan" to Mid-T'ang (c. 756-820), the Third Period from Ch'ang-ch'ing 長慶 to Ta-chung 大中 (c. 821-859), and the Fourth Period from Hsien-t'ung 咸通 to T'ien-yu (c. 860-905).⁹² Her identification of these periods, respectively, with a "Romantic," a "Realistic,"

---

⁹⁰ For an account of these views, refer to Cheng Pin-yü's 鄭賓于 *Chung-kuo wen-hsüeh liu pien shih* 中國文學流變史 (Shanghai: Pei-hsin, 1936), pp. 240-46, or to other histories of Chinese literature (Cheng's review is more detail).

⁹¹ The original passage is as follows: 有唐三百年詩，眾體備矣。故有往體、近體、長短篇、五七言、律句、絕句等製，莫不興於始，成於中，流於變，而陊之於終。至於聲律興象，文詞理致，各有品格高下之不同。畧而言之，則有初唐、盛唐、中唐、晚唐之不同。詳而分之，貞觀永徽之時，虞魏諸公，稍離舊習；王楊盧駱，因加美麗；劉希夷有閨帷之作，上官儀有婉媚之體，此初唐之始製也。神龍以還，洎開元初，陳子昂古風雅正，李巨山文章宿老，沈宋之新聲，蘇張之大手筆，此初唐之漸盛也。開元天寶間，則有李翰林之飄逸，杜工部之沈鬱，孟襄陽之清雅，王右丞之精緻，儲光羲之真率，王昌齡之聲俊，高適岑參之悲壯，李頎常建之超凡，此盛唐之盛者也。大曆貞元中，則有韋蘇州之雅淡，劉隨州之閒曠，錢郎之清贍，皇甫之沖秀，秦公緒之山林，李從一之臺閣，此中唐之再盛也。下暨元和之際，則有柳愚谿之超然復古，韓昌黎之博大其詞，張王樂府得其故實，元白序事務在分明，與夫李賀盧仝之鬼怪，孟郊賈島之饑寒，此晚唐之變也。降而開成以後，則有杜牧之之豪縱，溫飛卿之綺靡，李義山之隱僻，許用晦之偶對；他若劉滄馬戴李頻李羣玉輩，尚能黽勉氣格，將邁時流，此晚唐變態之極，而遺風餘韻，猶有存者焉。是皆名家擅場，馳騁當世，或稱才子，或推詩豪，或謂五言長城，或為律詩龜鑑，或號詩人冠冕，或尊海內文宗，靡不有精麤邪正長短高下之不同。觀者苟非窮精闡微，超神入化，玲瓏透徹之悟，則莫能得其門而臻其壼奧矣。("The General Preface" 總敘, *T'ang-shih p'in-hui* 唐詩品彙, 1782; rpt. Taipei: Shang-wu, 1976, 1a-2b). According to his interpretation, four periods can be discerned as following: (1) Early T'ang: from Chen-kuan 貞觀 to K'ai-yüan 開元 (c. 627-713); (2) High T'ang: from K'ai-yüan to Ta-li 大曆 (c. 713-766); (3) Mid-T'ang: from Ta-li to T'ai-ho 太和九年 (c. 766-836). (4) Late T'ang: from K'ai-ch'eng 開成 to T'ien-yu 天祐三年 (c. 836-908). For elucidation, consult Yang Ch'i-kao's 楊啓高 *T'ang-tai shih-hsüeh* 唐代詩學 (1935; rpt. Taipei: Cheng-chung, 1967) and Hu Yün-i's 胡雲翼 *T'ang-shih yen-chiu* 唐詩研究 (1930; rpt. Hong Kong: Shang-wu, 1959), which adopted the quadripartite scheme.

⁹² (Tai-chung: Kuang-ch'i, 1971), pp. 124-42. This periodization scheme is different from that proposed in her *T'ang-shih kai-lun* 唐詩概論 (Shanghai: Shang-wu, 1934), which contains five periods: 1) The Post-Classical Period 繼承齊梁古典作風的時期, from Early T'ang to K'ai-yüan (c. 618-713), major writers include Wang Chi 王績, Wang Po, Yang Chiung, Lu Chao-lin 盧照鄰, Lo Pin-wang 駱賓王, Shen Ts'üan-ch'i 沈佺期, Sung Chih-wen 宋之問, Ch'en Tzu-ang 陳子昂, and Chang Chiu-ling 張九齡; 2) The Romantic Period 浪漫文學隆盛的時期, from K'ai-yüan to "An-shih chih luan" (c. 713-756), major writers include Li Po, Wang Wei, Meng Hao-jan 孟浩然, Kao Shih 高適, Ts'en Shen 岑參, Li Ch'i 李頎, Ts'ui Hao 崔顥, and Wang Ch'ang-ling 王昌齡; 3) The Realistic Period 寫實文學的誕生, from "An Shih chih luan" to Ch'ang-ch'ing 長慶 (c. 756-821), major writers include Tu Fu, Han Yü, Meng Chiao 孟郊, Chia Tao 賈島, Po Chü-i, Yüan Chen 元稹, Wei Ying-wu 韋應物, Liu Ch'ang-ch'ing 劉長卿, Chang Chi 張籍, Wang Chien 王建, Ta-li shih ts'ai-tzu 大曆十才子; 4) The "Aestheticistic" Period 唯美文學發達的時期, from Ch'ang-ch'ing to Ta-chung (c. 821-847), major writers include Li Shang-yin, Tu Mu 杜牧, Wen T'ing-yün 溫庭筠; and 5) The Declining Period 唐詩衰頹的時期, from Hsien-t'ung to the third year of T'ien-yu (c. 860-906), major writers include Han Wo 韓偓, Lu Kuei-meng 陸龜蒙, P'i Jih-hsiu 皮日休, Ssu-k'ung T'u 司空圖. This quinquepartite periodization of T'ang literature is based on Hu Shih's attempt made in his *Pai-hua wen-hsüeh shih* 白話文學史 (Shanghai: Hsin-yüeh, 1928), with a distinction in labeling the first period—one calls

and an "Aestheticistic" period (she has no label for the Fourth Period) is basically the same as T'an Cheng-pi's 譚正璧 and Liu Ta-chieh's categories.[93] The tetradic divisions were represented in John C. H. Wu's 吳經熊 *The Four Seasons of T'ang Poetry*[94] by Spring (early T'ang poets, Wang Wei 王維 and Li Po, the Prince of Spring), Summer (Tu Fu), Autumn (Po Chü-i, Han Yü, Chia Tao, Meng Chiao, Li Ho 李賀) and Winter (Li Shang-yin, Tu Mu, Wen T'ing-Yün, Hsü Hun 許渾, Han Wu, Lo Yin 羅隱, and Li Yü, the Prince of Winter). He saw parallels between the associations of the seasons and the expressions or moods of the periods which were characterized in this vague, romantic manner: "On the whole, we may say that in the Spring of T'ang poetry, there were tears without griefs; in its Summer, the poets were so angry at the phenomena of social injustice and the uncalled-for miseries of their fellow-beings that they had very little time to weep for themselves; in its Autumn, griefs were assuaged by copious tears; and in its Winter, there were griefs without tears" (p. 36), and "Spring is cosmically-minded, Summer historically-minded, Autumn philosophically-minded, and Winter cosmetically-minded" (p. 173). Wu's description of the development of T'ang poetry was very similar to Jean J. Jusserand's remarks on Elizabethan literature, who referred to the late sixteenth-century years as "the Autumn of the Elizabethan period—darker days and season of fruits," and to the early seventeenth-century years as the Winter: "After a resplendent summer, a fruitful autumn; then clouds rise in the sky, and winter tempests loom in the distance."[95] Literary historians who adopt the "Three T'ang" divisions can be represented earlier by Huo I-hsien 霍衣仙, Hu Yün-i, and more recently by Li Yüeh-kang[96] 李日剛 whose chronological divisions are the same as Hu's (c. 618-712, 713-824, and 825-906). Besides these two views, there are others which propose to divide T'ang literature into two periods (Lu K'an-ju and Feng Yüan-chün's *Chung-kuo wen-hsüeh shih chien pien*[97] 中國文學史簡編; Chao Ts'ung's 趙聰 *Chung-kuo wen-hsüeh shih kang*[98] 中國文學史綱), regarding "An Shih chih luan" as the dividing line, and into five periods (e.g., *Chung-kuo wen-hsüeh shih,* ed. Chung-kuo k'o-hsüeh yüan wen-hsüeh yen-chiu so wen-hsüeh pien-hsieh tsu[99] 中國科學院文學研究所文學編寫組; c.

---

it "Vernacular," the other, "Post-Classical." To Su Hsüeh-lin, "Chinese literature of the Han Dynasty (c. 206 B.C.-A.D. 220) with *fu* as its major genre approximated to Western Classicism; the period between Chien-an and Wei-Tsin 魏晉 (c. 196-420) was an age of Romanticism. . . . Classicism reemerged during the Ch'i-Liang-Ch'en era 齊梁陳 (c. 479-589) when poetry was marked by 'bewitchingly beautiful' language and 'harmoniously attractive' rhythm with pages and cases of moons and dews, winds and clouds . . . . " (p. 14). Obviously, she appeared to have adopted the Classicism *versus* Romanticism dichotomy concept of literary evolution. It is, to a certain extent, justifiable to regard the Early T'ang period as the extension of the Ch'i-Liang-Ch'en era. Nevertheless, the term *Classicism* is improperly adopted, if not misapplied, here.

[93] See T'an's *Chung kuo wen-hsüeh shih ta-kang* 中國文學史大綱 (1925; rpt. Shanghai: Kuang-ming, 1947), pp. 43-46 and Liu's *Chung-kuo wen-hsüeh fa-ta shih,* pp. 393-491.

[94] (Tokyo: Charles E. Tuttle, 1972).

[95] *A Literary History of the English People,* (1895; rpt. London: T. F. Unwin, 1925-26), pp. 463-64.

[96] Huo I-hsien, *Chung-kuo wen-hsüeh shih t'ung lun* 中國文學史通論 (Hong Kong: Pei-cheng, 1940); Hu Yün-i, *Hsin chu chung-kuo wen-hsüeh shih* 新著中國文學史 (Shanghai: Pei-hsin, 1932); Li Yüeh-kang, *Chung-kuo wen-hsüeh shih* 中國文學史 (Taipei: Pai-yün, 1971).

[97] (Shanghai: Tai-chiang, 1932).

[98] (Hong Kong: Yu-lien, 1959).

[99] (Peking: Jen-min wen-hsüeh, 1962).

618-712, 713-756, 742-779, 780-859, and 860-905). All these views are primarily based on a static and synchronic conception of literary periods. If we interpret the historical process of Chinese literary development from a diachronic standpoint, we shall realize that the Early T'ang can be included in the Six-Dynasties (however labeled) period, and the Mid-Late T'ang in the Five-Dynasties-and-Early Sung period (which I propose to label, before an appropriate Chinese term is established, as "Chinese Baroque period"[100]) for their shared stylistic, generic, and thematic characteristics. In other words, we shall not encounter the particular problem of periodizing T'ang literature.

Yu Kuo-en 游國恩 in his essay "Tui yü pien-hsieh chung-kuo wen-hsüeh shih ti chi-tien i-chien"[101] 對於編寫中國文學史的幾點意見 made a more constructive proposition. Bearing in mind the dialectic instead of the causal relationship between social and literary development, he attempted to divide the history of "classical" Chinese literature into six distinctive periods:

> First Period: Antiquity to the end of Ch'un-ch'iu (18th century B.C.-4th century B.C.)—marked by the transitions in literature from oral composition to writing, from society to court, and from non-hierarchy to hierarchy.
> Second Period: Chan-kuo to Tung Han 東漢 (3rd century B.C.-2nd century)—a flourishing period of poetry and prose, marked by the stylistic innovations in the works of the pre-Ch'in masters 先秦諸子 and Ch'ü Yüan, and by the generic traditions of the *tz'u-fu* and the philosopher's prose.
> Third Period: Chien-an to High T'ang (3rd century-8th century)—marked by the development of *wu-yen shih* 五言詩 from emergence to maturity and of prose toward *p'ien-ou* 駢偶, and characterized by the pursuit of ornateness in diction, balance in form, and perfection in technique.
> Fourth Period: Mid-T'ang to the end of Northern Sung (9th century-early 12th century)—marked by plurality of styles and emergence of new literary genres, such as *tz'u, ch'uan-ch'i*.
> Fifth Period: Southern Sung to the "Opium War" (Early 12th century-mid 19th century)—a flourishing period of drama and novel, marked by the decline of "orthodox" 正統 literature and the rise of folk literature 市民文學, such as *chu-kung t'iao* 諸宮調, *hua-pen* 話本, *nan-hsi* 南戲, which serves as a mirror of reality.
> Sixth Period: The "Opium War" to May-Fourth Movement (mid 19th century-1919)—marked by the flourishing of social satire.

Evidently, this hexadic division has departed from the traditional "dynasty-period" concept, and demonstrated the awareness that the evolutionary rhythm of literature does not always coincide with that of society and history. Unfortunately, its dialectics still rests too much upon social factors, and its temporal referents are still predominantly "dynasty labels." To single out the emergence of "folk literary" genres (*chu-kung t'iao, hua-pen*) and the "Opium War" as the main criteria for determining the

---

[100] For information and discussion on this topic, please see my essay, "Toward Defining Chinese Baroque Poetry," *Tamkang Review*, 8 (1977), 25-72.
[101] *Wen-hsüeh i-ch'an hsüan-chi* (Peking: Chung-hua, 1960), III, 68-80.

last three periods is to underemphasize the importance of the *tz'u* genre in the first instance and to overlook the significant changes in stylistic tendencies during Mid-Ming when novel and *tuan-chü* 短劇 begin to replace *tsa-chü* in the literary scene. In my opinion, the Fourth Period should end around the second decade of the eleventh century for the reason that the early Sung writers often reflect a literary taste similar to their immediate predecessors; the Fifth Period should begin with the appearance of *man-tz'u* 慢詞 which is characterized by a narrative mode (middle decades of the 11th century), and end with the decline of *tsa-chü* (mid 15th century); and the Sixth Period, from then on until 1919.

More recently, Lee Chen-tong 李辰冬 in his essay "The Comparative Method in Periodization of Chinese Literary History"[102] proposed a system of periodization based on the particular consciousness of writers. By comparing the attitude toward life reflected in Juan Chi 阮籍 and Ts'ao Chih's poetry, he identifies "escapism" and "loyalism" as the two kinds of consciousness shared by two "schools" of writers: from Juan Chi to Li Po is the *Expressionist* period, and from Tu Fu to Wen T'ien-hsiang 文天祥, the *Anomalist* period. He further labels the period before Ch'ü Yüan as *Melic*, from Ch'ü Yüan to Ts'ao Chih as *Classical*, and from Kuan Han-ch'ing on as *Colloquial*. The terminology, according to him, has been arrived at by "taking one or two works which are most representative of the spirit of the respective periods, and using the title of the work to name the period."[103] Of course, such a system of periodization is undoubtedly derived from intrinsic factors. However, to define the achievement of major writers spanning over five centuries in terms of a common consciousness may run the risk of oversimplifying the complex process of literary evolution and slighting the roles of stylistic tendencies in period-formation; and it can be very arbitrary—for the individual consciousness is constantly affected by the milieu and the time, and a writer's attitude towards life may undergo several dramatic changes (it is not uncommon that we find in a writer's work contradictory views on the same theme). Besides, it is not made clear in what sense is the period label *Anomalist* related to "loyalism," and "loyalism" to the poets thus labeled. Poets like Li Shang-yin and Liu Yung 柳永 are at least as well-known as writers like Lu T'ung 盧仝 and Wen T'ien-hsiang. Since they are not included in the *Anomalist* period, where do they belong then? All in all, Lee's proposition is not groundless, but it needs elaboration and further examination of the problems it involves.

Generally speaking, periods in histories of Chinese literature[104] are usually given as a dynasty (e.g., Han, T'ang, Ming), or go by the name of the major literary figure/figures (e.g., The Age of Tu Fu, of Wen Li 溫李) or by the title of the reigning monarch (e.g., The Age of Chien-an, of Ta-li), or by literary genres (e.g., the Age of *tz'u-fu*, the Golden Age of Poetry, the Rise of *Tz'u*, the Development of Novel), or by literary groups/movements (e.g., *Chiang-hsi shih-p'ai* 江西詩派, *Kung-an p'ai* 公安派, *Ku-wen yün-tung* 古文運動). Among the works under survey, nearly all of

---

[102] *Tamkang Review*, 2, No. 2 & 3, No. 1 (1971-1972, Proc. from International Comparative Literature Conference held on 18-24 July, 1971 at Tamkang College of Arts & Sciences, Taipei, Taiwan, Republic of China), 193-97. Unfortunately it is an abstract from Chinese (tr. into English by George Lindberg). My discussion is based on the abstract.

[103] Ibid., 195. His method is similar to Brunetière's (note 20).

[104] About fifty histories of Chinese literature were included in the survey. For bibliographical information, see Liang Jung-jo and Huang Te-shih's 黃得時 "Ch'ung ting chung-kuo wen-hsüeh shih shu mu" 重訂中國文學史書目, *Yu-shih hsüeh-chi* 幼獅學誌, 4, No. 1 (1967), 1-36.

them adhere to a broad and stationary pattern of periodization. Most of the literary historians base their period scheme on dynastic divisions[105] or organize their materials by literary genres.[106] A few adopt a quadripartite scheme, the "periods" of which are usually referred to as "Early Ancient 上古, Medieval Ancient 中古, Near Ancient 近古, and Modern 近世";[107] occasionally as "the Ancient Period 古代, Han-Wei-Six Dynasties 漢魏六朝, T'ang-Sung 唐宋, and Yüan-Ming-Ch'ing & Modern Era 元明清及近代";[108] and infrequently as "the Age of Enlightenment 啓蒙時代, the Golden Age 黃金時代, The Silver Age 白銀時代, and the Dark Age 黑暗時代,"[109] with the first period extending from the eras of myth and "epic" to Chien-an times, the second to Late T'ang, the third to Yüan, covering mainly the poetic genres and philosophical writings, and the fourth to Late Ch'ing, dealing primarily with vernacular literature (*pien-wen* 變文, *hua-pen, tsa-chü, t'ung-su hsiao-shuo* 通俗小說, *chang-hui hsiao-shuo* 章回小說). Poetic styles mentioned in these literary histories are labeled either after reign-titles, such as Chien-an t'i 建安體 (Han), Huang-ch'u t'i 黃初體, Cheng-shih t'i 正始體 (Wei), Yüan-chia t'i 元嘉體 (Sung), Yung-ming t'i 永明體 (Ch'i), Yüan-ho t'i 元和體 (T'ang), Yüan-yu t'i 元祐體 (Sung), Yung-lo t'i 永樂體, Cheng-chia t'i 正嘉體 (Ming); or after dynastic divisions, such as Ch'u-T'ang t'i 初唐體, Wan-T'ang t'i 晚唐體; or after the name of an anthology, such as, Yü-t'ai t'i 玉臺體, Hsi-k'un t'i 西崑體; or of a place, such as, Ching-ling t'i 竟陵體, Kung-an t'i 公安體, Chiang-hsi t'i 江西體; or of literary figures, such as, Hsü-Yü t'i 徐庾體. All these belong more to the category of "group style" than to "period style," and none of the labels have been clearly defined in terms of the particular stylistic features shared by the literary group. The only exception is probably Chu Wei-chih's 朱維之 *Chung-kuo wen-i ssu-ch'ao shih lüeh* 中國文藝思潮史畧,[110] which periodizes Chinese literature according to *currents,* with dynasty-chronological periods overlapping one another to represent the undulating movement of literary development, so that Early T'ang literature, for example, would be included in the period when Buddhist thoughts flourished (from Eastern Han to High T'ang, early 1st century-early 8th century), and Mid-T'ang literature in the period when Aestheticism 唯美主義 was in full swing (from Mid-T'ang

---

[105] Consult the histories of Chinese literature by Ko Tsun-li 葛遵禮 (Shanghai: Hui-wen t'ang, 1921), T'an Cheng-pi (1935; rpt. Shanghai: Kuang-ming, 1936), Hu Yün-i (Shanghai: Pei-hsin, 1932), Liu Lin-sheng 劉麟生 (1931; rpt. Hong Kong: Nan-tao, 1956), Li Ting-i 李鼎彝 (Taipei: Wen-hsing, 1966).

[106] Consult the histories of Chinese literature by I Chün-tso 易君左 (Hong Kong: Tzu-yu, 1959), Yeh Ch'ing-ping 葉慶炳 (Taipei: Kuang-wen, 1965-66), and Li Yüeh-kang (Taipei: Pai-yün, 1971), the outlines of Chinese literary history 中國文學史大綱 by Yang Yin-shen 楊蔭深 (Ch'ang-sha: Shang-wu, 1938), Jung Chao-tsu 容肇祖 (1935; rpt. Shanghai: K'ai-ming, 1939), and T'an Cheng-pi (1925; rpt. Shanghai: Kuang-ming, 1947). See also Chang Chen-yung's 張振鏞 *Chung-kuo wen-hsüeh shih fen lun* 中國文學史分論 (Ch'ang-sha: Shang-wu, 1934), T'ing Ssu-wen's 丁思文 *Chung-kuo wen-hsüeh shih-hua* 中國文學史話 (Hong Kong: Chin-hsiu, 1960), and Ts'ao Chu-jen's 曹聚仁 *Chung-kuo wen-hsüeh kai-yao* 中國文學概要 (Hong Kong: Shih-chieh, 1956).

[107] Consult the histories of Chinese literature by Tseng I 曾毅 (Shanghai: T'ai-tung, 1915), Ch'ien Chi-po 錢基博 (1936; rpt. Hong Kong: Lung-men, 1965), and Hsieh Wu-liang's *Chung-kuo ta wen-hsüeh shih* (1918; rpt. Shanghai: Chung-hua, 1924).

[108] Consult Su Hsüeh-lin's *Chung-kuo wen-hsüeh shih*.

[109] Consult Lin Keng's *Chung-kuo wen-hsüeh shih* (Amoy, Fukien: National Amoy Univ. Press, 1947; rpt. Taipei: Ch'ing-liu, 1972 under the title *Chung-kuo wen-hsüeh fa-chan shih* 中國文學發展史, by Lin Wen-keng 林文庚).

[110] (Shanghai: K'ai-ming, 1946).

to Northern Sung, late 8th century-early 12th century), while High T'ang and Mid-T'ang literature would also constitute the period when social concerns and the *Fu-ku* movement came to the foreground. Western terms such as Classicism 古典主義 (Yüan and Ming literature,) Romanticism 浪漫主義 (Ming and Ch'ing literature), and Realism 寫實主義 (Ch'ing literature) were adopted to designate the major phases of a literary process similar to that of European literature. Such a scheme is diachronic and suggestive of relations with historical and social development. Unfortunately, the adopted period labels were not defined and modified to represent the characteristics of their respective literature in the context of Chinese tradition. And the scheme failed to include literary criteria other than ideological ones as underlying principles of period-formation.

To conclude, the problem of periodization in Chinese literature lies in the area of terminology, and in the lack of an actual scheme of literary periods that are built upon a compromise between chronology and the phases or "periodicity" of the literary process. One of the practical solutions is to use *period style* indicative of certain stylistic idiosyncracies and metaphysical concerns shared by writers of a time-span as a major criterion to determine literary periods and as an index to the spirit of an age so reflected in literature. Of course, the immediate difficulty that confronts the literary historian is how to establish the period styles with reasonable objectivity and reliable validity. As the study of period styles in Chinese literature, which treats not only *major* but also *minor* writers and therefore involves a complicated procedure of analysis and reevaluation, has not yet become popular, the contribution that the literary historian can make will be to attempt at diachronic periodization of Chinese literature in a much larger scale than Chu Wei-chih's, incorporating analyses of individual as well as group styles with commentaries on writers' thematic preoccupation and exploring the possible affinities between the different styles in terms of rhetorical characteristics and form-content unity.

The Bird as Messenger of Love in Allegorical Poetry

C. H. Wang

Lust, jealousy, and slander are three principal enemies of Friendship depicted in the Fourth Book of the *Faerie Queene* by Edmund Spenser. The estrangement of Timias from Belphoebe is obviously because of jealousy; slander vexes Arthur, Aemylia, and Amoret; whereas lust, before the other interweaving episodes take place, attacks Aemylia and Amoret. I attempt in this essay to investigate a specific attribute of allegorical literature by isolating the story of Timias and Belphoebe, which identifies the meaning of jealousy, from other narratives about the problem of Friendship, and in place of the Arthur-Aemylia-Amoret tangle, bringing in an examplar victimized by slander in Chinese poetry. To be certain, my focus will not be on the vices causing disasters to Friendship, but rather on the means of reunion when alienation is already existent. I intend to observe the image, or symbolism, of the bird in two allegorical poems, which share neither chronological nor cultural parallels. The aim of this study, therefore, is not to correlate two individual poems, but to single out for identification a singular agent, the bird, which appears to play a significant role in the making of allegorical literature.

The bird in the Timias-Belphoebe incident is a turtledove, flitting to reconcile the grieving young squire and his beloved lady.[1] And the birds invoked by Ch'ü Yüan 屈原, in *Li sao* 離騷 are called *chen* 鴆 and *chiu* 鳩, respectively. These two birds enter the poem when the courtier's wish for the entreatment of love is pronounced.[2] Whereas Timias and Belphoebe attain their romantic reunion with the assistance of the turtledove, Ch'ü Yüan fails in the pursuit of love, by and large, due to the ineptness of the *chen* and *chiu*. The importance of the messenger in the pursuit of love is thus betrayed. It is comparable with that in *Le Roman de la Rose* where the Duenna, acting as a go-between, presents to the imprisoned Fair Welcome a chaplet in behalf

---

[1] Book IV, Canto 8. The text I follow is that of the Globe Edition, *The Works of Edmund Spenser*, ed. R. Morris (London: Macmillan, 1910). The episode is found on pages 267-69.
[2] *Ch'u tz'u pu-chu* 楚辭補注 (Taipei: Chung-hua, 1966), 25b-26a.

of the Lover, and in so doing she creates a new hope for the imprisoned and the Lover. The Duenna's matchmaking, moreover, saves the *Roman* from stylistic stagnancy.³

Li sao is, similarly, a poem about the quest. The object of the quest is literally the beautiful woman, *mei-jen* 美人, and allegorically the Prince of Ch'u 楚 who, taking in slanderous words, has rejected the poet's service and sent him into exile.⁴ The poem starts with Ch'ü Yüan's account of his respectable genealogy, indicating that he is descended from a divine ancestor, the illustrious Kao-yang 高陽. The poet elaborates in the immediate ensuing passages to manifest his high personality in the finest allegorical structure. As the good plant symbolizes virtue and the bad one represents vice (e.g., the orchid in contrast with the mugwort), his effort to attain a high personality is usually expressed by his cultivation of the orchid and melilotus and, furthermore, by decorating himself with fragrant herbs and flowers, such as the selinea and angelica, gathered from the river bank. But, unfortunately, his aspiration for virtuous integrity turns out to be the cause of his wretchedness. His is a time of injustice. Dispirited in this world, Ch'ü Yüan determines to go on a quest for the Beauty (the wise prince) in another world.⁵ Before he sets out upward for heaven and other ethereal realms, he visits the tomb of Ch'ung-hua 重華 (or Shun 舜), the sage-emperor in Confucian classics:

> Looking to the ancient sages for appropriate guidance,
> I sighed with a bursting heart as I reckoned these.
> Crossing the Yüan and Hsiang, I journeyed to the south,
> And came to Ch'ung-hua, to whom I made my plaint.⁶

> 依前聖以節中兮，喟憑心而歷茲。
> 濟沅湘以南征兮，就重華而陳詞。

Eric Auerbach believes that the Vergil in the *Divina Commedia* is a *figura* rather than an allegory of reason, as other scholars claim.⁷ Ch'ung-hua in the *Li sao* is equivalent to Vergil in Dante's epic. However, I hesitate to say that Ch'ung-hua is absolutely a *figura* but not an allegory of the ideal government. The comparison must end here. For whereas Dante's poetical scope serves as a Renaissance reflection of the Judeo-Christian *past* and *future,* Ch'ü Yüan's turns out to be an observation of the *present* moral relationship between a courtier and his prince. The observation is, of course, much more meaningful and inspiring in the light of the classical Chinese norms of socio-ethical obligation than any pattern of the "allegory of theologians."

There is, nevertheless, a significant change of figural identity and, for that matter, ethical reciprocity in Ch'ü Yüan's poem. Distributing the multifold characteristic of the *tao* 道, *I Ching* 易經 prescribes that *k'un* 坤 is that of the earth, the wife, the courtier whereas *ch'ien* 乾 is the heaven, the husband, the prince.⁸ The allegorical

---

³ *Le Roman de la Rose,* trans. Harry W. Robbins (New York: Dutton, 1962), pp. 303-7.
⁴ See *Shih chi* 史記 (Peking: Chung-hua, 1959), 84 (pp. 2481-91).
⁵ Cf. C. H. Wang, "Sartorial Emblems and the Quest: A Comparative Study of the *Li Sao* and the *Faerie Queene*," *Tamkang Review*, 2, No. 2 & 3, No. 1 (1971-72), 309-28.
⁶ *Ch'u tz'u pu-chu*, 16ab.
⁷ "Figura," trans. Ralph Manheim, in *Scenes from the Drama of European Literature* (New York: Meridian, 1959), p. 71.
⁸ *Chou I cheng-i* 周易正義 (SSCCS ed.), 1.27a.

system in *Li sao,* however, espouses that the fair one, *mei-jen,* is the prince, associated with feminine attributes, and, in contrast, the poet in quest of "her" is the courtier. The former is King Huai of Ch'u 楚懷王, historically, and the latter, Ch'ü Yüan (343?-278 B.C.). The change of positions in this monumental poem of complex imagery and symbolism may prove that the poet was greatly influenced by folk literature, namely *Chiu ko* 九歌, or the *Nine Songs,* in which the quest of the goddess is a major theme.[9] That is, the elusive fair one sought after by the shaman is more often than not the goddess. This is one of the "shamanistic" features of Ch'ü Yüan literature.

Accordingly, Ch'ü Yüan's quest of the fair one in the other world is, in the complex allegory of love and politics, his solicitation for King Huai's readmitting him into official service, his wish for reconciliation. The birds, *chen* and *chiu,* occur in one of the three attempting proposals for the individual women living separately in the ethereal realms. Like the turtledove in the Timias-Belphoebe incident and the Duenna in the *Roman,* the birds in the *Li sao* are instrumental in the quest:

> I gazed at the lofty splendor of a jade tower,
> And saw the sweet Princess of the Kingdom of Sung.
> I bade the *chen* to be the messenger of love,
> But the *chen* returned saying that my suit was amiss.
> The male-*chiu* flew swiftly with much chattering,
> And I disliked it for its sly knavish manner.[10]

> 望瑤台之偃蹇兮，見有娀之佚女。
> 吾令鴆為媒兮，鴆告余以不好。
> 雄鳩之鳴逝兮，余猶惡其佻巧。

"The sweet Princess of the Kingdom of Sung," like Danaë of Argos, lives solitarily in a tower. In Chinese mythology, she swallowed an egg laid by a black bird, became pregnant, and gave birth to Ch'i 契 the ancestor of the House of Shang 商. According to *Shih Ching* 詩經 303 玄鳥, the black bird is a messenger sent from heaven to give start to the Shang; and according to other interpretations of lesser authority, it is the metamorphosis of Ti Chün 帝俊 approaching the chosen woman in order to open up a heroic age.[11] The legend is obviously similar to that of Leda and the Swan.

Before I discuss the nature of the bird as matchmaker in allegorical literature generally, it is necessary for me to examine the reason why Ch'ü Yüan's quest in the *Li sao* must fail. A close observation of the identity of the birds in comparison with Spenser's turtledove is in order. The *chen,* all the *Li sao* annotators and critics agree, is a certain ominous bird. Also called *yun-jih* 運日, its wings are believed to bear poison. It is like the owl in shape, purple-green in color, and fond of serpent as its diet. "The barbarian's lands," the author of the *History of the Sung* 宋史 writes, "are swampy, rugged, jungly, and malarious; those are no lands for human beings, but

---

[9] Cf. David Hawkes, "The Quest of the Goddess," in *Studies in Chinese Literary Genres,* ed. Cyril Birch (Berkeley: Univ. of California Press, 1974), pp. 42-68.

[10] *Ch'u tz'u pu-chu,* 25b-26a.

[11] For *Shih Ching,* see Ch'en Huan 陳奐, *Shih Mao-shih chuan shu* 詩毛氏傳疏 (Taipei: Kuang-wen, 1968), 30.3b-4b (pp. 910-12). Cf. *Shih chi,* 3 (p. 91). The myth of Ti Chün is told exclusively in *Shan hai ching* 山海經.

for the *chen* and poisonous serpents."¹² In modern ornithology it is identified as the snake-falcon 蛇鷹 (*Spilornis cheela*).¹³ Probably because of its diet, the bird has acquired an evil reputation. It is poisonous not only in folklore but also in philology; in Chinese ideography the bird's name, *chen* 鴆, has developed to mean "poison," since the sixth century B.C., if not before.¹⁴ In later literature the derivative meaning of the character seems to supersede the original, as the bird has gained itself a new name, snake-falcon, categorized in *Falconiformes*. The snake-falcon "hovers over the hills from Hainan to Burma, looking for the reptiles on which it feeds."¹⁵

The *chiu,* on the other hand, is by and large an auspicious bird. It is invoked as a symbol of passion and virtue in *Shih Ching* 1 關雎, and it is the first *hsing* 興 element in traditional Chinese poetics.¹⁶ The bird is illustrious for its melodious chatterings suggestive of love. Ornithologists identify it in the genus *Streptopelia* esp. *S. turtur*. It is the turtledove. This Chinese turtledove (*turtur orientalis Lath.*) is almost identical with its English counterpart in that it is also noted for its fidelity of love. Therefore, we may assume that Ch'ü Yüan did not mention the bird by accident when he was writing about the proposal of love in *Li sao*. The reference to the *chiu* in this place may very well be premeditated. The fact, as it were, proves that Ch'ü Yüan was well versed in the *Shih Ching* tradition, too, and the *Li sao* can be regarded as a post-Confucian convergency of northern and southern poetry in terms of imagery and other references, such as mythical personages. The poem did not generate itself directly from Ch'u shamanism.

Ch'ü Yüan's turtledove is, however, still different from that of Spenser's. The first apparent difference is that the former is a male while the latter is a female. In the *Faerie Queene,* Timias was estranged from Belphoebe by jealousy. He bemoaned the loss of his love.

>   Till on a day, as in his wonted wise
>   His doole he made, there chaunst a turtle Dove
>   To come where he his dolors did devise,
>   That likewise late had lost her dearest love,
>   Which losse her made like passion also prove:
>   Who, seeing his sad plight, her tender heart
>   With deare compassion deeply did emmove,
>   That she gan mone his undeserved smart,
>   And with her dolefull accent beare with him a part.
>   (IV, viii, 3)
>
>   Amongst the rest a jewell rich he found,
>   That was a Ruby of right perfect hew,

---

¹² *Sung shih* 宋史 (*SPPY* ed.), 348.14b.

¹³ Cheng Tso-hsin 鄭作新, *Chung-kuo niao-lei hsi-t'ung chien-shuo* 中國鳥類系統簡說 (Peking: K'e-hsüeh, 1964), p. 26.

¹⁴ See for example, *Kuo yü* 國語 (Taipei: Chung-hua, 1966), 8.2b.

¹⁵ Edward H. Schafer, *The Vermilion Bird: T'ang Images of the South* (Berkeley: Univ. of California Press, 1967), p. 245.

¹⁶ For the interpretation of the *hsing* in *Shih Ching* poetics, see Shih-hsiang Chen 陳世驤, "The *Shih Ching*: Its Generic Significance in Chinese Poetics," in *Studies in Chinese Literary Genres*, pp. 8-41. Cf. also, C. H. Wang, *The Bell and the Drum: Shih Ching as Formulaic Poetry in an Oral Tradition* (Berkeley: Univ. of California Press, 1974), pp. 102-8.

>   Shap'd like a heart yet bleeding of the wound,
>   And with a little golden chaine about it bound.
>
>   (IV, viii, 6)
>
>   The same he tooke, and with a riband new,
>   In which his Ladies colours were, did bind
>   About the turtles necke, that with the vew
>   Did greatly solace his engrieved mind.
>
>   (IV, viii, 7)

As the squire was practicing lovesick fallacy with her, the bird eventually understood his grief. She flew away "untill she came where wonned his Belphoebe faire" (IV, viii, 8). She guided Belphoebe back to Timias. The episode is written with such a sweet undertone that A. A. Jack claims, "The turtledove that effects the reconcilement is Spenser himself." His interpretation is based on the so-called historical allegory. So he continues:

> One is amused at the boldness of the allegory. . . . Yet in the whole *Faerie Queene* there is nothing more perfect than this courtier-like performance. It is perfection, this pleading of Spenser's for his friend, under the guise of a [turtle] dove, perfection diplomatically and equally perfection poetically.[17]

At this point, Jack is referring to the assumption that the meaning behind the "perfect" scene is concerned with Sir Walter Raleigh's criminal intrigue and his attempt to be reconciled with Queen Elizabeth of England. A nineteenth century annotator of the *Faerie Queene,* John S. Hart, concludes that "at length . . . the unfortunate squire recovers the favour of his Mistress, and is once more admitted to her service."[18] Still, Hart hints at historical allegory. When C. S. Lewis, writing with specific regard to allegory of love, finds this passage "quite free from allegory,"[19] he probably overlooks the importance of historical allegory as a division of allegorical literature in general. For whereas he dismisses the episode in question as allegory according to his definition, he, on another occasion, writes with fanciful emphasis about Belphoebe's "Lilly handës twaine" crushing "virtuous herbs." Lewis finds that the herbs are "for the healing of wounds."[20]

The Timias-Belphoebe incident, in which the turtledove plays the role of the matchmaker, is a historical allegory. Neither Timias nor Belphoebe is a *figura*. In terms of the allegory of history, as A. A. Jack notes, the bird is Spenser the poet, a friend of Raleigh; and in terms of the allegory of love, the bird is a matchmaker between two estranged lovers. On the other hand, the bird remains an element in a symbolism, and therefore, the allegory could not appear complete without further revealing its generic convention in the practice of direct naming—the squire's name

---

[17] *A Commentary on the Poetry of Chaucer and Spenser* (Glasgow: Maclehose, Jackson & Co., 1920), p. 219.
[18] *Spenser and the Faerie Queene* (Philadelphia: Hayes and Zell, 1854), p. 283.
[19] *The Allegory of Love* (New York: Oxford Univ. Press, 1958), p. 346.
[20] Ibid., p. 316.

is derived from τίμιος (the worthy). In addition, Spenser uses Belphoebe "to symbolize the life of maindenhood," as Kate M. Warren remarks, "and as a compliment to the queen." The turtledove is a symbol, but not a real bird, although Warren considers it "real" because, as she says, "it only uses bird-methods . . . to help its friend."[21] The bird cannot be "real" because a real bird, without being affected by pathetic fallacy, cannot make "a lamentable lay" for the squire and itself simultaneously. And pathetic fallacy is hardly possible in an allegorical poem like the *Faerie Queene*. Supported by the practice of direct naming of the squire and the lady, the bird is an agent in a complete allegory—it is, at the same time, a thought separated from Timias and Belphoebe. It is the most efficient and effective agent in the allegory of love. The turtledove can be compared to the swan which rapes Leda, or the black bird which causes pregnancy to the Princess of the Kingdom of Sung.[22] When we take the turtledove in the Timias-Belphoebe episode as a thought or desire formulated by the common contribution of the lovers, we recognize the so-called matchmaker as an agent of love appointed by both and, with this understanding, we can affirm the episode as literature transcending historical events. The turtledove as a matchmaker led Belphoebe back to Timias, and the estrangement was consequently dissolved:

> . . . her inburning wrath she gan abate,
> And him receiv'd againe to former favours state.
> (IV, viii, 17)
>
> In which he long time afterwards did lead
> An happie life with grace and good accord,
> Fearlesse of fortunes chaunge or envies dread . . .
> (IV, viii, 18)

At this point the bird exited. In fact, it disappeared from the poem as soon as Belphoebe reached the spot where Timias was.

There is yet another question to answer. Why is it that Spenser chooses this specific bird to act as a go-between? The turtledove is attributed with much fidelity to its mate. This is probably true. But there must be some mythical or literary reasons for the poet to choose it as a poetic device, too. John Upton believes that in this case "Spenser had his eye on Virgil, *Aen.* 6, 190ff."[23] Upton refers to the scene in which the doves of Venus guide Aeneas to the golden bough. The annotation, purporting to explicate an important literary allusion, is a dangerous one. Venus is Aeneas' mother, and we shall not be misled into construing an Oedipus complex in which the doves of Venus guide Aeneas to the golden bough. The annotation, reference to Spenser's poetry alone, we find that the turtledove is a most passionate, gentle, and amorous bird. It is the bird that flies in the "Epithalamion" and the "Prothalamion," which are songs celebrating nuptials.[24] At least twice in the *Faerie Queene* itself, moreover, the name of the bird is used as a metaphor to denote Cupid,

---

[21] *The Works of Edmund Spenser, A Variorum Edition,* ed. E. Greenlaw, C. G. Osgood, and F. M. Padelford (Baltimore: Johns Hopkins Univ. Press, 1935), IV, 283.

[22] For a relevant treatment on the topic, see Albert Mordell, *The Erotic Motive in Literature* (New York: Boni and Liveright, 1919).

[23] *The Works of Edmund Spenser, A Variorum Edition,* IV, 210.

[24] *The Works of Edmund Spenser* (The Globe Edition), 587-91, 605-7.

"the winged god of love." In one place the poet describes the way Cupid flies "as a very dove" (III, vi, 11), and in another, he puts Cupid in apposition to "Venus dearling dove" (IV, pr. 4). More than twenty centuries after the Chinese poet had determined on the turtledove to embellish and intensify his nuptial poem (*Shih Ching* 1), Spenser did the same in his lyrical celebrations of marriage and romantic narrative of the reunion of love. Spenser was, of course, not inspired by Chinese poetry; he was nourished by another great civilization, which in the making of this particular image parallels Chinese civilization.

The turtledove fulfills its mission in the Timias-Belphoebe incident, but it is somehow rejected by the poet in his difficult quest in *Li sao*. Ch'ü Yüan rejects it, calling it sly and knavish, and this judgment consequently leads him to one of the failures in the pursuit of the *mei-jen*. Ch'ü Yüan denies the service of the turtledove, and in so doing he denies his hope. But why does he reject the loving, amorous bird? While Spenser writes to achieve "the romantic conception of marriage"[25] in the Third Book of the *Faerie Queene* and much of the Fourth, Ch'ü Yüan works in a totally different direction. The *Li sao* is, in the final analysis, a poem intended as the last will of a frustrated man, a poetic testimony of his loyalty to a king distracted by the evils of the time. Ch'ü Yüan, at the writing of the poem, had come to a point of no return. He was no longer attempting to use it to effect a reconciliation with the king; rather, he wished to use it to make known to posterity his integrity and aspiration, to warn the future of any more mistakes. He may fail in reality, but he succeeds in poetry and what poetry conveys—the perfection of a truly loyal courtier in exile. The purport of *Li sao* is therefore quite different from that of the *Faerie Queene,* and, for the precision of it, Ch'ü Yüan mentions the turtledove in order to reject it. In other words, Spenser uses the turtledove for its affectionate nature in matchmaking, whereas Ch'ü Yüan, knowing that it is able to fulfill the mission, still rejects its service for this very reason. The bird as matchmaker, as noted earlier, is one's thought—or personality—in conceit; it is the lover's aggressive desire in action. Ch'ü Yüan may be aggressive and insistent in the quest, and yet he cannot identify his agent with the turtledove because the bird, though able, would break up his principle by its slyness and knavish behavior.

Instead of the turtledove, Ch'ü Yüan sends the snake-falcon as a messenger of love. The choice is a tragic one, because the snake-falcon is inept for such a mission. It can never be received with grace by society. When the snake-falcon returns and tells that the suit is amiss, it actually says that the lady in the tower refuses to accept its entreatment. The snake-falcon, obviously a *persona non grata,* may not even have the chance to present the case to the lady. There is, however, always something upright in *persona non grata;* and, in choosing the snake-falcon and rejecting the turtledove, Ch'ü Yüan shows his appreciation of the quality of uprightness—over slyness—in his messenger. For the messenger of love ought to be compatible with its master in heart and mind. The bad reputation of the snake-falcon is probably due to slander, too, as that of Ch'ü Yüan definitely is.

Between the slandered and the sly birds, Ch'ü Yüan chooses the former, the non-comformist, because he himself, though not literally "poisonous," is as mistreated as the bird is by society. He realizes that he is "alone at a loss" in the world where everything has turned upside down, and once he even compares himself to the eagle:

---

[25] *The Allegory of Love,* p. 298.

> Eagles do not flock like other birds—
> So it has been true since antiquity.²⁶

鷙鳥之不羣兮，自前世而固然。

The snake-falcon resembles the eagle in certain respects; for instance, it does not seek to flock with others like the lesser birds. Ch'ü Yüan uses it for its independent spirit, despite bad reputation. The choice, therefore, reveals a certain degree of pathetic fallacy on the part of the frustrated courtier. Perhaps out of protest, he identifies himself with the snake-falcon, the bird which is much slandered for its refusal to please the self-deceiving majority in a chaotic age. Ch'ü Yüan has been deprived of his title, but he does not believe it is appropriate to regain it at the cost of honor and justice. There is at the same time despair and pride in his search of truth throughout *Li sao*. His determination not to compromise with the wicked but to attack them, therefore, elevates him to a point where he is both high and lonely. Still, he refuses to succumb to ignorance, though he can succumb to death. Even at the very end of his life, he does not seem to be silenced; he maintains despair and pride to the end, like Socrates when he speaks to the Athenians: "Why do I mention this? Because I am going to explain to you why I have such an evil name."²⁷

---

²⁶ *Ch'u tz'u pu-chu,* 12b-13a.
²⁷ Plato, *Apology of Socrates and Crito,* ed. Louis Dyers and rev. Thomas Day Seymour (Waltham, Mass.: Blaisdell, 1908), 21a. The quote is from the Jowett translation.

Carolyn Kizer and Her Chinese Imitations

Dominic Cheung

In the acknowledgements which preface her book *Knock upon Silence,* Carolyn Kizer confesses the debt she owes to Arthur Waley's translations of Chinese poems.[1] It is from Waley's translations that Kizer derives the material for the group of her own poems which appear in the section of her book titled "Chinese Imitations." These eight poems are dedicated to Waley whose translations Kizer has read, she frankly admits, since her childhood, adding that "like so many of my contemporaries, my debt and my devotion to him is incalculable."[2]

Admittedly, it would be difficult to talk about the impact of the Chinese poems themselves on Carolyn Kizer's poems since her "imitations" are essentially imitations of Arthur Waley's translations. However, although the risks of any influence study run high, an examination of the sources available to Kizer is appropriate in order to furnish a clearer appreciation of what Kizer has undertaken.

Waley modestly assures us in the preface of his translations that his Chinese friends attest to the closeness of his translations, "closer, they have sometimes been kind enough to say, than those of any other translator."[3] Nevertheless, certain inac-

---

[1] Carolyn Kizer, *Knock upon Silence* (Seattle and London: Univ. of Washington Press, 1968). These are the words found in the beginning paragraph of her acknowledgments: "I have been reading the poetry of Arthur Waley since childhood, and, like so many of my contemporaries, my debt and my devotion to him is incalculable."

[2] Ibid. In her notes following the poems, Kizer has singled out each poem's originality as follows: "The first three poems in the book are written in the style of Po Chu-I. *Hiding Our Love* is modeled on a poem of the Emperor Wu-Ti. *Night Sounds* and *Summer near the River* are based on themes in the Book of Songs."

[3] In preparing for an illustrated edition of his translations, Waley confidently states, "Since then [translations made over twenty years ago] my own knowledge of Chinese and the general study of it in America and Europe have made enormous progress. In arranging the poems for this illustrated edition I have corrected a certain number of mistakes. . . . There is a great deal that specialists might quarrel with; but not much, I hope, that will be definitely misleading to the general public. . . . " See Preface, in *Translations from the Chinese* by Arthur Waley (New York: Vintage, 1971). Incidentally, the earliest edition was published by Alfred A. Knopf, Inc. in 1919. Therefore, the translation made by Waley twenty years ago must have been sometime around 1900.

curacies do exist in Waley's work; quite inexplicably, for instance, the Chinese poem "Reciting Alone in the Mountain" 山中獨吟 is translated as "Madly Singing in the Mountain."[4] Twice removed from the original, Carolyn Kizer's "Singing Aloud" is evidence of yet another stage in the metamorphosis of the poem.[5]

In another instance, Kizer claims that two of her works are derived from Arthur Waley's translation of *The Book of Songs,* a selection of ancient odes which were composed around the tenth century B.C. In actuality, Kizer's poems are based on the Waley translation of the "Tzu-yeh Songs" 子夜歌, ballads written in the third century A.D. The confusion is compounded further by the fact that the fourth of the five "Tzu-yeh Songs" which Waley translated is in fact taken from the tenth-century A.D. "Mo-ch'ou Songs" 莫愁樂.

However, the effect of these inaccuracies on Carolyn Kizer's poems is minimal since she is engaged in the creation of imitations derived from the Chinese works rather than translating the works from the original. On the other hand, considering the conciseness of the Chinese language and the resulting ambiguities and indirectness such a language poses when employed in poetry, it is rather amazing (particularly for those versed in the Chinese poems themselves) to note that Carolyn Kizer has effectively captured the subtlest nuances of the Chinese works while often bringing latent connotations to full and precise imagistic expression.

It is never a matter of referring Kizer's pieces to the Chinese poems themselves or vice versa since Kizer's works successfully demonstrate her sensitive explorations of material available to her. What she finally voices in her own poems is no longer the solitary cry of the oriental woman, but that which belongs neither to the east nor to the west and is not confined in terms of either space or time. Three stanzas of Kizer's "Summer near the River" are modelled after the "Tzu-yeh Songs." The last stanza, which actually belongs to the "Mo-ch'ou Songs" and which Waley mistook as belonging to the "Tzu-yeh Songs" is gracefully combined with the "Tzu-yeh" verses in the form of a dramatic monologue which utilizes all the episodes inherent in the original poems.

The word "Tzu-yeh" is a somewhat meaningless title of one of the largest group of songs from the Six Dynasties in China. According to a historical treatise, one of the original songs was said to have been written by a maiden named Tzu-yeh. The treatise goes on to describe, in all seriousness, the singing of two ghosts in two households of the T'ai-yuan 太元 period (A.D. 376-396). Since the ghosts kept singing the words "Tzu-yeh," the historians concluded that Tzu-yeh must have been the creator of these songs!

Carolyn Kizer's version of the "Tzu-yeh" assumes the title of "Summer near the River." In this work, two images immediately present themselves: the image of summer and that of a flowing river. Traditionally, summer symbolizes passion, the season of ripening love. In Kizer's poem, it is a season when life forces surge strongly but are counteracted by the cold determinism of the river, a symbol of the relentless flow, the clearly defined course of life. Where summer presents a wide variation of color in nature, the river, on the other hand, suggests a certain fixedness by virtue of its defined path.

---

[4] Waley, ibid., p. 197. The title of this poem has also been adopted for a posthumous volume in memory of Arthur Waley's works. See Ivan Morris, ed., *Madly Singing in the Mountains: An Appreciation and Anthology of Arthur Waley* (New York: Harper & Row, 1970).

[5] Kizer, pp. 4-5.

The river and summer are thus two antithetical images which Carolyn Kizer uses, tying them together through the use of internal rhymes such as "Sum*mer* ne*ar* the Ri*ver*." By persistently stressing the grief which is inherent in the symbol of summer, the poet is able to extend herself into the realm of dramatic details. The first two stanzas:

> I have carried my pillow to the windowsill
> And try to sleep, with my damp arms crossed upon it
> But no breeze stirs the tepid morning.
> Only I stir . . . Come, tease me a little!
> With such cold passion, so little teasing play,
> How long can we endure our life together?
>
> No use. I put on your long dressing-gown!
> The untied sash trails over the dusty floor.
> I kneel by the window, prop up your shaving mirror
> And pluck my eyebrows.
> I don't care if the robe slides open
> Revealing a crescent of belly, a tan thigh.
> I can accuse that non-existent breeze . . . [6]

In Arthur Waley's translations of two of the "Tzu-yeh Songs" we read:

> I have brought my pillow and am lying at the northern
>   window,
> So come to me and play with me awhile.
> With so much quarreling and so few kisses
> How long do you think our love can last?
>
> I will carry my coat and not put on my belt;
> With unpainted eyebrows I will stand at the front window.
> My tiresome petticoat keeps on flapping about:
> If it opens a little, I shall blame the spring wind.[7]

A word-for-word translation of the Chinese original reads:

> carry—pillow—north—window—lie
> you (man/boy)—come—to—me (woman/girl)—play/tease
> little—joy—more—clashes
> to pity each other—can—how long.
>
> carry—gown—not—tie—sash
> lightly—brows—out—front—window
> gauze—dress—easy—wavers
> little—exposure—blame/accuse—east-wind.

---
[6] Kizer, p. 11.
[7] Waley, p. 35.

擎枕北窗外，郎來就儂嬉。
小喜多唐突，相憐能幾時。

擎裙未結帶，約眉出前窗。
羅裳易飄颺，小開駡春風。

When compared to Waley's translation of the Chinese work, Kizer's verses are, psychologically, much richer in their depiction of the dejected woman. The opening lines "I have carried my pillow to the windowsill / And try to sleep, with my damp arms crossed upon it," direct our attention immediately to the meanings associated with the heat of summer. Physically confined to her chamber, the woman's discomfort is heightened by the oppressive warmth which, in turn, creates a sense of stasis since "no breeze stirs.../ Only I stir." On the psychological level, there is the same sense of oppression which is manifested by physical reality. Thus when the woman moves toward the window, she is not only seeking physical relief from the "tepid" morning, but, locked in her own ego, is trying to establish contact with the outside world. By providing her own details, Kizer thus amplifies the emotional tenor of the original work without departing from the basic thrust of Waley's "I have brought my pillow and am lying at the northern window."

Although each stanza of Kizer's poem is in fact an independent poem, she has managed, by reversing the order of the original poems, to melt the disparate elements into a single unified poem. The invitation "Come, tease me a little!" followed by "With such cold passion, so little teasing play, / How long can we endure our life together?" for instance, successfully prepares us for the actions which follow in the next stanza, where the woman, having failed to engage the man in a "little teasing," rises and slips on his dressing gown. Kizer's own use of the pronoun "your" with regard to the man's dressing gown, may, at first glance, seem immaterial. Several suggestions are implied, however, by the woman's use of her companion's dressing gown. The malaise which is created by the heat in the first verse is now paralleled by an emotional lassitude: the woman does not bother to dress, but merely slips on her companion's dressing gown allowing the untied sash to trail on the floor. It might have been suggested, too, that by wearing her companion's robe, the woman subconsciously strives for the physical contact which is not in the offing from the man whose passion is "cold" and who is so little inclined toward the "little teasing play."

By having the woman wear her lover's robe, Kizer effectively sets the stage, so to speak, for the crucial closing lines in the second verse where the woman says "I don't care if the robe slides open / Revealing a crescent of belly, a tan thigh." Elsewhere in her poem "Hiding Our Love," a modification of Wu-ti's "People Hide Their Love" 有所思, Kizer again uses the seemingly casual detail as a means of bringing certain facts to light without overt reference to them. In Waley's translation of Wu-ti's poem we read:

Round my waist I wear a double sash
I dream that it binds us both with a same-heart knot.[8]

腰中雙綺帶，夢爲同心結。

---

[8] Waley, p. 104. A clarification is needed here. The Wu-ti who wrote this poem is Liang Wu-ti 梁武帝 (A.D. 464-?), or Emperor Wu of the Liang Dynasty.

In Kizer's version she says:

> The sash of my dress wraps twice around my waist
> I wish it bound the two of us together.[9]

In Wu-ti's poem, the sash is a symbol of platonic love, the illusory bond between two hearts. In Kizer's poem, the sash is utilized to convey two levels of meaning: a separation between lovers has affected the woman; that the sash can be wound twice around her waist suggests that her health has failed and that she has grown thin. By winding the sash around her waist, the woman, undoubtedly, is reminded of the binding power of love, hence her words "I wish it bound the two of us together."

Similarly, in "Summer near the River," the trailing sash, a seemingly small detail, is utilized to convey several levels of meaning. Where the sash in "Hiding Our Love" is a symbol of the woman's desire to be bound in love, the trailing sash in "Summer near the River" suggests a deteriorating relationship, a slackening of love on the part of the woman's companion. It is also a means of leading into the last lines of the verse where the robe slides open, blown apparently by a "nonexistent breeze" to reveal the "crescent of belly, [and] a tan thigh." The untied sash in Kizer's poem is a parallel to the fluttering gauze dress worn by the lady in the Chinese poem. In both instances, the seemingly casual dishabille is an attempt at seduction, but where the sliding robe reveals belly and thigh, the diaphanous gauze dress is allowed to flap open in the spring wind and perhaps "open a little."

The defiance in Kizer's "I don't care if the robe slides open / Revealing a crescent of belly, a tan thigh" is absent in the Chinese poem. The woman's defiance as well as the subjunctive mood in which she states that she "can accuse that non-existent breeze" is weak because there is only the remotest possibility that a breeze would stir the "tepid morning." In the Chinese poem, whatever the "wavering" dress reveals is not mentioned and neither are reasons given as to what causes the dress to "waver" in the first place. The attention is thus drawn not to what the opening dress reveals, but rather, to why the spring wind is being used as an excuse for the dishabille and not the gauze dress or the deliberately unfastened sash.

In Kizer's poem, we learn of a waning interest on the man's part and the woman's suspicion of his infidelity later in the poem. Laying the blame on the "non-existent breeze" for the exposed belly and thigh thus lends a poignant air to the situation in the poem. For although she is aware of the "cold passion," the woman's pride is maintained sufficiently to the extent that the efforts to win back the man must appear casual and not actively sought. True desperation over an impending loss cannot be revealed, hence the feeble lie, that a wind, and a non-existent wind at that, has caused the robe to fall open.

In the third verse of "Summer near the River," the woman's pride is affirmed in the midst of her fears over her vagrant lover. She reveals that:

> I am as monogamous as the North Star
> But I don't want you to know it. You'd only take advantage.
> While you are as fickle as spring sunlight.[10]

---

[9] "Hiding Our Love," Kizer, p. 8.
[10] "Summer near the River," Kizer, p. 12.

Her love and desire to hold on to her companion cannot be revealed to him, for in contrast to her steadfastness he is "as fickle as spring sunlight."

In comparing her lover to the spring sunlight, Kizer, once again, stays close to the astrological imagery used in the Chinese poem. In the "Tzu-yeh Songs," fidelity and faithlessness are described in terms of the North Star and the sun:

> Where I am the dawn star of the North
> Never shifting for thousands of years,
> You bear the heart of the bright sun
> East in the morning, west at dusk.[11]
>
> (my translation)

儂作北辰星，千年無轉移。
歡行白日心，朝東暮還西。

As an archetype, the sun is a representation of truth, righteousness and supremacy. Used in the "Tzu-yeh," the sun conceit is similar to the image employed by Donne in "A Valediction, Forbidding Mourning." In Donne's poem, lovers are bound as one by their love. As two separate entities, the poet sees himself as the active half which, when it "far doth roam," "leans and hearkens after" "the fixed foot," which "in the center sit."[12] In the "Tzu-yeh" and "Summer near the River," the path taken by the sun each day from east to west suggests not only the man's infidelity, but perhaps his natural inability to remain constant. For just as the sun may pass through northern skies at certain times of the year, it must, inevitably, move on in its established course leaving the Northern star which never shifts in a thousand years. The very inevitability of such a course in nature only heightens the harsh reality which exists in terms of the human love relationship.

It is not until the last two verses of the poem that Kizer introduces the image of the river, and where the passion associated with summer is identified with the man who is seen "striding toward the river," while the woman petulantly exclaims, "The cat means more to you than I." When he returns "reeking of fish and beer," the woman notes that:

> There is salt dew in your hair, where have you been?
> Your clothes weren't that wrinkled hours ago, when you left.
> You couldn't have loved someone else, after loving me.[13]

In her distress at the sight of her returning lover, all of the woman's senses are brought into play as she smells the beer and fish, notes the wrinkled clothes and salt dew in his hair.

---

[11] The original Chinese poem can be found in Kuo Mou-ch'ien 郭茂倩, ed., *Yüeh-fu shih chi* 樂府詩集 (Taipei: Shang-wu, 1968), II, 521.

[12] *The Complete Poetry and Selected Prose of John Donne,* ed. Charles M. Coffin (New York: Random House, 1952), pp. 38-39. Other examples that demonstrate love triumphing over the inconstancy of the sun can be found in Donne's other poems like "The Anniversarie," and "Song: Sweetest Love, I Do Not Goe."

[13] Kizer, p. 12.

The river is mentioned again in the closing lines of the poem when the man embraces the woman, causing her to say, "for a moment, the river ceases flowing."[14] The river, as we have previously noted, is a symbol of unrelenting fate. Specific applications of the symbol are made in turn to the man and the woman in "Summer near the River." The man, for instance, strides toward the river, and figuratively the act may be seen as the control he has over his life and fate. The woman's fate, on the other hand, rests on the man himself, her happiness and peace of mind depend on his uncertain love. Fate, like the relentless flow of the river, has already decreed a change in the relationship, but in the moment that the man embraces her, the woman feels that what is foreordained cannot possibly occur. In the light of her present ecstacy, the future without him is stalled, hence "for a moment, the river ceases flowing."

In the Chinese poem, the stilled river is placed in context of a separation between a woman and her lover. She sees him off on his journey, going "with him as far as Ch'u-shan." When he, against all social conventions, embraces her in public, she ecstatically says:

> For a moment you held me fast in your outstretched arms.
> I thought the river stood still and did not flow.[15]
>
> 探手抱腰看，江水斷不流。

Here, as in "Summer near the River," a parting of the ways is in the offing, harshly determined perhaps by fate. The breach of socially accepted behavior is sufficient reason for the woman's ecstatic "I thought the river stood still and did not flow," but in terms of the river as a symbol of predetermined factors in life, it would seem that here, as in Kizer's poem, the ecstasy can, and does momentarily, halt the tide of fate. In the Chinese poem, the moment is crystallized by the illusion of the river's stillness, and the setting of mountains surrounding the embracing pair is fixed in a perfectly harmonious whole. While Carolyn Kizer's poems are not exact translations, they do utilize the substance, stylistics and subtle nuances of Chinese works. Where basically oriental allusions with no English equivalent appear, they are used as points of departure for Kizer's own personal experiences without jeopardy to the essential details of the original Chinese works. The graceful artistry of Kizer's poems lies on the strength of the balance she has struck between her vision and that which is inherent in the Chinese poems, for her poems are never merely accurate copies of the Chinese poems, nor are they simply a vehicle.

It cannot be said that Kizer lacks originality in what she has undertaken to write, since what she has taken from the Chinese is synthesized by her own passion and sensitivity. The extent of this synthesis is seen in a comparison of her lines from "Winter Song" with those of Arthur Waley:

> (1) So I go on, tediously on and on . . .
>   We are separated, finally, not by death but by life.[16]
>   (Kizer)

---

[14] Waley, p. 35. The original poem can be found in *Yüeh-fu shih-chi*, II, 574.
[15] Waley, p. 35.
[16] "Winter Song," Kizer, p. 14.

> On and on, always on and on
> Away from you, parted by a life-parting[17]
>
> (Waley)

行行重行行，與君生別離。

> (2) How can you and I meet face to face
> After our triumphant love?
> After our failure?[18]
>
> (Kizer)

> The way between is difficult and long,
> Face to face how shall we meet again?[19]
>
> (Waley)

道路阻且長，會面安可知。

In the lines quoted above, we see that Waley, like many established sinologists, has tended to present the original poem as closely as possible. With Carolyn Kizer's renditions, we sense for the first time an attempt at exploring the poems for meanings which go beyond the linguistic representations. With her lyric temperament and acute sensibilities, Kizer peels away at the different layers of metaphor, exhausting words and allusions of their ultimate meanings. Thus, although her works may be deemed interpretative, they, on occasion, exceed even the Chinese poems themselves, for the vibrancy which Kizer has infused into them.

---

[17] "Seventeen Old Poems," Waley, p. 37.
[18] Kizer, p. 14.
[19] Waley, p. 37.

The Reception of Cold Mountain's Poetry in the Far East and the United States

Ling Chung

> When men see Han Shan
> They all say he's crazy
> And not much to look at—
> Dressed in rags and hides.
> They don't get what I say
> And I don't talk their language.
> All I can say to those I meet:
> "Try and make it to Cold Mountain."
> —Han Shan, translated by Gary Snyder

時人見寒山,各謂是風顛。
貌不起人目,身爲布裘纏。
我語他不會,他語我不言。
爲報往來者,可來向寒山。

Han Shan, or Cold Mountain 寒山, has been a puzzling literary figure. The reception, and in some sense, the rediscoveries of his poetry probably fare well among the most phenomenal literary cases. In his native land—China—he was not even considered a minor poet prior to the eighteenth century. Not until the 1970's was his reputation as a poet firmly established in Taiwan. Yet in the classical periods, he was deified by some Chinese religious sects as the reincarnation of a bodhisattva, or of a Taoist immortal. Surprisingly, his fortune as a poet fares much more impressively abroad. For centuries the Japanese honored him as a major Chinese poet. In spite of the great cultural divergence of the East and the West, he suddenly turned into an ideal hero of the Beat Generation of the United States in the late 1950's.

Han Shan's identity is as enigmatic as literary titans such as Shakespeare and the author of *The Dream of the Red Chamber*. There are practically no extant historical materials about Han Shan's life. The earliest source on his life is a preface to his collection, presumably written by Lü Ch'iu-yin 閭丘胤. Scholars such as Yü Chia-hsi 余嘉錫, Wu Ch'i-yü 吳其昱, and Ch'en Hui-chien 陳慧劍 have proven that this preface was a forgery, probably written in the ninth century.¹ The name of the poet, Han Shan, literally means "Cold Mountain." It apparently is a pen name. No scholar has yet pinned down his real name and his birth place. Scholars of different nationalities dated Han Shan from the sixth to the ninth century.² Wu Ch'i-yü in his article "A Study of Han Shan" tries to prove that the legend of Han Shan grew from a historical figure, a monk named Chih Yen 智嚴, the Wise Cliff (547-645).³ Though interesting enough, he could not supply his theory with substantial evidence. E. G. Pulleyblank in "Linguistic Evidence for the Date of Han Shan" presents a survey on the rhyming patterns of the three hundred odd poems in Han Shan's collection, and concludes that the poems fall into two categories: the larger portion of the poems were composed in the late sixth and the seventh centuries, while the smaller portion in the eighth and the ninth centuries.⁴ His discovery supports the theory that Han Shan's poems were written in different ages by at least two poets. This is so far the most convincing theory on the authorship of the Cold Mountain poems. Hence, in this study I will refer to "Cold Mountain Poems" instead of "the poet Han Shan."

In China, Cold Mountain Poems were denied recognition by orthodox traditions for six hundred years, that is, from the twelfth to the eighteenth centuries. During this period there were no government-sponsored collections containing Cold Mountain Poems, nor were they included in important privately printed anthologies of T'ang poetry.⁵ Cold Mountain Poems were imitated by poets such as Wang An-shih 王安石, and the poets of the Sung Dynasty (960-1279), such as Chu Hsi 朱熹, Wang Ying-lin 王應麟, and Lu Yu 陸游, passed favorable remarks on the style of the poems.⁶ However, these poets still did not take Cold Mountain Poems as serious poetry; rather they viewed most of the poems as doggerels on religion and life philosophy.

Cold Mountain Poems not only were denied recognition by the orthodox men of letters, but they were also excluded from the anthologies of religious traditions. These poems were not included in the government-sponsored collections of Buddhist

---

¹ Yü Chia-hsi, *Ssu-k'u ch'üan-shu t'i-yao pien-cheng* 四庫全書提要辯證 (Taipei: I-wen, 1961), 20 (p. 1259). Ch'en Hui-chien, *Han-shan-tzu yen-chiu* 寒山子研究 (Taipei: Hua-hsin, 1974), pp. 10-15, 18-21. Wu Ch'i-yü, "A Study of Han Shan," *T'oung Pao*, 45 (1957), 398-400.

² To give a few examples: Hu Shih 胡適 dates him in the late eighth century in *Pai-hua wen-hsüeh shih* 白話文學史 (Shanghai: Hsin-yüeh, 1928), pp. 242-243; Iriya Yoshitaka 入矢義高 dates him in the eighth century in *Kan Zan* (Tokyo: Iwanami, 1961), p. 9; Arthur Waley dates him in the eighth and ninth centuries in "27 Poems by Han Shan," *Encounter*, 12 (September, 1954), 3; and Wu Ch'i-yü dates the poet in the sixth and seventh century in "A Study of Han Shan," 399-410.

³ Wu Ch'i-yü, "A Study of Han Shan," 400-08.

⁴ E. G. Pulleyblank, "Linguistic Evidence for the Date of Han-shan," forthcoming in *Chinese Poetry and Poetics*, ed. Ronald Miao (Taipei: Ch'eng-wen).

⁵ The following anthologies do not include any Cold Mountain Poems: Chi Yu-kung's 計有功 *T'ang-shih chi-shih* 唐詩紀事 (the 12th Century) which selected one hundred and fifty T'ang poets; Yang Shih-hung's 楊士宏 *T'ang yin* 唐音 (the 14th Century); Kao Ping's 高棅 *T'ang-shih p'in-hui* 唐詩品彙 (the 15th Century); Wang Shih-chen's 王士禎 *T'ang-jen wan-shou chüeh-chü hsüen* 唐人萬首絕句選 and Shen Te-ch'ien's 沈德潛 *T'ang-shih pieh-ts'ai* 唐詩別裁. Not until the government-sponsored *Ch'üan T'ang shih* 全唐詩 was published in 1707 were the Cold Mountain Poems included.

⁶ Yeh Ch'ang-chih 葉昌熾, *Han Shan shih chih* 寒山寺志 (1922 ed.), 3.15a-20a, 2.9a, 3.29ab, 3.30a, 3.30b-33b.

writings, nor in the government-sponsored collections of Taoist writings. Here I refer to religious Taoism, as opposed to philosophical Taoism. Philosophical Taoism which consists of the doctrines of Lao-tzu 老子 and Chuang-tzu 莊子 as well as Neo-Taoist interpretations, permeates, in various degrees, the poetic works of all three major orientations as they—Confucianism, religious Taoism, and Buddhism—were institutionalized. In a word, Cold Mountain Poems were rejected by all orthodox literary trends. Fortunately, they survived, because in every age, they had a great number of readers among Buddhists and Taoists, and sometimes, among the men of letters. In fact, Cold Mountain Poems enjoyed immense popularity as early as the ninth century.[7] Furthermore, fabulous legends about Han Shan grew like a snowball from the ninth to the twelfth centuries. In Lü Ch'iu-yin's preface, Han Shan was depicted as a reincarnation of bodhisattva Meitreya 文殊菩薩, who visited a temple in the disguise of a crazy man. Later, he became the master of Zen Buddhism enlightening people with his profound, witty dialogue. He was described in a source quoted by Tu Kuang-t'ing 杜光庭 in the eleventh century as a Taoist immortal who reproved a Taoist disciple for his quick temper and narrow-mindedness. Han Shan in this legend mastered the Taoist magic of transformation: he first appeared as a poor man, then a wealthy man.[8] Han Shan and his companion Shih Te 拾得 were so popular that they became favorite subjects of Chinese painters through the centuries.[9]

What then is the reason for these divergent responses to Cold Mountain Poems, that on the one hand they were rejected by the orthodox traditions while on the other they gained immense popularity? In the 1920's Yü Chia-hsi pointed out that from the internal evidence of Cold Mountain Poems, the persona of these poems upholds the doctrine of Buddhism as well as that of Taoism; however, because this persona did not live in a temple, he is not necessarily a monk, and since he ridiculed Taoist alchemy, nor is he a wholehearted religious Taoist.[10] This persona never proclaimed himself to be a Buddhist monk, nor a Taoist priest. Perhaps this is the reason why Cold Mountain Poems were not selected in the government-sponsored collections of Taoist and Buddhist writings. The Cold Mountain Poems speak of the Wheel and retribution, so they would certainly be sneered at by the Confucianists who follow the teaching of "never speaking of prodigies, violence, disorders and spirits" 子不語怪力亂神. Thus, Cold Mountain Poems were denied legitimacy by the three main trends in classical China, namely, Confucianism, Taoism, and Buddhism.

Paradoxically, because these poems attracted so many readers, and because the Han Shan legend in Lü's preface was so intriguing, both the Taoists and Buddhists claimed Han Shan to be their sage for their own propaganda. Eventually, Han Shan was deified, and a temple in Su Chou 蘇州 called Han Shan Temple 寒山寺 enshrined him. In addition to the rejection from the three main orthodox orientations, Cold

---

[7] Wu Ch'i-yü, "A Study of Han Shan," 445. Pen Chi 本寂 (830-901) published a commentary on the Cold Mountain Poems, which was very popular at his time. Ch'en Hui-chien, *Han-shan-tzu yen-chiu*, pp. 47-49, Ch'i Chi 齊己 (870-950) mentioned the popularity of the Cold Mountain Poems.

[8] For an English translation of these legends, see Gary Snyder's version of Lü Ch'iu-yin's Preface, *Anthology of Chinese Literature*, ed. Cyril Birch (New York: Grove, 1965), pp. 194-96, and see Wu Ch'i-yü's "A Study of Han Shan," 410-20.

[9] The famous painter Liang K'ai 梁楷 did many portraits of Han Shan and Shih Te. There is also a list of the portraits of Han Shan and Shih Te in *Han Shan shih chih*, ed. Yeh Ch'ang-chih, 1.17b-20a.

[10] Yü Chia-hsi, 20 (pp. 1254-56).

Mountain Poems were denied fair judgment by the literary establishment. The Chinese literary traditions emphasized refinement and implicitness. The language in most Cold Mountain Poems is colloquial, their style outspoken, while some even were composed in vulgar diction. No wonder that the men of letters seldom gave credit to the artistic qualities of some Cold Mountain Poems. Furthermore, the Chinese poetic traditions emphasize direct, and objective presentation of the great mystery through natural objects in the landscape. Chinese poetry inclines to involve the sensory activities of a reader rather than to convince the reader with philosophized argument. Wai-lim Yip in his "Aesthetic Consciousness of Landscape in Chinese and Anglo-American Poetry" (*Comparative Literature Studies*, Fall, 1978) illustrates this point in full detail and depth. Only a small portion of the Cold Mountain Poems meets this criterion of Chinese poetic traditions.

In Japan Cold Mountain Poems have been admired for centuries. As a matter of fact, the earliest extant edition of Cold Mountain Poems is currently kept in the Palace Library of Japan.[11] Unlike the Chinese poetic traditions, the religious elements, especially those of Zen Buddhism such as poetic *kung-an* 公案 (*kōan*) verse, all from China, have been an integral part of Japanese poetry. Many major poets, including the Haiku 俳句 master Matsuo Bashō 松尾芭蕉, were Buddhist monks. Because of their religious and philosophical flavor, Cold Mountain Poems were neglected by the orthodox traditions in China while in Japan for the same reason Han Shan was hailed as a superb poet and holy man. In addition, Japanese readers were inclined to appreciate Chinese poetry written in colloquial style rather than that written in erudite and refined language, simply because, I think, the former is easier to learn. Thus, the colloquial style of Cold Mountain Poems, like those of Po Chü-i 白居易, evoked a popular response in Japan, whereas in China, it caused resistance from the literary establishment. In conclusion, the divergent responses to the Cold Mountain Poems in China and in Japan are largely due to the cultural and linguistic differences of these two nations.

In the twentieth century, the reception of Cold Mountain Poems borders on legend. Cold Mountain Poems have gained a large following in Japan, the United States, and Taiwan. In the 1920's and 1930's a temporary revival of Cold Mountain Poems was launched in China and Japan. The May Fourth Movement of 1919 involved changes in almost all the cultural spheres of China. In language and literature, colloquial style was promoted to replace the written medium of classical language. Therefore, many writers of colloquial style who had been overlooked in the past were unearthed to be placed in a prominent position. Han Shan was one of them. Scholars such as Hu Shih and Cheng Chen-to 鄭振鐸 hailed Han Shan as the pioneer of vernacular poetry.[12] Subsequently Yü Chia-hsi published his scholarly research, and Cold Mountain Poems were included in the *Ssu-pu ts'ung-k'an* 四部叢刊, a voluminous collection of classical Chinese masterpieces, published by the Commercial Press in 1929. Strangely enough, after 1938, hardly any scholarly study on Han Shan was published in China. Cold Mountain Poems again were forgotten in his native land. In Japan during this period, in addition to the two newly published editions, Shimada Kan 島田翰 did an extensive study on the ancient editions of Cold

---

[11] It is the 1189 edition published by Kuo Ch'ing Temple 國清寺.
[12] Hu Shih, *Pai-hua wen-hsüeh shih*, p. 242. Cheng Chen-tuo, *Chung-kuo su-wen-hsüeh shih* 中國俗文學史 (Changsha: Shang-wu, 1938), pp. 124-25.

Mountain Poems.[13] The renowned novelist Mori Ogai 森鷗外 (1862-1922) wrote a short story "Han Shan and Shih Te" 寒山拾得 based on Lü's preface.

In the 1950's the cult of Cold Mountain Poems finally reached the West. Cold Mountain Poems in fact were introduced to the United States when Zen Buddhism was "growing more chic by the minute," as phrased by Stephen Mahoney.[14] According to Thomas Parkinson, by 1960 Zen became so popular that "some beat generation have taken to calling themselves Zen Hipsters, and Zen Buddhism has spread like Asian flu, so that now you can open your fortune cookie in one of the real cool Chinese restaurants of San Francisco and find a slip of paper with the straight poop: "Dig the Crazy Zen Sukiyaki."[15] Although to sort out the reasons for Zen's popularity in a radically different cultural climate is extremely difficult, Alan Watts has given a bird's-eye view summary for the reasons behind Zen's sudden popularity during the period from 1938 to 1958. His speculations serve well as a background to understanding the environment into which Han Shan was born as a holy man:

> The appeal of Zen arts to the "modern" spirit in the West, the work of Suzuki, the war with Japan, the itchy fascination of "Zen-stories," and the attraction of a non-conceptual, experiential philosophy in the climate of scientific relativism—all these are involved. One might mention too the affinities between Zen and such purely Western trends as the philosophy of Wittgenstein, Existentialism, General Semantics, the metalinguistics of B. L. Whorf, and certain movements in the philosophy of science and in psychotheraphy. Always in the background there is our vague disquiet, with the artificiality or "antinaturalness" of both Christianity, with its politically ordered cosmology, and technology, with its imperialistic mechanization of a natural world from which man himself feels strangely alien.[16]

In this climate a figure like Han Shan, with his intuitive sensibility and his defiance of social ties echoes truly the need of a whole generation.

Cold Mountain Poems were first introduced in the United States in 1954. Arthur Waley published "27 Poems by Han Shan" this year. Gary Snyder's "Cold Mountain Poems" appeared in the autumn of 1958 in *Evergreen Review*. Waley discovered Cold Mountain Poems probably through his reading of Japanese publications while Snyder's interest was aroused by a Japanese painting of Han Shan. Snyder said in the preface to his translation, "in the Japanese art exhibit that came to America in 1953 was a small sumi sketch of a robe-tattered wind-swept long-haired laughing man holding a scroll, standing on a cliff in the mountain. This was Kanzan, or Han Shan." Burton Watson published his translation of one hundred poems in 1962 and his translations are considerably indebted to Iriya Yoshitaka's *Kan Zan* pub-

---

[13] Iwanami 岩波 Company published in 1925 the 1189 edition kept in the Palace Library; this version was edited by Shimada Kan.
[14] Stephen Mahoney, "The Prevalence of Zen," *Nation*, 187 (November, 1968), 311.
[15] *A Case Book on the Beat* (New York: Thomas Y. Crowell, 1961), p. 253.
[16] Alan W. Watts, *Beat Zen, Square Zen and Zen* (San Francisco: City Lights, 1959), pp. 3-4.

lished in 1958.[17]   Thus, it was the Japanese art and literary studies that introduced Cold Mountain Poems to the United States. And among these three translated versions, Snyder's enjoyed immense success among the youth.

In the 1960's if you asked a university student who looked somewhat like a hippie, "Have you read Cold Mountain's Poems translated by Gary Snyder?" Most likely his answer would be:

> "Woo, yah."
> "Do you like the poems?"
> "Yah, sure!"
> "Why?"
> "Why?" he would look at you as if you were incredibly stupid, "because he is BEAT, man!"

However, Snyder could not claim to be *the* advocate of Han Shan. It was Jack Kerouac's *The Dharma Bums* (1958) that made Snyder and Han Shan launch the modern hipster and hippie world.[18] This biographical novel centers on Kerouac's friendship with Snyder. It describes how Snyder translated Han Shan's poetry at Berkeley and introduced it to Kerouac, and how Snyder led Kerouac to the mountain and to his enlightenment.

On the front page of *The Dharma Bums* was printed "Dedicated to Han Shan" —a strange dedication indeed, to a foreign poet who died one thousand years ago. Kerouac in fact dedicated this book to Gary Snyder, because in this novel, Snyder, whom Kerouac called Japhy Ryder, is identical with Han Shan.[19] At the very end of the book, after Japhy Ryder has left for Japan, Kerouac goes to the mountain to seek his ideal hero Han Shan and see his image:

> I called Han Shan in the mountains: there was no answer.
> I called Han Shan in the morning fog: silence, it said. . . .
> And suddenly it seemed I saw that unimaginable little
> CHINESE BUM standing there, in the fog, with the expressionless humor on his seamed face. It wasn't the real-life
> Japhy of rucksacks and Buddhism studies and big mad parties
> at Corte Madera, it was the realer-than-life Japhy of my
> dreams.[20]

In this passage Han Shan and Snyder merge into one personality. This personality is a mixture of a late 1950's American literary bum as well as a crazy Chinese monk. The similarity between a hippie and the Han Shan as depicted in Lü's preface is obvious. Han Shan is a mad man, "walking the long veranda, calling and

---

[17] Waley, *Encounter*, 3-8; Snyder, *Evergreen Review,* 2 (Autumn, 1958), 69-80; Watson, *Cold Mountain: One Hundred Poems by the T'ang Poet Han Shan* (New York: Grove, 1962); for Watson's indebtedness to Iriya Yoshitaka, see the preface.

[18] *The Dharma Bums* was first published by the Viking Press in 1958.

[19] Kerouac, "Meditation in the Woods," *Chicago Review*, 22, No. 2 (1958), 17-22; this is an excerpt from *The Dharma Bums,* in which the real names of the characters are used instead of the disguised ones.

[20] Kerouac, *The Dharma Bums* (New York: New American Library, 1959) pp. 190-91.

shouting happily, talking and laughing to himself,"[21] while the bums in Kerouac's novel run, jump and shout madly in the mountain. In fact, the similarity in appearance between Han Shan and modern hipsters and hippies is probably the chief reason why Han Shan appealed to them: they both dress in rags and wear worn-out shoes; laugh, sing and talk as if they were mad. Kerouac gives Han Shan an additional touch—Han Shan has an "expressionless humor" on his face; this is a real Beat version of Han Shan, for the hipsters are inclined to be cool, expressionless, and detached in their involvement in life.[22] In this novel Kerouac attempts to portray the image of "a great new hero of American culture."[23] He did not fail, because Han Shan and Snyder did become the new heroes of the Beat Generation. This hero is calm, cool and self-contained. He is also Alan Watts' hero who refuses to participate in "the American way of life," and instead involves himself in "a revolt which turns to find the significance of life in subjective experience rather than objective achievement."[24] He strives to liberate himself from social reins. Perhaps this primitivism is the congeniality in spirit between Han Shan and the Beat Generation. In this novel, the halo of the modern hero was actually granted to all bums, all hippies. Snyder also said: Han Shan and Shih Te "became Immortals and you sometimes run into them today in the skidrows, orchards, hobo jungles, and logging camps of America."[25] This modern version of Han Shan demonstrates the rise of a mass hero in America. Alan Watts says, "We like this [Zen Saint] because here, for the first time, is a conception of the holy man and sage who is not impossibly remote, not superman, but fully human."[26] Han Shan's popularity is also due to his down-to-earth image as depicted in Lü's preface, because it answers the need of the Beat Generation for a mass hero.

As I mentioned previously that Han Shan and the Beat Generation share a similar non-conformity in their behavior and appearance while in spirit Han Shan and the Beat Generation share the primitivism, to liberate oneself from social reins, to recover one's original nature and to experience life in subjective terms. Based on the internal evidence of Cold Mountain Poems and on the legend in Lü's preface, Han Shan, if he ever existed, broke all his ties with the human world and lived alone on a cliff in the wilderness. The Beat Generation likewise broke their ties with family and society, and they exiled themselves into the open roads and wild woods. Furthermore, because of the pressure of the modern industrial, commercial and mechanical civilization, the yearning for nature and spirituality grew stronger in the mind of the young generation. Han Shan's spiritual union with nature is apparently reflected in his name, "COLD MOUNTAIN." This poet identified himself with the cliff where he lived for many years. The serenity and composure in a natural environment as reflected in Cold Mountain Poems promise an alternative for the search of the Beat Generation. It is because the image of Han Shan satisfies much of the expectation and search of the Beat Generation that Cold Mountain Poems became rooted in an alien culture. The cult of Han Shan declined as the Beat Generation passed into history. But Cold Mountain Poems have found their way into many anthologies of Chinese literature

---

[21] See Snyder's translation of Lü's Preface, *Anthology of Chinese Literature*, p. 194.
[22] Parkinson, *A Case Book on the Beat*, p. 250.
[23] *The Dharma Bums*, p. 27.
[24] Watts, *Beat Zen, Square Zen and Zen*, p. 9.
[25] See Snyder's brief preface to his translation, "Cold Mountain Poems," *Evergreen*, 69.
[26] Watts, *Beat Zen, Square Zen and Zen*, p. 5.

in English translation.[27] In these anthologies Han Shan appears together with masters of Chinese literature such as Li Po 李白, Wang Wei 王維, and Tu Fu 杜甫. Cold Mountain Poems have won a prestige in the States they have never attained in China.

When a relatively unknown poet becomes extremely popular abroad, his native land always responds favorably to him. In 1966 the first response came from Hong Kong. Hu Chü-jen 胡菊人 published an article written in Chinese called "the Rebirth of the Monk Poet Han Shan" 詩僧寒山的復活.[28] Hu's article attracted my attention and curiosity. Subsequently in 1970 I published in Taiwan "The Literary Position of Han Shan in the East and the West" 寒山在東方和西方的文學地位, an article written in Chinese.[29] This article has aroused unexpected enthusiasm and response. In the next six years more than two editions of the Cold Mountain Poems were printed and many articles as well as five books of secondary studies on Han Shan were published in Taiwan.[30] The fact that a Chinese poet attracted attention and recognition in the United States must have flattered the ego of the Chinese men of letters in Taiwan, which had been a military and political protégé of the United States for many years. There was a touch of political overtone in Han Shan's triumphant homecoming.

In addition to the enchantment of the fabulous legends, the colloquial style and the philosophical dimension of the Cold Mountain Poems, some of these three hundred odd poems also bear superb poetic qualities such as vivid imagery and unique powerful usage of symbolism. This poetic excellence, I believe, has contributed to the popularity of the Cold Mountain Poems throughout the ages and across national boundaries.

Nevertheless, a great portion of these three hundred odd poems are written in the style of *chi* 偈, or *gatha,* that is, Buddhist didactic verse. They usually start with a description of mundane life in a satirical tone, and end with a simple Buddhist idea such as "female beauty is ephemeral," or "death shall conquer all." The didacticism eventually reduces these poems to mere epigrams. This poem could serve as a sample of this category of the Cold Mountain Poems:

> You have seen the blossoms among the leaves;
> Tell me, how long will they stay?
> Today they tremble before the hand that picks them;
> Tomorrow they await someone's garden broom.
> Wonderful is the bright heart of youth,
> But with the years it grows old.

---

[27] Gary Snyder's "Cold Mountain Poems" are anthologized in Cyril Birch's *Anthology of Chinese Literature* and in *Literature of the Eastern World* (Glenview: Scott and Foresman, 1970).

[28] *Ming Pao Monthly* 明報月刊, 1 (November, 1966), 2-12.

[29] Ling Chung 鍾玲, *Central Daily News* 中央日報 (March 8-11, 1970).

[30] After my article was published in *Central Daily News,* during the following month, five articles on Han Shan were published in the same newspaper. The following books were published from 1970 to 1976: Chao Tzu-fan's 趙滋蕃 *Han Shan te shih-tai ching-shen* 寒山的時代精神 (1970); Tseng P'u-hsin's 曾普信 *Han Shan shih chieh* 寒山詩解 (1971); Ch'en Hui-chien's *Han-shan-tzu yen-chiu* 寒山子研究 (1974); Ch'eng Chao-hsiung's 程兆熊 *Han-shan-tzu yü Han Shan shih* 寒山子與寒山詩 (1974), and Sun Ch'i's 孫旗 *Han Shan yü hsi-p'i* 寒山與西皮 (1974). Two editions of Han Shan's poetry were published by Han Sheng Publishing Company in 1973 and by Wen Feng Publishing Company in 1974, which is a pirate edition of Burton Watson's book. Chang Man-t'ao 張曼濤 also writes on the reception of Han Shan in twentieth century Japan in his *Jih-pen-jen te ssu* 日本人的死 (Taipei: Li-min, 1976), pp. 97-117.

> Is the world not like these flowers?
> Ruddy faces, how can they last?[31]

君看葉裏花，能得幾時好？
今日畏人攀，明朝待誰掃？
可憐嬌艷情，年多轉成老。
將世比於花，紅顏豈長保？

It is perhaps this homiletic aspect that had initially disenchanted the poets and critics of the T'ang Dynasty, whose central aesthetic concern was concreteness. Some of these didactic poems use unconventional, or even vulgar colloquialism and yet convey an outlandish sense of humor:

> Pigs devour dead men's flesh.
> Men devour the intestines of dead pigs.
> Pigs won't regard men stink.
> Sure men think pigs tasty.
> Dead pigs were thrown into the ditches,
> And we dug a hole to hide the dead.
> If you stop swallowing one another,
> Lotus flowers will grow in the boiling soup.

猪吃死人肉，人吃死猪腸。
猪不嫌人臭，人反道猪香。
猪死抛水內，人死掘地藏。
彼此莫相噉，蓮花生沸湯。

In the Cold Mountain Poems there are also some conventional modes of poetry such as imitation of the Ch'u tz'u 楚辭 style and verse in praise of objects 詠物詩. However, noteworthily, there are approximately seventy poems directly dealing with a hermit's life in a high mountain, and some of these poems possess incredibly moving force and dazzling beauty.

These mountain poems are always imbued with living experience, such as this one:

> For countless years
> I had desired to climb up the East Cliff.
> I climbed it yesterday, clinging to the creepers.
> Halfway up, I am trapped in the blasts and fog.
> Hard to squeeze through the path with my clothes on.
> The soggy moss sucked back my shoes.
> I'd like to live under that cinnamon tree
> And pillow my head on the white clouds.

---

[31] This poem and the following six poems are translated from *Han-shan-tzu shih-chi* 寒山子詩集. *SPPY* ed. (Shanghai: Shang-wu, 1929), 23a, 7a, 23a, 13a, 22b, 3a, and 4b. The first poem was translated by Burton Watson, *Cold Mountain*, p. 25. The sixth poem was translated by Gary Snyder, *Anthology of Chinese Literature*, p. 198. The other five poems were translated by myself.

欲向東巖去，于今無量年。
昨來攀葛上，半路困風煙。
徑窄衣難進，苔粘履不前。
住茲丹桂下，且枕白雲眠。

Only a mountain climber could have so vividly depicted how one felt walking on soggy moss, or squeezing between rocks. In addition to sight, this poem also evokes tactile physical experience. Therefore, it possesses the power to directly involve the sensory activities of a reader.

These mountain poems dwell not merely in human spheres, but they also reach the celestial realms. The mountain itself becomes a revelation of the great mystery and the persona here turns into a visionary. In the following poem, the persona presents the mountain in a spell-binding vision:

> Cold Mountain has many mysterious wonders.
> People who climb it are always scared.
> When the moon shines, water sparkles.
> When the wind blows, grass rustles.
> On the bare plum branches, snow was changed to flowers.
> On the dead stump, clouds are transformed into leaves.
> At the touch of rain, the mountain becomes fresh and alive.
> You can only climb it in good weather.

寒山多幽奇，登者皆恆懾。
月照水澄澄，風吹草獵獵。
凋梅雪作花，枯木雲充葉。
觸雨轉鮮靈，非晴不可涉。

A spell is cast on the ordinary water, grass, plum branches, and dead stumps. The living and the dead, the withered and the growing, are but one in this magical world, a world of eternity and total liberation.

However, this world of eternity and total liberation is not just an external phenomenon as manifested in mother nature. The persona of these mountain poems absorbs the essence of this world into his mind.

> Today I sat at the foot of a cliff.
> Sat till the mist and clouds drew apart.
> Clear cold water formed one solid stream
> Thousands of feet from the jade-green ridge.
> The still morning light shines through the white clouds.
> Under the bright moon, luminous evening mist adrift.
> My body is free of dust and strain;
> What cares could trouble my mind?

今日巖前坐，坐久煙雲收。
一道清谿冷，千尋碧嶂頭。
白雲朝影靜，明月夜光浮。
身上無塵垢，心中那得憂？

In this poem, the persona "sat," probably in Zen meditation, from morning till night. He observed the natural elements—mist, clouds, and waterfall—until they cleansed his mind and freed him from all mental entanglements. Here the tranquil, keen observing eye as well as its harmonious interaction with nature echo the best of Wang Wei's 王維 nature poems.

In this way, nature, or more precisely, the Cold Mountain, is absorbed and internalized into the mind of the persona. This Cold Mountain cliff, which is situated in Southeast China, is not only his abode, but has become part of himself. This poet, according to the legend, forsakes his own name, and names himself after the mountain where he lives, because he has totally identified himself with the mountain, instead of with his family, his clan, or his society. The following poem shows the merging of his subjectivity with an objective external object—Cold Mountain:

> Men ask the way to Cold Mountain.
> Cold Mountain: there's no through trail.
> In summer, ice doesn't melt.
> The rising sun blurs in swirling fog.
> How did I make it?
> My heart's not the same as yours.
> If your heart was like mine
> You'd get it and be right here.

> 人問寒山道，寒山路不通。
> 夏天冰未釋，日出霧矇矓。
> 似我何由屆，與君心不同。
> 君心若似我，還得在其中。

The first four lines seem to describe the landscape of the mountain. But the last four lines clearly indicate that Cold Mountain is no longer a locality, but a projection of his state of mind. Therefore, Cold Mountain comes to symbolize the alter-ego of an introspective man, alone and alienated from his society. In this sense Cold Mountain resembles well-known symbols of the modern era such as Franz Kafka's beetle and Hermann Hesse's steppenwolf. This probably is another reason why the Cold Mountain Poems could have reached our modern audiences so easily. However, unlike its modern counterparts, the symbol Cold Mountain does not suggest an alienated self. On the contrary, it signifies the reconciliation between the self and its environment, and between the alter-ego and the ego. This symbol crystalizes the personal salvation of the persona. The following poem suggests the process of his spiritual journey to salvation:

> I climb up the Cold Mountain path.
> The Cold Mountain trail goes on forever.
> In the long gorge, boulders pile up.
> By the wide creek, grass is mist-blurred.
> The moss is slippery, but there has been no rain.
> The pine hums, though there is no breeze.
> Who can transcend the worldly burden
> And sit with me among the white clouds?

登陟寒山道，寒山路不窮。
谿長石磊磊，澗闊草濛濛。
苔滑非關雨，松鳴不假風。
誰能超世累，共坐白雲中。

The mountain climber moves upward from the creek, the gorge to the mountain top covered by pines and clouds. Likewise, the mental state of the persona is transcended from the mundane world to a state of self-sustaining spiritual liberation which fills the mountain poems with eloquent grace and persuasive serenity.

The reception of Cold Mountain Poems has been exceptional. No other minor figure in Chinese literature has ever attracted so much attention in Japan, and no other Chinese poet has ever had such a large following in the United States, not even Li Po and Tu Fu who have been read in recent years by an increasing number of American poets and students. Furthermore, no other Chinese poet has aroused so much enthusiasm at home because he gained recognition abroad. The diverse responses to the Cold Mountain Poems in China, Japan and the United States result from the complicated cultural milieu as well as from the excellent qualities of some of the poems, which have been largely ignored. The Cold Mountain Poems have lasting aesthetic value, because they embody living experience, they capture mystic beauty, and furthermore, they present a symbol—Cold Mountain—which signifies the marriage between the subjective mind and the objective environment, and which signifies sheer spiritual liberation. I hope this study has cast some light on the complex reasons behind all these intriguing international literary phenomena.

The Tragic Theme in *Li sao*

Ping-leung Chan

Among the *Ch'u tz'u* 楚辭 poems, *Li sao* 離騷 is undoubtedly the best and the most famous. In it the poet, Ch'ü Yüan 屈原, powerfully and unreservedly expresses his feelings and his moral disposition. In this paper, I will analyze this masterpiece as a tragic work. The word "tragic" is used here in the original sense, despite the fact that *Li sao* is not a play. Some people may object to my suggestion, saying that in China there has existed no tragedy. In *The Psychology of Tragedy,* published in 1933, Chu Kuang-ch'ien 朱光潛 points out that there is no tragedy in Chinese literature.[1] Ch'ien Chung-shu 錢鍾書, after examining four plays in the Yüan and Ch'ing Dynasties, is of the same opinion that there is an absence of tragedy in traditional Chinese literature.[2] Yet in an article Ch'en Shih-hsiang 陳世驤 contradicts these two famous critics by saying that *Li sao* portrays the desperation in tragic human glory. He unequivocally declares that Ch'ü Yüan was a tragic hero. He says, "This purity [of the personal heroic character] the poet knows to be frail, but it is all the more heroic as it is pitched with pain of death against a changing, hence constantly compromising, impure, and fickle world at large."[3] This seeming contradiction between these two theses can be solved by the theory advanced by Charles H. Glendinning that a society which is capable of producing tragedy should have different systems of values, different classes of people, and different choices for every one.[4] It is a well-known fact that from the unification of the Ch'in Dynasty in 221 B.C. to the downfall of the Ch'ing Dynasty in A.D. 1911, China was a "monolithic" society, in which no one had absolute freedom to choose what he valued most. Therefore, it is small wonder that during this long period no tragedy was written, because people had to submit them-

---

[1] *The Psychology of Tragedy*: *A Critical Study of Various Theories of Tragic Pleasure* (Strasbourg: Libraire Universitaire d'Alsace, 1933), pp. 216-23. Herbert J. Muller and Ralph J. Hallman also share the same idea; see Muller, *The Spirit of Tragedy* (New York: Alfred A. Knopf, 1956), pp. 328-30; Hallman, *Psychology of Literature*: *A Study of Alienation and Tragedy* (New York: Philosophic Library, 1961), p. 47.

[2] "Tragedy in Old Chinese Drama," *T'ien Hsia Monthly,* 1 (August, 1935), 37-46.

[3] Shih-hsiang Ch'en, "The Genesis of Poetic Time: The Greatness of Ch'ü Yüan, studied with a New Critical Approach," *Ch'ing-hua hsüeh-pao* 清華學報, N.S. 10 (June, 1973), 29.

[4] "The Tragic Hero: A Re-evaluation," Diss. Case Western Reserve 1972, p. 19.

selves to authority, which, except in the Ch'in Dynasty, embodied the social values set by the Confucian School. Anyone straying from the "right path" would be frowned upon, much less approved. Such a person, of course, could not be a tragic hero. However, in the Chan-kuo period China was undergoing a tremendous social change. With the decline of the aristocracy, the rise of a merchant class and the proliferation of knowledge, philosophical and technical, the Chinese people enjoyed much freedom, especially in the Ch'u state where, because of her geographic and economic situation, the native culture and the culture of North China existed side by side.[5] This society had different classes, different cultures and different sets of values. Therefore, in light of Glendinning's thesis, this society is likely to produce tragedy. And produce it did this tragic poem *Li sao*. To prove this point, I would like to show that Ch'ü Yüan, the poet, is a tragic hero, and that *Li sao* fits into the concept of tragedy.

As explained in Aristotle's *Poetics,* tragedy is an imitation of serious action in life, written in embellished language. It invokes in the audience pity and fear, through which catharsis results. As a literary form it must have six parts: plot, character, diction, thought, spectacle, and song. Of these plot and character are the most important. By plot Aristotle means the sequence of incidents. In this sequence *peripeteia,* or reversal of situation, and *anagnorisis,* or recognition, are two elements which will draw emotional responses from the audience. As to character, he is the agent to action. The protagonist should be of good stature and fortune. His suffering is due to some flaw in his character or unintended error in his conduct.[6]

The tragic hero, according to Glendinning, must be typical of the people of his own class, which has the recognition of his society. He must be excessive in some emotional trait approved of by his class, and he must be aware that his punishment goes beyond his guilt.[7] As for Ch'ü Yüan, he was born a member of the royal families, and he was knowledgeable, well-versed in politics, and good at speech. With these qualifications, he was trusted by the king. We therefore can say that he had inherited and acquired position and since he was the top adviser to the king, he was typical of his class. Even after he had been estranged, he was still sent by the king to Ch'i as an envoy. This appointment proved that his talents and his service were useful. He might have been overzealous in trying to help his king, but this is understandable, because he wanted to accomplish something before he became old (11.9-12). After all, his action was at first approved by the king. Yet, his overzealousness later became his *hamartia,* the error which brought about his misfortune.

---

[5] Kwang-chih Chang 張光直, *The Archaeology of Ancient China,* revised and enlarged ed. (New Haven: Yale Univ. Press, 1968), p. 408; Wen Ch'ung-i 文崇一, *Ch'u wen-hua yen-chiu* 楚文化研究 (Nankang, Taiwan: Chung-yang yen-chiu yüan min-tsu-hsüeh yen-chiu-so, 1967), p. 97.

[6] There are many translations of Aristotle's *Poetics*. The most thorough one is Gerald F. Else's *Aristotle's Poetics: The Argument* (Cambridge: Harvard Univ. Press, 1967).

[7] Glendinning, pp. 23-30. Mitchell A. Leaska suggests, "The hero must possess more of those qualities than the average man to inform himself of the impulsive nature of other human beings; enough intelligence to make him introspective in his attempts to understand the world and eventually to become conscious of its irony. He must be superior enough to be aware of his worth, to want his freedom and at the same time to sense his freedom as the degree of individuation that separates him from nature, from other men." See *The Voice of Tragedy* (New York: Robert Speller & Sons, 1963), p. 12. For the discussion of some "tragic heroes" in China, see K'o Ch'ingming 柯慶明, "Lun pei-chü ying-hsiung" 論悲劇英雄, *Wen-hsüeh p'ing-lun* 文學評論, 4 (Taipei: Shu-p'ing shu-mu, 1977), 1-68.

> Others all fight to get into [the court] and become greedy,
>> Quite insatiable in exacting [bribes].
> They all give themselves excuses, but impose high standards on other people;
>> Each of them has evil intentions and is jealous of [others].
> Suddenly, I gallop and chase after them;
>> This [actually] is not what I am eager to do.
> [Only because] old age is creeping in and will come,
>> I am afraid my good fame will not be established [by then].
>
> (ll.30-33)

眾皆競進以貪婪兮，憑不厭乎求索，
羌內恕己以量人兮，各興心而嫉妒，
忽馳騖以追逐兮，非余心之所急，
老冉冉其將至兮，恐脩名之不立。

His enthusiasm is naturally interpreted by self-seeking people as an attempt to compete with them. They then succeed in removing him from the court by slandering him. Besides overzealousness, the poet has another weakness—stubbornness. Shamaness Nü-hsü 女嬃 warns him that Kun 鯀 was executed (or confined) because of his stubbornness, and she advises him to be more flexible. Well aware of his obstinacy, he still clings to his own standard. In *Li sao* he takes pride in himself.

> Outspoken, I follow the example of the former sages,
>> Which is not what the people in this world would accept.
> Even though I cannot accord with [every one of] my contemporaries,
>> I wish to attach to the principle bequeathed by P'eng Hsien.
>
> (ll.38-39)

謇吾法夫前脩兮，非世俗之所服，
雖不周於今之人兮，願依彭咸之遺則。

He also knows that in a corrupt society, uprightness and incorruptibility will not make him popular. But unpopularity does not warrant a severe punishment. In "Chiu chang" 九章 he resents:

> What is the crime of being loyal, and why am I punished for that?
>> This is not what I expected.
>
> ("Hsi sung" 惜誦, l.15)

忠何罪以遇罰兮，亦非余心之所志。

> I believe it was not my crime that caused me to be banished;
>> How can I forget about it in daytime and at night.
>
> ("Ai Ying" 哀郢, l.33)

信非吾罪而棄逐兮，何日夜而忘之。

It is Ch'ü Yüan's uncompromising attitude that gives rise to his tragedy. As the chorus in *Antigone* sings, "Thy self-willed temper hath wrought thy ruin."[8] This uncompromising attitude is not agreeable to Yang Hsiung 揚雄 and Pan Ku 班固. The former thought that a gentleman should submit to Fate[9] and the latter, that Ch'ü Yüan's exposure of the king's mistakes amounted to advertising himself,[10] which was not permissible in a Confucian society.

Being a tragic hero, Ch'ü Yüan is in a difficult situation. There are three options open to him: (1) he submits to the authority and cooperates with the corrupt officials; (2) he clings to his ideal and fights to the end; and (3) he transcends these difficulties by leaving his homeland. Nü-hsü and Shaman Fen 巫氛 advise him to take the first or the third choice, and warn him of the consequence of taking the second option. He rejects the first, however, because he abhors other officials' avarice and sycophancy. He has given some thought to the third, which we may call the "golden mean," but he, as a tragic hero, would not like to buy time.[11] He is in fact torn between two forces—the pressure of the collapsing social and moral order on the one hand, and the implacable urge of his inner passion for establishing a new order on the other. It is his passion, his stubbornness and his tragic pride, or *hubris,* that make him choose to fight for his ideal. In so doing, he reaches for a greater moral order, which he calls "P'eng Hsien's principle." We can accuse him of extremism, but not defeatism, as T'ang I-ch'iao 唐一帚 does in his book,[12] because even in his defeat a new order is born and human dignity shines forth.

Whether *Li sao* can be considered a tragic poem is the next topic of our discussion. Let me recount the life of Ch'ü Yüan, to whom the authorship of this poem is attributed. He was a member of the royal families and served at first as an important adviser to King Huai of Ch'u 楚懷王. He was possibly a shaman,[13] and was trusted by the king. Another office he held was *san-lü ta-fu* 三閭大夫, an official in charge of the domestic affairs of the royal families. Being a palace official, or *nei kuan* 內官, he became the target of innuendoes, fabricated by the court officials, or *wai kuan* 外官. He was once commissioned by the king to draft some legislation. His political rivals slandered him, charging that he had committed *lèse majesté* by claiming all the credit for this assignment. This accusation struck home, and, as a result, he was estranged by the king. After this political debacle, he wrote this poem *Li sao.*[14]

---

[8] Whitney J. Oates and Eugene O'Neill, Jr., eds., *The Complete Greek Drama* (New York: Random House, 1948), I, 447.

[9] *Han shu* 漢書 (Hong Kong: Chung-hua, 1970), 87A (p. 3515).

[10] Pan, "*Li sao hsü*" 離騷序, in Yen K'o-chün 嚴可均, ed., *Ch'üan shang-ku San-tai Ch'in Han San-kuo Liu-ch'ao wen* 全上古三代秦漢三國六朝文 (Peking: Chung-hua, 1958), I, 611.

[11] Henry A. Myers, *Tragedy: A View of Life* (Ithaca, N.Y.: Cornell Univ. Press, 1956), p. 141.

[12] T'ang, *Ch'ü Yüan—chen-te mei-yu che ko jen* 屈原——真的沒有這個人 (Taipei: Li-jen, 1969). Roy Morrell points out, "But in the tragic end of the hero, and of the hopes we had in him, there is nothing defeatist; for only in his failure is some connection, some 'transference' between us and our fantasy life in the play, broken, and our own energies set free." See "The Psychology of Tragic Pleasure," in Robert W. Corrigan, ed., *Tragedy: Vision and Form* (San Francisco: Chandler, 1965), p. 214.

[13] This is suggested by Ch'en Meng-chia 陳夢家, Wen I-to 聞一多 and P'eng Chung-to 彭仲鐸. See Ch'en, "Kao-mei chiao she tsu-miao t'ung k'ao" 高禖郊社祖廟通考, *Ch'ing-hua hsüeh-pao,* 12 (July, 1937), 452-70; P'eng, "Ch'ü Yüan wei wu k'ao" 屈原爲巫考, *Heüeh-i* 學藝, 14 (November, 1935), 1-8.

[14] *Shih chi* 史記 (Hong Kong: Chung-hua, 1969), 84 (pp. 2481-82).

Some Japanese scholars call it a piece of autobiographical literature,[15] as it describes the poet's life from his birth to his political demise.

In the beginning, the poet points out that Kao-yang 高陽 (or Chüan-hsü 顓頊) was his first ancestor, and declares with pride that he is endowed with inner beauty as well as good abilities, which are also reflected by his names, Cheng-tse 正則, "right standard," and Ling-chün 靈均, a possible allusion to his shamanic profession.[16] He uses fragrant flowers to symbolize his virtues of righteousness and justice. He always fears that there will not be enough time for him to do what he wants to do (11.7, 9-10 and 33). Like many talented people, he has his ambitions. His primary concern is to help the king rule the country, fearing that the latter would be led to failure by evil ministers (11.17-18). This combination of pity and fear,[17] which the poet apparently wants his reader to share with him, is truly Aristotelian.[18] His reader also pities and fears for him for his quixotic fight against a pack of greedy and corrupt officials. Most Chinese literary men in Imperial China were in the same situation, so this poem evoked great empathy in them. They pitied his vain effort to help the king, and feared for him the retaliation of evil ministers. In this poem he insists on his disinterestedness.

> Pointing to the nine skies as my witness,
>   [I swear that what I do] is only for the Fair One.
>   (1.22)

指九天以為正兮，夫唯靈脩之故也。

Yet, after the estrangement by the king, the result of the evil ministers' slander, Ch'ü Yüan is aware of the inevitability of encountering strong opposition, and anticipates the doomed failure of his quixotic struggle. This sounds ironic, but irony is essential to tragedy.[19] It is this sense of inevitability that makes the situation tragic, as Oscar Mandel asserts that inevitability is the *sine qua non* of tragedy.[20]

During his struggle with his rivals, Ch'ü Yüan tries hard to regain the king's lost confidence in him, but his efforts are thwarted by the opposition party (11.107 and 127). Eventually, he is alienated by the king. The resulting sufferings described in the poem were a common experience of the scholar-officials in Imperial China. Thus, this poem brought to their mind their forgotten or repressed sorrow. This process of identification explains why Yang Hsiung of the Later Han Dynasty could not help weeping whenever he read this particular poem.[21] It reminds its

---

[15] Fujino Iwatomo 藤野岩友, *Fukei bungaku ron* 巫系文學論, rev. ed. (Tokyo: Daigaku shobō, 1969), pp. 84-89; Asano Michiari 淺野通有, "Jijokei Sōji bungaku no keitō" 自序系楚辭文學の系統, *Kokugakuin zasshi* 國學院雜誌, 68 (September, 1967), 1-12; Fukino Yasushi 吹野安, "Shikan bungaku josetsu" 仕官文學序說, *Sagami jōshi daigaku kiyō* 相模女子大學紀要, 31 (December, 1958), 30-49; 32 (March, 1959), 1-23.

[16] *Ling* means "shaman"; see Hung Hsing-tsu 洪興祖, *Ch'u-tz'u pu chu* 楚辭補注 (*SPPY* ed.), 2.3a.

[17] Walter Kaufmann translates the Greek terms into "ruth" and "terror"; see *Tragedy and Philosophy* (Garden City: Doubleday, 1969), pp. 49-56.

[18] S. H. Butcher, *Aristotle's Theory of Poetry and Fine Art*, 4th ed. (New York: Dover, 1951), p. 256.

[19] Oscar Mandel, *A Definition of Tragedy* (New York: New York Univ. Press, 1961), p. 24.

[20] Ibid.

[21] *Han shu*, 87A (p. 3515).

reader that a noblemen such as Ch'ü Yüan, who had once enjoyed the king's confidence, also had to suffer. As a result, the reader would undergo catharsis, which, as interpreted by F. L. Lucas, purges the human soul of its excessive passions.[22]

The reversal of fortune in the poem is scarcely dramatic. As mentioned above, Ch'ü Yüan had been commissioned to draft some legislation. This should be considered a serious and significant responsibility.[23] But the evil ministers, out of jealousy, accused him of self-conceit. Consequently, he was alienated by the king. In *Li sao* the poet laments,

> Earlier, he made an agreement with me;
> > But later, he broke it, evaded [his responsibility], and had other ideas.
> In fact, it is not difficult for me to leave him,
> > [I am only] saddened by the Fair One's frequently changing attitude.

初既與余成言兮，後悔遁而有他，
余既不難乎離別兮，傷靈脩之數化。

Obviously, he recognizes that his sense of righteousness and his incorruptibility have made him the archenemy of the irresponsible officials (1.153). Yet he insists on upholding these virtues and is ready to accept the consequences (11.41-53). The triumph of his moral aspiration over his will to live is analogous to what Eugene Falk terms "renunciation,"[24] which is the turning point in a tragedy. Psychologically speaking, inside Ch'ü Yüan's mind there is a conflict between the *id* and the superego.[25] Finally, the instinct for self-preservation (i.e., the *id*) is suppressed. In fact, the poet repeatedly says in the poem that he is not afraid of death (11.43, 53, 65 and 88). The acceptance of death does not necessarily mean submission to Fate.[26] Rather, it makes him stronger to defy Fate.

Before long, he realizes that his hope for rapprochement with the king becomes dimmer and dimmer (1.128). Lost and disenchanted in the world of corruption that surrounds him, he searches for spiritual guidance, which will give him strength to cope with the forces that have been destroying him politically. He consults Nü-hsü, a shamaness, Ling Fen, a shaman, and Wu-hsien 巫咸, the supreme god of the Ch'u people, and they all advise him to be flexible or to leave his country and serve other kings (11.66-71, 131-134, and 143-151). But he hesitates to follow their advice.

---

[22] Lucas, *Tragedy in Relation to Aristotle's Poetics* (New York: Harcourt, Brace, 1928), p. 26. Leon Golden points out that catharsis can also mean "intellectual clarification"; see "The Purgation Theory of Catharsis," *Journal of Aesthetics and Art Criticism,* 31 (1973), 473-79.

[23] In his book *Hamartia* J. M. Bremer asserts that *"hamartia* here must be understood to mean 'mistake,' 'blunder,' i.e. a well-intentioned action (or at least one not maliciously undertaken) which proves harmful and therefore wrong because too little was known about its nature of effect." See *Hamartia: Tragic Error in the Poetics of Aristotle and in Greek Tragedy* (Amsterdam: Adolf M. Hakkert, 1969), p. 195.

[24] *Renunciation as a Tragic Focus* (Minneapolis: Univ. of Minnesota Press, 1954), pp. 4-6.

[25] Albert T. Sawyer, "A Psychoanalytic Approach to Tragic Drama," Thesis Ohio State 1958, p. 18.

[26] Ralph J. Hallman maintains, "Tragedy expresses the need to die as the only means of regaining the spontaneity which life loses under the alienating, repressive systems created by intelligence." See Hallman, p. 11. D. D. Raphael prefers "Necessity" to "Fate"; see *The Paradox of Tragedy* (Bloomington: Indiana Univ. Press, 1960), p. 25.

His hesitation and indecision represent vividly and forcefully the acuteness of the inner conflict between his moral aspiration and the will to live.[27] He finally starts his journey, and looks for, but fails to meet, his ideal lady. His distrust in pretended friendship and his disgust of the treachery prevailing in the court make him stop his futile search. He decides to stay in Ch'u and abide by the principle of P'eng Hsien (11.39 and 187).

Allegorically speaking, the search is a quest for fulfillment.[28] It has a mystical meaning too.[29] First, we do not know precisely who P'eng Hsien actually was. Was he a loyal minister in the Shang Dynasty, a water-god or a shaman ancestor?[30] In the second place, what his principle was is also a baffling question. This is not unusual, however. The revelation of the absolute truth, be it *jen* 仁 in Confucianism or *satori* in Zen Buddhism, is always a mystical experience. It sounds esoteric, but what is more appropriate to describe the highest order of human dignity than in inscrutable and ambivalent words? After all, who can give an accurate definition of, say, "humanity"? Moody Prior is right in saying that "Motives, conflicts of will, and emotional responses to events are in their nature too involved, even too little understood, to be reduced to plain and self-evident clarity without destroying their essential nature or giving them a narrow and false simplicity."[31]

The poet's eventual rejection of the advice given by God Wu-hsien and people in the shamanistic profession indicates that he is not willing to follow what seems to be the easy way out, and that, like Euripides, he is doubtful whether gods should interfere with human affairs, despite the fact that he believes in their existence.[32] This spirit of defiance is essential in a tragedy. Human determination crashes head on with the Will of Heaven. Although man always suffers in this conflict, the noble value of humanity is thus revealed. Furthermore, these advisers, or arbiters, to borrow Albert Sawyer's term,[33] help the reader know that Ch'ü Yüan's action is irrational to the common people. That is why Shamaness Nü-hsü expostulates him for his aloof attitude and impracticable plan.

The reaffirmation of moral principles at this point gives the reader tragic pleasure.[34] He is sorry to see his hero suffer; yet he is also pleased to realize that

---

[27] This reminds us of Hamlet's hesitation; see Maynard Mack, "The World of Hamlet," in Cleanth Brooks, ed., *Tragic Themes in Western Literature* (New Haven: Yale Univ. Press, 1955), pp. 30-58.

[28] Jerah Johnson interprets *Li sao* as the poet's search for meaning in life and truth in universe and as an account of his personal struggle for individuation or self-completion; see *Li sao: A Poem on Relieving Sorrows by Ch'ü Yüan* (Miami: Olivant Press, 1959), p. 11.

[29] In discussing the *Book of Job* as a proto-tragedy, Sidney Lamb remarks, "When Job is confronted by the voice of God speaking out of the whirlwind, we are in the world, not of tragedy, but of mystical affirmation. . . . The voice out of whirlwind transcends human reason and asserts the mystery of Creation." See *Tragedy* (Toronto: Canadian Broadcasting Corporation, 1965), pp. 10-11.

[30] Hashikawa Tokio 橋川時雄, "Risō to wa nani ka" 離騷とは何か? *Jimbun Kenkyū* 人文研究, 4 (August, 1953), 308; David Hawkes, *Ch'u Tz'u: The Songs of the South* (London: Oxford Univ. Press, 1959), pp. 24, 68.

[31] Moody E. Prior, *The Language of Tragedy* (Bloomington: Indiana Univ. Press, 1947), p. 12.

[32] A. E. Haigh, *The Tragic Drama of the Greeks* (New York: Dover, 1968), p. 270.

[33] Sawyer, pp. 45, 46.

[34] There are many discussions of "tragic pleasure." The following books deal exclusively with this subject: P. K. Guha, *Tragic Relief* (London: Oxford Univ. Press, 1932); Joseph F. O'Conner, "Aristotle and the Pleasure Proper to Tragedy," Thesis Ohio State 1967.

he (the hero) does not succumb to oppressive authority. He is in a state of exaltation, after perceiving from the hero's behavior "greatness of spirit," to use Corneille's phrase.[35] He identifies himself with the hero. But at the same time, he disapproves of the hero's emotional trait. Thus, through identification and projection catharsis results.[36] From the socio-religious point of view, he has undergone a rite of passage, through which he is admitted into a new and greater world of humanity.[37]

The poet devotes about three fifths of the poem to the presentation of his hesitation, in which he describes his consultation with god and shamans and his celestial flight. These supernatural elements serve to neutralize the pain invoked by the poem.[38] The shamanistic practices and magic journey are what Nietzsche calls Dionysian.[39] In the realm of religion, the poet sees suffering as something common to all people. This outlook on life palliates the pain of suffering for both the poet and the reader.

The first part of the celestial journey can be called a "bride quest," but it is different from that in the Mediaeval European epics,[40] in that the poet in *Li sao* does not really want a bride, he merely wants to show his uncompromising attitude in politics through his imaginary search for an ideal lady. To Ch'ü Yüan, any compromise on his part is unacceptable. He would feel embarrassed if he were to propose a rapprochement with the king. Even if he were to do so, he would have made some biting criticism (1.117), which is inappropriate for an official to say to the throne. Yet, he would not do less than that. Therefore, he hesitates and has some "foxy suspicion."

> I order *chen* (a poisonous bird) as my matchmaker, [but]
> It tells me that the idea is no good.

---

[35] Dorothea Krook also says, "We feel, extraordinarily, liberated from pain and fear (Aristotle's 'purgation' of the emotions of pity and terror); not depressed or oppressed, but in a curious way exhilarated; not angry and bitter but somehow reconciled; our faith in man and the human condition not destroyed or underminded but restored, fortified, reaffirmed. This is the psychological fact of our final response to tragedy; and the reason behind it is what I have named as the fourth universal element of tragedy—the affirmation of the dignity of man and the worthwhileness of human life. . . . " See *Elements of Tragedy* (New Haven: Yale Univ. Press, 1969), p. 14. Joseph Campbell says in the same vein, "It is the function, the power and fascination of the tragic art, as indeed of all art when turned to art's proper task . . . to render an experience in affirmation of life as it is, in form and in depth, in this vale of tears: over and above the terror, the pity, and the pain, communicating an exhilaration of the will's affirmation of life in its being and becoming, here and now." See *The Masks of God: Creative Mythology* (New York: Viking, 1970), p. 355.

[36] Sawyer, ch. 3.

[37] Sawyer observes, "Catharsis is also the relief achieved as a result of real or fancied insight into one's own nature." Sawyer, p. 58.

[38] Guha, pp. 165-84. Charles E. Whitmore says in *The Supernatural in Tragedy* (1915; rpt. Manaroneck, N.Y.: Paul P. Appel, 1971), "We must agree that tragedy is that form of drama which seeks to penetrate as far as possible into the mystery of existence, and to reveal the secret sources of human action. . . . When a writer has penetrated to the very verge of human existence, he must confront the question, what lies beyond? And it is in some respect of the supernatural that he will find whatever answer he chooses to give" (p. 356).

[39] Friedrich Nietzsche, *The Birth of Tragedy and the Genealogy of Morals*, tr. Francis Golffing (New York: Doubleday, 1956), pp. 3-146.

[40] William Calin, *The Epic Quest: Studies in Four Old French Chansons de Gestes* (Baltimore: Johns Hopkins Univ. Press, 1966), pp. 3-56.

> A male turtle dove flies away [as my messenger], chirping,
>   I still hate its trickiness.
> My heart is hesitant and suspicious like a fox,
>   I wish to go by myself, but it is improper.
>
> (11.120-122)

吾令鴆爲媒兮，鴆告余以不好，
雄鳩之鳴逝兮，余猶惡其佻巧，
心猶豫而狐疑兮，欲自適而不可。

He then stops to consult Shaman Fen and God Wu-hsien. The second part of the journey is a kind of pageantry. There are dragons, phoenixes, carriages inlaid with jade and ivory, music and dance. And the places he passes include the K'un-lun Mountain 崑崙縣圃, Shifting Sands 流沙, Pu-chou Mountain 不周山 (the mythical mountain against which Kung-kung 共工 knocked his head), and, of course, the Bright Heaven. This pageantry not only gives aesthetic distancing,[41] but also serves as a contrast to the human world, which, though full of sufferings, is the place where the poet wants to live and die.

We have found thus far that many important elements of tragedy are present in the poem—inevitability, reversal and tragic effect; and we are therefore convinced that *Li sao* may be called a tragic poem. In the beginning, the poet, a hero of high mimetic tragedy,[42] recalls his birth and the name-giving ceremony. He is endowed with unusual talent and ability.[43] His ambition is to help his king run the government, and thus establish his reputation. But his fellow officials are jealous of him and accuse him of depravity. As a result, he is alienated by the king. He is then urged by god and shamans to leave his country and seek another master. He hesitates and finally decides to cling to his cherished moral principle and stay. To alleviate the reader's feeling of distress, the poet uses several devices of "artistic distancing," namely, flower and female images, history, divination and magic flight. Throughout the poem he uses flower images to "build the tragic perspective."[44] They conjure up in the reader's mind the idea that the poet is faultless and incorruptible. His recourse to history and his frequent reference to Time reflect that there is a force which has pushed him into his present situation; and his rejection of the advice given by God Wu-hsien and others signifies his defiance against Fate. At this point, the poet seems to be locked up in a small place where he can hardly breathe, and the reader would worry about him. Nevertheless, the reader is soon relieved of this tense feeling,

---

[41] Spectacle is one of the six elements in tragedy; see S. H. Butcher, pp. 29-31. Susanne K. Langer says, "Tragedy, which expresses the consciousness of life and death, must make life seem worth while, rich, beautiful, to make death awesome. The splendid exaggerations of the stage serve tragic feeling by heightening the lure of the world." See *Feeling and Form* (London: Routledge, 1953), p. 364.

[42] Northrop Frye, *Anatomy of Criticism: Four Essays* (Princeton: Princeton Univ. Press, 1957), pp. 37-38.

[43] The hero of tragedy "is usually conceived and presented his exceptional personality, his clash with outer circumstance, his inner conflict, and the domination of the plot of the play by the sway of his character." See Guha, p. 47. William Van O'Conner remarks, "He [the tragic hero] is a symbol of strength, of revolt, of spiritual resiliency." See *Climates of Tragedy* (Baton Rouge, Louisiana: Louisiana Univ. Press, 1943), p. 46.

[44] T. R. Henn, *The Harvest of Tragedy* (New York: Barnes & Noble, 1966), p. 145.

because the poet takes him on a celestial flight. This flight is "an illusion of freedom, of space to maneuver, even a sense of companionship with others in misfortune, and a strengthening of course thereby."[45] After his travel from this finite world to the infinite sky and back to the finite,[46] the poet feels reassured and unequivocally proclaims that he is to abide by his moral principle. All in all, *Li sao* is a unique piece of literary writing, which can be interpreted by various theories of tragedy.

Generically, I have tried to show that this poem may be considered a tragic poem, and as such it takes the reader onto a higher level of understanding—an intellectual understanding of human reality through the empathetic process. The poet's seemingly blind emotional drive rouses in the reader great pity, and his cool and calculated struggle with his adversaries instills in the reader fear for him. Through pity and fear the reader comes to an understanding of his limitations and potentialities. This self-understanding will make one prefer to cut short his life rather than become a slave of Fate. Ch'ü Yüan's decision to stay and stand by P'eng Hsien's principle despite its futility illustrates his preference for a high humanistic ideal over a meaningless life.

Structurally speaking, *Li sao* has all the elements of a tragedy. It has a tragic hero, who in the beginning is at the top of the wheel of fortune, but is totally defeated in the end. There is a tragic flaw, or *hamartia,* which is the poet's overzealousness, and tragic pride, or *hubris*. The reversal of fortune, or *peripeteia,* happens after 1.16. From the point of view of existentialism, this reversal presents the absurdity of human life. That the king turns a deaf ear to the poet who eagerly wants to serve him is the sharpest irony. Instead of resigning himself to Fate, the poet presents his case to his reader and demands that there should be a certain order in the human world. There ensues the tragic conflict, a conflict between the poet's ideal and the collapsing order. Many people think that this conflict is between good and bad people. If this be the case, then the downfall of the hero is not tragic, as maintained by Aristotle, because he is brought down by unworthy people.[47] In fact, it is the king, the embodiment of the existing social order and values, who is the antagonist in the conflict.[48] In the poem he often criticizes and complains against the king. It is his high moral standard and personal integrity that is in conflict with society as represented by the crown. The conflict between self and society, to both of which high value is attached, is the basic theme of tragedy.[49]

Attendant on the reversal is *anagnorisis,* or the recognition of truth, which in this poem is P'eng Hsien's principle. If tragedy and myth have an intricate relationship with each other, as suggested by Richmond Hathorn, who says that a tragedy has as its chief emphasis the revelation of mystery,[50] it is appropriate for Ch'ü Yüan to lead his reader to the mystery of P'eng Hsien. Since tragedy deals with reality and

---

[45] Ibid., p. 37.

[46] The "finite" and the "infinite" are two basic ideas in Fr. William F. Lynch's book, *Christ and Apollo: The Dimensions of Literary Imagination* (New York: Mentor-Omega Book, 1963).

[47] S. H. Butcher, p. 45.

[48] Lionel Abel maintains that "tragedy is never caused by what is unambiguously evil. It is sheerly positive in conflict with the sheerly positive that destroys the tragic protagonist." See "Is there a Tragic Sense of Life?" in Lionel Abel, ed., *Moderns on Tragedy* (New York: Fawcett, 1967), p. 183.

[49] See Michael Hinden, "Ritual and Tragic Action: A Synthesis of Current Theory," *Journal of Aesthetics and Art Criticism,* 32 (1974), 357-73.

[50] *Tragedy, Myth, and Mystery* (Bloomington: Indiana Univ. Press, 1962), p. 223.

not abstraction, the mystery of P'eng Hsien is in fact the mystery of the existence of man. In the Old Testament we come across this question, "What is man?"—a question asked by Job,[51] who, like Ch'ü Yüan, was brought down by a slanderer. This question comes up again in a different form in the myth of Oedipus, the classic tragic hero. That is the famous Sphinx riddle. In *Hamlet* the protagonist puts the question in still another way:

> What is a man,
> If his chief good and market of his time
> Be but to sleep and feed? A beast, no more. (IV, iv)

Like Job, who "would order [his] cause before [God], and fill [his] mouth with arguments," Ch'ü Yüan in *Li sao* kneels down to present his argument and demands justice even in the shadow of death, because he has the clear conviction that he is right (1.92). In the verbal conflict (or *agon*) with Shamaness Nü-hsü, Shaman Fen and God Wu-hsien, Ch'ü Yüan is not convinced by the idea of getting along with others in this world. To him Heaven is just, and the good will be rewarded. He therefore doubts the intelligence of these supernatural agents. Although the tragic hero's cause does not prevail in the end, the reader, nonetheless, perceives the mystery of human existence. Short of any solution, the tragic poet and his reader realize the truth that in the end wisdom comes to men after their sufferings, as sung in Aeschylus' *Agammenon*.[52] This wisdom helps them perceive the complexity of life. Furthermore, it comes with strength. This dichotomy, wisdom and strength, as mentioned in the Book of Job (12:13), is the root of tragic pleasure. Having wisdom, the reader knows that life is not just "to sleep and feed"; and with strength he has the capability to fight for his ideal. With these newly acquired virtues, the reader enters into a higher level of humanity.

---

[51] Book of Job 7:17.
[52] Arthur S. Way's translation renders the passage as follows:
>   From suffering's root the flower instruction groweth.
>   Yet even in sleep the heart sees only pain
>   Dropping from memory's winepress: still is given
>   Wisdom to scholars loth to understand:
>   The God from thrones of majesty in heaven
>   Must force their boon into the unwilling hand.

See *Eleven Plays of the Greek Dramatists* (New York: Grosset & Dunlap, 1969), p. 6.

"Lord, Do Not Cross the River":
Literature as a Mediating Process

Ying-hsiung Chou

"Great" literary works are very often valued more than their "minor" counterparts by critics who abide by some principles in the sociology of literature as their critical norm. As is often the case, "great" works are treasured for their coherence and organization which embody the world view of a certain society at a particular juncture of history. "Minor" pieces, on the contrary, and especially works with folk connections, are very often downgraded for the simple reason that they only reflect particular problems and thus fail to present a unified outlook on life. Either a "minor" poet's access to society as a whole is thought to be too limited, or, as in the case of folk literature or literature with folk connections, the communal participation in the creation and transmission necessarily destroys its unity. Hence, the "reflection" produced at this level of literary activities is considered partial or ill-focused, and thus of little value as a documentation of society.

In a way this attitude is understandable. "Great" works generally occupy a privileged position in that they command a panoramic view of a certain sector of society with some degree of intensity. "Fu on Shang-lin Park" 上林賦 is a perfect example of comprehensiveness as well as intensity in its depiction of the uppermost layer of Han society. In fact, the masterpiece is characterized by such complexity and intensity that it is in a sense no longer the work of an individual poet. It is, in fact, the aesthetic representation of a type of social consciousness.[1]

By contrast, less ambitious works of the period cannot boast the same dimensions and depth achieved in court literature. We cannot, for instance, expect a simple *yüeh-fu* 樂府 ballad of the period, titled "Shadowy, Luxuriant" 攤離 to rival "Fu on Shang-lin Park."

---

[1] Lucien Goldmann in his "Genetic Structuralism and the History of Literature," claims that the "great writer is precisely the exceptional individual who succeeds in creating in a certain field, that of the literary . . . work, an imaginary, coherent—almost rigorously coherent—universe . . . . " Such a coherence is what he refers to as the "world vision." See *Velocities of Change*, ed. Richard Macksey (Baltimore and London: Johns Hopkins Univ. Press, 1974), p. 94.

> Shaded, clustered, by the foot of Chung-nan,
> Go build houses;
> Why bother with constructions,
>   Constructions of *Hui* and *Lan* Orchid Halls?
> Shaded, clustered, by the foot of Chung-nan.

> 中趾離擁
> 室築可
> 之葺用何
> 蘭用蕙
> 中趾離擁

"Fu on Shang-lin Park" is characterized by a complex, but coherent, procedure in which the absolute monarch goes through an elaborate ritual of first accumulating wealth from all quarters of the universe and later giving it up in exchange for the title of a sage king who shares all his possessions with his subjects. Here in this simple ditty, the folk artist sings, from the core of his heart, his practical concern: a complaint on the unfair expropriation of his farming land and an appeal to the emperor not to expand his constructions. Admittedly, what is presented is a rather partial glimpse of the Han society. Yet, limited as it is, this perspective of content sociology, moreover, coincides with what Lucien Goldmann calls the genetic structural interpretation. While "Fu on Shang-lin Park" is characterized stylistically by its grand unity (which in turn symbolizes a unified world view endorsed by the predominant State Confucianism of Han), the folksong here is fluid and open in form. Structurally, the song proceeds more or less on the basis of extension, with one line giving rise to another. Line 1 flows into line 2 by incorporating the last syntactic unit of line 1, "the foot of Chung-nan" 趾中, as the subject of line 2. Line 3 further builds upon line 2 by simultaneously asking a rhetorical question and offering an alternative in the fashion of "since/why?" At this point, line 3 does not come to a halt. It goes on to generate line 4 by allowing one of its lexicons (i.e., *yung* 用) to be repeated and manipulated in the succeeding line.[2] By permutation, the heart of the issue is unfolded and the singer makes a blunt comment on the ruler's unnecessary expansion of the imperial residences. Finally, line 5 repeats verbatim line 1. Coming after line 4, line 5 as a refrain accentuates the singer's opinion that the two new palaces are uncalled-for and that even if the emperor is insistent upon the project the site should be relocated in the south where land is abundant. Structurally, of course, the two refrains nicely put two "aural bookends" to the piece and thus instate a nice poetic closure. Compared with the elitist poem, a greater degree of spontaneity is evident throughout the lines. And given its relatively loose structure, the singer no less than the reader can be said to be better able to experience reality as it comes along. In other words, despite its limitations in delineating a unified vision of a particular sector of society, the folksong is capable of deriving working solutions to the oppositional forces in life. In this case, it is the emperor's love for the imperial reserve

---

[2] Lines 3 and 4 may very well be emendated as, "何用葺之, 用蕙用蘭." As such, the syntactic parallelism between the two lines becomes clear and line 4 is obviously a structural outgrowth of line 3. Another interpretation sets line 4 as a response to line 3; as, "What should be used to repair (build) it? / Use *hui* and *lan* orchids." The second reading seems to be less relevant, for "hui" and "lan" obviously refer to two of the fourteen palaces in the imperial park.

versus the peasants' need for the fertile land. A simple rhetorical solution to the conflict is offered in the singer's plea to relocate the park in the less populated part of the empire. The song, in other words, offers a temporary solution to the conflict between the ruler and his subjects.

In what way, then, does the aesthetic system exemplified in these *yüeh-fu* ballads provide working solutions as the author and reader experience the oppositional, and often irreconcilable, forces in nature? To answer this question, one would have to first place literature in its original stage of inception. Primitive men tried to possess the natural world by transforming it into something more immediate and more manageable. For this purpose, tools were invented and improved. In fact, men became eventually so efficient with their tools that they distinguished themselves from ordinary animals by virtue of this ability. They were able to shape events in their own designs, as ordinary animals could not. From the state of the natural, they were thus advanced to the cultural. Now, among the tools they invented and mastered, language was the most far-reaching in its impact. Aside from its most fundamental and primordial function as a medium of communication in the early men's communal activities, language was also used as magic. Presumably, by arousing the subconscious power of the collective will to act, language was used as if endowed with extraordinary powers. Furthermore, to achieve the greatest of its arousing effects, language was often refined and intensified into art. And in a cyclical manner, this communal use of language was heightened to the degree that people began to see this linguistic art as actually capable of conferring magic power over men's enemies as well as nature. And true enough, a large amount of primitive art did serve as magic formulas in man's hunting or agricultural activities.[3]

Even in a later stage of society when individuality started to evolve from the primordial collectivity and art was in the process of becoming an expression of alienation, the task of the individual poet was frequently to restore unity and harmony with the outside world. Often in a frenzied state of creativity, the artist communicated his highly sensitized and concentrated experience which was fundamentally similar to that of his audience. The result of his heightened use of language was the arousal of the audience's communal awareness. Viewed in this light, the function of poetry was, in a highly symbolic manner, primarily problem-solving. In its earliest stage, poetry served the purpose of bridging the gap between man and nature, thereby ensuring the procurement of his foodstuff. To a certain extent, the basic contradiction between man and nature was reconciled with the use of language as magic. In a more advanced stage, poetry restored human consciousness to its communal origin. The opposition between society and individuals was again mediated through language as art.

In its primordial state, life is literally made up of sets of oppositions: life/death, love/hate, man/nature, culture/nature, art/nature and so on. The mythic thought, according to Lévi-Strauss, generally "progresses from the awareness of oppositions toward their solution."[4] However, the oppositions are at times so polarized that movement of any kind is extremely difficult. Mediating processes are therefore called for to reconcile the polarization. One or two opposite terms, for instance, are replaced

---

[3] For a detailed discussion of the origin of art, see Ernst Fischer, *The Necessity of Art* (Middlesex: Penguin, 1964), pp. 15-48.

[4] Claude Lévi-Strauss, *Structural Anthropology* (New York: Basic Books, 1963), p. 224.

or transformed so as to admit of the mediator, and form a new triad which embodies the tension as well as harmony of life. In the same manner, we can view literature in its primitive and folk states not as an empirical object yielding a reflection of society from which it springs. We can instead treat it as a conceptual entity capable of bodying forth a process of mediations among the oppositions of life. The structure of literature itself, in other words, is an experiential mode in which the subject comes to terms with his object, and in which man establishes with nature or with his fellow men a complex of relationships which are more conducive to a rewarding living than the pre-mediated stage.

II

The ancient oral ballad of "Lord, Do Not Cross the River" 公無渡河 is tucked away inconspicuously in *chüan* 26 of *Yüeh-fu shih chi* 樂府詩集 within the prose epigraph to Li Ho's 李賀 (A.D. 791-817) "The Tune of the K'ung-hou Harp" 箜篌引, which gives an account of the genesis of this ancient song.

> Ts'ui-pao in *Ku chin chu* says, "So far as 'The K'ung-hou Harp Tune' is concerned, it was the creation of Li Yü, the wife of Ho-li Tzu-kao, who was a guard at a ford in Korea. Tzu-kao got up one morning, to pole his boat. There was a gray-haired, deranged person, with his hair down, and carrying a gourd-shaped container. He tried to wade across against the stream. His wife followed behind and tried to stop him, but to no avail. As a consequence, he was drowned in the river. At that the wife took a K'ung-hou harp and sang:
>
> *Kung mi̯wo d'âg g'â*
> *Kung ki̯ang d'âg g'â*
> *D'i̯wəd g'â ńi̯ag si̯ər*
> *Tsi̯âng nâd kung g'â*
>
> Lord, do not cross the river.
> Lord, you did cross the river.
> You fell into the river and died.
> What could I do with you, Lord?
>
> The tune was quite pathetic, and at the end of the song she also committed suicide by drowning herself. Tzu-kao went home and told Li Yü about the incident. Li Yü was so moved by it that she wrote down its tune to the accompaniment of the K'ung-hou harp. Those who heard the song, without any exception, shed their tears and cried. Li Yü taught her neighbor, Li Jong, the tune and named it 'The K'ung-hou Harp Tune.'"

崔豹古今注曰：箜篌引者，朝鮮津卒霍里子高妻麗玉所作也。子高晨起刺船，有一白首狂夫，被髮提壺亂流而渡，其妻隨而止之不及，遂墮河而死，於是援箜篌而歌曰：

公無渡河，公竟渡河
墮河而死，將奈公何

聲甚悽愴，曲終亦投河而死。子高還以語麗玉。麗玉傷之，乃引箜篌而寫其聲。聞者莫不墮淚飲泣。麗玉以其曲傳鄰女麗容。名曰箜篌引。

Kuo Mao-ch'ien 郭茂倩, the Sung editor, does not quote exactly from *Ku chin chu* verbatim though, for in the third item on music of the said work, Ts'ui Pao only mentions that the old man's wife sings a song before her death; the text of the song is actually not recorded. As a result, the texts of the song vary extensively from collector to collector. So far as I have been able to discover, there are at least four versions.[5] Of course, in oral literature, this is not altogether unexpected, for any version is as good as another. In the world of oral transmission no such thing as a fixed text really exists.[6]

As a matter of fact, we find variants not only in the texts of the song itself but also in the prose introductions that are supposed to go with the song. The prose section has three variants. Aside from *Ku chin chu*, *Ch'in ts'ao* 琴操 and *Yüeh-fu tsa-lu* 樂府雜錄, among others, also keep records of the story. Yet for all the varia-

---

[5] Line 2 has two variants:
    公竟渡河 —Tu Wen-lan 杜文瀾, *Ku yao yen* 古謠諺 (Taipei: Shih chieh, 1963).
    公終渡河 —Yang Wei-chen 楊維楨, *Ch'ien-yai ku yüeh-fu chu* 錢崖古樂府注 (Taipei: Chung-hua, 1971).

Line 3 has four variants:
    渡河而死 —Lo Ken-tse 羅根澤, *Yüeh-fu wen-hsüeh shih* 樂府文學史 (Taipei: Wen-shih-che, 1972).
    Li Ch'un-sheng 李純勝, *Han Wei Nan-pei-ch'ao yüeh-fu* 漢魏南北朝樂府 (Taipei: Shang-wu, 1971).
    公墮河死 —Tu Wen-lan, *Ku yao yen*.
    墮河而死 —Cheng Chen-to 鄭振鐸, *Chung-kuo su-wen-hsüeh shih* 中國俗文學史 (Taipei: Shang-wu, 1970).
    Liang Ch'i-ch'ao 梁啓超, *Chung-kuo chih mei-wen chi ch'i li-shih* 中國之美文及其歷史 (Taipei: Chung-hua, 1968).
    Ting Fu-pao 丁福保, *Ch'üan Han San-kuo Nan-pei-ch'ao shih* 全漢三國南北朝詩 (Taipei: Shih-chieh, 1969).
    Chang Shou-p'ing 張壽平, *Han tai yüeh-fu yü yüeh-fu ko-tz'u* 漢代樂府與漢府歌辭 (Taipei: Kuang-wen, 1970).
    公墮而死 —Yang Wei-chen, *Ch'ien-yai ku yüeh-fu chu*.

Line 4 has two variants:
    將奈公何 —Liang Ch'i-ch'ao, *Chung-kuo chih mei-wen chi ch'i li-shih*.
    當奈公何 —Yü Kuan-ying 余冠英, *Yüeh-fu shih hsüan* 樂府詩選 (Peking: Jen-min, 1953).

If we treat the varied elements as v and the rest as x, the poem can be seen as,

    x x x x
    x v x x
    v v v v
    v x x x

The variants in line 2 and 4 are synonyms and are, therefore, of little significance. Line 3, though containing four variants, can be further reduced to two types:

    I. v x x x
        渡河而死
        墮河而死
    II. x x v x
        公墮河死
        公墮而死

Significantly, the existence of the variants does not change the basic structure of the ballad. The leaping lines exist in all versions. The displacement of $g'â$ in the third line is generally valid. And, of course, the transformation—the punning of $g'â$—remains unchanged in all versions.

[6] This is true of Mrs. Brown's two versions of "Lass of Roch Royal," for instance, which were transcribed respectively in 1783 and 1800 and are very different from each other. The essential idea remains unchanged, but the two versions differ in their methods of composition. See David Buchan, *The Ballad and the Folk* (London and Boston: Routledge, 1973), pp. 155-56.

tions, a consistent pattern persists throughout. And in going through the various versions in the following pages we shall see how a structural model multiplies itself from a simple opposition to a full-fledged human drama involving complex human relationships as well as mediations.

The most simple narrative skeleton is given in *Yüeh-fu tsa-lu*:

> There was once a gray-haired old man who was drowned in the river. The song was in commemoration of him. Li Yü, who was versed in the K'ung-hou harp, created this tune to express her sad feelings.

> 昔有白首翁，溺於河，歌以哀之。女麗玉善箜篌，撰此曲以寄哀情。

We see two sets of basic human conflicts like,

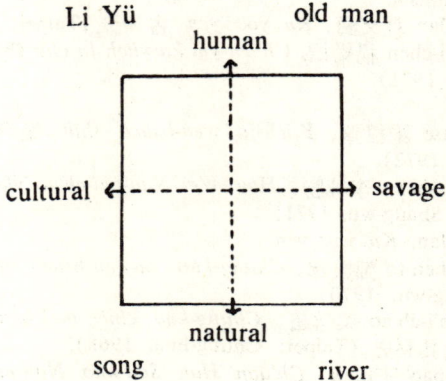

The savage, vertical line on the right signifies the tragic event. It is counterbalanced by the cultural, vertical line on the left which represents the verbal reproduction of the tragic event. In the same oppositional manner, the human, horizontal line on top is related to the human world of the tragic old man and the compassionate artist. As a contrast, the line in the bottom describes the impersonal world of the song and the river which are again in conflict with each other for reasons which we will give later.

In *Ch'in ts'ao* the event is further elaborated:

> So far as "The K'ung-hou Harp Tune" is concerned, it was the creation of Ho-li Tzu-kao, who was a ford guard in Korea. There was a gray-haired, deranged person, with hair down, carrying a gourd-shaped container, and he tried to cross the river. His wife ran after him, but could not overtake him. He fell into the river and was drowned. The wife thereupon sighed with her head lifted toward heaven and sang while strumming the K'ung-hou harp. At the end of the song, she also died by drowning herself in the river. Tzu-kao took the harp and sang the song. Therefore, it was called "K'ung-hou Harp Tune."

> 箜篌引者朝鮮津卒霍里子高所作也。子高晨起刺船而濯，有一狂夫被髮提壺而渡，其妻追之不及，墜河而死，乃號天歔欷，鼓箜篌而歌，曲終投河而死。子高援琴作其歌聲，故曰箜篌引。

Notice how Li Yü, the artist, is replaced by the old man's wife. And since she follows and dies a martyr of love, there arises a need to have an outsider to transmit the song as we have it today. For that reason, Tzu-kao appears on the scene and repeats what the wife has sung. The event must now be represented as,

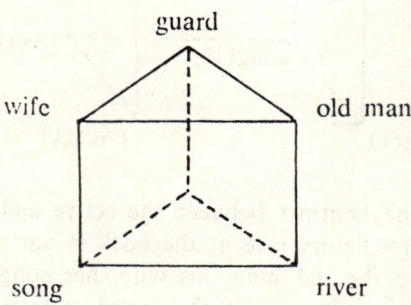

The figure changes from a two-dimensional plane to a square pyramid with five planes. The plane in the front—constituted of the old man, his wife, her song and the river—are directly involved with the tragic event. On the other hand, the official, vertical side of the guard is only indirectly involved in the incident—he watches as an onlooker and repeats the song as it is. (The introduction does not tell us specifically if he is even moved at all.) Symbolically, we see a sharp contrast between these two sets of life situations. Yet it is also a contrast transformed from the first figure we have just mentioned. In that two-dimensional plane, we see the contrast between these two states of being as existing between the sides of "old man / river" and "Li Yü / song." Now in this complicated scheme, the cultural role of Li Yü creating and singing her song is taken over by the guard repeating the tune. At the same time, the old man's wife now participates actively in the events and, because of her inability to distance herself, is actually destroyed. As for the old man, he is given even a larger tragic role to play. In the previous case, he is simply drowned in the river—there is no dramatic conflict of any kind involved. In this case his action is not only unpremediated. It is even reckless and wilful, because he is probably intoxicated and crosses the river against his wife's admonition. It thus follows that the outcome is inevitably tragic. As to the guard, he is diametrically in opposition against the "savage" couple. While the couple go out and encounter nature in the most primitive manner, the guard's contact with nature is official, being safely in a boat carrying out his daily routine. Likewise, just as the river is of no vital concern to him, so the song he repeats has no real psychological impact on him. To him the river is psychologically just as insignificant as the song. That is why in the figure they are actually treated as one entity, and are focused into one point. Nonetheless, for all his insensibility to nature and art, what he does is probably the most fundamental form of creativity—sheer repetition of the event and its concomitant artistic product. As a mediating act, however, the song enables the guard to play the double roles of participant and observer. The difference between mediations and unreconciled opposition should be self-evident by now.

As we move on to Ts'ui Pao's introduction given in its entirety above, the situation is further developed into a full-fledged human drama, represented with a cubic form.

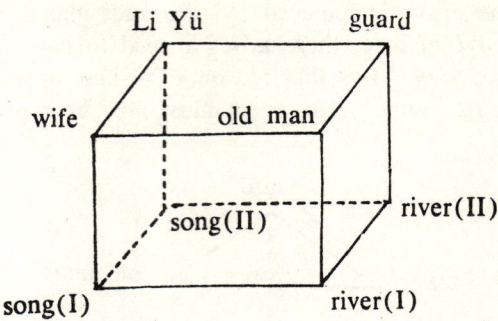

In the second situation, the contrast between the active and oppositional plane in the front and the passive and mediatory side in the back is not balanced in the sense that the active drama involving the old man, his wife, her song and the river dominates the situation. The non-committal role of the guard is overshadowed by the intense personal conflicts in the foreground. It is only in the third situation here that the relationship in the front plane is properly balanced by the one in the back. (Li Yü is recalled back to the scene, in the capacity of the guard's wife.) As a matter of fact, the plane in the back is almost a carbon copy of the plane in the front. As a result of such a repetition, an artful miming of human conflict, reality—be it the one in the front or the one in the back—as we shall soon see, can be treated as a structural unit within which its constituents are essentially interrelated, and are symptomatic of the all-pervasive contradictions in life. This interrelated quality generally remains unchanged regardless of the dramatis personae involved. The drama enacted by the old man and his wife against the backgrounds of the song and the river, for instance, establishes a model after which the life of the guard with his wife is also constructed.

In this elaborated scheme, we also see for the first time that the guard's double functions of witnessing and singing are shared by this wife. Instead of singing the tune himself, he relays the happening to his wife who recreates the song and then in turn transmits it to a girl in the neighborhood. Such a division of function consequently entails the separation of the song(II) from the river(II), thus developing the situation in the back as a full-fledged reality. As such, just as the unruly old man is in sharp contrast to the dutiful ford guard, so is Li Yü a reversal of the old man's wife. The latter attempts in the first place to dissuade her husband from committing such an impulsive act. When her advice is not heeded, she resorts to singing and eventually allows the pathos of the song to consume her life. On the contrary, Li Yü receives the story only indirectly from her husband. Besides, her song is only a recreation of the original voice of agony and even that is soon relayed to other singers; thus the agony is several times removed. In this way, she unloads the emotional burden evoked by the tragic event while at the same time bringing the audience back to the communal sense of tragedy. Since such oppositions exist within the human world, they must also exist in the natural world. Just as the river is domesticated for the guard—which is not the case with the old man's river—so is Li Yü's song a cultural product, not a song of total disillusionment which metaphorically drains the life force of the old man's wife and forces her to end her life. In other words, in the fashion of the contrast between the cultural world and the savage world, the river(I) and the song(I) of the savage world are to be distinguished from their counterparts in the cultural world. Here both the song(II) and the river(II) are tamed. Both are domesticated and exist as cultural products to serve man: the song assumes the functions of catharsis as well as the arousal of communal consciousness, and the river also connects the two shores as it is under the jurisdiction of man.

Aside from the front-back opposition mentioned above, the contrasts also exist between the plane on the right and the plane on the left. As men are made to deal physically with the river, so are women made to handle the song. Even though there are two basic ways of dealing physically with nature—the cultural and the savage ways which determine how the events will turn out to be—the male members are basically men of action and are incapable of creativity. On the contrary, the female members generally take the passive role in the drama of life and choose to internalize their desires by means of creativity rather than action—a creativity which may be constructive or destructive, depending on their attitude toward art. Graphically, this bipolar division between action and creativity can be seen as,

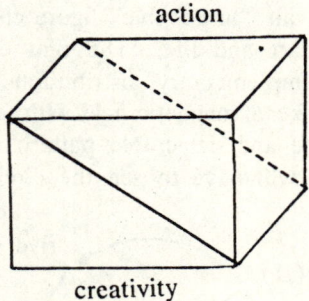

The lower wedge represents creativity involving mainly the songs of the river by women. Conversely, the upper wedge stands for action, involving the two male members in their encounters with the river, without the company of women. As for the relationship between the two wedges, one can very well say that creativity is a dynamic verbal "reflection" of the world of action, while the pattern of action also manifests itself in the process of creativity. The song in a microcosmic form bodies forth the conflict and love in life, and lessens the impact of the tragic event, as we shall soon see. In the same way, the action also determines the mode of creativity—the way a song is formalistically created. The two mirror forms, the upper and the lower wedges, can be distinct, for the purpose of analysis, but they are certainly inseparable. The song sung by the old man's wife, for instance, suggests in the fourth line the course of action she plans to take in life.

Nonetheless, if one were to overstress the lower wedge of creativity, one might simply develop an attitude that art as form is capable of taking up and actually subsuming all subject matters in life. The reification of a certain genre as pure form is the outcome of such an attitude. On the other hand, if one were to side with action and see creativity as a mechanical reflection of reality and that alone, the result would be to treat art as a subsidiary document of life. Obviously, neither attitude is altogether correct.

A more meaningful way to treat these two realms of human operations is to see them as open-ended and fluid, in the sense that each of them keeps intruding into the other, thereby constantly transforming their relationships. For this reason, a better graphic representation of creativity in relation to action would be to see the lower plane as being transformed, surrealistically, into a circle,

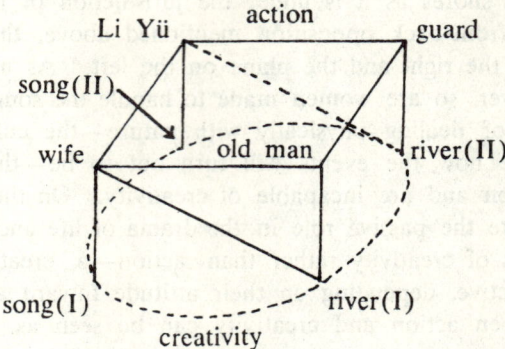

The present representation in an "impossible" figure eliminates, at the outset, the unnecessary dichotomy between art and life. Different elements exist in a fluid state along the circle and form complementary distributions with each other. The entire plane, in other words, exists like a magnetic field with forces running in different directions, yet maintaining a definite and detectable pattern.

To see how it works, we will have to see the circle transversely as,

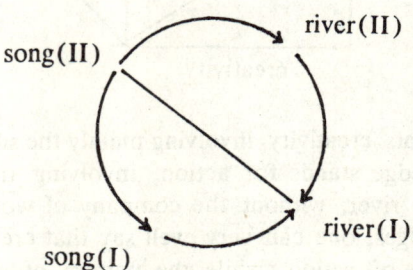

Song(II) is the text or, in this particular case, the four variants we have found. Song(I) can be said to be an *ur*-text. Consequently, Song(II) awaits being reconstructed into its prototype, Song(I)—hence the arrow on the left side of the circle.⁷ Song(I), according to the most complete prose introduction, is a verbal re-enactment of what happens at River(I)—therefore, the arrow pointing from Song(I) to River(I). Song(II), on the other hand, is a retelling of the entire action from the viewpoint of River(II). The arrow on top pointing to the right indicates such a secondary approximation. Be that as it may, River(II) is also tinged with the tragic coloring of River(I), especially from the point of view of Li Yü, who is after all "moved," and perpetuates the event by teaching her neighbor, an outsider, to sing the song. For this reason, the arrow on top runs beyond the medial point and reaches River(I),

---

⁷ Some critics actually believed that "The K'ung-hou Harp Tune" 箜篌引 was in fact a cultural product, inspired by the primitive "The K'ung-hou Harp Song" 箜篌曲 that is no longer existant. In other words, at a certain time in the ancient past there did exist two versions, Song(I) and Song(II). See Huang Chieh 黃節, *Han Wei yüeh-fu feng-chien* 漢魏樂府風箋 (Hong Kong: Shang-wu, 1961), p. 46.

which serves as the thematic core of the entire event. And one would not be surprised if in recomposing or reexperiencing Song(II), a singer or an audience strikes a direct passage from Song(II)—the text of the Song—directly to River(I)—an almost spontaneous, eye-witness response to the situation at the river bank, way back in the Han dynasty. In other words, the song as it is enables the reader to return to the communal feeling aroused by the tragic event of the demented husband. The diameter cutting from Song(II) to River(I) represents an ideal and total identification with the tragic event, either as a historical or a mythical experience.

III

We have so far considered all the possible passages from the song to the river. Next a consideration of the reversed passages is in order to ascertain the ways in which the river as an external reality makes its way into the song. (But before going into it, we must note that this approach is rather limited in effectiveness, unless one investigates the insertion of social formations into literary works. In other words, reality cuts into literature on a very specific sociocultural level and unspecified matching of the two realms of literature and society sheds little light. Short of a knowledge of the dynamic relationships between different classes, it is much more advisable to go back to the text.) Historically, according to *Feng-ch'an chi* 封禪記, the K'ung-hou harp as a musical instrument was not invented until after Emperor Wu of Han conquered what is present-day Vietnam in the sixth year of Yüan-ting 元鼎 (111 B.C.).[8] Based on this record, the song was probably not created before this time. In addition, it is also in the same period that Emperor Wu defeated the descendents of Wei Man 衞滿, who fled the Middle Kingdom in the beginning years of the Dynasty and established himself as the King of Korea. Korea, presumably the locale of the song, was in other words not annexed before this time and remained a relatively peripheral area in the Chinese civilization during the second century B.C. As such, the milieu of the song is probably seen as a rather uncultured state. In the minds of the singers, it is quite probable that the river poses a threat to their lives.

As a matter of fact, the river is so menacing that it appears as a lexical or a phonetic item in each and every line of a ballad made up of four four-character lines. The first two lines end with the word for "river" $g'\hat{a}$ and, therefore, rhyme with the simplest repetition, a kind of homoeoteleuton. Used in literate poetry, the device might appear mechanical; yet here in this spontaneous song, the repetition is designed to carry the perceptual repetition to the phonetic level so as to physically demonstrate the presence of the river in the song. The river's presence is constantly referred to for a very good reason. In Bruce F. Kawin's classification of different categories of repetition, this may very well belong to "the Falsification of Reality," which he sees as problem-solving:

> Freud pointed out that by repeating an experience we may become master of it.... Repetition in this case is operating to remove the emotional content from a mental experience.[9]

---

[8] Chang Shou-p'ing, pp. 45-46, 100.
[9] *Telling It Again and Again, Repetition in Literature and Film* (Ithaca and London: Cornell Univ. Press, 1972), pp. 26-27.

In other words, by repeating *g'â* in line 2, the singer wishes to create from a harsh, intimidating reality an illusion which might provide some temporary relief. But as we move on to line 3, *g'â* is placed in a different position and thereby destroys the illusion that has been built up so far.¹⁰ The change in position also changes the value of *g'â*. In the first two lines, *g'â* serves as the object of the transitive verb 渡 "to cross." In its new position in line 3, the river no longer follows a transitive verb. As a matter of fact, 墮 "to fall into" as an intransitive verb in the locative case puts the river in a new light. Instead of the objective or neutral case in which an item in the objective world waits to be acted upon—to be "crossed," specifically—the river is no longer the recipient of an action initiated by the agent. In other words, in the first two lines, the river is "crossed," but in the third line, the river is not exactly "drowned"; it "drowns [people] within." The river changes from a passive object to a receptacle of action. It now demands to be heeded immediately and, indeed, the reader does feel the dramatic change, for in the same line the hero meets his death in the river. Up to this point, the river operates on a factual level and possesses its full physical entity. Yet as we move into the last line (line 4), the *g'â* in our daily life is metamorphosed phonetically into a disillusioned attitude toward life in general. The way this metamorphosis is done is through the punning of "river" 河 with "how" 何, both sharing the same pronunciation *g'â*. Logically, this is like turning A into Ā, by treating the two terms as having the same phonetic value but semantically opposing one with the other; and by treating the river as the antonym of "how," an ultimate questioning of the meaning of life.¹¹ The question, "What could I do with you, Lord?" means more than what it asks. If the ballad is seen as a part of the larger reality, we can say that the line asks something to the effect, "What am I to do with life"? And judged from the implicit message of this line, her eventual suicide certainly comes as no surprise. If we take a second look at the lines, the song is actually a description of the erosion of life by *g'â*, first as an object to be defied by man, then as a recipient of the human action, and finally as an empty echo of man's disillusionment toward human relationships as well as life as a whole.

One of the characteristics of the English traditional ballad is the so-called "fifth-act" beginning. Lord Randal is found poisoned at the very beginning of the story. Edward starts the action by surprising us with a sword dripping with blood. In most cases, no attempt is made by the singer to provide us with the background information.¹² He does not tell us what goes before, for instance. And often he does not reveal to us what follows either. One way to account for this phenomenon is to see folk poetry as a product which springs up in a homogeneous environment between

---

¹⁰ Based on a different version of the third line which reads, "Fallen into the river, Lord, you died" 墮河公死, Yang Mu 楊牧 [C. H. Wang] compares the line to the peripeteia in a tragedy in the sense that the line marks a climactic point in the relationships between man and nature. Unlike the first two lines in which *"Kung"* precedes *"gâ,"* here the order is reversed —a linguistic reversal which parallels the turn of the tragic event. See *Ch'uan-t'ung ti yü hsien-tai ti* 傳統的與現代的 (Taipei: Chih-wen, 1974), pp. 1-14.

¹¹ For a more detailed analysis of this aspect, see Yang Mu.

¹² Among the laws of folk narratives Axel Olrik described, the Laws of Opening (*das Gesetz des Einganes*) specifies that the *Sage*, which includes practically all oral folk genres, does not begin with sudden actions. It begins by moving from calm to excitement. Obviously Olrik had in mind the emotional development of the narrative, not the purely narrative progression of the plot. See *The Study of Folklore*, ed. Alan Dundes (Englewood Cliffs: Prentice-Hall, 1965), pp. 129-41.

the singer and his audience. In a ballad such as this, with the listeners highly knowledgeable about the "goings-on" of the event, the singer naturally seeks to excel by recounting only the essential core of the story. And in doing so, not only is the beginning made abrupt. Even the main body of the story told in the ballad is liable to be given a "leaping" treatment. M. J. C. Hodgart compares this to Eisenstein's treatment of juxtaposing shots, as in

> He's throw the dark and throw the mark
> And throw the leaves of green.[13]

The three stages are given to us as three shots, and the listeners are supposed to infer a progression from it. In some cases the omission is such that one even gets the impression that events are rushing along. Notice, for example, the omission of the relative pronoun in a stanza from "Sir Patrick Spence":

> The king was written a braid letter,
> And signed it with his hand,
> And sent it to Sir Patrick Spence,
> Was walking on the sand.

In the same ballad the tragic climax is treated with a sleight of hand, as it were,

> O our Scots nobles wer richt laith
> To weet their cork-heild schoone;
> Both lang owre a' the play wer playd,
> Thair hats they swam aboone.

Such a leaping device is used primarily with the knowledge that the specific ballad community is capable of grasping the way the story develops—the dramatic effect through juxtaposition is probably only a secondary concern.

So far as homogeneity is concerned, the Chinese ballad in question seems to illustrate the situation. If we treat the guard and his wife as the first audience of the event as well as the song, we should expect them to know so much about the actual happening as not to crave for full details. In the same way, we as the present-day readers are but the audience several times removed. Nonetheless, what we are given is still an "in-person" report in the sense that the story is relayed to Li Yü, who recreates it for her neighbor who in turn goes on transmitting the story until it is written down in the present forms. The part on background information is recorded in the prose introductions which keep us informed of the genesis of the song. As a result, the song is capable of maintaining its original tacit quality without suffering from ambiguity.

IV

Very often the prose introductions are ignored by critics who see them as extrinsic, and not directly related to the ballads themselves. They have failed to see that the

---

[13] *The Ballad* (New York: Norton, 1962), p. 28. "Throw the mark" means "Through the murk."

introductions provide necessary background information upon which the ballads are built. What is even more significant is the fact that under the pressure of the introductions, the ballads themselves are forced to slough off unnecessary details and develop in the "leaping" manner, as in the case of "Sir Patrick Spence." It is sometimes not surprising to see these specimens bypassing, in their narrative development, the basic rule of cause-and-effect relationships. We have seen the aversions of Sir Patrick Spence and his men to getting their cork-heeled shoes wet followed immediately by a scene with their hats floating on the water. One act does not give rise to another on the basis of strict causality. In a way the hats substitute, rather than predicate, the shoes. In a humorous song in China, causality is even reversed and we see the sequence completely reshuffled,

> I was born earlier.
> My elder brother later.
> While Dad and Mom were getting married,
> I played the gong.
> In Grandma's Selection Rite, I held the box.
> I walked by my maternal uncle's house,
> And saw my maternal uncle rocking my Grandma.

> 先養我，後生哥
> 爹討媽，我打鑼
> 家公抓週我捧盒
> 我走舅爺門前過
> 舅爺在搖我家婆[14]

Admittedly this is not a typical case of the narrative progression in ballads, but it does show that one single mechanical causal relationship cannot possibly account for the folk genres. Take "Lord, Do Not Cross the River" for example. The song, when paraphrased, reads: I asked you not to cross the river/but you eventually crossed the river./ You fell into the river and died;/What could I do with you? Using Alan Dundes' model of morphology which he borrowed from V. Propp, we can see the four lines as a four-stage narrative progression.[15] Line 1 is an interdiction. Line 2 stands for violation. Line 3 indicates consequence and line 4 concludes with an attempted escape. In this particular case, to simplify the typology, line 3 can be seen as consequence I and line 4 consequence II, because the attempted escape does not actually take place until the old man's wife is through with her song. To further simplify the scheme, the four stages can further be grouped into bipolar narrative units. In terms of physical actions, line 3 is a direct consequence of line 2—the old man crossed the river(line 2) and as a result was drowned(line 3). On the emotional plane, however, line 2 is an outcome of line 1 in the sense that the old man's crossing of the river is a wilful contradiction of his wife's interdiction. Line 4, in the same way, is a direct emotional response to line 3—the death of her husband(line 3) gives rise to her mourning(line 4). The two bipolar pairs are further paralleled because what line 1

---

[14] The Chinese text is taken from Chu Tzu-ch'ing 朱自清, *Chung-kuo ko-yao* 中國歌謠 (Taipei: Shih-chieh, 1974), p. 147.

[15] "Structural Typology in North American Indian Folktales," *The Study of Folklore,* pp. 206-15.

is to line 2 is also what line 3 is to line 4. In both cases, action gives rise to reaction —one deed creates an emotional impact. Just as her interdiction meets with his violation, his consequence is also reciprocated by her mourning—a mourning which definitely contains a certain degree of disillusionment over their relationships. In graphic terms the narrative development can be seen as,

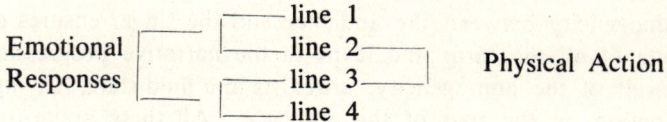

A relation like this is not exactly what one would call a direct and straightforward causality. Nor is the process of thinking what one would call lineal.[16] The song clearly builds itself up line by line and unit by unit, without following a pre-designed direction. In a sense, it tests different options until one comes to the end where some escape from the basic contradictions in life is found. Notice, for example, how the dramatis personae leap from the first person in line 1 to the second person in lines 2 and 3, and finally back to the first person in line 4. Notice also how the song shifts from an affirmative interdiction(line 1) to a negative violation(line 2) and consequence(line 3) and finally to her reaffirmation of her commitment.

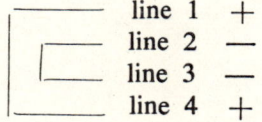

All these go to show that the song moves in a rather roundabout way in several aspects. The lines seem to progress by means of permutations. Line 1 flows into line 2, but not without an about-face twist (interdiction vs. violation). In the same way, line 2 finds its way into line 3, with a vital addition(the old man's death). Line 3 makes its secret entry into line 4 by transforming the substantive *g'â* "river" into a merely functional *g'â* "how." The same meandering method is also used in "South of the River" 江南, where the lotus in line 1 gives way to the lotus leaves in line 2. And in time the lotus leaves as objects are transformed into the lotus leaves indicating the space in which the fish sport.

---

[16] According to Pierre Maranda and Elli Göngäs Maranda,
> Analogy . . . is essentially "linear." Continuous analogy, A:B::B:C, "A is to B as B is to C," or discontinuous analogy, A:B::C:D, "A is to B as C is to D," cannot formalize the twists found in myths and which call for a non-linear formalization . . . . Lévi-Strauss' formula
> $$f_x(a):f_y(b)::f_x(b):f_a^{-1}(y)$$
> should be understood as the figuration of a mediating process where some dynamic roles are expressed more accurately than in a simple analogy model.

See "Structural Models in Folklore," *Structural Models in Folklore and Transformational Essays* (The Hague: Mouton, 1971), pp. 25-26. Even though the progression in this Chinese ballad does involve certain exchanges of role and the story does not progress on a straightforward basis, one would have to amass a large corpus of materials and impose upon them what Lévi-Strauss calls "Transcendental reduction" before one can confirm if the Chinese songs operate strictly on this model. In an intensive study of a song, it is inappropriate to generalize to that extent.

V

In sum, the oral ballads seem to employ a method which requires a constant shifting of attention as a mediating strategy. And this seems to be caused by the following factors. The spontaneous oral composition encourages a narrative progression on a local basis. The comprehensive structure is put in a secondary position. Secondly, the homogeneity between the audience and the singer ensures effective communication in spite of all the turns and leaps in the narrative progression. Last but not least, as a result of the homogeneity, art exists in a fluid state, leaving ample room for direct participation on the part of the audience. All these make it easy for folk poetry to serve as a communal act and to mediate between the oppositional forces between nature and man.

To further elucidate these characteristics, let us now examine a literate counterpart of this oral ballad. As in the case of "South of the River," the folk piece is also followed in *Yüeh-fu shih chi* by no less than seven literary imitation pieces, all under the same titles of either "The K'ung-hou Harp Tune" 箜篌引 or "Lord, Do Not Cross the River" 公無渡河. Without any exceptions, they all deal with the same subject matter, but in a much individualized way. Liu Hsiao-wei 劉孝威 of the Liang dynasty (A.D. 502-83) expands the original into,

> Please do not cross the river.
> The river is wide, the wind harsh.
> The mast topples, the Gold Crow sets.
> The boat capsizes, the rhino oars sink.
>
> Blue carriages offered, to no avail.
> White horses sacrificed, in vain.
> Picking stones hurts the unmated heart.
> Tumbling Wall buries the widow's sleeves.
>
> The coupled swords will be reunited in the same water.
> With the spirit drowned, the principles pass away.
> You be the courtier of the River God.
> And I be the concubine of the stream.[17]

請公無渡河，河廣風威厲
檣偃落金烏，舟傾沒犀枻

紺盖空嚴祀，白馬徒牲祭
銜石傷寡心，崩城掩孀袂

劍飛猶共水，魂沈理俱逝
君爲川后臣，妾作姜妃娣

One cannot deny that the literate ballad here is of a longer length than the original and, as such, elaborations can be easily made and a greater totality achieved. None-

---

[17] The "Gold Crow" refers to the sun. The "blue carriages" are used in the sacrificial ceremony paying tribute to the river spirits.

theless, what is significant is that the leaping progression in the original is here replaced by a lineal, three-section structure. Section I (lines 1-4) informs us of the interdiction and the consequence of the violation. Section II (lines 5-8) continues by first reviewing the fruitless sacrifices made previously and next by invoking mythical models of romantic love. Section III (lines 9-12) concludes with a reaffirmation of their love eterne and by alluding to her wish to rejoin her husband by serving in the same court in the watery realm. Basically the progression here follows that of a typical elegy in which the departure of the hero is described but not accounted for. Then in the second stage of the narrative progression, the tragic event is followed by a ritual of mourning in which the entire universe is enlisted to share the personal sentiment of the poet. Finally, as the last stage, the entire elegiac cycle concludes with a compromise that despite death there is such a thing as glory. The development clearly follows distinctly a beginning, a middle and an end—a tripartite construction based on the development of the heroine's feelings.

In the second place, unlike the original where the details are trimmed down to the essential core, here the creative principle is one of expansion and multiplicity rather than contraction. As a matter of fact, the descriptive details are generously employed—so much so that sometimes the narrative line tends to be drowned by lyrical strains. The result is the "lyricalization" of the narrative lines. Lines 3 and 4, for example, are noted for visual perspicuity: one is made to witness the shipwreck in very elaborate detail. The details which include images and allusions are, moreover, usually so carefully juxtaposed that they form an emotional unity of their own. The images in Section I dramatize the glorious death of the hero. On the contrary, the allusions in Section II are designed to bring to the fore the sentiment of universal mourning that we have mentioned earlier. In the same way, Section III also uses details to convey the glory to be achieved after death. In other words, the major portion of the poem (lines 3-10) relies on descriptive details to impose the tripartite structure. And, with the use of juxtapositions, technically called coupling—lines 3 vs. 4; 5 vs. 6; 7 vs. 8; 9 vs. 10—the narrative entities succeed in expressing unified ideas that are then fitted into the formal scheme of the poem. The result is the fullness of details, the continuity of the narrative structure, the closedness of form, and the prevalence of individual visions that are seldom found in the oral ballads.

For all the differences that might exist between the oral and the literate modes of presentation, when a literary poet such as Liu sets out to imitate the original ballad, there is an unmistakable connection between them. The original ballad is treated as an emotional core which varies from one imitating poet to another.[18] In Liu's case he sees the first line as the core, for he does not hesitate to use the first line in the original, almost as it is, thus provoking among his readers the original response to the prototype. And as he goes on, he is mainly concerned with the tragic consequence of man's confrontation with the inevitable. As a solution Liu advocates entrusting one's hope to the other world—a highly personalized vision which is quite far removed from the original situation. The recreated literary poem is, in short, a symbolic reenactment of the original ballad. To put it in a slightly different way, the literate imitation, though seeking to evoke the original communal awareness in which the fate of

---

[18] For a study of the "emotional core," see Tristram P. Coffin, "Mary Hamilton and the Anglo-American Ballad as an Art Form," *The Critics and the Ballad,* ed. MacEdward Leach and Tristram P. Coffin (Carbondale: Southern Illinois Univ. Press, 1961), pp. 245-56.

mankind depends on the mediations of oppositional forces, merely uses the prototype as a point of departure. As the lyrical line is developed and elaborated, personal vision is injected and soon takes over the universal landscape, which is to a certain extent internalized. The universal conflict between man and nature is abstracted into a Platonic love between the "courtier of the River God" and the "concubine of the stream."

The Substantive Level Revisited: Concreteness and Nature Imagery in T'ang Poetry

William Tay

I

In his essay "The Substantive Level," W. K. Wimsatt proposes the following "new table of styles . . . in description" to account for the concreteness and abstractness of poetry:

1. The abstract or less than specific-substantive style: e.g., *implement*.
2. The minimum concrete or specific-substantive style: e.g., *spade*.
3. The extra-concrete, the detailed, or more than specific style: e.g., *rusty garden spade*.[1]

In poetry, however, the "detailed, or more than specific style" of the third level may appear in a more complicated and elaborate manner than the simple example provided by Wimsatt. Fully aware of this fact, Wimsatt moves on to say that "most adjectival elaboration shows at least a tendency toward the more than specific. . . . " But even on the third level, some descriptive expressions naturally are more detailed than others. In Wimsatt's opinion, "violets dim" and "lady-smocks all silver-white" are not as detailed as "cowslips wan that hang the pensive head" and "the coming musk-rose, full of dewy wine," and even less so than the following two descriptive expressions, which Wimsatt considers to be "the most characteristic examples of twentieth century imagism": "Rose, harsh rose, marred and with stint of petals," and "purple grackles —shining and bulging under leaves." Surely one can find descriptions even more detailed, but for the convenience of discussion, descriptions with minute differences in elaborateness are all classified under the same category.

There is, however, one kind of concreteness which proves to be a slippery problem for the classifier of descriptive styles. This is the kind of concreteness "some-

---

[1] W. K. Wimsatt, Jr., *The Verbal Icon* (1954; rpt. New York: Noonday, 1958), p. 138.

times achieved within the general decorum of 'poetic diction.'" The poetic diction of eighteenth century English writing usually replaces the class name by a more generic name, which is preceded by a qualifier just sufficient to denote the original class name. For instance, "fish" is substituted by "scaly breed," and "sheep" by "fleecy kind." In Wimsatt's opinion, this kind lies somewhere "between the more and the less concrete, with the precise point of specific and substantial concreteness unmentioned but present between."[2]

The second level of concreteness, "the purely specific or substantive," according to Wimsatt, "may be the rarest." Examples of this level of minimum concreteness are difficult to find. "A few lines together may be found in a nature poet whose slant is toward the simplicities and honesties of rustic labor. . . . The style has been employed for effects of a certain severity." The instance cited by Wimsatt is as follows:

> Under some mulberry trees I found
> A little pool; and in brief space
> With all the water that was there
> I fill'd my pitcher and stole home.
> —*The Sick King in Bokhara*[3]

In giving us a table of styles with three levels of concreteness, Wimsatt by no means implies that one level is necessarily more valuable or more "poetic" than the other; he is merely trying to provide a scheme to differentiate the various styles of description in a systematic and objective way. In the "second half of the eighteenth century," Wimsatt observes, "as Scottish associational rhetoricians moved away from the more Platonic forms of neoclassicism," the "schoolbook rule that verbal discourse, and especially description, ought to be particular or concrete" began to prevail.[4] And in modern times, the "imagist view of poetry and related modern views have tended to see precisely [the third] level of concreteness as the poetic level."[5] But Wimsatt declines to be judicial and states clearly that his analysis and description in the essay are to remain neutral and be void of value judgement. This stance will be adopted in the present paper.

In Wimsatt's table of levels, specificity of description is linked with concreteness; and the two terms at times seem to be interchangeable. One question immediately arises: is descriptive specificity an indispensable attribute of concreteness? The answer is positive. Concreteness is conveyed by the use of a "concrete term," which linguistically can be defined as "denoting a person, animate or inanimate being, or in general anything physically real and perceptible by the senses or organs of perception." Opposing the concrete term is the "abstract term," which is, "in general, any term, word or expression which denotes a notion, concept, idea."[6] "Implement" is too general a term to evoke a visual form in the imagination, but not so once the "implement" assumes the specificity of a "spade." Furthermore, according to one ex-

---

[2] Ibid., p. 142.
[3] Ibid., p. 139.
[4] Ibid., p. 133.
[5] Ibid., p. 139.
[6] Mario Pei and Frank Gaynor, *A Dictionary of Linguistics* (New York: Philosophical Library, 1954), p. 44 and pp. 4-5.

planation, "to think concretely is to represent general relations as embodied in particular instances; and so to delineate the object thought of after the fashion and with the determining details of immediate perceptive experience."[7] "Spade" is an "implement," but by calling an "implement" a "spade," it assumes a "particular" identity. A "spade" is a "concrete term" because it is perceptible and has a particular shape, which can be physically known. The expression "rusty garden spade" is the "extra-concrete," when compared with simply "spade," for it provides more "determining details" of specificity. Hence, when a description is considered as concrete, the things and qualities it describes must be physically perceptible. The level of concreteness is then determined by the specificity conveyed by the details.

II

In his book *Chinese Lyricism,* Burton Watson devotes part of a chapter on T'ang poetry to a study of the nature imagery.[8] The method employed is the statistical count of the frequency of the nature images. The material used is the eighteenth century anthology *T'ang-shih san-pai-shou* 唐詩三百首. The anthology has been very popular among the general reading public ever since its compilation. Although it has a few drawbacks, such as the total omission of Li Ho's poetry, the anthology, actually containing 317 poems, includes works from all the important periods of T'ang poetry. The dominant forms are the *lü-shih* 律詩 (five- or seven-character "regulated" poems usually in eight lines) and *chüeh-chü* 絕句 (five- or seven-character four-line "curtailed" poems). In his counting, Watson has left out all the place names, as he believes that "it is naturally difficult for a foreigner to assess the emotional effect which such names may have for the Chinese reader."[9] Apart from emotional effect, place names in T'ang poetry, due to the continuous cultural tradition, often carry "historical or legendary associations," which can evoke "dramatic or nostalgic overtones."[10] Most relevant to the present study is the visual quality some of the place names harbor. A few examples will suffice: "Yellow Flower Rill" 黃花川, "Green Stream" 青溪, and "White Rock Rapids" 白石灘.[11] The result is that some of the place names may contribute certain visual effects to the texture of the poetry.

In Watson's discussion of the nature images, the term "imagery" is used interchangeably with "image." An "image" can be defined as "the reproduction in the mind of a sensation produced by a physical perception." But "more specifically in literary usage, imagery refers to images produced in the mind by language, whose words and statements may refer either to experiences which could produce physical perceptions were the reader actually to have those experiences, or to the sense-impressions themselves."[12] This definition limits the production of image to the medium of language and confines the image within the sphere of physical perceptions. Since many critics

---

[7] James M. Baldwin, ed., *Dictionary of Philosophy and Psychology* (Gloucester, Mass.: Peter Smith, 1925), I, 209.

[8] *Chinese Lyricism* (New York: Columbia Univ. Press, 1971), pp. 122-37.

[9] Ibid., p. 129.

[10] Ibid., p. 128.

[11] Wai-lim Yip, *Hiding the Universe* (New York: Grossman, 1972), pp. 55, 120.

[12] Alex Preminger, ed., *Encyclopedia of Poetry and Poetics* (Princeton: Princeton Univ. Press, 1965), p. 363.

have, like Watson, used the two terms alternatively to refer to the same thing, here I propose to do the same, with the definition quoted above as the general guideline.

Critics have repeatedly proclaimed that Chinese poetry is replete with the so-called "simple images."[13] In Watson's statistical study, the T'ang images are divided into eight groups: land formations, water (and related images), weather, heavenly bodies, tree, flower, plant, and bird. Most of the images counted, one notices, are represented in Chinese only by one character, which, needless to say, is a noun. In the following discussion, these one-character nouns will be referred to as "simple images." To call a noun a simple image is seemingly awkward in English. This kind of image, however, enjoys a fairly high frequency in the nature poetry of Wang Wei 王維; and some kind of a term is needed to classify it. Often the simple noun image is modified either by an adjective (e.g., "long river" 長河) or another noun (e.g., "pine wind" 松風). These are also considered as simple images, since the modifier attributes a quality to the noun and becomes an integral part. From a comparative perspective, these images are indeed "simple," for they often consist of only one or two characters, and never more than three, while their counterparts in the Western languages may be formed by several words or one statement. When critics like James Liu and Wai-lim Yip describe Chinese poetic image as "simple," I believe it is this verbal economy that they have in mind.

Watson's counting finds the weather imagery as the largest single group of images among the eight. As Watson has woven all his figures into running commentaries, and it is cumbersome to quote long passages, the figures are tabulated according to the frequency of appearances. (The plural numbers assigned to the nouns are deleted here in most cases.)

Weather Images

wind	:	115
cloud	:	89
rain	:	52
snow	:	32
mist	:	29
dew	:	23
frost	:	13
haze	:	7
fog	:	6

After the weather images comes the land formations group. The most favored image of this group is that of "mountain ranges." Here Watson has not made it clear which particular Chinese noun or compound he is counting, nor has he informed us whether synonyms are grouped under the same heading. But since the counting of Wang Wei's nature images in the next section finds the noun "mountain" 山 leading all other mountain images by a large margin, it is safe to speculate that Watson's figure refers to this noun and possibly other synonymous noun compounds such as "mountain range" 山嶺. The table for this group is as follows:

---

[13] For example, James Liu in *The Art of Chinese Poetry* (Chicago: Chicago Univ. Press, 1962), p. 104.

Land Formations Images

mountain range	:	150
mountain (with "wind")	:	115
stone	:	23
ravine	:	11
stream valley	:	10

Since Watson has left out place names, which include a large number of mountain names, the number of mountain images is considerably smaller than it should be.

The next largest group of images is that of water. The character "water" 水, when used by itself or with a modifier, may sometimes mean a river or stream. Again, Watson has not explained or clarified his rules for the counting, and there is no way of knowing whether the figure for water includes those words literally meaning "water" but contextually referring to a river. In Chinese, the term "river" may be represented by these different words: *chiang, ho, ch'uan,* 江, 河, 川; since Watson has not given any explanation, it is likely that they are lumped into the same category.

Water Images

river	:	81
water	:	79
sea	:	36
waves	:	29
spring	:	18
lake	:	9
pond	:	8

After this group comes the images of heavenly bodies. Moon, sky, and sun outnumber all other images.

Heavenly Bodies Images

moon (or moonlight)	:	96
sky	:	76
sun	:	72
stars	:	13
Milky Way	:	8
Big Dipper	:	4

The figures for the images of tree, plant, flower, and bird are listed in the following. Placing them together, instead of separating them with brief comments, may reveal the popularity of the generic names in T'ang nature images more effectively:

Tree Images

tree	:	51
willow	:	29
pine	:	24
bamboo	:	12
peach	:	10

mulberry	:	7
cypress	:	6
maple	:	6
cassia	:	5
pear	:	5
plum	:	4

Plant Images

plant (*ts'ao*)	:	42
p'eng (wild raspberry)	:	8
moss	:	6

Flower Images

flower	:	87
fu-jung (hibiscus)	:	9
lotus	:	4
orchid	:	3
chrysanthemum	:	3

Bird Images[14]

bird	:	31
wild goose	:	23
phoenix	:	13
crane	:	6
mandarin duck	:	5
luan	:	5
oriole	:	5
swallow	:	5
gull	:	4
egret	:	4

It is obvious that the T'ang poets, rather than naming and identifying the species of the trees, plants, flowers, and birds specifically, are more in favor of the general reference to the genera. In the four groups, only the bird images offer the greatest variety and maximum particularity. Still, the generality of the "bird" is preferred over the particularity of the species. The generic name of the "tree" also outnumbers all other species by quite a wide margin, but the multiplicity of the species can be regarded as quite sufficient, if it is to be compared with that of the flower and plant groups. These two groups are the poorest in variety and specificity—this probably will startle readers familiar with the myriad profusion of flowers and plants in, say, Shakespeare and Milton.

In the T'ang poets' choice of nature images, Watson concludes, the highly specific is generally avoided. In his counting, he has noticed that the highly abstract is also absent: "Almost never does one encounter a term or concept as broad, for example, as the English 'nature' or 'natural world,' or even our 'scenery' or 'landscape.' "[15] As

---

[14] Both phoenix and *luan* are mythical creatures and perhaps should not be counted as nature images. Since Watson has done so, they are listed for reference.

[15] *Chinese Lyricism*, p. 128.

such, the natural world presented by T'ang poets tends to be very much generalized. "There is, after all," Watson continues to observe, "only one moon and one sun, and, unless we are meteorologists, we tend to think of wind, clouds, rain, or snow as entities that are not subject to further division."[16] These images, however, are quite frequently modified by an adjective or another noun. Modification is not considered in Watson's statistics; and his figures for the images make no distinction between the qualified and unqualified simple images. Hence it is impossible to determine the level of description of these images. "White snow" and "white clouds," two popular images in T'ang poetry, cannot be more specific than simply "snow" and "clouds," since they are generally white; but "dawn wind" and "pine wind" certainly are more specific than "wind."

Watson's conclusion of generality being preferred over specificity in the selection of nature images is based upon the popularity of the genus in the flower, plant, tree, and bird groups. The level of descriptive concreteness, however, involves not only the distinction between genus and species, but also the degrees of specificity in modification. In Wimsatt's scale, "dawn wind" is descriptively more concrete than "wind." In order to find out more about the level of concreteness in T'ang poetry, the images of one collection of Wang Wei's nature poems will be counted and classified.

III

Wai-lim Yip's 葉維廉 *Hiding the Universe,* a collection of Wang Wei's poems in English translation, is the text used in the counting. The reason for choosing this anthology instead of others is obvious: it has selected the major nature poems of Wang Wei with the sole purpose of introducing him as a nature poet. The more discursive poems written by this poet on various other subjects are excluded. Such exclusion, however, helps to ensure the "purity" of the material for our statistics. The collection contains fifty-two poems by Wang Wei, a letter to P'ei Ti, and twenty poems written by P'ei Ti in response to Wang Wei's works. The Chinese text reproduced *en face* to the English translation is from the *Ssu-pu pei-yao* 四部備要 edition. The dominant forms are the five-character *lü-shih* and *chüeh-chü*. In my counting, noun compounds in co-ordination are split into two characters and considered as two simple images: e.g., *t'ien ti* 天地 are separated into "heaven" and "earth." In the case of *yün-shan* 雲山 "cloud mountain," "cloud," though a noun itself, is the modifier of "mountain," thus not counted as an independent image. Similarly, when "flower" 花 is used with the name of a species, as in "peach flower" 桃花, it is not counted separately. My figures have distinguished the modified nouns from those not modified. Some translators tend to consider static verbs as modifiers and render them likewise, as in the line "Cold weather: red leaves are sparse"[17] 天寒紅葉稀. Word-for-word the line reads like this: "sky / cold / red / leaves / sparse." In my counting, "cold" will remain as a static verb.

Following Watson's precedent, the nature images of Wang Wei's poems are divided into eight groups. In the tree group, the genus "tree" appears 15 times in the synonymous forms of "tree" 樹, "wood" 木, and "forest" 林. In every appearance this simple image is modified by an adjective or another noun.

---

[16] Ibid., p. 129.
[17] Yip, p. 85.

Tree Images	Q.	Unq.	T.[18]
tree	15		15
pine	2	4	6
willow	2	3	5
bamboo	1	4	5
peach		3	3
mulberry		2	2
cassia		2	2
cypress		1	1
hemp		1	1
sycamore	1		1
plum	1		1
ashtree	1		1
apricot	1		1
dogwood		1	1
	24	21	45

Comparing these figures with Watson's, the results actually concur. The generic term assumes the highest frequency of appearance, with pine, willow, and bamboo being the most popular species in both tables.

In the plant group, "grass" leads the list, and the general term "vegetation" appears 3 times in different characters. Ten other species are mentioned only once, so the specific names are not listed.

Plant Images	Q.	Unq.	T.
grass	2	1	3
vegetation	2	1	3
moss	2		2
10 other species	4	6	10
	10	8	18

The outcome here is not so unequivocal, but it is still safe to surmise that, as in Watson's findings, "grass" is the most prominent genus in Wang Wei's plant images.

As for the flower images, the high frequency of the genus again coincides with Watson's statistics.

Flower Images	Q.	Unq.	T.
flower	2	4	6
hibiscus	1	3	4
catkin		1	1
lotus		1	1
	3	9	12

---

[18] Q = Qualified, Unq = Unqualified, and T = Total.

The figures for the bird images once more find the genus dominating and the species lagging behind.

Bird Images	Q.	Unq.	T.
bird	6		6
oriole	1	1	2
wild goose	2		2
pheasant		2	2
egret	2		2
seagull	1		1
magpie		1	1
eagle		1	1
	12	5	17

It is obvious that Wang Wei, like his fellow T'ang poets, prefers to use the generic names in the description of trees, plants, flowers, and birds. These inhabitants of his natural landscape tend to remain unidentified, vague and general, though they can also appear distinctly and vividly with particular names.

In the figures for the images of land formations, 16 times out of a total of 27, the simple image "mountain" is not modified. The total of the unqualified images also exceeds that of the qualified.

Land Formations Images	Q.	Unq.	T.
mountain	11	16	27
valley		4	4
peak	2	1	3
stone	2		2
field	1	1	2
islet		1	1
bank	1		1
desert	1		1
	18	23	41

In the group of water images, this situation is reversed. Though the leading images are frequently modified, the unqualified images hold a large proportion. Six different characters denoting "stream" or "river" are grouped together (澗，溪，川，津，河，江), as are the synonymous terms for waves (波，漪). Among the 13 mentions of "water," 6 are joined by "pond" or "stream" to form compounds, 4 are unqualified and 3 qualified. The word *"p'u"* 浦 usually refers to a cove, but in Wang Wei it sometimes is used to mean a "stretch of water." These two meanings, along with 淼漫, a compound synonymous with a "stretch of water," are all put under *p'u*.

Water Images	Q.	Unq.	T.
river (stream)	9	5	14
water	9	4	13

waves		5	5
p'u	2	3	5
lake		3	3
spring	1	1	2
pond	1		1
sea		1	1
ferry	1		1
	28	17	45

Only three images can be located for the heavenly bodies group, and the figures for the qualified and unqualified images are almost a tie.

Heavenly Bodies Images	Q.	Unq.	T.
sky	2	7	9
sun	4	3	7
moon	5	2	7
	11	12	23

As for the weather images, more appear in the modified form, but the margin is not wide.

Weather Images	Q.	Unq.	T.
cloud	5	5	10
rain	4	2	6
wind	3	1	4
mist	2		2
snow		2	2
fog		1	1
haze	1		1
smoke	1		1
	16	11	27

For these four groups, the qualified and the unqualified images appear to have a 55% versus 45% distribution. But if the first four groups are included, the unqualified images are lowered to roughly 40%. Most noticeable among the first four groups is the fact that the generic names of "tree" and "bird" always appear with modifiers. "Flower," however, appears to be unmodified most of the time. The trend of the leading images, one also notices, is crucial to the outcome of the total figures. In all eight cases, when the leading image is qualified, the total favors the qualified too. The proportions of the unqualified and qualified in the leading images are reflected in the total. This leads one to conjecture that certain rules of description in Wang Wei can be derived from these figures. Mountains and flowers tend to remain unmodified. Images of birds, weather, and water are usually modified. Trees, plants, and heavenly bodies waver between the two poles.

The unmodified mode of description in Wang Wei is, according to Wimsatt's scale, the second level of descriptive specificity, the minimum concrete. This level is considered by Wimsatt to be the rarest in English poetry. Since this style amounts to roughly 40%, it is not so "rare" in Wang Wei's nature poems. Among the modified images, the two-character type is the most prevalent, and the structure is either noun-noun or adjective-noun. These simple images possess specific names, but they are only described by one modifier, thus limiting the specificity. Wimsatt would probably view them as staying near the "beginning of [his] list of examples"—the "violets dim" and "lady-smocks all silver-white" rather than the marred and stinted rose. Occasionally the modifier in a simple image may be a noun compound, as in "peach-flower water" 桃花水, but the "peach-flower" can only be counted as one detail. In other words, a Chinese nature image can be on the level of extra-concrete with an English one, but the latter may have more specific details.

IV

One cannot help but wonder why the descriptive specificity is restricted in Wang Wei's, or speaking in broader terms, the T'ang poets' nature images. Perhaps the answer can be found through an examination of the form of T'ang poetry, which is also known as "Recent Style Poetry" 近體詩. In *T'ang-shih san-pai-shou,* 227 poems are in *lü-shih* or *chüeh-chü* form; and the line numbers are usually limited to eight and four respectively. These two most popular forms of T'ang poetry can be regarded as limited in length when compared with English poetic forms. Another reason may be the brevity of the line, which generally consists of five or seven characters—since Chinese is monosyllabic, the numbers of words then correspond with that of the syllables. Compactness and density become the inherent characteristics of this kind of poetry. This has long been noticed by many Western critics, and by now seems to be a point overly belabored. The succinctness, one suspects, is forced upon the poets by the terseness of the line, since each line is a complete syntactic unit with enjambment totally absent from T'ang poetry.[19] In a line of five characters, the restriction or sacrifice seems to be on the descriptive details, providing space for other elements.

The semantic structure of the pentasyllabic line appears to have helped limit the descriptive specificity and create the modifiers in their present forms. As Wang Li has stated in *Han-yü shih-lü-hsüeh,* the metrical structure is almost always 2-2-1, with the main caesura after the second word, but the semantic structure has more variations: 1-1-3, 2-1-2, 1-3-1, 2-3, 3-2, 4-1, 1-4. The most prevalent, however, is the 2-3 structure, because the 2-1 of the metrical structure can be easily combined to provide parallelism on both metrical and semantic levels.[20] The metrical 2-2-1 or the semantic 2-3 structure naturally confines the length of the modification, thereby prompting the predominance of the monosyllabic modifier. Let us now examine closely Wang Wei's oft-quoted poem "Bird-Singing Stream" 鳥鳴澗, and hopefully it will illustrate these observations effectively by itself:

---

[19] Wang Li 王力, *Han-yü shih-lü-hsüeh* 漢語詩律學 (1957; rpt. Shanghai: Chung-hua, 1964), p. 11.
[20] Ibid., pp. 230-233.

```
man         leisure     cassia      flower      fall
night       quiet       spring      mountain    empty
moon        rise        startle     mountain    bird
at-times    sing        spring      stream      middle
```

Man at leisure. Cassia flowers fall.
Quiet night. Spring mountain is empty.
Moon rises. Startles—a mountain bird.
It sings at times in the spring stream.[21]

人閒桂花落，夜靜春山空。
月出驚山鳥，時鳴春澗中。

The grammatical structure of the first two lines is as follows:

> noun/static verb—noun compound/verb
> noun/static verb—noun modifier/noun/static verb

There are four simple images and four verbs. Only one simple image has a monosyllabic modifier. The "man," "cassia flower," and "night" are presented in a bare, essential, and sketchy manner. What kind of a man is he? What are the flowers like? And how is the night? These are all unsaid and left for the reader's imagination. The conciseness of the line is such that details like these find no room in the poem at all.

In Wang Li's opinion, metrically and semantically, the heptasyllabic line is an extended form of the pentasyllabic. Often two characters can be deleted from a heptasyllabic line with no drastic alteration of the meaning. Seven ways of "extending" a line from five to seven characters are listed.[22] Naturally this is only an exercise used to illustrate a point in discussion; it does not imply that poets actually compose in this manner. The seven ways are quoted here with examples from Wang Wei's works. The words underlined are those that can be deleted.

(a). Disyllabic modifier added before the subject.

> *protect Chiang* (tribe) colonel morning station fort
> *crush capture* general night cross Liao (river)

> The Protector of Chiang, in the morning, reported at the fort.
> The General of Victory, at night, crossed the River Liao.[23]

護羌校尉初乘障，破虜將軍夜渡遼。

(b). Adverbs of time or place added at the beginning.

> *tree below* water sound clamor word laugh
> *crag among* tree color hide house lattice

---

[21] Yip, p. 81.
[22] Wang Li, pp. 234-35.
[23] Wang Wei 王維, *Wang-yu-ch'eng chi chien-chu* 王右丞集箋注, ed. Chao Tien-ch'eng 趙殿成 (Hong Kong: Chung-hua, 1972), I, 176. All subsequent page numbers from (b) to (g) refer to this edition, and all the translations are mine.

Below the trees, sounds of water clamor with talk and laughter.
Among the crags, colors of trees hide the latticed houses from sight.

(p. 177)

林下水聲喧語笑，巖間樹色隱房櫳。

(c). Monosyllabic modifier added before the subject or the verb.

gold cup *slowly* drink clear song revolve
painted boat *lightly* move glamorous dance turn

Golden cup, drinking slowly—clear song roams.
Show boat, moving lightly—glamorous dance circles.

(p. 264)

金杯緩酌清歌轉，畫舸輕移艷舞廻。

(d). Monosyllabic modifier added before the verb and the Goal (this term includes the direct and indirect object, and the locative).

morning wave jade pendant approach gold palace
evening hold imperial book bow ornate living-quarter

Morning—waving jade pendant, approached golden court.
Evening—carrying Imperial documents, bowed to ornate palace.

(p. 184)

晨搖玉珮趨金殿，夕奉天書拜瑣闈。

(e). Reduplication as modifier or 連緜字 (alliteration and/or riming compounds) added at the beginning or in the middle. (The example is a reduplication).

mo-mo (overcast) water paddy fly white egret
shade shade summer tree sing yellow oriole

Mist over mist: water paddies, flies a white egret.
Shade upon shade: summer trees, sings a yellow oriole.

(p. 187)

漠漠水田飛白鷺，陰陰夏木囀黃鸝。

(f). Adverbial, predicate, or verb phrase with preceding adverbial added at the beginning or in the middle. (The example belongs to the third case).

how like jade palace born three fragrant-herb
how have brass pool rise five cloud

How can it be compared with the three fragrant herbs sprouting in the jade palace?
How can it be matched with the five noble clouds rising from the brass pool?

(p. 174)

豈如玉殿生三秀，詎有銅池出五雲。

(g). Verb phrase added at the beginning, with the next five words as the Goal.

how dislike Shang P'ing marriage marrying-off early

but detest T'ao Ling leave office late

Shang P'ing's swift handling of children's marriages is admired (i.e., retiring early to be a hermit).
T'ao Ling's lingering in office is detested.

(p. 187)

豈厭尚平婚嫁早，卻嫌陶令去官遲。

In the first five cases, the addition (or deletion) are all descriptive details. They all contribute specificity and extra-concreteness to the simple images. In (a), the general is identified as the one with the title meaning "enemy-crushing and captive-taking." In (b), the trees are located among the crags. In (c), the boat is painted and the movement is light. In (d), the documents are those from the court and are carried away in the evening. And finally in (e), the summer trees are presented as exuberant and shady. The last two examples (f and g), however, have only increased the syntactic complexity. In other words, when the poet is given the space, nearly always he attributes more modifying details (i.e., specificity and concreteness) to his images. This, in turn, proves the point noted earlier: the limitation and simplicity of the modification are mainly due to the brevity of the line and, though not as significant, the shortness of the poem.

V

In modern English, according to Thomas Bever and Peter Rosenbaum, there is a regular rule which "extends surface quality adjectives which are drawn from a restricted set of abstract qualities."[24] This can be formulated as:

$$\begin{Bmatrix} \text{adjective concrete} \\ \text{surface quality} \end{Bmatrix} \longrightarrow \text{adjective abstract}$$

Such an extension usually enlarges the usage of the adjective. This, explain the two linguists, is why the adjective "colorful" can be applied to both the concrete noun "ball" and the abstract noun "idea." A diagram is devised to analyze and explain this fact:

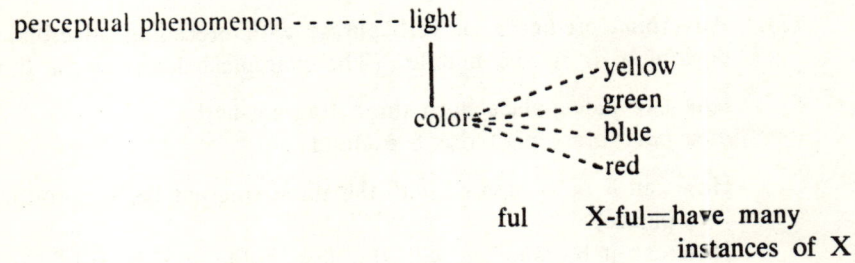

Hence, the statement "the ball is colorful" means that the ball possesses the several qualities of X. But when the word "colorful" is applied to "idea," as in "the idea is

---

[24] Thomas Bever and Peter Rosenbaum, "Some Lexical Structures and Their Empirical Validity," in *Readings in English Transformational Grammar,* ed. Roderick Jacobs and Peter Rosenbaum (Waltham, Mass. and London: Ginn, 1970), p. 15.

colorful," this adjective is interpreted as "having simultaneously a large set of potentially distinguishing characteristics." This broadening of usage is seen as the "metaphorical extensions of certain words from their original lexical structure."[25] One cannot physically perceive an "idea" in several different colors, but one can infer the abstract interpretation from the concrete phenomenon, which may have been visually experienced before. When applied to "idea," the concrete adjective "colorful" is "metaphorically extended" to become an "adjective abstract."

As we have noted earlier, a simple image in T'ang poetry can be modified by another noun. In the Chinese language, a noun when used grammatically as an adjective needs no verbal alteration. Generally this is not so in English and quite often orthographical changes are required. A concrete noun is the linguistic sign of an actual thing in the world. Inherent in a physical thing may be several surface qualities. Once a noun is used to describe another noun, these qualities may be implied without being specifically pinpointed. In short, when the ball is described as "colorful," it is not entirely clear what and how many colors are actually referred to. The impression created is general and unspecific, though one can assume that "several" colors are meant here. At this level, however, the adjective is still a concrete one. Many of the noun-modifiers in T'ang poetry operate in a similar way—creating general but not specific impressions, implying several qualities but not pinning down the particular one (or ones). This reminds us of the generality produced by the pervasiveness of the generic names in T'ang nature images.

One such noun-modifier from a poem by Tu Fu 杜甫 will be analyzed.

"Moonlit Night"
Tonight, moon over Fu-chou.
My wife watches it alone there,
I think of my children across such distance;
They don't understand why I am in Ch'ang-an.
Fragrant mist wets cloud-locks.
Clear moonlight chills white arms.
When can we lean on the open casement together,
Doubly shone, as tears dry up.[26]

今夜鄜州月，閨中只獨看。
遙憐小兒女，未解憶長安。
香霧雲鬟濕，清輝玉臂寒。
何時倚虛幌，雙照淚痕乾。

A word-for-word translation of the sixth line is: "clear ray jade arm cold." The noun "jade" is used to describe the human "arm." As a concrete object, jade possesses several surface qualities. Its visual quality is either white or green. Its tactile quality is smoothness and coolness (the latter can also be classified as thermal quality). Using jade to describe the human arm, the poet may mean one, two, or all of the qualities contained in the "adjective concrete." At the same time, jade is often "metaphorically extended" to suggest abstract qualities, such as beauty (e.g., "beautiful person" 玉人

---

[25] Ibid., p. 16.
[26] Wai-lim Yip, ed. and tr., *Chinese Poetry: Major Modes and Genres* (Berkeley and Los Angeles: Univ. of California Press, 1976), p. 268.

or "fair lady" 玉女), chasteness (e.g., "behaving virtuously" 玉立), and preciousness and delicacy (e.g., "jade body" 玉體). When an abstract term is modified by a concrete adjective, it is not difficult to decide that it is the "metaphorically extended" meaning being actually implied. But when a concrete image is modified by a concrete adjective, sometimes it is not easy to determine which qualities are actually intended. Ambiguity is then created.

Wai-lim Yip's rendition of this line chooses "white" from the other qualities. This is quite a logical selection, denotatively as well as contextually. Two other translators also favor this interpretation:

> Bynner: "Her jade-white shoulder is cold in the moon."[27]
> Hawkes: "and her white arms chilled by the cold moon-light."[28]

William Hung 洪業, however, opts for the "metaphorically extended" abstract quality: "The air may be too chilly on her delicate arms."[29] Contextually, the brightness of the moon stated by the first adjective of the line already suggests whiteness. Since it is night time, the chilliness of the air can be surmised. So the visual and tactile qualities of "jade" are evoked and reinforced by an adjective and an verb. In applying "jade" to "arm," however, it seems that both the concrete qualities and the "metaphorically extended" abstract qualities are at work. The whiteness, coldness, and smoothness of a lady's arms can be physically perceived, felt, and experienced. Delicacy and preciousness are understandable "extensions" in ancient China. So the context of the line allows the noun-modifier to operate on both levels. Perhaps for once the literalists may have accidentally hit upon the right note:

> Amy Lowell and Florence Ayscough:
> "The *jade* arm must be chilly
> In this clear, glorious shining."[30]

In Wang Wei's "Bird-Singing Stream," the noun-modifier "spring" is also capable of operating on both levels. Generally the word "spring" is a seasonal indicator. Sometimes it can be "metaphorically extended" to mean various abstract qualities, for example, *ch'un-hsin* 春心 "sensual or lewd mind." Literally "spring mountain" refers to "a mountain in spring" (line 2). Apart from being just a season, by convention, spring has acquired and actually possesses some perceptual and sensory qualities, such as the sprouting greenness when used to describe a mountain, and the renovating of the torrential water when associated with a stream (line 4). And one is tempted to say that perhaps the concept of spring is "metaphorically extended" from the concrete activities of nature.

When Tu Mu 杜牧 modifies "wind" by "flute" in his famous line "Sinking sun, tower and terrace, flute-sound in the wind" 落日樓臺一笛風, another kind of generality

---

[27] Witter Bynner, *The Jade Mountain* (1929; rpt. New York: Knopf, 1945), p. 148.
[28] David Hawkes, *A Little Premier of Tu Fu* (London and New York: Oxford Univ. Press, 1967), p. 32.
[29] William Hung, *Tu Fu, China's Greatest Poet* (Camb., Mass.: Harvard Univ. Press, 1952), p. 101.
[30] Amy Lowell and Florence Ayscough, *Fir-Flower Tablets* (New York: H. Mifflin, 1921), p. 118.

is involved. Syntactically, on the first reading of the line, "one flute wind" (the last three words) may create the illusion of "a flute-ful of (or a flute's) wind." Almost immediately, knowing that wind does not come by "a fluteful" or a "flute's wind" being unlikely (though the playing of a flute requires blowing air into it), a reader may understand the situation as "flute-sound *in* the wind." This understanding, however, needs the addition of a preposition and the transformation of an adjective into a noun. As an image, "flute wind" can startle and puzzle the reader because of the very unusual combination of "flute" modifying "wind." Apparently the music of the flute is heard with the blowing of the wind being felt simultaneously, thus allowing the sound quality to be assigned to the wind. The two readings coexist congruously. Similarly, in Wang Wei's "pine-winds blow—my girdle is loosened" 松風吹解帶,[31] the "pine wind" does not mean "pine's wind" or "pine-ful of wind," but "wind blowing through (or in) the pines." (Bynner translates it as "a wind from the pine-trees.") When the preposition is not employed—its function being to indicate time, space, and the relations between the nouns—and one concrete noun is used to modify another, the relationship between the two is understood in a general way and not specifically spelled out. (When an adjective is used to describe a noun image, e.g., "red leaves," the quality of red is an inherent one, and no spatial or temporal relationship is implied.)

This kind of generality is different from the previous one. In "jade arms," the generality is due to the unspecification of the concrete qualities. In "flute wind" or "pine wind," the generality is created by the abstract relation between the two objects remaining undefined. To specify is to destroy the intriguing ambiguity and the surprise effect. In these two examples, unlike that of "jade arm," even when the relation is explicitly stated, there is no increasing of concrete details. Both kinds of generality, however, tend to produce ambiguity. In the "jade" instance, one meaning appears to be dominant, but several others (including an abstract one) cannot be dismissed simply as over-reading. In the latter case, where grammatical relation is not specified, sometimes the ambiguity created can be confusing, and interpretations, most obviously shown by translations, may vary greatly.

VI

In their brilliant and pioneering essay on T'ang poetry, Yu-kung Kao and Tsu-lin Mei argue that the Chinese language "lacks most of the accumulative processes of English. Post modification is rare." Consequently, the objects described in English poetry can acquire more details, whereas "the absence of accumulative processes prevents details from accruing to noun-objects" in Chinese poetry.[32] Wordsworth's "Daffodils" is briefly analyzed to demonstrate their arguments:

> The focal image, the daffodils, is presented with a wealth of details—where they are, how they line the shore, and how they dance; in this sense the poem is oriented toward an object, the daffodils. Individual details are attached to the

---

[31] Yip, *Hiding the Universe*, p. 39.
[32] Yu-kung Kao and Tsu-lin Mei, "Syntax, Diction, and Imagery in T'ang Poetry," *Harvard Journal of Asiatic Studies*, 31 (1971), 87.

>object mainly by the pronouns; after the occurence of "golden daffodils," it is successively referred to by "they," "them," "their." . . . In addition, there are the relative pronouns ("that," "when," "which"), participial phrases ("fluttering and dancing"), prepositional phrases ("beside the lake, beneath the trees"), which function as the links between the noun-objects and their added detail.[33]

By "post modification," the two critics apparently mean these three syntactic structures: relative clause, participial phrase, and prepositional phrase. "Accumulative processes" then refer to post modification and pronouns. They believe that this lack of "accumulative processes" explains the limitation and compactness of the image and its modification.

It is true that post modification by relative clause does not exist in T'ang poetry. But does this absence (as well as the two other forms of post modification) necessarily mean that a T'ang poet cannot assign to his natural objects descriptive details by other means? A relative pronoun generally functions as either a connective or a subject/object. In "I wandered lonely as a cloud / That floats on high o'er vales and hills," "that" serves as a connective conjoining two clauses and a subject of the second clause. "The grammatical meaning of subject-predicate in a Chinese sentence," notes the linguist Yuen Ren Chao, "is not that of actor-action, as in most Indo-European languages, but topic-comment, which includes actor-action as a special case."[34] This means that a sentence—in T'ang poetry, a line is always a complete sentential unit—can make perfect sense without the specification of the agent of the action. This is why the translators of Chinese poetry are often burdened with the strenuous task of identifying the protagonist or speaker. The last two lines from Wang Wei's "Bird-Singing Stream" exemplify this problem vividly:

>moon   rise   startle   mountain   bird
>at-times sing   spring   stream   middle
>
>Moon rises. Startles—a mountain bird.
>It sings at times in the spring stream.

There is no subject in the last line, nor is there a "that" which can function as a subject. And in T'ang poetry there is no enjambment. In this case, as in most cases, one decides by the context that it is the bird "that" sings in the spring stream. Modification by relative clause in the strict Western sense (using "that" or "which") indeed does not exist in T'ang poetry, but this does not forbid the poet from employing a subjectless (or pronounless) line to ascribe details to the noun-object appearing in the preceding line. As to the other function of "that"—the conjoining of two clauses, often it is taken care of by mere juxtaposition.[35]

---

[33] Ibid., 84.

[34] Yuen Ren Chao, "Notes on Chinese Grammar and Logic," *Philosophy East and West*, 1 (1955), 38.

[35] This reminds us of the fact that in Chinese there is no true co-ordinate conjunction "and"; juxtaposition again is the solution. All "and-" like words are structurally verbs and modifiers. See Chao, 34-35.

The Western-styled prepositional phrase is absent in Chinese poetry. In the previous section, it has been noted that prepositional relation between two nouns is usually left unspecified. The absence of prepositions, however, does not mean that the relation between the two noun-objects is annihilated; rather it is implied and not explicitly stated. For instance, the line

> mo-mo(overcast) water paddy fly white egret
>
> Mist over mist: water paddies, flies a white egret.

may be read, as Yip does, like this: "*Across* water-paddies / a white egret flies."[36] In the original, the prepositional function is served without actually employing a preposition to form a phrase.

There is no participial phrase in Chinese as well as in Chinese poetry. Since Chinese is an uninflectional language, the verbs do not have tense changes. In Kao and Mei's argument, however, the main function they assign to the participial phrase is the accumulation of details (A host of golden daffodils; / . . . / Fluttering and dancing in the breeze.") To a certain extent, a subjectless Chinese line, though without verb changes, can serve the same purpose. The last two lines of Wang Wei's "Mount Chung-nan" 終南山 are:

> want   to-stay   man('s)   place   sleep
> across water   ask   wood-cutter
>
> 欲投人處宿，隔水問樵夫。

Again the two lines do not have subjects, but an "I" can be assumed. In both Bynner's and Yip's translations, the penultimate line is turned into a participial phrase modifying the "I":

> Needing a place to spend the night,
> I call to a wood-cutter over the river.
>
> Wanting to stay over in some stranger's house,
> Across the river, I call out to ask the woodcutter.[37]

In the opinion of Kao and Mei, in a poem like "Daffodils," "individual details are attached to the object [daffodils] mainly by the pronouns." Classical Chinese prose has a few pronouns, but they do not seem to appear in T'ang poetry. As we have already demonstrated in the discussion on post modification by relative clause, a Chinese sentence can make perfect sense without the naming of the action-performer, so it is possible to have a line describing the main object without using a pronoun. The following poem is Wang Wei's "Willow-Waves" 柳浪, which has willow as its central image:

> separate line   connect silk   tree
> reflect   shadow   enter   clear   wave

---

[36] Yip, *Hiding the Universe*, p. 77. Italic mine.
[37] Bynner, p. 193; Yip, *Hiding the Universe*, p. 43.

| no | learn | imperial | moat | upon |
| spring | wind | sorry-for | fare-well | |

In rows, silken trees after silken trees,
Their shadows thrown upon limpid waves.
Unlike those upon the palace moat——
Spring winds: sorrow, sorrow at farewell.[38]

分行接綺樹，倒影入清漪。

不學御溝上，春風傷別離。

"Willow" is actually only mentioned in the title. The last line invokes the symbolic signification of the "parting sorrow" conventionally attributed to willows. All the lines in the poem except the first transmit some information about the willows without employing pronouns or utilizing a synonymous term.

"The accumulative devices exemplified in Wordsworth's poem," according to Kao and Mei, "clearly enjoyed wide currency in English poetry."[39] Although these "accumulative processes"—the three ways of post modification and the different kinds of pronouns—in the strict Western sense and form are absent in Chinese poetry, it does not follow, as we have just seen, that descriptive details cannot be accrued to the noun-objects by other similar means. The unique structure and syntactic freedom of the Chinese language must be taken into consideration in any comparison of Chinese and English poetry. Even if post modification were totally impossible, pre-modification would be an alternative. But as Kao and Mei have rightly observed: "In theory a noun can be preceded by any number of modifying phrases or adjectives, but in practice the number is severely limited."[40] This is very true, and an explanation is attempted in section IV. To recapitulate: the brevity of the line and the poem, and the metrical and semantic structure of the line seem to be the main factors restricting extensive modification.

Chinese does not have definite and indefinite articles. In English, indefinite articles can help to specify the singularity of the noun-objects, while definite articles can sometimes make the images assume a more specific character. "In Wordsworth's poem, for example, the definite article in 'beside the lake, beneath the trees,' not only makes the lake and the trees specific, but also confers definiteness upon the daffodils by fixing their precise location." But the "*li-hua* 梨花 [in Li Po's line "pear blossom white snow fragrance" 梨花白雪香] is literally 'pear blossom,' and nothing more. It is not 'a pear blossom' nor 'the pear blossom'; nor is it 'pear blossoms' or 'the pear blossoms.' "[41] Though it can be used to specify, "the" is an abstract pointer, and no concrete detail is added by its appearance. Singular and plural in number, however, can contribute to the details of concreteness, since visually one wild goose and several of them can make a crucial difference.

In Chinese poetry, the singular or plural in number is often decided by context or left to the reader's imagination, as in

---

[38] Yip, *Hiding the Universe,* p. 115.
[39] Kao and Mei, 87.
[40] Ibid.
[41] Ibid.

> shade shade summer tree sing yellow oriole
>
>   Shade, shade
>   summer trees:
>   a yellow oriole sings.[42]

One can easily decide that there is more than one summer tree in the scene. However, while Yip hears only one bird singing, Witter Bynner has heard differently: "And *several* mango-birds are singing in the full summer trees."[43] Like the pronouns and prepositions, the singular and plural in number are absent in Chinese poetry, but their function is served in another way.

"Definite and indefinite reference, singular and plural in number, modification by relative clause—all these have to do with individuation and individuals."[44] To this list we can add the following conspicuous absences: prepositions, pronouns, verb inflections, demonstratives, and often subjects of sentences. The combined effect of all these exigencies missing is the referential generality of the Chinese language. Along with the practice of favoring generic terms and modifying noun-objects with qualities-unspecified modifiers, it is only natural that the kind of concreteness one finds in T'ang nature imagery mediates somewhere between the Wimsattian levels of the extra-concrete and the minimum concrete. The imagery can be "more than specific" or extra-concrete, but the entire impression created by first the image, then the line, and finally the poem, can hardly be "more than specific." Consequently, the concreteness of T'ang nature poetry cannot yield the kind of specific impression one can procure from Wordsworth's landscape. In short, on the imagistic level, concreteness is shared by both English and Chinese poetry, but the total impression provided by a Chinese nature poem is oriented toward generality.

VII

Apart from referential generality, the lack of syntactic exigencies also creates ambiguity or multi-signification, which compensates for the restrictive brevity of the line and the poem. Along with syntactic freedom, categorical flexibility, which allows words to shift from one form class to another, helps to promote multi-signification into a norm. Li Po's line quoted by Kao and Mei is such an instance: "pear blossom white snow fragrance." Every word in the line is basically a noun. "Pear" is combined with "blossom" to form a compound. "White" is used as a modifier, and "white snow" is, like "pear blossom," a simple image. "Fragrance" is an olfactory impression, while the whiteness of the snow and pear blossoms are visual. The multi-signification of this line mainly results from the strategic position of the last character, which is flexible enough to be used as both noun and adjective. Reading this word as a noun, one can connect it with the preceding "white snow," and the semantic structure of the line becomes 2-3. Then "white snow" will become the modifier of "fragrance," and the line now reads: "Pear blossoms; snow-white fragrance." This is synaesthesia, describing an olfactory sensation by a visual quality. Changing the last

---

[42] Yip, *Hiding the Universe,* p. 77.
[43] Bynner, p. 197. Italic mine.
[44] Kao and Mei, 87-88.

word categorically into an adjective, the line becomes, as Kao and Mei have it, "pear blossoms (are) snow-white fragrant." And the synaesthesia is still retained.

Another example is Tu Fu's line which has been discussed earlier: "clear ray jade arm cold." Notice that both Yip and Hawkes translate the word "cold" as a verb in their versions, thus pivoting it before "jade arm." But the word "cold," like the last word in Li Po's line, can also be interpreted as an adjective—for example, Bynner's translation. Another possible reading is to consider "cold" as a noun and translate the line as "Clear moonlight; jade arms' coldness." This mode of multi-signification, due to the more restrictive and specific categorical and syntactical structure of the Western languages, is difficult to preserve in translations. Often a translator is forced to select one reading from several possibilities.

Roughly at the same time when Ezra Pound was experimenting with the translation of Chinese poetry, T. E. Hulme was advocating a new kind of poetry which would have concreteness as its main objective. Hulme's theory considers syntax as "unpoetical," and apparently asks for some kind of dislocation of syntax. According to Hulme, there are two reasons which make syntax "unpoetical." Firstly, syntax is the means used to organize words into small units, and small units into larger ones. When concrete images are embedded in syntactic constructions, their visuality tends to be blurred by the on-flowing movement created by syntax. Full attention to the visual objects presented is not possible, and the reader is carried by the forward flow of syntax to move from one linguistic unit to another, "gliding through an abstract process." Hulme wants poetry to be "not a counter language, but a visual concrete one. It is a compromise for a language of intuition which would hand over sensations bodily. It always endeavours to arrest you, and to make you continuously see a physical thing, to prevent you from gliding through an abstract process."[45] Secondly, the manipulation of syntax creates rhythm in poetry. And "the effect of rhythm, like that of music, is to produce a kind of hypnotic state, during which suggestion of grief or ecstasy are easily and powerfully effective. . . . This is for the art of chanting, but the procedure of the new visual art is just the contrary. It depends for its effect not on a kind of half sleep produced, but on arresting the attention, so much so that the succession of visual images should exhaust one."[46] Hulme describes the result of his theory as follows: "This new verse resembles sculpture rather than music; it appeals to the eye rather than to the ear."[47]

The method suggested by Hulme to avoid "abstract process" and "hypnotic effect" is juxtaposition of concrete images: "Say the poet is moved by a certain landscape, he selects from that certain images which, put into juxtaposition in separate lines, serve to suggest and to evoke the state he feels."[48] Hulme, however, had never accomplished his ideal and method in his own poetry. Pound is the one who had scored a success with visual perspicuity and the juxtaposition method, as exemplified by these lines:

---

[45] T. E. Hulme, *Speculations*, ed. Herbert Read (London: Routledge and Kegan Paul, 1924), p. 134.
[46] T. E. Hulme, *Further Speculations*, ed. Sam Haynes (Minneapolis: Univ. of Minnesota Press, 1955), p. 73.
[47] Ibid., p. 75.
[48] Ibid., p. 73.

>   Rain; empty river, a voyage
>   . . . .
>   Autumn moon; hills rise above lakes
>   . . . .
>   Broad water; geese line out with the autumn.
>
>   (canto 49)
>
>   Prayer: hands uplifted
>   Solitude: a person, a Nurse
>
>   (canto 54)
>
>   Moon,   clouds,   tower,   a patch of the battistero all
>   of whiteness.
>
>   (canto 79)[49]

By now it should be obvious that the kind of visual perspicuity and juxtaposition of concrete images vigorously advocated by Hulme and brilliantly achieved by Pound is a common norm in T'ang poetry. The absence of syntactic exigencies and categorical restrictions have not only created multi-signification, but have also sharpened the visual effects of the poetry. It is not uncommon for a Chinese line to have only noun images, as Hulme would have preferred. Li Po's line is one vivid example, and this line by Tu Fu is another: "Fine grass; light breeze; shore" 細草微風岸. Compare this with Hawkes' version: "By the bank where the fine grass bends in a gentle wind."[50] The prepositional phrases and the modification by relative clause have indeed generated a syntactic flow which has greatly damaged the perceptual images and completely destroyed the juxtaposition. The syntax, as in Li Po's line, is minimal; and the images are simply juxtaposed to each other with their relationship unspecified. The images stand out sharply and distinctly. Neither is there syntactic connection "obscuring" the visual perspicuity, nor syntactic movement "sweeping" the reader into an "abstract process."

Consequently, though concreteness is a common property shared by both English and Chinese poetry, the unique structure of the Chinese language allows the images to be presented in such a way that visual perspicuity is an easily achievable quality. Again this is compensation for the limitation of the modification and the brevity of the line. English nature images may be more oriented toward specificity in impression, but the sculptural and visual interests common to the Chinese counterparts are rare to find in pre-modern English poetry. As we have seen in the case of Pound, it is possible for a modern poet to achieve the same effects, but it would demand the deliberate dislocation of normal syntax in English. Dislocation of syntax may not increase the degrees of concreteness, but it can certainly compel the reader to be more aware of the concreteness contained by the images. As such, it is obvious that the structure of language is one of the vital forces shaping and determining the modes and possibilities of poetry.

---

[49] *The Cantos of Ezra Pound* (New York: New Directions, 1972).
[50] Hawkes, p. 202.

A Cinematic Interpretation of Wang Wei's Nature Poetry

Thomas Yuntong Luk

The concept of comparative literature has come a long way; it has weathered numerous cold receptions and browbeating from the purists to build up its credibility as a respectable discipline, one standing not on its own but drawing on all other disciplines to form its theory and methodology. As it stands, comparative literature, as a study of literary expressions, has broadened its horizon by transcending itself from influence or affinity studies in the literatures compared, to the study of the kinships between literature and the other arts. It is a step in the right direction that will result in a larger vista, where a truly cosmopolitan sensibility is to be gained by studying literature and "other spheres of human expression" comparatively.

In this context, the study of film and literature is definitely within the perimeter of comparative literature. Like painting, sculpture and poetry, film is an art form, an attempt at understanding reality. The study of film and poetry is just as valid an endeavor as the study of film and the theatre. As a more recent art form, film has often been considered indebted to literature for its content and form, a creature living under the nourishing umbrella of literature. This statement, however, cannot be accepted without qualification, what with the full-fledged growth of film as an art form in its own right, and what with film's indigenous techniques. Yet, the implication that film is indebted to and complemented by literature is fairly true, even up to this date. One can take a look at the number of adaptations from literature to film to be convinced. Nevertheless, one has begun to witness a reverse process taking place, a process in which film feeds literature with form and content. This is how film has managed to repay its debt. Richard Wilbur, the American poet, has openly acknowledged his indebtedness to film for some of his poems, just to mention a case in point.[1] Thus, the idea of using filmic technique in the analysis of poetry does not appear an outlandish but rewarding venture from the perspective of the aforementioned reverse process. One may well bear in mind that both poetry and film

---

[1] Richard Wilbur, "A Poet and the Movies," in *Film and the Liberal Arts,* ed. T. J. Ross (New York: Holt, Rinehart and Winston, 1969).

are forms of communication and that the poet's pen spells out paragraphs, sentences and commas, just as the director's "caméro-stylo" spells out the equivalent sequences, shots and cuts.² If one can call Jean Cocteau's films "cinematographic poetry," one can, with the same equanimity, call the poetry by Wang Wei 王維, the Chinese painter-poet, "cinematic poetry."

This article is an attempt to analyze some of the nature poems of Wang Wei from a cinematic perspective. By "cinematic," I mean, among other things, the impulse towards the visual and the spatial. As a poet-painter, Wang Wei is very pictorially conscious; he is susceptible to colors, and to composition in his poetry; most important of all, he is conscious of the spatial in the temporal, and vice versa. The conception of "The Twenty Poems on the Wang River" 輞川二十首 is the offspring of Wang Wei's aesthetic make-up. In drawing the scenery of the Wang River in his painting, *Wang-ch'uan t'u* 輞川圖 and in describing it in "The Twenty Poems of the Wang River," Wang Wei had in his artistic mind a strong sense of space-time continuum. By composing these twenty poems on the model of their pictorial counterpart, *Wang-ch'uan t'u,* Wang Wei succeeded essentially in transforming a spatial continuum into a temporal one. Nevertheless, both continuums conspire to create the visualness on their respective ocular and cerebral levels. Wang Wei's attempt at composing the poems in reference to the painting reveals on the one hand a poet-painter's practice in the "convertibility" between poetry and painting, and on the other, as the scenic descriptiveness of these poems might suggest, a painter's obsession with the visual and the spatial.

In these poems Wang Wei retains the fluidity and successiveness of scenery—a technique comparable to the cinematic succession of shots—with which the painting is blessed either in its scroll or wall-painting forms. The attention paid to the description of the topography of these "specifically named locales" renders the poems cinematically adaptable:

> My country retreat is in the valley of the Wang River. From there I have made excursions to nearby places such as, Meng-ch'eng Valley, Mountain Hua-tzu, Apricot Wood House, Bamboo Hill, Deer Park, Magnolia Park, Dogwood Bank, Sophora Walk, Lake Pavilion, South Hill, Lake I, Willow Waves, the Rapids by the Luans', Gold Powder Spring, White Stone Bank, North Hill, Bamboo Grove House, Hsin-i Village, Lacquer Garden, and Pepper Garden; and I have composed poems with P'ei Ti about these excursions at our leisure.
> (Preface to the "Twenty Poems on the Wang River")³
> 余別業在輞川山谷。其遊止有孟城坳，華子岡，文杏館，斤竹嶺，鹿柴，木蘭柴，茱萸沜，宮槐陌，臨湖亭，南垞，欹湖，柳浪，欒家瀨，金屑泉，白石灘，北垞，竹里館，辛夷塢，漆園，椒園等。與裴廸閒暇，各賦絕句云爾。
> （輞川集幷序）

---

² Ralph Stephenson and J. R. Debrix, *The Cinema as Art* (Middlesex: Penguin, 1965), p. 17.
³ All the translation in this article is done by the writer himself.

These poems are a recovery from the imaginative mind of Wang Wei, the poet, of what Wang Wei, the painter, had earlier seen, by placing in words the scenes before the mind's eye of the reader. They are a conversion from the "material continuum," i.e., the scenery painted on the original wall-painting or scroll, into a "mental continuum," i.e., the poems. Most of the twenty poems are purely scenic descriptions, such as "Apricot Wood House," "Bamboo Hill," "Magnolia Park," "Dogwood Bank," "Lake Pavilion," "South Hill," "Deer Park," "Sophora Walk," "Willow Waves," "Lake I," "Rapids by the Luans'," "White Stone Bank," "North Hill," "Hsin-i Village," and "Bamboo Grove House," with the exception of a few such as "Meng-ch'eng Valley," "Mt. Hua-tzu," "Lacquer Garden," "Golden Powder Spring," and "Pepper Garden," where the poet blends the scenic description with a certain sentimental strain.

In the poem, "Apricot Wood House," Wang Wei gives an architectural description of the house, pointing out the solidity and depth of its layout—the pillars and the height of the roof—as well as its odoriferous texture. The effect is a synaesthetic fusion of the tactile and the oderous senses. Moreover, the height of the house is suggested by the cloud-circled pillars, an example of how successfully Wang Wei, the painter, manipulates the spatial dimension.

> Apricot trees carved into beams,
> Fragrant reeds plaited into a roof,
> With no knowledge of clouds among pillars,
> Making rain in the world.
>
> 文杏裁爲梁，香茅結爲宇。
> 不知棟裏雲，去作人間雨。

In "Deer Park," "Bamboo Hill," and "Willow Waves," Wang Wei shows his pictorial realism by revealing his awareness of the optical reflection of an object and the gradation of colors:

> Empty mountain, no one is seen.
> Human voices are heard.
> Reflected sunlight enters the deep woods
> And shines upon the green moss.
>
> 空山不見人，但聞人語響。
> 返景入深林，復照青苔上。
>
> Tall bamboos reflected in the empty river,
> With green and blue ripples.
> Secretly entering the Shang Hill path,
> Where even woodcutters do not know.
>
> 檀欒映空曲，青翠漾漣漪。
> 暗入商山路，樵人不可知。
>
> Rows of silken trees
> Fall reflected in the limpid waves.
> Unlike those planted in the palace moat,
> Saddened at parting, in spring breeze.

分行接綺樹，倒影入清漪。
不學御溝上，春風傷別離。

In "Sophora Walk," he shows his awareness of shadows cast by objects and his flair for contrast between light and shade:

> Sidewalk shaded with sophora trees,
> Shadowy, deep and very mossy.
> Answering the door, sweeping the place to welcome
> The probable arrival of the mountain monk.

仄徑蔭宮槐，幽陰多綠苔。
應門但迎掃，畏有山僧來。

In "Magnolia Park," Wang Wei, the painter, is again at work, giving the reader a mental picture in which he could feel and "see" through his mind's eye the movement of the retreating sun and the flying birds, and the blinking tints of green in the middle of a greyish white:

> Autumn mountains retract the lingering glow,
> Flying birds chase after their mates,
> Green hue blinks from time to time,
> Evening dusk spreads everywhere.

秋山斂餘照，飛鳥逐前侶。
彩翠時分明，夕嵐無處所。

Perhaps, this poem is a better example of the temporalization of space mentioned at the beginning of the article. The movement of the setting sun, the flying birds and blinking color creates a process of continuous visualization of the scenery at the mental level. These images, like shots on the screen, lead to a temporalization of space on the screen of the reader's mind. This similar cinematic quality can be found in some other poems as well.

In "Lake Pavilion," for example,

> A light boat to welcome guest,
> Leisurely coming from the lake,
> Before the windows, toasting,
> Hibiscus blooms on all sides.

輕舸迎上客，悠悠湖中來。
當軒對樽酒，四面芙蓉開。

One can discern that the movement of images in the poem is analogous to a distant shot gradually zooming into a close-up, namely, the long shot of the lake and the approaching boat with the guests changing first into a medium shot of the window scene inside the pavilion, and then into a close-up of the blooming hibiscus around the pavilion. Moreover, this poem is purely descriptive of a physical reality, a very cinematic subject matter, as "it pictures such elements of physical reality as the camera alone can capture."⁴ Thus, a cinematic reenactment of this scene is easily done.

Like "Lake Pavilion," the description of "South Hill" can be considered cinematic:

> A light boat to South Hill,
> North Hill, there, water too deep to reach,
> Across the river homes are sighted
> But too far away to be distinct.

> 輕舟南垞去，北垞淼難卽，
> 隔浦望人家，遙遙不相識。

The journeying to a distance, described in the poem, is capable of being re-enacted by means of a long shot of the lake or by a soft-focus shot, which can create the haziness of the distance on the cinematic screen.

In "Rapids by the Luans'," the visual imagery is reinforced by the auditory imagery—the howling of the wind, the pattering of the rain, and the splashing of the waves—so much so that one can almost tangibly feel the impact of the ferocity of the movement. Again, this pure physical description is easily converted from the mental screen of the reader to the scenic shots projected on the cinematic screen; and the effect of the poem is cinematic, as it hinges very much on the visual and the spatial:

> Pattering, the autumn rain,
> Skimming through the slippery rocks,
> Jumping ripples splash themselves,
> The white egret, startled, descends again.

> 颯颯秋雨中，淺淺石溜瀉。
> 跳波自相濺，白鷺驚復下。

From some of these poems so far discussed, one can easily infer that Wang Wei has a predilection for the expanse and the far-reaching scenery, such as stretches of waters and mountains, the distance and the height, the two dimensions that his painterly instinct does not allow him to miss. This predilection is seen again in the following poems:

> Flying birds toward the distance,
> Mountain upon mountain, all autumn hue,
> Up and down Mountain Hua-tzu,
> Sad sentiment, endless.
>
>   (Mt. Hua-tzu)

> 飛鳥去不窮，連山復秋色。
> 上下華子岡，惆悵情何極。

---

⁴ Siegfried Kracauer, *Theory of Film: the Redemption of Physical Reality* (New York: Oxford Univ. Press, 1960), p. 270.

> Flute music floats across the waters to afar,
> At sunset, seeing my friend off,
> On the lake, turning my head,
> Green mountains curled by white clouds.
>
> (Lake I)

吹簫凌極浦，日暮送夫君。
湖上一迴首，山青卷白雲。

It is interesting to note that the clouds in "Lake I" possess a quality of suddenness, not dissimilar to those that Wordsworth saw on the lake; however, it should be noted that these clouds that Wang Wei saw on Lake I do not seem to convey any omens or visitations by which Wordsworth was haunted. There is a sense of sublime in these clouds, but it is one of a quietistic and soothing nature, not one of those breath-taking kinds.

The poem, "North Hill," is still concerned with the far-reaching distance.

> North Hill, north of the lake,
> Clumps of trees reveal a red fence,
> Winding, the waters of the South River,
> Flickering at the edge of the green forest.

北垞湖水北，雜樹映朱欄。
逶迤南川水，明滅青林端。

The landscape conjured up by the imagery here is one of the distance alternated with a watery white and dark-greenness. The emergence and disappearance of the river and the gradation of colors are similar to those mentioned earlier in the blinking hues of "Magnolia Park." Wang Wei's use of color is never dull, for he knows how to find something to contrast with. For example, in "Dogwood Bank,"

> Bearing fruits, red and green,
> Like flowers in bloom.
> If a guest stays over in the mountain,
> Put this in his hibiscus cup.

結實紅且綠，復如花更開。
山中倘留客，置此茱萸杯。

the description of the dogwoods, "red and green," is synaesthetic, as "red" suggests the ripeness of the cornels and "green" the textural solidity of the cornels. It also shows the poet's botanical discernment, his sensitivity to colors and their impact upon the viewer.

Wang Wei is also good at luxurious, colorful descriptions. In "Gold Power Spring," the images are more flamboyant and gaudier than usual:

> A daily drink from the Gold Powder Spring,
> At least a thousand years to live.
> Variegated phoenix flies with striped dragon,
> Plummage, staff, tribute to the Jade Emperor.

> 日飲金屑泉，少當千餘歲。
> 翠鳳翔文螭，羽節朝玉帝。

The flight of the phoenix and dragon, with all its colorful pomposity, symbolizes the Taoist upward yearning for immortality and supernaturalness. The effect of this poem is not only contingent upon its colorful images but also upon its underlying sense of motion, the spatial reinforcement of the desire for elevation, if not complete release, from time, suggested in the first two lines.

The most characteristic feature of Wang Wei's cinematically adaptable poems, in addition to the pure description of physical nature, already mentioned in some of the poems cited, is the absence of any tinge of complex psychological depiction. Two poems, "Hsin-i Village" and "Bird-singing Stream" suffice to serve as examples of this deinteriorization:

> High on the treetops, the hibiscus
> Sets forth red calyces in the hill.
> A quiet stream hut, with no one around.
> It blooms and falls, of its own accord.
>
> 木末芙蓉花，山中發紅萼。
> 澗戶寂無人，紛紛開且落。
>
> Man at leisure, cassia flowers fall,
> Quiet night, spring mountain empty.
> Moon rises, startling a mountain bird.
> It sings from time to time in the spring stream.
>
> 人閒桂花落，夜靜春山空。
> 月出驚山鳥，時鳴春澗中。

Without any tinge of intellectualization, Wang Wei is able to reveal in these poems a physical phenomenon in its native purity. One may well say that Wang Wei in these poems becomes "Nature (phenomenon) as it is: no trace of conceptualization."[5] This representation of nature as it is conforms to the cinematic approach, insofar as the phenomenon as it is, i.e., non-conceptual, is the most cinematic.[6]

It should be noted that Wang Wei's attention to the pictorial composition through poetic imagery demonstrates his use of chiaroscuro and manipulation of color and lighting. The following lines culled from various nature poems of Wang Wei can bear testimony to his compositional and color awareness:

> Pheasants sing, barley grows fine,
> Silkworms sleep, mulberry leaves are sparse.
>   (Farming Home in the Wei River)
>
> 雉雛麥苗秀，蠶眠桑葉稀。 （渭川田家）

---

[5] Wai-lim Yip, *Hiding the Universe* (New York: Grossman, 1972), p. 5.
[6] Siegfried Kracauer, p. 263.

In the rain the grass is green-dyed,
On the water the peach blossom is bright-red.
                    (Villa on the Wang River)

雨中草色綠堪染，水上桃花紅欲然。（輞川別業）

The distant trees guide the traveller,
The solitary wall confronts the setting sun.
    (Farewell to Mr. Ch'i Mu-ch'ien Upon His Homeward
        Journey, After Failure in the Civil Examination)

遠樹帶行客，孤城當落暉。（送綦母潛落第還鄉）

The bright moon shines through the pine-trees,
The clear stream runs over the rocks.
                (Living in the Mountain in Autumn)

明月松間照，清泉石上流。（山居秋暝）

Looking back to the eagle-hunting ground,
A thousand *li* of evening clouds on the horizon.
                                    (Hunting)

回看射雕處，千里暮雲平。（觀獵）

The sun sets over the edge of the desert.
                            (On General Li Ling)

日暮沙漠陲。（李陵詠）

In the vast desert the lone smoke is straight,
On the long river the setting sun is round.
                        (Delegated to the Frontier)

大漠孤烟直，長河落日圓。（使至塞外）

In the two lines from "Farming Home in the Wei River," Wang Wei describes the pheasants, the barley, the silkworms and the mulberry leaves with a very observing eye to minute details; his eyes function like a close-up shot that includes everything in view within one single frame. The common feature of these examples is that they all pay attention to the subtle gradation of colors, light and shadow, and that they describe a physical reality that is photographable. Perhaps it is interesting to note that the magnificence and sublime in the lines from "Hunting," "On General Li Ling" and "Delegated to the Frontier" conjure up visual equivalents enacted on the horizontal frame of a cinemascope screen.

    Another cinematic quality found in Wang Wei's poems of the Wang River and other nature poems is a dreaminess, a kind of lull, comparable to the one usually created by slow-moving camera on the screen. In reading the twenty poems of the Wang River, the reader could get a vicarious feeling of touring the locales in the footsteps of the poet. Or he could feel he is being led on a guided tour. This dreaminess is originally imbedded in the painting, the viewing of which sent Ch'in Shao-yu 秦少游

into a dreamy journey to all the places on the scroll.[7] This dreaminess is retained in the poetry, thanks to the succession of scenery in the poetic imagery, and is comparable to what Pasolini calls "Oniricita," a dreamlike effect resulting from the successive sequence of shots.[8]

This lulling, slow-moving camera effect can be found in other poems as well. In "Journey to the Peach-blossom Spring" 桃源行, Wang Wei keeps shifting his scenic description back and forth, near and far:

> A fishing boat sails up the river; lovely spring in the hill.
> On both banks peach blossoms line the flowing water.
> The fisherman sits and looks at the red trees, not knowing the distance.
> Reaching the end of the green stream, seeing no one.
> At an opening in the hills, he skulks through some twists and turns at first.
> Then the hills open up to a vast, flat land.
> Looking to a spot of clusters of cloud-topped trees afar,
> He approaches thousands of houses among flowers and bamboos.
> . . . .
> Spring comes, peach-blossom waters overflow.
> That idyllic village, nowhere to be found.

漁舟逐水愛山春，兩岸桃花夾去津。
坐看紅樹不知遠，行盡清溪不見人。
山口潛行始隈隩，山開曠望旋平陸。
遙看一處攢雲樹，近入千家散花竹。
....
春來偏是桃花水，不辨仙源何處尋。

At the beginning of this poem, Wang Wei describes the fisherman's boat gliding through the water until it discovers the village. The reader, while reading this portion of the poem, can feel and "see" the movement of the boat gliding on the river, flanked by peach-blossoms. While the red trees on both sides of the river move away from the fisherman, the reader may get an effect comparable to that of a landscape moving past a gliding boat on a cinematic screen. A sense of the moving camera is felt up to the arrival at the source of the stream, and the appearance of hills, twisting and turning. Cinematically, lines seven and eight from the poem are comparable to a long shot and a close-up. The two images in these lines, like the image of peach-blossom water at the end of the poem, are profoundly poetic by creating an aura of dreaminess befitting the idyllic nature of the locale.

The poem, "Mountain Chung-nan" 終南山, also exudes this sense of moving camera effect.

---

[7] This anecdote is recorded in Appendix III (秦少游書輞川圖後) of *Wang-yu-ch'eng chi chien-chu* 王右丞集箋注 ed. Chao Tien-ch'eng 趙殿成 (Hong Kong: Chung-hua, 1972), II, 527.

[8] See *Pasolini on Pasolini: Interview with Oswald Stack* (Bloomington: Indiana Univ. Press, 1969), p. 153.

Mt. Tai-i is near the Capital,
Stretching its ranges to the edge of the sea.
White clouds circle, viewed from a distance, and coalesce
    around the peaks,
Green mist becomes invisible, viewed inside the mountains.
Each peak is under a different stardom,
Reflecting a variegation of light and dark in its valley.
For lodging accomodation,
Ask the woodcutter across the river.

太乙近天都，連山到海隅。
白雲廻望合，青靄入看無。
分野中峯變，陰晴眾壑殊。
欲投人處宿，隔水問樵夫。

The first three lines, cinematically equivalent to long shots, draw the eyes of the viewer to roam over a distant landscape, while the fourth line, cinematically equivalent to a close-up, transports the viewer's eyes from the hazy, distant cloud-circled peaks to a close-ranged scrutiny inside the mountains. This visionary switch, comparable to a camera tracking and panning, is also found in the following two poems, "Green Stream" 青溪, and "To P'ei Ti from the Cottage on the Wang River" 輞川閒居贈裴秀才迪.

Sailing into the Yellow Flower Stream,
Following the green water,
Along the mountain's numerous curves;
Straight waterway, less than a hundred *li*.
Noise stirs among disarrayed rocks.
Quiet color hides in the pines.
Ripples over water-chestnuts and weeds
Clearly reflect the reeds.
My mind, ever peaceful, is unworried,
So is the clear stream.
Please stay on the rocks
And fish the day away.

言入黃花川，每逐青溪水。
隨山將萬轉，趣途無百里。
聲喧亂石中，色靜深松裏。
漾漾汎菱荇，澄澄映葭葦。
我心素已閒，清川澹如此。
請留盤石上，垂鈎將以矣。

The chilly mountains turn bluish-green.
The autumn stream flows murmuring all day long.
Leaning on a cane, outside the wooden gate,
Listening to the windborne tittering of cicadas at dusk,
Over the ferry the setting sun lingers,
Lone strand of smoke rises above the village.

> Meeting drunken Chieh Yü,
> Singing wildly in front of the Five Willows.

> 寒山轉蒼翠，秋水日潺湲。
> 倚仗柴門外，臨風聽暮蟬。
> 渡頭餘落日，墟里上孤烟。
> 復值接輿醉，狂歌五柳前。

However, the effect of the visionary switch upon the reader in these two poems is quite different. The more sequential and gradual description of scenery in "Green Stream" creates a tracking camera effect by moving along with the subject described; the reader seems to move bodily along with each scene described, while reading the poem. However, the more random description of scenery in "To P'ei Ti from the Cottage on the Wang River" creates an effect more like panning shots, which has less a sense of continuous movement, but makes the reader take view of far and near scenes from a fixed point, like a camera pivoting round on a vertical axis. All in all, the switch from the far and the near or vice versa in Wang Wei's poems produces an irrational and discontinuous logic of space, which is comparable to what a shifting camera can do on a cinematic screen.

In the context of the analysis of Wang Wei's poem thus far, one can perhaps feel justified to assert that Wang Wei's poems are cinematic, without unduly fearing to incur criticisms such as "historical anachronism," "inter-media promiscuity" or the like, that probably would question this cross-media approach—using the techniques of one form of human expression to invigorate the content of another. In fine, judged from the cinematic viewpoint, Wang Wei's nature poems, with their impulse towards visual successiveness and spatial fluidity, and their lack of abstraction, lend themselves very easily to cinematic representation.

Full-length *Hsiao-shuo* and the Western Novel: A Generic Reappraisal

Andrew H. Plaks

As students of the masterworks of Chinese fiction within the framework of comparative literary studies, we have become accustomed to referring to major texts such as *Chin P'ing Mei* 金瓶梅, *Hung-lou meng* 紅樓夢, and others as Chinese "novels." Given the relative imprecision of that term which allows it to encompass a variety of literary products—from Fielding and Sterne to Robbe-Grillet—it has been adopted with few qualms as a label of convenience for the genre of extended fictional narrative that flourished in China from the sixteenth to nineteenth centuries.

Any more thorough consideration of the theoretical bases of this generic category, however, immediately raises a number of serious reservations regarding the transfer of the term to the Chinese works. When one reviews the copious Western critical writings on the novel, it is easy to form the conclusion that in certain respects the novel form is unique to its own tradition—that it is conditioned by and inextricably bound to the literary heritage and general aesthetics of post-Renaissance Western civilization.[1] But the striking fact remains that even after one has discounted those elements in the theory of the novel which are peculiar to the fortuitous configurations of the Western tradition, there still can be observed a certain core area of overlapping concerns which continues to justify the use of the term "novel" in the Chinese context. This area of overlap becomes even more sharply defined in the writings of more recent Western theorists,[2] whose attempts to cut away the non-essential factors and penetrate to the generic marrow of the novel form have laid bare a number of defining

---

[1] Serious criticism of the novel genre dates back at least to the late-eighteenth and early-nineteenth centuries: e.g., Friedrich Schlegel's "Brief über den Roman" and Friedrich von Blanckenburg's *Theorie des Romans;* and continues right down to the formalist and structuralist narrative theory of the twentieth century. For a historical review of critical comments on the novel form by novelists themselves, see Miriam Allott, *Novelists on the Novel* (London: Routledge, 1959).

[2] See, for example, Georg Lukács, *Theory of the Novel,* trans. Anna Bostock (Camb., Mass.: M.I.T., 1971); Ralph Freedman, "The Possibility of a Theory of the Novel," in Peter Demetz et al., ed., *The Disciplines of Criticism* (New Haven: Yale Univ. Press, 1968), pp. 57-77; Jonathan Culler, "Poetics of the Novel," in his *Structuralist Poetics* (Ithaca: Cornell Univ. Press, 1975), chapter 9; and Robert Scholes, ed., *Approaches to the Novel* (San Francisco: Chandler, 1961).

criteria which can be applied without undue distortion to non-Western forms of prose fiction as well. In the following paper, we will discuss some of these key points of recent Western novel theory and consider their applicability to the extended vernacular prose narrative of China, in order to justify the continued use of the term "novel" for the latter corpus. In conclusion we will treat briefly some possible speculations on the "inevitability" of the appearance of the novel, and on the cross-cultural significance of this particular literary genre.

Before proceeding, let us review the place of the novel in the overall literary histories of the respective cultures. Perhaps the simplest way of dealing with the novel is to take it as merely the "newest," or most recent, phase of a continuous tradition of narrative art—to whose "novelty" its generic designation in English refers. This sense of inherent continuity within a larger narrative tradition is even more obtrusive in nearly all of the other languages of Europe, which continue to refer to the novel by the term "roman," presumably derived from the designation for the prose romance which had existed since antiquity and flourished during the Medieval and Renaissance periods. Many critics who hold this view of the novel have also gone on to trace its line of descent back to the epic, so that the three forms: epic, romance, and novel, fall together into a single integral narrative tradition. This explanation has enabled literary scholars to sidestep the confusion caused by the fuzzy generic divisions which make the romance form often quite indistinguishable from "synthetic epics" of the post-Classical period, and which lead to the polemics surrounding the parturition of the novel out of the romance in the eighteenth century. One particularly far-reaching conclusion drawn by some Western theorists is the notion that in the novel we witness the reappearance of an "epic synthesis" of classical civilization which had been submerged, or fragmented, during long centuries of cultural instability, but was bound to surface again as a medium for expressing the new intellectual synthesis of the Enlightenment—a theory which was explicitly stated as early as the eighteenth century and which finds later expression in the writings of a number of twentieth century scholars.[3] For those scholars who adhere to this view of the origins and significance of the novel in the West it has been logical to approach this newer form of narrative with classical—largely Aristotelian—critical canons of structural unity, temporal ordering, and representation of character derived mainly from the experience of the epic.

This theory of the origins of the novel has proven to be quite stimulating for an overview of Western literary history; but its usefulness in the Chinese context is immediately cancelled out by the simple fact that no epic narrative exists in early Chinese literature with which to bracket the later genre of prose narrative which we call the novel. This, however, does not close the door to our comparative inquiry, for while the Chinese novel cannot be linked to an earlier epic form, it, too, is firmly embedded in its own literary heritage.

Here, by way of contrast, scholars of Chinese fiction have generally preferred to relate the appearance of the full-length works of the Ming and Ch'ing periods to pre-

---

[3] This idea was especially popular in German Romantic criticism, where it was stated explicitly by Schlegel, "Brief," in *Sämmtliche Werke,* 2nd ed. (Wien: I. Klang, 1846), V, 221, and in Friedrich von Blanckenburg's *Theorie* (see Freedman, p. 60), and is also reflected in certain passages in the writings of Hegel and Schiller. More recently, it has also contributed to the central conceptual scheme of Robert Scholes and Robert Kellogg's *Nature of Narrative* (New York: Oxford Univ. Press, 1966).

existing or contemporary colloquial language genres, especially the drama and the short story. The fact that the term *hsiao-shuo* is extended to apply to both the shorter and the full-length forms (while continuing to bear its original reference to classical-language anecdotal fiction and quasi-fictional writings of various sorts) bears out the conception of the generic commensurability of the short story and the novel, an understanding based on the common use of the simulated rhetoric of the oral storyteller in both forms, and emphasized in the use of the term *chang-hui hsiao-shuo* 章回小說 for the latter.

But it may be more useful for the purposes of the present discussion to focus attention instead on the genetic relation between the Chinese novel and the vast tradition of historical narrative which forms perhaps the central textual corpus of its literary and intellectual heritage. Unfortunately, too many scholars of Chinese literature have overemphasized the relation between the novel and the popular tradition evidently reflected in its colloquial sources, and have understated or even overlooked the more crucial role of historiography in the development of the tradition. This central role must be stressed not only because a large portion of the corpus of Ming-Ch'ing fiction can be called "historical fiction" either in terms of its central figures or its documentary sources, but also because it continues to draw upon "official" historiography for a variety of formal and structural devices (e.g., biographical form, multiple foci of narration, conventional narrative *topoi* and motifs, etc.), as well as for its overall sense of the broader context and significance of human events. This close kinship between historical and fictional narrative in China is reflected in the use of terms such as *pai-shih* 稗史 to refer to a wide variety of fictional works, and is noted with due gravity by the best traditional Chinese fiction critics such as Chin Sheng-t'an 金聖嘆 and Mao Tsung-kang 毛宗崗.[4] One might also mention here, as another link between the novel and the classical Chinese literary tradition, the fact that many aspects of the technical art of the novel as outlined by the Ming-Ch'ing critics—the conception of larger structural divisions as well as the fine weaving of textural linkage—are modeled directly after the critical theory and practical training in the prose essay which constituted a primary focus of education and scholarship in late Imperial China.

Despite the fact that from the point of view of literary history both the Chinese and the European novel must be viewed as genres organically and genetically linked to their respective literary systems rather than as completely new forms created *ex nihilo* to reflect unprecedented realities at the dawn of the modern era, it still remains intuitively obvious that there is something fundamentally different about the novel which sets it off from the forms of extended narrative which preceded it: the epic and romance in the one tradition, historiography and folk narrative in the other. Because of the difficulty of differentiating between the novel and its predecessors on purely formal generic grounds, Western scholars have tended to fall back upon a variety of features of content which set the novel apart as a recognizable narrative category. For example, a number of eighteenth-century writers, including practitioners such as Fielding and Richardson and critics such as Clara Reeve, emphasize the novel's allegiance to "real life" as opposed to the flights of fantasy associated with the romance.[5]

---

[4] See, for example, Chin Sheng-t'an's *tu-fa* 讀法 introduction to various editions of *Shui-hu chuan* 水滸傳 (*ti-wu ts'ai-tzu-shu* 第五才子書), and Mao Tsung-kang's similar *tu-fa* which is reproduced in many editions of *San-kuo chih yen-i* (*ti-i ts'ai-tzu-shu* 第一才子書).

[5] Cited in Allott, pp. 41-43, 45-47, and 49-61.

The recent critic Northrop Frye, on the other hand, distinguishes between the novel and romance primarily on the basis of characterization, citing the "glow of subjective intensity" which illuminates the latter form.[6]

Such arguments become strongest when they abandon distinctions on the basis of structure, characterization, or degree of fictionality, and attempt instead to account for the special quality of the novel in terms of the particular aspects of social and intellectual history which form the backdrop to the formative period of the novel from the seventeenth to the nineteenth centuries in Europe. For example, when Lukács somewhat glibly speaks of the novel as the "epic of a world abandoned by God," he not only asserts that the novel and epic are inherently commensurable genres, but also implies that the distinction between the two lies in the ideological gulf which separates the novel from the past "heroic" ages associated with the epic. In spite of the fact that the Chinese novel obviously does not share the same intellectual background as its European counterpart, the interesting thing is that it is precisely in the relation between the novel and intellectual history that we find the most striking parallels between the two traditions, and the greatest justification for applying the term "novel" to the Chinese works, notwithstanding the vastly different features of structuration, characterization, etc. which would otherwise disqualify the use of that term.

One of the aspects of the extraliterary background of the appearance of the novel which has been brought forward to account for the difference between this literary form and what preceded it is the matrix of interrelated elements of social and economic history of the centuries in question: urbanization, commercialization, the industrial revolution, the spread of education, printing, etc.—which unite to give rise to the consolidation of bourgeois culture in early modern Europe, as described in Ian Watt's theoretically-flawed but still useful little book *The Rise of the Novel*. Interestingly enough, very nearly the same sort of factors of social and cultural history cited by Watt as responsible for the appearance of the novel in Europe can be observed in China of the sixteenth-eighteenth centuries, where they also coincide with the rise of a comparable genre of prose narrative in that culture. In China such factors as rapid urbanization, the switch to a money economy based on new-world silver, increased trading possibilities opened up by maritime exploration, and the meteoric rise of great printing houses, indicate a clear link with the world of vernacular fiction, all the more so since these factors were largely concentrated in the cities of the Yangtze delta and the Southeastern coast where fiction publishing had its impetus in that period. This lends strong support for Watt's thesis that these extraliterary factors, rather than the purely literary qualities mentioned earlier, may indeed be credited with the emergence of the novel form, stronger than if these correspondences appeared in the European context alone. (One might add that the case becomes very nearly watertight when one notes the identical conjunction of urban culture and a flourishing market for prose fiction in the rapid rise of *kanazōshi* 假名草子 and other genres in the cities of Tokugawa Japan.)

The problem with the application of Watt's valuable study lies not so much in his thesis of the interrelation between social and literary history as in the conclusions which he and others seem to draw from this connection. The perception of the common element, in these various social and economic developments, of a certain

---

[6] Northrop Frye, "Specific Continuous Forms," in *Anatomy of Criticism* (Princeton: Princeton Univ. Press, 1957), p. 304, reprinted in Scholes, *Approaches*, pp. 41-54.

diffusion or democratization of culture—whether one chooses to account for such phenomena in terms of "seeds of capitalism," "bourgeois mentality," or "social mobility,"—has led to the widespread misconception that the novel is an essentially "popular" form of cultural expression. This assumption is implicit in a number of studies of Western narrative (even Auerbach, for example, implies in his *Mimesis* that the "high and low styles," which he isolates as purely rhetorical features, may be associated with the social classes whose speech they seem to imitate), and has become the dogma for nearly all students of Chinese colloquial fiction ever since its "rediscovery" by twentieth-century literary reformers. In the latter tradition, the highlighting of the colloquial-language medium, the narrative focus on parvenu merchant or military figures, or on bandits, outcasts, and other disenfranchised types, and most important, the imitation of the rhetoric of the streetside oral-storyteller as the normative narrative mode, have naturally led generations of readers to conclude that this is the true literature of the "broad masses"—or at least of the rising middle classes—as opposed to the classical poetry and prose of the "scholar-official" elite. This view is, furthermore, reinforced by the notion of the much-publicized contempt for fiction on the part of the arbiters of literary culture, a point we will return to shortly.

There is no doubt a certain amount of validity to this picture of the Chinese novel: certainly the rapid spread of colloquial fiction in the last few generations of the Ming owes much to the spread of printing establishments and to the wider reading public, with the leisure and the means to indulge in literary pastimes afforded by the growth of trade and the money economy. But it will be argued here that the great Chinese novels we are dealing with here—and any discussion of literary genres must, in the final analysis, base itself on the best works of a tradition, those whose stature and influence contribute most to the conception of genre and the establishment of generic conventions—lend themselves to the most meaningful interpretation when they are treated not as examples of a "popular" counter-culture, but rather as major documents in the mainstream of Ming and Ch'ing literati culture.

Just as in the case of European fiction, the use of a less restrictive linguistic medium (in the Chinese case the colloquial language, in Europe the vernacular of the respective national languages, cf., "romance") does not in itself prove anything about class affinities. For one thing, the actual linguistic medium of the Chinese novel is not identical with common speech but rather represents a new hybrid literary language drawing on both classical diction and the jargon of the marketplace.[7] It is no accident that most of the great fiction writers of Ming and Ch'ing China were also acknowledged masters of various classical literary forms,[8] much as Chaucer, Boccaccio, Dante, Milton, and other pioneers of European vernacular narrative were also known as great Latin stylists. The retention of the rhetorical tags of the oral

---

[7] In many novels it is the classical idiom which predominates over colloquial expressions, either carrying the main narrative function (as in *San-kuo, Yeh-sou p'u-yen* 野叟曝言, and others), or even forming the basis of an entire narrative (as in *Yen-shan wai-shih* 燕山外史). Significantly enough, those works which can truly be called "chapbooks" (i.e., the cheap small editions of *ts'ai-tzu chia-jen* love stories, many of which survive in present-day collections) are more often written in a stilted classical style than in the literary colloquial developed by the great novels.

[8] Cf. Feng Meng-lung's 馮夢龍 *Ch'ing-shih lei lüeh* 情史類畧, Li Yü's 李漁 *Hsien-ch'ing ou-chi* 閒情偶寄, Wu Ch'eng-en's 吳承恩 collection of classical-language anecdotes, and the classical prose works by nearly every candidate for the authorship of the *Chin P'ing Mei*.

storyteller, therefore, signals not the low-born origins of authors, subjects, and readers, but rather a deliberate aesthetic choice which is put to work for special ironic effects in the manipulation of their material, and has little or nothing to do with any class solidarity between authors and a "popular" audience.

It should also be added at this point that the traditional bias for colloquial *hsiao-shuo*, which would seem to brand that genre as an essentially popular medium, was never as great among leading literati as twentieth-century literary historians have led us to believe, and in any event is more a specifically Ch'ing phenomenon which was far less prevalent among sixteenth- and seventeenth-century writers.[9] One might perhaps conclude from this that those particular literati were simply more liberally disposed towards the popular tradition, but since so many of the major cultural figures of the period were themselves involved in one way or another in the dissemination of colloquial literature—as writers, publishers, critics, and readers—it may be more to the point to say that this new "genre" was in fact felt to be an integral part of the serious literary heritage, an understanding confirmed in numerous prefaces, colophons, and personal notes which rank works such as *San-kuo yen-i* 三國演義, *Hsi-yu chi* 西遊記, etc. along with the greatest classical works in the tradition.[10] Interestingly enough, the same sort of double standard—facile condemnation accompanied by sincere enthusiasm and creative participation in the genre—also describes the situation in Europe at the time of the rise of the novel, where the new form came up for considerable abuse—particularly in France—while continuing to engage some of the best minds and talents.[11]

The real objection against writing off the Chinese novel as "popular" fiction, however, has less to do with its provenance than with its intellectual content: i.e., its projection of meaning through the representation of human experience. In both China and Europe the emergence of the novel form is undeniably related to a greater diffusion of culture making possible a wider reading audience; but in both cases a close examination of the major texts reveals a far greater affinity with the sophisticated wit and philosophical vision of the high cultural tradition than with the wisdom or the aesthetics of folk literature. Once again, we are speaking here of the *great* novels—the innumerable works in both traditions which fail to develop a dimension of intellectual depth must of necessity be considered either as minor examples of the genre or else as works which fall outside of these generic criteria.

One central feature of the novel form which has tended to reinforce the impression that it is in some sense conditioned by its more broad-based audience is the fact that in both China and Europe the novel carries with it the aesthetic expectation of a "realistic" representation of some phase of human existence. This expectation is so central that many scholars have cited "realism" as the principal defining feature

---

[9] A careful reading of the documents collected by Wang Hsiao-chuan 王曉傳 in *Yüan Ming Ch'ing san-tai chin-hui hsiao-shuo hsi-ch'ü shih-liao* 元明清三代禁毀小說戲曲史料 (Peking: Tso-chia, 1957) reveals that the majority of pre-Ch'ing documents refer to drama or anecdotal *hsiao-shuo* rather than to colloquial prose fiction. On the other hand, many very formidable classical scholars, e.g., Yü Yüeh 俞樾, Chiao Hsün 焦循, Chang Hsüeh-ch'eng 章學誠, Chu I-tsun 朱彝尊, etc., were quite willing to acknowledge their interest in the novel in their personal writings.

[10] See, for example, Chin Sheng-t'an's *ts'ai-tzu shu*, evidently modelled after a similar list by Li Chih 李贄.

[11] See André Lévy, "La condamnation duroman en France et en Chine," in *Études sur le conte et le roman chinois* (Paris: Maisonneuve, 1971), pp. 1-14.

of the novel genre.[12] Of course, the specific focus of realism in a given work may vary from social mores and manners or economic realities, to the portrayal of the inner workings of the human mind; but the reader of the novel has been trained to expect a more or less faithful representation of day-to-day reality in a credible external context on at least some level of existence. As for those fictional works whose subject matter is removed from the normal sphere of human experience, critics who accept this definition of the novel may then reassign them to another generic type—such as romance, allegory, or the fantastic[13]—or else may choose to tolerate the non-realistic narrative framework and focus attention on their ability to convey nevertheless a "realistic" dimension of historical or philosophical truth. In the Chinese tradition, for example, some scholars may prefer to label works of broad historical sweep such as *San-kuo yen-i* as "romances," or to categorize works such as *Hsi-yu chi* under the rubric of allegory, thus reserving the term novel for "domestic fiction" such as *Chin P'ing Mei* and *Hung-lou meng*.

The expression "realism," however, is an extremely loaded term: we use it rather freely for a wide range of varying concepts. In attempting to sort out these various levels of meaning here, it may be useful to distinguish between two major areas of significance: first, the nature of the objects that are depicted in a given work, and second, the actual manner of depiction that is employed. To use the analogy of representational painting, the impression of realism is sometimes due primarily to the subject of the picture: a still-life bowl of fruit, a domestic scene, a well-known historical event; and at other times resides more in the technical devices selected by the artist: sharp outlines accented by shadings of color, manipulation of light and shadow to evoke the illusion of three-dimensional depth, maintenance of "natural" proportions and postures of subjects, and most important, the use of the illusionistic convention of perspective.

In the medium of *literary* representation, where visual images are replaced by words on a page, the perception of realistic portrayal becomes even more subtle and complex. With regard to the nature of the objects depicted, the impression of realism in fiction often arises when we read about more "familiar" aspects of experience—the sights, sounds, and smells of daily life. This may apply even in works whose basic setting may be removed to geographically or historically exotic spheres (e.g., Chateaubriand, Melville, etc.) or focused on unfamiliarly high or low social strata, in which cases the impression of familiarity may be maintained by depicting intimate or quotidian scenes in substantial detail within those less familiar settings. It is this aspect of realism in fiction which Northrop Frye evidently has in mind when he assigns the novel to what he terms the "low mimetic level," on which "the hero is one of us."[14] Although this particular criterion is far too reductive to serve our purposes as a generic distinction for the novel, it does cast an interesting light on the development of the Chinese novel, where the transition from *San-kuo yen-i* to *Shui-hu chuan* to *Chin P'ing Mei* to *Ju-lin wai-shih* 儒林外史 traces a nicely-ordered progression down Frye's scale, from a higher to a lower mimetic level.

---

[12] See, for example, Ian Watt's article "Realism and the Novel Form," in Scholes, *Approaches*, pp. 55-82, esp. p. 56. Cf. Clara Reeve's definition of the novel cited above.

[13] For a definition of the fantastic as a generic category, see Tzvetan Todorov, *La littérature fantastique* (Paris: Seuil, 1970), translated as *The Fantastic* (Ithaca: Cornell Univ. Press, 1975).

[14] Frye, *Anatomy*, p. 34.

As to the manner of depiction which gives rise to the illusion of realistic representation in the novel, we may cite a wide range of techniques: exhaustive attention to fine details, maintenance of an orderly scheme of temporal movement,[15] articulation of a consistent narrative perspective—i.e., point of view, and emphasis on credibility in motivation and personality. Of course, there is nothing to stop the fiction writer from applying this sort of techniques of realistic depiction to unreal objects, or conversely, treating objects in the real world in the manner of the unreal, as in impressionism, surrealism, and other recent aesthetic movements. The fact that in much of contemporary fiction such inversion of realistic conventions becomes the dominant mode need not, however, alter this conception of the novel as a genre, as the attempt to subvert these conventions in itself reaffirms the centrality of the canons of realism in the novel form during its core period.

Whether we choose to emphasize the subject matter of the novel or its narrative conventions, we may isolate as a fundamental feature of the genre its attempt to create in fiction an entire "world" that corresponds to the intellectual, historical or personal experience of the reader, and that may be convincing in spite of its departures from the strictly familiar. This ability of the novel to create a convincing world often revolves about the logical rather than the formal structure of a given work, so that a plausible chain of causality may be evoked even where the subject matter has moved beyond the pale of normal human experience (as in many of Kafka's novels, or in the best of science fiction).

This tendency of the novel to move out into the unreal in spite of its essentially realistic foundations brings us to a second major defining feature of the genre. In attempting to faithfully represent or convincingly fabricate an entire world in all its fullness of detail, novelists (at least the great ones) are inevitably forced to confront some of the deeper issues regarding the nature of that reality. What may start out as a pursuit of objectivity sooner or later becomes entangled in the paradox that objective reality presupposes a perceiving subject, and hence an ultimately subjective and relative point of view. That is why the realistic foundations of the novel nearly always give way to an exploration of the intangibles of existence, or of the vagaries of the subconscious. In the West, this process begins as early as Sterne, with his witty assault on the "hobby-horses" of his age, and finally arrives at a point in the present century at which the exploration of consciousness becomes the central focus of the novel. In Ming-Ch'ing China, the novel begins with a serious questioning of the interrelation between historical, supernatural, and personal forces, and quickly moves into the twilight areas of the contingency between dream and waking reality or the tensions between individual ideals and collective consciousness.

In terms of the central characters in the novel tradition, we observe that the genre in the West has been rather consistently marked by the presence of ambiguous heroes. From Julien Sorel to Moses Herzog the pages of the Western novel are peopled with figures that on one point or another are disqualified from the role of the fully-realized hero: sometimes because of their own social position (foundling, criminal, adulteress, etc.), sometimes because of the pressures of a hostile environment. In China, likewise, the cast of characters of the novel corpus reads like a rogues'-

---

[15] Cf. Ian Watt, p. 69: "The novel's closeness to the texture of daily experience directly depends upon its employment of a much more minutely discriminated time-scale than had previously been employed in narrative."

gallery of *manqués* individuals: Liu Pei 劉備, Sung Chiang 宋江, Hsi-men Ch'ing 西門慶, Chia Pao-yü 賈寶玉, To Shao-ch'ing 杜少卿, etc. Even such popular heroes as Kuan Yü 關羽, Chu-ko Liang 諸葛亮, or Wu Sung 武松 are severely cut down to size by their own individual flaws or by the invincible force of circumstances when their popular sagas reach the pages of the novel form (from this point of view *San-kuo* and *Shui-hu* clearly qualify as "novels").

The point here is not simply that the heroes of novels tend to be misfits, or even anti-heroes (as they become in much of contemporary fiction), but rather that they are nearly without exception what Lukács has termed "problematic individuals."[16] In other words, they are no longer merely individuals who face *problems*, which they can then proceed to overcome in accordance with their own degree of heroic resourcefulness but, more important, are figures through whose situations and perceptions the very meaning of existence is called into question. In the Western tradition, this *problématique* revolves about a set of ontological and epistemological issues: the problem of knowledge, the alienation of the individual self, the impossibility of communication, and similar problems, typically conceived in terms of the stormy issue of love which forms the thematic core of the entire corpus.[17] In the Chinese novel, the particular theme of human love is less than central, but the same sort of basic issues can still be recognized in the recurring theme of mutual appreciation of individual worth (*chih-chi* 知己)—whether between ruler and minister, general and warrior, man and woman, or friend and friend, as well as in the central intellectual problem in Neo-Confucian civilization, that of self-cultivation.

The fact that the major examples of the Western novel revolve so predominantly about a core struggle for self-realization, or the validation of the individual personality in external relations, has led a number of theorists to conclude that the *bildungsroman*, in which this striving of the self towards its own identity is explicitly dramatized in terms of the maturation of a youthful consciousness, may be taken as the paradigmatic form of the novel genre as a whole.[18] Other critics, stressing instead the problematics of the reflection of the outside world in individual consciousness, have concluded that the picaresque should be viewed as the chief progenitor of the vision of the novel.[19] In the Chinese tradition, in spite of the abundance of novels whose episodic structure may be reminiscent of certain examples of picaresque fiction, the fact that such works generally lack the unifying consciousness of a *picaro* figure, the essential defining characteristic of the picaresque genre, effectively rules out the use of that particular label (the misapplication of many students notwithstanding). The pattern of the *bildungsroman*, on the other hand, may perhaps be seen in embryonic form in numerous works of the *ts'ai-tzu-chia-jen* 才子佳人 type, and blossoms into full fruit in the acknowledged masterpiece of the tradition *Hung-lou meng*.

Turning again from the narrative subject to the mode of narration, we can now see that the predominant feature of the treatment of individual character in the novel form—and one more of our defining criteria of the genre—is the normative rhetorical stance of *irony*. That is, the novelist's growing self-consciousness as to the

---

[16] Lukács, pp. 78ff.

[17] Cf. Dr. Johnson's definition of the novel as "a smooth tale, generally of love," quoted by Sir Walter Scott, in Allott, p. 49.

[18] For this view, see Freedman, pp. 58ff and 65ff, and Lukács, pp. 80, 89.

[19] See Freedman, pp 75ff. For a similar definition of the picaresque, see Claudio Guillén, *Literature as System* (Princeton: Princeton Univ. Press, 1971), pp. 72-85, esp. p. 80.

problematic nature of his heroes inevitably surfaces in the form of ironic reflection on the products of his own creation.[20] In the Chinese novel, the identification of irony as a central characteristic of the genre not only helps to account for the incessant undercutting of the ideals and aspirations of its major "heroes," but also sets off the novel to a certain extent from the historiographical and popular narrative traditions, at the same time linking it more closely to the intellectual milieu of the late-Ming and early-Ch'ing. Although I realize that works such as *San-kuo, Shui-hu, Hsi-yu chi* and *Chin P'ing Mei* are most often read as straightforward renderings of their respective mimetic worlds, I believe that in each case a careful textual analysis in fact reveals a radically ironic revision of the popular source materials in question.

In this context we can reassess the actual function of the simulated rhetoric of the oral storyteller which is maintained as an artificial pose in most of the novel tradition, in spite of the fact that its authorship, readership, and general level of sophistication mark it as a cultural form far removed from the streetside raconteurs. In the final analysis, what the use of such rhetoric in the literary novel achieves is the interposition of a strong sense of ironic detachment, which enables the author-narrator to modulate between private and public sensibilities, between his individual consciousness and the outlines of his traditional source material, in order to project further levels of meaning into his work. While this set of techniques is fundamentally different from the Western novelist's manipulation of point-of-view or the focusing on centers of consciousness within his narrative, it nevertheless shares in its reliance on the ironic discrepancy between several angles of perspective in shaping its overall literary vision.

It need hardly be pointed out that the rhetorical stance of irony is no less central in the autobiographical form of the novel (whether explicit or implicit) which increasingly comes to dominate Western fiction, from Rousseau and Goethe to the first-person syndrome of the twentieth century. In fact, one might say that the turning of novelists toward themselves as central subjects for mimetic presentation is simply the logical conclusion of the fundamental tendencies of the genre, and interestingly enough the history of the Chinese novel also evinces an overwhelming shift to the autobiographical focus in the Ch'ing period.

Ultimately, the ironic perspective of the novel form cuts not only against the individual figures within the text, or even against the author himself, but calls into question the existential foundations of the entire world which he has so painstakingly assembled through the devices of mimetic representation. It seems that the more the novelist exercises his own free will in the manipulation of his fictional text, the more he comes into confrontation with the basic rules of the game: the bounds of logic and credibility grounded in the essential realism of the novel form. Thus, in the history of the Chinese novel, one observes an increasing self-consciousness in the use of various storyteller's devices (e.g., chapter titles, post-chapter summations and forecasts, narrator's intrusions, etc.) which superficially refer to the contingencies of circumstances involved in a given plot, but actually indicate precisely those points at which the author calls attention to his own problematic role in the imposition of a credible structure on the flux of human events.

In light of this point, the fact that the course of the Western novel progresses

---

[20] Cf. Lukács, p. 75: "The irony of the novel is the self-correction of the world's fragility," and p. 90: "Irony is the objectivity of the novel."

from a static world-view to the disorder and meaninglessness of modern fiction does not simply reflect a realistic representation of the breakdown of traditional values in Western civilization during those centuries, but also indicates the novelists' gradual coming to grips with the problem of self-consciousness implicit in the novel form.[21] To say that the novel as a genre deals with human consciousness, of course, does not set it off from other literary genres, but, as a matter of proportion, the degree to which the novel does so is indeed rather unique. In effect, as the focus of the novel turns inward[22] (or more accurately, as the focus on the individual self-consciousness expands to squeeze out the rest of the world), the net result is that the problematical nature of the individual self becomes identified with the tottering foundations of the entire world-view of the civilization.

In the history of the European novel, falling as it does astride the seventeenth to twentieth centuries, it is easy to see a causal interrelation between this particular aspect of the theory of the novel and the general intellectual and philosophical movements of that period. The connection between Lockean Empiricism and Sterne, for example, or that between Bergson and Proust, is well documented, and few would dispute the influence of post-Kantian phenomenology on most of the serious fiction of the twentieth century (much as the romance narrative of the Renaissance period takes on its fullest significance in the context of the various strains of Neo-Platonic thought current at the time). Moreover, the very fact that the broader artistic and literary movement to which we apply the term "Romanticism" also happens to coincide rather neatly with the formative period of the novel, may be extremely suggestive with respect to a number of features of the novel, notably its intense focus on individual subjectivity as a means for the reconstruction of a shattered world-view.[23]

In the case of the Chinese novel, the entire history of post-Renaissance Western thought, with its baggage of empiricism, phenomenology, Freudianism, etc. is not of direct relevance. But we have seen that the Chinese novel evinces a number of features in the nature and treatment of the fictional character that are strikingly similar to those in the Western tradition. Even granting certain fundamental differences in the conception of the hero in Chinese civilization: the greater emphasis on learning and wisdom than on physical exploits, the stress on flexibility over steadfastness, the tendency to present composite groups of heroes rather than zeroing in on what Hegel has termed the "world-historic individual,"[24] etc.—there still seems to be a large ground of common concerns which links Chia Pao-yü to Goethe's Werther or Proust's Marcel as much as to his own models within the Chinese tradition.

The ground of similarity becomes even more significant when one notes that the problematic hero of the Chinese novel is also the product of a period which saw startling developments in the area of intellectual history. Although any attempts to draw close parallels between literary works and philosophical thought can be dangerously distorting, it seems fair to say that the exploration of the bounds of individual fulfillment in Ming-Ch'ing fiction is not unrelated to the tendencies towards heterodoxy,

---

[21] For discussions of the novelists' attempts to come to grips with the meaning of their world, see Culler, p. 189: "The novel is the primary semiotic agent of intelligibility," *et passim*.

[22] For a treatment of this aspect of the development of the novel form, see Erich Kahler's essays in *The Inward Turn of Narrative,* trans. Richard and Clara Winston (Princeton: Princeton Univ. Press, 1973).

[23] Schlegel makes this connection in his "Brief," p. 221.

[24] See Lukács, *The Historical Novel* (Atlantic Highlands, N.J.: Humanities, 1965), pp. 38ff.

pluralism, and what Professor William T. deBary has labelled "individualism" in post-Wang Yang-ming Neo-Confucianism.[25] As in the case of the Western novel, the ironic treatment of the central figures in the Chinese works ultimately reflects on the problematic nature of the author's entire "world," so that in each major text the aesthetics of narrative suspense, structural patterning, and mimetic recognition eventually give way to a serious exploration of some of the central issues of the civilization: conflicts between commitment to social order and withdrawal for individual fulfillment, relations between the self-contained microcosm of the private world and the larger structure of meaning in the world at large, the perception of patterns of order and meaning within an apparent chaos of temporal flux.

Unfortunately, the potential resolution of these various issues raised in the great Chinese novels, as in their Western counterparts, remains forever beyond reach. By the very nature of the form, any attempt at a final synthesis must itself stand vulnerable to ironic reevaluation, so that even what may appear to be the most unambiguous oracular pronouncements of meaning in a given text—most often through the medium of Buddhist or Taoist philosophizing—must necessarily remain at best tentative, superceded by the "realistic" contingency of a mimetic world fraught with problematics. This last point cannot be emphasized enough, as too many readers of Ming-Ch'ing fiction have tended to either take the words of such oracles at face value as the expression of the author's own "message," or else have rejected such ideas out of hand, and with them, the acknowledgement of any level of intellectual seriousness in the works in question.

The fact that the novel is essentially an open-ended form may perhaps be responsible for the tendency of many novels in both China and the West to run on to great length, as if to substitute sheer plenitude of mimetic detail for the intellectual synthesis which remains by definition elusive. This tendency towards encyclopedicity is all the more striking in the Chinese novel, where there is no prior tradition of full-length continuous narrative, except perhaps in *pien-nien* 編年 histories or works of the *pen-mo* 本末 variety. In any event, the exigencies of the task of ordering the vast canvases which result from this tendency have led novelists in the two traditions to come up with a number of comparable structural devices—the use of cyclical structures often based on multiple generations of characters, attempts at building up a polyphony of textual motifs, balancing of narrative and non-narrative elements, etc.—in spite of the very different conceptual models by which these patterns are interpreted.

A further outgrowth of the monumental size and open-ended form of many examples of the novel genre may be seen in the critical interpretations and commentaries which have accompanied both Chinese and Western novels from an early point. In the Chinese case, the practice of printing novel texts together with marginal or interlinear commentaries, and with extensive prefatory and post-chapter discussions, highlights the fact that these works were intended from the very start to be read with critical reflection. At its shallowest, this critical material amounts to little more than hit-or-miss remarks on the style or content of a given passage; but at its best it includes full-scale attempts to set forth the meaning of the works in question, using allegorical or other types of interpretive schemes. Moreover, in the writings of such great critics as Chang Chu-p'o 張竹坡, Chin Sheng-t'an, and Mao Tsung-kang, we find a sophisti-

---

[25] Cf. Watt, p. 59.

cated adaptation of the language of Chinese criticism of prose, poetry, and painting which, with fuller study, may in fact provide us with a comprehensive poetics of the Chinese novel.

This integral connection between the art of the novel and its critical interpretation is important not only because it supports the contention that the finest examples of the genre were conceived and executed by and for members of a highly sophisticated literary milieu, but also because it points to a more general characteristic of the overall intellectual climate within which the novel developed in both China and Europe. That is, the age of the novel in both of these traditions corresponds fairly neatly with what might be termed the "age of criticism," a period in which thinkers in a wide range of fields of art and learning were involved in a critical reevaluation of their classical heritage with a view towards readjusting it to new social and economic realities and to new standards of intellectual validity. In the European tradition, one need only think of such names as Dr. Johnson, the Schlegel brothers, or Madame de Staël to see the close link between this broad critical inquiry and the specific province of prose fiction, as the novel took shape from the seventeenth to the nineteenth centuries. In China this development begins and ends about a century earlier (roughly 1550-1750), and is marked by the keen interest in the emerging novel genre on the part of such leading figures as Li Chih, Yuan Hung-tao 袁宏道, Shen Te-fu 沈德符, Wang Shih-chen 王士禎, etc. If there is any validity to the statement that the central achievement of the novel is its ability to re-create its world *critically,* then this surely reflects the general critical spirit of the centuries in which the novel appeared, and may further help us to distinguish between the novel and other genres of prose fiction.

Before concluding, let us review some of the major points which we have seen to link the Chinese and the Western novel as members of the same generic class in spite of their sharp divergence in the areas of structure, characterization, and literary history. First, we have noted that the relation demonstrated by many Western scholars between the rise of the novel and the social and economic development of the pre-modern period also describes quite well the context of the emergence of full-length prose fiction in China. We have also seen that the Chinese novel shares with its Western counterpart a basic grounding in realistic representation, but that in both cases the inherent limitations of realism lead to an increasing preoccupation with the more problematical aspects of human character and experience. This attempt to grapple with the issue of the nature of reality is sharpened by the use of irony as the central narrative mode of the novel, and the focus of this ironic perspective in both cases ultimately turns to the broader intellectual foundations of the respective traditions. We have suggested that the coincidence between the novel form and a broad spectrum of critical inquiry in both China and Europe further illuminates the essentially critical nature of the mimetic representation of reality in the great examples of the genre.

Finally, let us consider certain possible conclusions to be drawn from this striking correspondence between the essential qualities of the novel form in the two traditions. Given the fact that these comparable developments occur at a time of limited mutual influence,[26] it would be tempting to conclude that the emergence of such a genre of realistic prose fiction may represent an inevitable function of human culture, bound

---

[26] In this context, we cannot really say that the Chinoiserie which finds its way to expression in Voltaire, or the early translation of such Chinese works as *Hao ch'iu chuan* 好逑傳 or *Yü chiao li,* 玉嬌梨 had any significant effect on the development of the European novel genre.

to appear in any literary civilization regardless of its particular course of historical development. To do so, however, would be to commit the same fallacy as that of scholars of the epic who observed the appearance of that form in widely separate cultures and therefore assumed it to be an inevitable phenomenon of human creativity.

Since we have seen that the putative relation between the Western novel and its social and economic background is nearly duplicated in the Chinese context, it may be more useful to speculate further on the causal relation between the literary and extraliterary factors involved in the development. On this point, some critics have argued that the novel form reflects the positive aspects of dynamic growth and development (e.g., Lukács: "The Novel is the art form of virile maturity, in contrast to the normative childlikeness of the epic.")[27]; while others have taken the opposite tack and attempted to relate the novel to a breakdown in social order and traditional values during the same period.[28] What both of these views have in common is the notion that the novel form in some sense grows out of the increasing cultural complexity of the modern era, that it is, so to speak, a response to the sheer weight of history and culture at a certain stage in the development of civilization. In terms of intellectual history, at any rate, it does make some sense to see in the novel a manifestation of the need for some kind of a synthesis, a comprehensive reevaluation of the sum total of past cultural experience, in order to adapt that to the perception of emerging new directions. (Such speculations, however, cannot satisfactorily account for a work such as the *Tale of Genji* 源氏物語, which partakes of a number of the defining characteristics of the novel form enumerated above, yet appeared in the vastly more restrictive social and intellectual context of the Heian court in eleventh-century Japan.)

A final possible attempt to account for the novel might shift the burden of explanation to the European side, and argue that Chinese civilization—with its essentially organic world-view and long-standing emphasis on the problematic nature of individual character—was ripe for the appearance of the novel at least by the time of the Neo-Confucian synthesis from Sung times on; but that a literary genre grounded in critical realism could not have appeared in the European context until after the fundamental shifts in intellectual history which mark the sixteenth and seventeenth centuries. Whether or not such speculations may prove to be of any value remains to be seen, but it is clear that it is in the area of intellectual history that we find the most fertile ground for speculation on the factors responsible for the formation of the essential features of the novel genre.

---

[27] Lukács, *Theory of the Novel,* p. 71.
[28] Cf. the remarks by Abel Rémusat cited in Lévy, p. 1.

Some Rhetorical Conventions of the Verse Sections of *Hsi-yu chi*

Francis K. H. So

Until recently the unique verse sections of *Hsi-yu chi* have remained unexplored. Without applying a specific theory of the epic, Anthony Yu pioneers to read the novel with an eye on the dimensions of the epic.[1] Yet the verse[2] sections still escape proper attention although they manifest some far more established modes of operation than the emergence of dimensions of heroic poetry. Indeed, this 100-chapter vernacular novel demands a more thorough investigation of its verse than the present article can aspire to. However, for the sake of focussing, the complication points of Tripitaka's westward journey are chosen for this study, i.e., chapters 1, 19 and 22 where Sun Wu-k'ung 孫悟空, Chu Wu-neng 猪悟能 and Sha Wu-ching 沙悟淨 make their debut. Since rhetoric is fundamentally persuasion at work,[3] the effectiveness of these verses as rhetoric will be examined. Furthermore, conscious the while that Western literatures are mainly mimetic in interpretation whereas Chinese literature is not, it is hoped that through explicating the rhetorical scheme of composition, a non-mimetic perspective for reading works of non-Western tradition can be found. Ultimately, these instruments of rhetorical conventions will be evaluated as to their applicability to the text analyzed.

---

[1] "Heroic Verse and Heroic Mission: Dimensions of the Epic in the *Hsi-yu Chi*," *Journal of Asian Studies*, 31 (1972), 879-97.

[2] By verse is meant the patterned sequence of linguistic sounds that carry prosodic features regardless of their poetic merit.

[3] The idea of persuasion in rhetoric has had its ups and downs but is still crucial in modern times. See Hoyt H. Hudson, "The Field of Rhetoric," *Quarterly Journal of Speech Education*, 9 (1923), 167-80, reprinted in *Historical Studies of Rhetoric and Rhetoricians*, ed. Raymond F. Howes (Ithaca, New York: Cornell Univ. Press, 1961), pp. 3-15; Donald C. Bryant, "Rhetoric: Its Function and Its Scope," in *Philosophy, Rhetoric and Argumentation*, ed. Maurice Natanson and Henry W. Johnstone, Jr. (University Park: The Pennsylvania State Univ. Press, 1965), pp. 32-62 and "'Rhetoric: Its Function and Its Scope' *Rediviva*," in *Rhetorical Dimensions in Criticism* (Baton Rouge: Louisiana State Univ. Press, 1973), pp. 3-23; P. Albert Duhamel, "The Function of Rhetoric as Effective Expression," *The Journal of the History of Ideas*, 10 (1949), 344-56, reprinted in *Philosophy, Rhetoric and Argumentation*, pp. 80-92.

It has been noted that the story of *Hsi-yu chi* has been influenced more by *p'ing-hua* 平話 than by vernacular dramas.⁴ What people called *su-chiang* 俗講 in the T'ang and Five Dynasties, *chiang-shih* 講史, otherwise *shuo-hua* 說話 in the Sung dynasty, *p'ing-hua* after the Sung dynasty, and *tz'u-hua* 詞話 in the Yüan dynasty are actually the same thing with different names.⁵ Again, *tz'u-hua* and *shih-hua* 詩話 have been proved to have no difference.⁶ This being the case, the presentation of *tz'u-hua* in its entire corpus as antecedents of *hua-pen* 話本 may serve to shed light on some characteristics of the latter. Sun K'ai-ti summarizes six formations of *hua-pen* as follows:

1. Combining scripture passages, colloquial prose and Buddhist metrical chant song, *chieh tsan* 偈讚, to compose a vernacular tale.
2. Combining colloquial prose and Buddhist chant song to compose a vernacular tale.
3. Combining colloquial prose and *tz'u* to compose a vernacular tale.
4. Combining colloquial prose, Buddhist chant song and *tz'u* to compose a vernacular tale.
5. Combining colloquial prose, Buddhist chant song and occasionally accompanied by *tz'u, shih,* couplets, and four- and six-character parallel lines of short phrases to compose a vernacular tale.
6. Forming a vernacular tale with colloquial prose, interspersed with *tz'u, shih,* couplets, and four- and six-character parallel lines of short phrases.⁷

Noticeably the present novel owes its mode of existence to the sixth category as a predecessor in form. It is generally regarded risky to trace the motivations in the making of literary works, but fruitful for elucidation if they are put in the schemes of formalistic conventions. Whereas the former temptation is to be avoided the latter principle will be applied to show some of the rhetorical conventions of the work. In other words, the elements singled out will be placed within their respective conventions, and, at the same time, correlated to a symbiosis with the prose context which makes up the major bulk of the novel.

The novel opens with a poem:

When Chaos was undivided, sky and earth were confused,
Boundless and indistinct, that no man had ever seen.
But since P'an Ku broke through the primeval force,
Creation then had the clear and the murky separated.
All sheltered creatures looked up to the Supreme Benevolence,

---

⁴ Chao Ts'ung 趙聰, *Chung-kuo ssu ta hsiao-shuo chih yen-chiu* 中國四大小說之研究 (Hong Kong: Yu-lien, 1964), p. 152.
⁵ Sun K'ai-ti 孫楷第, *Lun Chung-kuo tuan-p'ien pai-hua hsiao-shuo* 論中國短篇白話小說 (Shanghai: T'ang-ti, 1953), pp. 46-47.
⁶ Ibid., pp. 42-43.
⁷ Ibid., pp. 54-55.

> Ten thousand things that were made became all good.
> If you want to know the Creation and its work in eras and epochs,
> You must read the *Deliverance from Perils in the West Journey*.[8]

> 混沌未分天地亂，茫茫渺渺無人見。
> 自從盤古破鴻濛，開闢從茲清濁辨。
> 覆載羣生仰至仁，發明萬物皆成善。
> 欲知造化會元功，須看西遊釋厄傳。

To begin with a poem is often seen as the story-teller's convention. It serves various purposes. Firstly, it demands attention which is particularly necessary for an audience which comes for entertainment rather than for a hortatory speech. Secondly, it is the preamble suggesting to the audience what the story is about. Thirdly, the presence of a poem signifies something lofty, that which is above the humdrum daily speech and hence a thing of beauty and of credibility.[9] Authors especially take the third function seriously to insert poetry or verse in their novel even when it is not written as a promptbook. For that matter, the venerable look of poetry releases an author from forcing himself to assume a didactic tone so that he can freely proceed to compose a work of artifice.

This kind of design in the opening of a narrative is not an isolated incident. *Shui-hu chuan* 水滸傳, for example, has it too. In narratives bearing close relation to oral tradition this rhetorical design seems to be a common device. A classic case is the thirteenth century English romance *Havelok the Dane*. Its first 26 lines read:

> Herknet to me, godemen,
> Wiues, maydnes, and alle men,
> Of a tale þat ich you wile telle,
> Wo-so it wile here and þer-to duelle.
> þe tale is of Hauelok imaked;
> Wil he was litel, he yede ful naked.
> Hauelok was a ful god gome:
> He was ful god in eueri trome;
> He was þe wicteste man at nede
> þat þurte riden on ani stede.
> þat ye mowen nou yhere,
> And þe tale ye mowen ylere,
> At þe beginning of vre tale,
> Fil me a cuppe of ful god ale;
> And wile [y] drinken, her y spelle,
> þat Crist vs shilde alle fro helle!
> Krist late vs heuere so for to do

---

[8] Wu Ch'eng-en 吳承恩, *Hsi-yu chi* 西遊記, 2 vols (Hong Kong: Shang-wu, 1974), p. 1. Hereafter citations are from this edition. It is based on the *shih-te t'ang* 世德堂 edition of the Ming dynasty (A.D. 1592) which besides being closest to the author's day is noted for its verse sections that are often deleted in later editions.

[9] Cf. Sun, pp. 11-13.

>   þat we moten comen him to;
>   And, witþat it mote ben so,
>   B[e]nedicamus Domino!
>   Here y schal biginnen a rym;
>   Krist us yeue wel god fyn!
>   The rym is maked of Hauelok,
>   A stalworþi man in a flok;
>   He was þe wihtest man at nede
>   þat may riden on ani stede.[10]

The functions of these verses have been pointed out by the editors as follows:

> The minstrel-prologue is unusually full. The customary items, all present here, are (1) a request for attention; (2) an announcement of the subject; (3) an interesting fact or two about the story, to whet the listeners' curiosity; and (4) a prayer for the listeners, or a wish that the story may prove edifying, or an assurance that it is told with a view to moral improvement. The fashion was French (cf. the openings of "L'Entree d'Espaigne," "La Mort Aymeri de Narbonne"). The lines in "Havelok" give a good idea of the conditions under which the romance was read in public.[11]

While Western rhetoric tries to include a religious message within the secular context, its Chinese counterpart attempts to lessen the density of the moral by the camouflage of verse. Yet its total intensity is not diminished. It is sustained through the combination of the plot and the venerable mode of verse which artfully earns an additional credibility and persuasiveness. But aside from the different approaches to the context, both the Chinese and the Western rhetors are concerned with telling a tale with the aids of verse narration.

The metrics of this 7-syllable regulated verse gives it an orthodox outlook. While hinting at the development of the story it has also grandiosely stated that the subject matter will be of the mystical and the supernatural. To strengthen the story's mythological outlook as well as its credibility, the passage immediately following is turned into antiquated prose with which all books of history are written. There are quotations from a renowned philosopher, the *Book of Changes,* and the *Book of History.* Stylistically these coupled characteristics are attributed to the educated readers and therefore, for most other people, such recourse to the mystical beginning like those of the classics make the story authoritative in speaking about the supernatural. In resorting to the form of *chin-t'i shih* 近體詩 the poem acquires the advantage of being placed in a more familiar stance of convention. By virtue of its governing principles of the leveled and deflected tones, the intonation tends to be more euphonious. Because its lines are relatively lengthy they enable the semantic level of the language to stretch out at ease, making themselves more readily understood

---

[10] Walter Hoyt French and Charles Brockway Hale, eds., *The Middle English Metrical Romances* (1930; rpt. New York: Russell and Russell, 1964), pp. 74-75.

[11] Ibid., p. 74, n. 1-26.

than the more condensed lines. But whatever front this poem has put on, it intends to be a facade in order to salvage the work from being taken too lightly. Immediate readers of this vernacular novel perhaps are the literate but not the very educated people. An internal evidence is the last couplet which retains traces of attempts to get the audience's attention. Therefore, the poetry cannot follow abstruse examples like some of the less read *sung* 頌 in the *Book of Songs,* or the *Ch'u tz'u.* This rule of abiding to the relatively colloquial language, as a whole, governs all the verses found in the novel.

Images of this *chin-t'i shih* are mythopoeic. It particularly emphasizes the notion of the "Supreme Benevolence." From this *Prime Mover* all other creatures are made. The story therefore will witness all kinds of the miraculous coming to pass. Furthermore, the tone is prophetic rather than a matter-of-fact evolution of things. Inevitably it has excused itself from explaining the logic of some later *deus ex machina* techniques and other lacunae. With this forewarning, the persona's interest falls on the presentation of a universal history and its interpretation[12] in terms of the liberation from perils and the straits in a westward journey. The domains of the story are therefore fixed at the outset within those of the legendary, the historical, and the human.

The following verse portion in the chapter has taken up a *fu* 賦 genre, which in the words of Pan Ku is a type of the ancient *shih*.[13] A fifth century critic Liu Hsieh 劉勰 has definitively explained that

> the reason for making "ascension to the height" the peculiar quality of *fu* is that it is the sight of concrete objects which excites the emotions. Since the emotions have been excited by concrete objects, the ideas associated with the objects always remain clear; and since the objects are viewed with feeling, the language used to describe them is always beautiful. Beautiful language and clear ideas complement each other as the symbol and the symbolized. They are like red and purple silk in weaving, and black and yellow pigments in painting. The patterns, though mixed, possess substance, and the colors, though variegated, are fundamentally based. This is the main principle of the *fu* writing.[14]

> 原夫登高之旨，蓋覩物興情。情以物興，故義必明雅；物以情觀，故詞必巧麗。麗詞雅義，符采相勝，如組織之品朱紫，畫繪之著玄黃，文雖新而有質，色雖糅而有本，此立賦之大體也。

Despite the various themes, episodes and characters of the novel, Monkey undoubtedly is portrayed as the hero. His birth, like that of the overhead binding force

---

[12] For an excursus on other mythopoeic works such as the Bible as a universal history and its necessitation for interpretation, see Erich Auerbach's "Odysseus' Scar," *Mimesis: The Representation of Reality in Western Literature,* trans. Willard R. Trask (Princeton: Princeton Univ. Press, 1953), esp. pp. 8-23.

[13] "Preface to 'Liang-tu Fu'" 兩都賦序, *Wen hsüan* 文選, chüan 1.

[14] *Wen-hsin tiao-lung* 文心雕龍, bilingual edition, trans. and annotated by Vincent Yu-chung Shih 施友忠 (Taipei: Chung-hua, 1970), p. 66.

Tripitaka, should be of importance. The place where Monkey was born therefore bears some significance:

> Its pomposity overpowers the vast ocean,
> Its majesty pacifies the jasper sea.
> Its pomposity overpowers the vast ocean.
> While tides of silvery crests rushing, fish enter the caves.
> Its majesty pacifies the jasper sea.
> While billows of snowy waves breaking, shellfish leave the deep.
> Flaming woods by the corner pile up on high;
> Where the East Sea stretches towers a soaring peak.
> There are reddened cliffs and strange rocks,
> Precipices and amazing summits.
> On top of the red cliffs
> The colorful coupled phoenixes sing;
> Before the precipices
> A unicorn singly rests.
> At the peak is heard the frequent song of flow'ry pheasants;
> At the stone caves are often seen the dragons passing in and out.
> In the forest are longevity deer and fairy foxes;
> On the trees are divine fowls and dark cranes.
> Precious herbs and rare flowers never wither;
> Green pines and emerald cypresses have their prolonged spring.
> Heavenly peaches always bear fruit;
> Lofty bamboos often invite clouds.
> A torrent bed with creeping vines so dense,
> Its embankments fuse with grassy color afresh.
> This is truly where a hundred rivers meet, the pillar of heaven,
> Unchanged for ten thousand *kalpas,* the Earth's root. (p. 2)

勢鎮汪洋，威寧瑤海。勢鎮汪洋，潮湧銀山魚入穴；威寧瑤海：波翻雪浪蜃離淵。木火方隅高積上，東海之處聳崇巔。丹崖怪石，削壁奇峯。丹崖上，彩鳳雙鳴；削壁前，麒麟獨臥。峯頭時聽錦鷄鳴，石窟每觀龍出入。林中有壽鹿仙狐，樹上有靈禽玄鶴。瑤草奇花不謝，靑松翠柏長春。仙桃常結果，修竹每留雲。一條澗壑籐蘿密，四面原堤草色新。正是百川會處擎天柱，萬劫無移大地根。

In this *fu,* there are extravagant diction, exotic animals, scenes unknown to the ordinary eye-sight and items of encyclopedic interest which contribute to a generally high style. The structure of this *fu* basically is not much different from that of the others though it is short of a *hsü,* or the introductory part.[15] Our author may not be interested in writing the *fu* simply for the sake of writing it or of displaying his knowledge

---

[15] The structure of *fu* is discussed in Suzuki Torao's 鈴木虎雄 *Fu shih ta-yao* 賦史大要, trans. Yin Shih-ch'ü 殷石臞 (Taipei: Cheng-chung, 1966), pp. 45-85. For the rhetoric of *fu,* see David R. Knechtges, *The Han Rhapsody: A Study of the Fu of Yang Hsiung (53 B.C.-A.D. 18)* (Cambridge, London, New York, Melbourne: Cambridge Univ. Press, 1975).

of exotic fauna and flora. But through the *fu*, he develops a highly imaginative form of description by the accumulation of details, *descriptio,* which is unattainable in other genres of classical Chinese poetry. Moreover, ordinary *fu* does become difficult to read on account of its unusual vocabulary and often obsolete terms. Inasmuch as it tries to be exotic, this *fu* maintains a fairly colloquial tone, using an easy flow of learned phraseology and romantic diction rather than tongue-twisters. For this reason alone it has avoided many pitfalls of the more familiar *fu* that tends to be recondite and becomes a simple sport of word game. Though not intended for oral delivery, it bears the traits of good oratory, *pronunciatio.* By virtue of its present form, effusive in nature, it also helps the author to develop elaborately a single *topos,* though an *exaggeratio,* without rapidly digressing to other reflections, so commonly found in other forms of Chinese poetry.[16] Virtually the theme is the exotic fauna and flora. However, by its very *dispositio,* or structural arrangement, it has smoothly understated another *topos,* the *locus amoenus* or a place of pleasance.[17] Through the scheme of *dispositio* and *elocutio*—style or choice of diction, therefore, this birthplace of Monkey leads to an expression of panegyric rhetoric. This characteristic of the poetry implies the writer's attitude toward Monkey even before he is formally ushered in front of the reader. Contextually, the author is having recourse to the geomantic belief that the landscape bears some influential factors on a man's luck and fortune. Without being given further foreshadowing, one is made aware that Monkey must turn out to be some very exceptional being. As one recalls Shakespeare's dramatis personae, one notices that the nobles almost always speak in verse whereas the commoners and villains speak in prose. Similarly, this poetic setting anticipates the autochthonous birth of Sun Wu-k'ung, resulting from his receiving the emittance of the essence of the sun and the moon.

Being unusually endowed by birth, he is by no means restrained by decorum and etiquette in daily activities. Along with the essence of heaven and earth, the blood of wild Nature also runs in his veins. Like the other monkeys he is ever so full of life in the crudest and instinctive way. In his frolickings he mixes with his fellow beings to:

> Leap on the tree and climb the branch,
> Pluck a flower and seek a fruit,
> To toss pebbles
> And play games with them.
> They rush at sand burrows

---

[16] The shorter the length of a poem is, esp. in *chin-t'i shih*, the more likely it will digress to other sentiments, using *pi* (比 analogy) or *hsing* (興 induction) as a mode of expression. One other genre besides *fu* I can recall offhand which does not digress that much is *yüeh-fu*. The reason may be this. In short verse forms, the number of lines are limited. In order to fill the poem with fully developed poetic sentiments, the poet has to condense his thoughts in a compact form, using either juxtaposition (*pi*) or induction (*hsing*) to extend the implications. Some examples are Li Po's "靜夜思," Ts'ui Hao's "黃鶴樓," Wang Wei's "雜詩," Wang Ch'ang-ling's "出塞," Li Yü's *tz'u* to the tune of "相見歡," and Liu Yung's to the tune of "少年遊," etc. Hence, these short poetic forms usually present a medley of feelings other than one stretch of imagination at its full play.

[17] Andrew H. Plaks has recently dealt with the *topos* in Chinese literary tradition in *Archetype and Allegory in the Dream of the Red Chamber* (Princeton: Princeton Univ. Press, 1976), pp. 146-77.

And pile up pagodas.
Chasing dragonflies
And pounding on locusts,
They pay homage to Heaven
And worship *Bodhisattvas.*
They pull the creeping vines
To plait grass mats.
They catch the lice
Bite and nip.
They fondle their hair clothes
And pick on their nails.
Those who lean on others are leaning,
Those who rub themselves are rubbing,
Those who push are pushing,
Those who press are pressing,
Those who tug are tugging,
Those who pull are pulling.
Under the pine grove they play at will;
By the green brook they bathe so carefree. (p. 3)

跳樹攀枝，採花覓果；拋彈子，邷麼兒；跑沙窩，砌寶塔；趕蜻蜓，撲𧍪蜡；參老天，拜菩薩；扯葛藤，編草𢯎；捉虱子，咬又掐；理三衣，剔指甲；挨的挨，擦的擦；推的推，壓的壓；扯的扯，拉的拉，青松林下任他頑，綠水澗邊隨洗濯。

This *demonstratio* is said to exhibit "realism and vivid delineation."[18] Truly, the liveliness of the monkeys characterizes what a monkey should be. It is more than a purely descriptive passage. But, its verse form does not fit into any known pattern. The closest metrical scheme one can trace to is a *ch'ü* 曲 to the tune of *kuei-chih-hsiang* 桂枝香 like that in *nan-ch'ü* (southern *ch'ü*) as Professor C. T. Lo has pointed out for me. However, Professor Lo emphasizes that this tune should only be taken as a metrical similarity to the quoted verse and not a categorization of it.[19]

---

[18] "Heroic Verse and Heroic Mission: Dimensions of the Epic in the *Hsi-yu Chi*," *JAS*, 31 (1972), 884; cf. also Wei Chien-kung 魏建功, "Lüeh lun *Hsi-yu chi* te chieh-kou hsing-shih he yü-yen kung-chü te ch'eng-chiu" 畧論西遊記的結構形式和語言工具的成就, in *Hsi-yu chi yen-chiu lun-wen chi* 西遊記研究論文集, Tso-chia ch'u-pan-she comp. (Peking: Tso-chia, 1957), p. 135.

[19] I am obliged to Professor Lo Chin-t'ang 羅錦堂 of the University of Hawaii, Honolulu, for his expert answer which removes my doubt on the metrical pattern of the passage. I was under the impression that it was more like a *ch'ü* than a *tz'u*, yet not exactly an orthodox one. Professor Lo's explanation of the passage is herewith gratefully cited: This verse does not seem to have any fixed pattern. If only for the sake of finding similarity, it resembles a *ch'ü* to the tune of *kuei-chih-hsiang* as in Southern *ch'ü*. The regular prosody of *kuei-chih-hsiang* is one of eleven lines, made up of 49 syllables. But, sometimes there can be 53 syllables. That is, the last two lines, with each of 5 syllables, change to those of 7 syllables, making the meter 4, 4, 6, 6, 4, 4, 4, 4, 3, 7, 7. As to the verse of *Hsi-yu chi*, it has added on an extra four 4-syllable lines but deleted the 3-syllable line. Instead of the 11 lines in *kuei-chih-hsiang* pattern, it now becomes 14 lines, bearing this metrical scheme: 4, 4, 6, 6, 4, 4, 4, 4, 4, 4, 4, 4, 7, 7. The verb in the original 3-syllable lines may be considered as a "tag on" word and when the "tag on" words are discarded, two 3-syllable lines will make one 4-syllable line. All the particles *te* 的, for that matter, are also "tag on" words. The extra 4-syllable lines are additional lines which are quite common in Southern *ch'ü*.

When criticizing the images in *shih* and *tz'u* verses, Wang Kuo-wei coins the terminology *pu ke* 不隔 or "not veiled"[20] to describe those that come out naturally.[21] However, he applied the term only to poetry that reflects poetic sentiments and scenes. But genres that often dwell on an action such as the *ch'ü* quoted above have escaped his attention. Despite the vulgar (dialectal) level of the language, the action illustrated, to use his terminology, is *pu ke*. As is generally recognized, *ch'ü* is closer to vernacular drama than *tz'u*. This being the form chosen, it befits all the more the description of a dramatic action. Essentially the rhetorical device of this verse portion is an *amplificatio*. It is not a descriptive amplification but a dramatic characterization that is presented in its full *energia*. There is no poetic *tour de force*; instead one finds it poetically some kind of pedestrian narrative verse. The *amplificatio* does not help create poetic sentiments or provide estheticism, but it surely vivifies the actions of the monkeys and conjoins itself tightly with the narrative skill. The same awareness is present in the description of the battle feats. But the *tz'u* form may be used, e.g., in chapter 19 the battle between Pigsy and Monkey, and in chapter 22 between Pigsy and Sandy. For choosing *tz'u* instead of *shih* the author can have long and short lines; hence the oscillating rhythms which are characteristic of the genre, to illustrate the action. Within a similar metrical framework, he can conveniently waive the *ch'ü* form, i.e., the use of dialect, since colloquial language will suffice in the illustration of action and recording of the dialogue.

The real poetry that one usually comes across is whenever a mountain, a waterfall, a river, a landscape or some natural thing becomes the focus of concern. In that case, the rhetorical situation requires a proper and more poetic treatment. A 5-syllable regulated poem on the waterfall curtaining Shui-lien Cave 水濂洞 from the outer world exemplifies this:

> A whole stretch of white rainbow arising,
> A thousand fathoms of snowy waves splashing,
> Sea breeze cannot blow through,
> Shone upon by river moon it still remains effuse.
> The cool air divides the green veil,
> Its remnants moisten the blue-green hill.
> This current known as a waterfall
> Is truly like a hanging drapery. (p. 3)

一派白虹起，千尋雪浪飛。海風吹不斷，江月照還依。
冷氣分青嶂，餘流潤翠微。溪溪名瀑布，眞似掛簾帷。

Here the rhetorical convention and rhetoric as a form become one. This *topographia*, to be exact, *effiguration*—elaborate description of an object or event—offers an opportunity for the author's imagination to ride and bounce. This is the place where his description and narration are equally taken care of. When a 5-syllable regulated verse

---

[20] Hsü Wen-yü 許文雨 ed., *Jen chien tz'u-hua chiang shu* 人間詞話講疏 (Shanghai and Nanking: Cheng-chung, 1937), pp. 25-26, 29-32.

[21] Lao Kan 勞榦 comments that when an image is propounded clearly it is *pu ke*, and when it is not propounded clearly it is *ke*. See "Lun shen-yün shuo yü ching-chieh shuo" 論神韻說與境界說, in *Chung-kuo te she-hui yü wen-hsüeh* 中國的社會與文學 (Taipei: Wen-hsing, 1968), p. 22.

is not used, a *tz'u* may be employed to describe the mountain like the one Wu-ch'ao *ch'an* master 烏巢禪師 lives on (Ch. 19), or a 5-syllable quatrain to expound on the flowing sand river over which Sandy reigns (Ch. 22). On the one hand the poetry dispels the monotony in style, on the other hand it helps bring out an outstanding impression and picture of the location where some happening will eventually occur. Furthermore, polite verse is also used to mark the pompous occasion when immortal peaches and gifts are presented to Tathāgata Buddha after his subduing Monkey (Ch. 7). It is noted that classical Chinese novels have spent too much effort on the narration of the plot at the sacrifice of the description of characters and scenes. *Hsi-yu chi* in this respect is an exception.[22] But when the verse is functioning to replace the narrator's comment, then the poetry spoils the work:

> Today his name begins to be renowned,
> The opportune moment comes and his fortune is won.
> Having the fortune to reside at this place
> Is like sending a king to an immortal palace. (p. 4)

今日方名顯，時來大運通。有緣居此地，王遣入仙宮。

The verse follows Monkey's coming out from the throng in response to the challenge of going into the water-curtain cave. It is a 5-syllable quatrain with the second and the fourth lines in rhyme as expected. Its tonal pattern is shown below on the left in comparison with the orthodox scheme on the right:

```
+ − + + −              − − + + −
+ + − − + R            + + − − + R
− + + − −              + + + − −
+ − − + + R            − − − + − R
```

It can be seen that the tonal pattern is quite regular, for its irregularities are within permissible limits. However, even though the general rhythmic beat of the lines is in the xx / xxx pattern, like that of most other 5-syllable quatrains, the language is prosaic and discursive rather than poetic. Secondly, the "poem" as a whole is devoid of any poetic sentiment which is its Achilles heel. The problem as to whether the tone is colloquial, or whether the pattern is standard, is not so important as the presence of sentiments which is the essence of poetry. The lines, despite their rhyme, may therefore be called doggerel verse. To say this, at this point, does not mean to condemn Wu Ch'eng-en's failure to compose poetry. Instead, the attempt is to point out that his rhymed lines are not necessarily poetry and hence the appellation "verse" seems more suitable to categorize the body of material at issue in these three chapters. If that verse fits the status of some personage at all, it is the story-teller's because he knows the form of poetry, the leveled tone and deflected tones, rhyme scheme, but perhaps not the spirit of poetry. The verse also suits the unsophisticated audience or readers who are easily satisfied with some lines of musical tonality. Therefore, despite its being doggerel, the verse in the novel binds itself closer to the narration through mock poetry.

---

[22] Chao, p. 198.

A similar incident occurs in the description of the first woodcutter whom Monkey has mistaken for an immortal (Ch. 1). The syntax is even closer to prose than to doggerel verse. However, the number of syllables in each unit structure are fairly symmetrical, 5, 8/5, 8/5, 8/5, 8/5, 5/5, 5, making the lines repetitive and the rhythm regular like those of the refrain of a ballad. There is the emphatic repetition of the alliterative stock-phrase *nai shih* 乃是 (which is; the very).

> On his head he wears a bamboo-leaved hat,
> *The very* first leaves of fresh tender shoots.
> On his body he puts on plain clothes,
> *The very* yarn twisted from cotton tree.
> Around his waist he ties a girdle,
> *The very* silk spun from old silkworms.
> On his feet he treads the straw-sandals,
> *The very* fabric knitted from dried sedge.
>
> (p. 8)

頭上戴箬笠，乃是新笋初脫之籜。身上穿布衣，乃是木綿撚就之紗。腰間繫環縧，乃是老蠶口吐之絲。足下踏草履，乃是枯莎槎就之爽。

The previous song, a *tz'u* to the tune of *man-t'ing-fang* 滿庭芳 that the woodcutter sings just before Monkey addresses him is one that depicts a mood of plain and self-satisfied life. But the verse above, though demonstrating simple contents, is employing a hyperbole. There is the double intention that our rhetor wants to transcend the image of the humble woodcutter by means of *conduplicatio*—repetition of words in succeeding clauses, and at the same time renders the character somewhat comical. His behavior is a superficial imitation of the immortal. Unimportant as a character, he is, however, essential and crucial in the development of the plot. Through his advice Monkey finds the real immortal Patriarch Subhūti from whom he learns how to override the control of transmigration and to acquire supernatural power. Even at this moment listening to the song, Monkey's fate is already decided: he will become an immortal some day; he will be punished by Tathāgata Buddha until the coming of Tripitaka; and he will successfully assist Tripitaka to bring back the sūtras. Such an imminent image of hyperbole, in conjunction with the kind of *tz'u* the woodcutter sings, makes it small wonder that the uninitiated Monkey mistakes him for an immortal. In the lines, no lyrical impulse can be detected, but the rudimentary form of music, i.e., recurrent cantillation, is present. In so far as the lines are rhythmical, metrical or rhymed, they still deserve to be called verse. The exaggerated verse therefore foreshadows some misleading encounters Monkey will have during his quest.

Ku feng 古風 makes up another form of verse uniformly used and remains uncorrupted throughout the text. It is found in the autobiographic and career background passages of Monkey when he addresses Tathāgata Buddha in Chapter 7, of Pigsy relating his past to Monkey in Chapter 19, and of Sandy boasting of himself in front of Pigsy in Chapter 22. Stylistically they have reiterated how each seeks his immortality. Therefore, terms of the five elements, alchemy and names of various celestial deities are mentioned. Other than that, the language is quite natural and comprehensible. By choosing this genre, the author can have the liberty of using more than one rhyme scheme which happens to be the case in the three passages. There is also no limit in the number of lines in so far as each line remains consistently 5-syllable or 7-syllable. A fixed tonal pattern is not required. Therefore the author can introduce the three characters to the reader as freely as he can and as lengthily as he desires. The genre then becomes particularly suitable for narrative purposes. When Li Po wants to write a critical essay on the development of Chinese poetry in verse, he, too, has to forsake all other lyric styles he has mastered and employs the *ku feng* (5-syllable) genre.[23] The choice of this genre has one added advantage in that it gives the content a touch of antiquity. Since all the three "selected disciples" have an ancient history behind them, the form therefore goes hand in hand with the content.

At this juncture it is apparent that Wu Ch'eng-en selects his form of verse deliberately and carefully to fit the function of his rhetoric. When at the end of Chapter 19, Tripitaka asks the Wu-ch'ao *ch'an* master the way to go west, the latter answers him in a poem. It is a 5-syllable poem with 22 lines rhyming in even numbers with two rhyme phonemes: /u/ and /ü/. It may be taken as *p'ai-lü* 排律, i.e., regulated poem having its middle couplets in *ad infinitum* display.[24] It may also be taken as a variant of *chieh tsan,* a kind of Buddhist hymn that usually serves as explication of the scripture in the Buddhist tale-telling. It can be in 5-syllable lines or 7-syllable lines. In its later development it becomes an independent genre not accompanying the explication of scriptures but assumes the form of 7-syllable lines or sometimes two 3-syllable lines followed by three 7-syllable lines, or two 3-syllable lines followed by seven 7-syllable lines.[25] It may again be taken for another form of the Buddhist verse, *gāthā* 偈, which is usually of 4, 5 or 7 syllables to a line and is complete in meaning in its every two-line unit. Many of these verses are commonly composed of a four-line entity. Yet the one chanted by Tripitaka, after gaining intuition to the *Hṛdaya sūtra,* in the beginning of Chapter 20, is much longer, like the verse below. The reply of the *ch'an* Buddhist priest reads as follows:

> The road is not difficult to travel,
> Just listen to my instruction:
> A thousand hills and a thousand waters deep,
> Where dwell many a plague and demon.
> When coming to a sky-reaching cliff,
> Be at ease and have no fear.
> Coming toward the "ear-rubbing rocks,"
> Walk on your tiptoes.
> Watch out for the "black pine grove,"
> Fairy-foxes often the road block.
> Spirits pack the nation's cities,
> Monster chiefs all over the mountain live.

---

[23] See No. 1 of his *ku feng,* or ancient style odes, in *T'ang Sung shih chü-yao* 唐宋詩舉要, Kao Pu-ying 高步瀛 comp. (Taipei: Kuang-wen, 1972), 1.12a. An exposition of the genre and its mode of operation may be found in Fang Yü 方瑜, *T'ang shih hsing-ch'eng te yen-chiu* 唐詩形成的研究, Ch. 3, "T'ang-tai te hsin yüeh-fu—ku feng"唐代的新樂府——古風(Taipei: Mu-t'ung, 1975), pp. 83-114.

[24] For a metric scheme of the array of the couplets, see *T'ang shih hsing-ch'eng te yen-chiu,* pp. 78-79; Wang Li 王力, *Han-yü shih-lü-hsüeh* 漢語詩律學 (Hong Kong: Chung-hua, 1973), pp. 23-33.

[25] Sun, pp. 49, 67-102.

>   Tigers preside in the court room,
>   Grey wolves become the magistrates.
>   Lions and elephants all turn to be kings,
>   Tigers and panthers join the royal train.
>   The boar has to carry the luggage load,
>   A water demon ahead to be met.
>   The many years old stone monkey,
>   What for to harbor a wrath?
>   If you ask that acquainted one,
>   He knows the westbound road.   (p. 221)

道路不難行，試聽我吩咐：千山千水深，多瘴多魔處。若遇接天崖，放心休恐怖。行來摩耳巖，側着腳踪步。仔細黑松林，妖狐多截路。精靈滿國城，魔主盈山住。老虎坐琴堂，蒼狼爲主簿。獅象盡稱王，虎豹皆作御。野猪挑擔子，水怪前頭遇。多年老石猴，那裏懷嗔怒。你問那相識，他知西去路。

The form combines regulated verse with Buddhist chant and is apposite since it appears immediately after the *Mahāprajñā-pāramitā-hṛdaya sūtra* 摩訶般若波羅密多心經. But unlike ordinary regulated verse that depicts a scene or concentrates on a single sentiment, this verse suggests some occurrence in the future. Like the *gāthā* again, it appears to be some kind of oral formula, suggesting an eternal or epiphanic moment. It is a secret code and a truism as *gāthā* always is. The words are simple, drawing from the immediate everyday and natural examples. Yet they bear a *significatio*. The tone which sounds playful, if not absurd, is in fact prophetic.[26] Tripitaka since leaving the capital has become somehow a dullard. He has nothing in mind except the unbending will to go west to fetch the consigned scriptures. In times of controversy and stress he often fails to make head or tail of the situation. His significance in the plot is as a symbol of persistent belief in the ultimate good, with a naive knack for sincerity, and as a victim always preyed upon by the treacherous evils. Thus characterized, he cannot envision the *significatio* in the *ch'an* master's messages. Pigsy is shrewd in practical matters, but is too mundane to perceive the less immediate. Though he notices the ambiguous statement "a water demon ahead to be met," he does not quite realize his being called a "boar." Much as this *accusatio* indicts his beastly nature, it foretells and helps him realize the many travails awaiting him and his fellow pilgrims. Monkey, the most enlightened of the three, however, perceives the allegory. He does anticipate that they have to encounter numerous perils. But he is undaunted and has determined to help Tripitaka to carry out the mission through every crisis. That explains why later when he is twice banished by Tripitaka, he still comes back to his master to help him prevail. Despite the fact that he surpasses others in intuition and perception, Monkey nevertheless carries a metamorphosed body of flesh and blood. In his anger to stop the *ch'an* Buddhist priest from leaving so easily, his rash act of pounding further indicates his understanding of the priest's satire as well as his possession of human emotions that keep the novel forever interesting.

---

[26] For an interesting account comparing and contrasting the world (*viṣaya*) of poetry and ch'an (*dhyāna*) see Huang Yung-wu 黃永武. "Shih yü ch'an te i-t'ung" 詩與禪的異同, *Yu-shih yüeh-k'an* 幼獅月刊, 44 (Sept. 1976), 22-26.

This genre also contains passages which have been neglected too long. They are the exuberant description of the weapons of Pigsy and Sandy. That of Monkey's has been rendered partially in dialogue and mainly in prose in Chapter 3. Like the *locus classicus* of the shield of Achilles (*Iliad*, XVIII. 478-607), the weapons of the two immortals have been treated in the novel as *ecphrasis*, i.e., description in verse of an object of art.[27] It is an epical dimension that has so far been overlooked by Chinese scholars and critics. As a matter of fact, the *topos* does not appear profusely in epics. It is affiliated with only the most renowned and the most worthy personages. In the two lengthy works of Homer, besides the above mentioned citation, there are only six other *ecphrases: Iliad*, III. 125 ff., Helen's robe; V. 738 ff., the war gear of Athena; XI. 24-28, Agamennon's corselet; XI. 32-40, the shield of Agamennon; *Odyssey*, XI. 607 ff., Hercules's sword belt and XIX. 299 ff., Odysseus's brooch.[28] To see how *ecphrasis* works in *Hsi-yu chi* let us turn to a portion in Chapter 19 in full:

> This is divinely refined ice-iron,
> Polished to craftsmanship of brilliance.
> Lao-tzu himself did the hammering,
> God of Fire, in person, attended the fuel.
> The Five Genius Kings have schemed it out,
> The Six Deities have taken their bout,
> Making this jade fang of nine teeth,
> Molding this double-ring gold pendant leaf,
> Decked with the Six Luminances and Five Stars,
> Embodied in tune with the Four Seasons and Eight Divisions.
> Its length and height settle Heaven and Earth.
> Its left and right, *yin* and *yang* mark the sun and moon.
> The Six Hexagrams and divine troops array in celestial rule,
> The Eight Diagrams and constellations all in place,
> And so named as Super Gold Rake.
> Was presented to Jade Emperor as guard of the Red Palace.
> But since I learned to be Grand Heaven Immortal,
> And became someone with longevity,
> I was dubbed a marshal entitled T'ien P'eng,
> And was granted by Imperial favor this rake as my staff.
> When held, it flames with vigor and beams with light,
> Put down, it blasts with wind and sheds ominous snow.
> Celestial officials and generals all are kept in awe.
> Hell and *Yama* thereupon become frightened.
> Where in the world can one find this kind of weapon?
> Mankind can by no means provide such iron.
> Changing with the body and harboring in the mind,
> It plays havoc in accordance with an oral formula.
> I have carried it without fail for years;
> It accompanies me and leaves me not a day.

---

[27] Examples of the *topos* in classical European literature may be found in George Kurman, "Ecphrasis in Epic Poetry," *Comparative Literature*, 26 (Winter 1974), 1-13.

[28] Ibid., p. 3, n. 7.

Three meals a day, it never gets lost,
At night lodging it is not cast aside.
I have taken it to the P'an T'ao Festival
And have carried it to the Imperial court.
Just because of the wine I acted in violence,
Relying on my strength I became reckless,
Heavens condemned me to the mundane world,
In this life I would indulge in sins.
In a stone cave, with evil intent, I ate human beings.
In village Kao, in exaltation I got married.
This rake, in the sea, stirs the dens of dragons and tortoises;
In the mountain, breaks asunder the lairs of tiger and wolf.
All weapons may be left unmentioned
But my rake comes out as the best fit.
In battle, what difficulty is there to win?
Betting and merit seeking, all the easier.
Your copper head, iron brain and steel body, I am not afraid of;
I'll rake you until your soul vanishes and your breath disperses. (p. 215)

此是煆煉神冰鐵，磨琢成工光皎潔。老君自己動鈐鎚，熒惑親身添炭屑。五方五帝用心機，六丁六甲費周折。造成九齒玉垂牙，鑄就雙環金墜葉。身妝六曜排五星，體按四時依八節。短長上下定乾坤，左右陰陽分日月。六爻神將按天條，八卦星辰依斗列。名爲上寶沁金鈀，進與玉皇鎭丹闕。因我修成大羅仙，爲吾養就長生客。勅封元帥號天蓬，欽賜釘鈀爲御節。舉起烈焰並毫光，落下猛風飄瑞雪。天曹神將盡皆驚，地府閻羅心胆怯。人間那有這般兵，世上更無此等鐵。隨身變化可心懷，任意翻騰依口訣。相携數載未曾離，伴我幾年無日別。日食三餐並不丟，夜眠一宿渾無撇。也曾佩去赴蟠桃，也曾帶他朝帝闕。皆因仗酒却行兇，只爲倚強便撒潑。上天貶我降凡塵，下世儘我作罪孽。石洞心邪曾喫人，高莊情喜婚姻結。這鈀下海掀翻龍鼈窩，上山抓碎虎狼穴。諸般兵刃且休題，惟有吾當鈀最切。相持取勝有何難，賭鬪求功不用說。何怕你銅頭鐵腦一身鋼，鈀到魂消神氣泄！

    This is the introduction by Pigsy himself when Monkey looks down upon his rake during the second confrontation. In regular 7-syllable *ku feng* pattern, save for some slight exceptions, the form offers the narrator unrestrained space and leisure to tell his tale. The same holds true for the other *ecphrasis* which sees the fighting between Pigsy and Sandy at the bottom of the Sand Flowing River. As in the first incident this passage is also put in the first person point of view:

This precious staff of mine is famous.
It was originally from the *suo* tree of the moon;[29]
Wu Kang chopped off a branch of it;

---

[29] The meaning of the Chinese, 本是月裏梭羅派, is obscure to me. Here I take *suo* 梭 as a kind of tree.

Lu Pan shaped it with his carpentry.
In its core passes a line of gold,
On the outside are thousands of stripes of jade silk.
It is named Precious Staff and good at subduing demons,
Ever to guard Ling Hsiao Palace and suppress monsters.
But as I was ranked the Grand General,
Jade Emperor allowed me to carry it by my side.
Be it long or short depends on my will,
Thin or thick follows my whims.
It has escorted the Emperor to P'an T'ao Festival
And has also followed the court to abide in Heaven.
While on court duty many a sage paid homage.
When the screen was rolled up immortals came to worship.
Thus it has nurtured its spirituality and become a divine weapon.
It is not an ordinary human utensil.
Since my demotion from the Celestial Gate,
I have been freely roaming over the seas.
It is too presumptuous for me to brag:
Worldly spears and knives are no match.
Look at your rusty nail rake,
It's only good for plowing fields and raking vegetables.

(pp. 250-51)

寶杖原來名譽大，本是月裏梭羅派。吳剛伐下一枝來，魯班製造工夫蓋。裏邊一條金趁心，外邊萬道珠絲玠。名稱寶杖善降妖，永鎮靈霄能伏怪。只因官拜大將軍，玉皇賜我隨身帶。或長或短任吾心，要細要粗憑意態。也曾護駕宴蟠桃，也曾隨朝居上界。值殿曾經眾聖參，捲簾曾見諸仙拜。養成靈性一神兵，不是人間凡器械。自從遭貶下天門，任意縱橫遊海外。不當大胆自稱誇，天下鎗刀難比賽。看你那個銹釘鈀，只好鋤田與築菜！

Unlike the European *ecphrases* which serve as Homeric similes, these two weapons are portrayed not at the expense of an extended metaphor, but to bring to the fore the veiled background of some incidents that have taken place. In each case the weapon has a name (so has Wu-k'ung's cudgel in Chapter 3), and specifically its majestic power is accounted for. It is an *objet d'art*. As an *artificium*, it therefore is responsible for the *topos* of *deus artifex*.[30] This god as maker is not the God; rather, he appears "now as weaver, now as needleworker, now as potter, and now as smith."[31] As in the case of the shield of Achilles which is made by Hephaestus instead of Zeus, Pigsy's rake and Sandy's staff are not made by Jade Emperor. They are the outcome of collective efforts of some heavenly deities. Besides enhancing our appreciation of the work as art, *artificium* also serves various purposes. (1) It stresses that the weapon is a divine one. (2) It exposes the secret of the beginning and the creation of some celestial ventures that heretofore have been hidden

---

[30] E. R. Curtius, *European Literature and the Latin Middle Ages,* trans. Willard R. Trask (Princeton: Princeton Univ. Press, 1953), pp. 544-46.
[31] Ibid., p. 545.

from man's knowledge. (3) It provides a scenario of a period of celestial history. (4) It details some personal involvements of the deities in a human manner. (5) It brings to the foreground the deities' individual destiny that conjoins both realms of Heaven and Earth. (6) Inevitably it implies the cosmic idea of karma. (7) It reveals important moments of the past; e.g., the stress on the P'an T'ao Festival. By making use of the present it not only recapitulates history in a short instant, but also increases our spatial and temporal awareness of the journey to the west, which is the major myth of *Hsi-yu chi*. Viewed in this light, the *ecphrases* are not merely some boastful verses of Tripitaka's would-be disciples. They also reinforce the significance of some leitmotifs throughout the novel.

To sum up, the various genres of verse in these three chapters almost represent the whole spectrum of Chinese poetry. They may be good poetry or doggerel verse, but one thing is always clear: the form and the content coalesce harmoniously. When the poetry is bad it does not mean that Wu Ch'eng-en fumbles in his composition of verse. It only shows that he is more concerned with *inventio,* the gathering of his materials and finding the fittest form to propound them, than with adopting the orthodox diction and prosody as expected. His taking up of the difficult *su-wu-man* 蘇武慢 tune to compose the introductory *tz'u* in Chapter 8 has proved his great literary skill.[32] Despite his capability of rendering the language more elegant if not more abstruse (the Imperial Edict on the Holy Religion in Chapter 100 is evidence of his potential), he prefers the language of the verse to be fairly colloquial and plain to suit the vernacular nature of the novel. Even if he has to sacrifice the poetry he still endeavors to choose the proper form to distinguish the verse portion from the prose. He has therefore successfully drawn our attention to the verse by displaying the proper convention of each of the genres—and unavoidably he also has displayed his eloquent treatment. Eloquence and poetry are often identified in the same realm of *belles lettres.*[33] Yet like Dante and Chaucer who do not hesitate to break away from medieval Latin, Wu Ch'eng-en also writes in "vulgar" language instead of classical Chinese. While Dante follows the vernacular formalistic convention of the *dolce stil novo,* sweet new style,[34] and Chaucer that of the French vernacular courtly school of Machaut,[35] Wu Ch'eng-en has recourse to *tz'u-hua*. Despite the language of their works being vernacular in spirit, all three pattern their verse after the more acceptable literature, *belles lettres,* of their time. While Dante patterns after Virgil, and Chaucer after Ovid, Wu Ch'eng-en incorporates all the extant poetic genres used by men of letters. Their points of departure coincide though the results are different. Wu Ch'eng-en specifically utilizes vernacular prose which makes him fundamentally different from his European counterparts. Yet ultimately, like these writers, he is able to formulate an eloquent vernacular style. The prominent factor that contributes

---

[32] Liu Ts'un-yan, *Wu Ch'eng-en: His Life and Career* (Leiden: E. J. Brill, 1967), p. 69.

[33] Donald C. Bryant, *Rhetorical Dimensions in Criticism* (Baton Rouge: Louisiana State Univ. Press, 1973), p. 130.

[34] For Dante's apprenticeship in rhetoric and his theory of diction, esp. as found in *De Vulgari Eloquentia,* see Alfred Ewert, "Dante's Theory of Diction," The Presidential Address, 1959, *Annual Bulletin of the Modern Humanities Research Association*, No. 31 (1959), 15-30.

[35] Cf. a recent doctoral dissertation on this medieval French figure, Margaret J. Ehrhart, "Chaucer's Contemporary, Guillaume de Machaut: A Critical Study of Four *Dits Amoureux,*" *Dissertation Abstract International,* 35 (1975): 4299A-4300A.

to his eloquence is his overwhelming concern with using verse for narrative purpose,[36] but less for esthetics though the latter is not entirely neglected. He has no need of writing *Hsi-yu chi* in the guise of a poetic fiction, less of writing a forced sterilized poetic style, still less of deleting the verse to make his novel appear more "realistic." But with the interspersed verse, he attains the necessary multidimensions, dexterity in turns of phrases and imagery, and even ambiguities in implications (such as the gāthā).

From the above exercises in Western classical rhetorical conventions, one can see that the compositional and esthetic criteria defined by rhetoric do not hamper the analysis of Wu Ch'eng-en's verse, nor do they cover him with an alien veil. Whereas Western critical tradition has ramified into levels of implications (e.g., there are four levels for interpreting the Bible), its rhetorical counterpart holds them to one predominant level. In effect, rhetoric deals with the artistic composition of literary works and its integral relationship with prospective readers. Ultimately, Western and non-Western literatures share their basic concern not so much with interpretation, but with their composition and their presentation. As such, if ever there is an artistic universal, rhetoric is one dimension of it. Indeed, from a rhetorical angle, Wu Ch'eng-en has provided his verses with *technoi pisteis,* i.e., artistic means of persuasion. And for that, he has exalted the work from the traditionally besmeared reputation of the vernacular novel.

---

[36] Speaking of *hua-pen,* John L. Bishop complained about the appearance of verse in prose narratives. "Originally such verses have had an integral function in the story; later they served as a commentary, a verification, a means of delaying a climax, or merely as an embellishment. The narrator felt free to intrude in his own person into the story, lecturing his auditors on some moral problems raised by the plot, answering questions which he assumed to be in their minds, even exhibiting to them some tour de force of narrative logic which they might have missed. . . . What is of interest is the fact that during these centuries [Sung and Yüan] of development from an oral to a written genre, the oral conventions persisted to such a degree in versions designed to be read. With the conservatism characteristic of Chinese literature, these once functional literary devices have been retained as unessential literary clichés. . . . [They] impeded the development of a realistic narrative technique toward its ultimate goal of producing an effect of actuality." See "Some Limitations of Chinese Fiction," in *Studies in Chinese Literature,* ed. John L. Bishop (Cambridge: Harvard Univ. Press, 1965), p. 241. The reason that Bishop denounced the interspersed verses as impediments seems to be that he was preoccupied with the idea of "realism" and "actuality" which when translated into Aristotelian terms become mimetic, or representational. But, long after the Sung and Yüan dynasties of the *hua-pen* era, Wu Ch'eng-en (c. 1500-1582) demonstrated that the Chinese narrative tradition can be approached from another perspective instead of the mimetic. In doing so, we are only being fair to Wu Ch'eng-en's work of art.

The *Yang Lin* Story Series: A Structural Analysis

Chang Han-liang

This paper attempts to analyze three related T'ang *ch'uan-ch'i* 傳奇 stories which are generated from a prototypal anecdote in the Six Dynasties. The methodology to be employed is the formalist-structuralist theory of narrative, especially its reductive operation to search for simple structure behind complex literary works. In the course of analysis, we shall refer to the theories and practices of Shklovsky, Tomashevsky, Propp, Barthes, Genette, Todorov, and Greimas. The original anecdote, entitled *Yang Lin* 楊林, is a legend recorded by Liu I-ch'ing 劉義慶 (403-444) of the Liu Sung Dynasty (420-477). The three derivatives of the T'ang Dynasty are *Chen-chung chi* 枕中記 by Shen Chi-chi 沈旣濟 (d. 781), *Nan-k'e t'ai-shou chuan* 南柯太守傳 by Li Kung-tso 李公佐 (fl. 810), and *Ying-t'ao ch'ing-i* 櫻桃青衣 supposedly by Jen Fan 任繁, a relatively obscure author who flourished around 840.

To compare these stories by tracing their origin and evolution would be to tumble into the pitfall of diachronic study, which the structuralist intentionally tries to avoid. But our study will be justified on the following accounts. First, as Lévi-Strauss has shown in his analysis of the Oedipal myth, we should define the myth "as consisting of all its versions," and "structural analysis should take all of them into account."[1] Or as Edmund R. Leach puts it in his study of Genesis as myth, "Every myth is one of a complex and that any pattern which occurs in one myth will recur, in the same or other variations, in other parts of the complex. The structure that is common to all variations becomes apparent when different versions are 'superimposed' one upon the other."[2] Likewise, Propp's structural formula of fairy tales consisting of thirty-one functions and seven spheres of action is arrived at after an examination of one hundred tales though none of them contains all.[3] This is especially true of the archetypal models of Frye, Rank, and Campbell, whose structural elements are not necessarily present in one literary work, but in all the works as a system. In the *Yang Lin* cycle,

---

[1] Claude Lévi-Strauss, *Structural Anthropology* (New York: Basic Books, 1963), p. 217.
[2] Edmund R. Leach, "Genesis as Myth," in *European Literary Theory and Practice*, ed. Vernon Gras (New York: Dell, 1973), p. 328.
[3] Vladimir Propp, *Morphology of the Folktale*, trans. Laurence Scott (Austin: Univ. of Texas Press, 1970).

each story makes some of the structural elements manifest; the more stories we have, the clearer an underlying structure appears.

Second, in linguistic study, the notion of diachronic development is most usefully applied *macroscopically*, that is, in the comparison of "states" of a language relatively far removed from one another in time.[4] On the other hand, much of the difference between two diachronically-determined "states" of language may be present in two "varieties" of the language existing at the same time. From the *microscopic* point of view, it is impossible to draw a sharp distinction between diachronic change and synchronic variation.[5] Following this concept, therefore, the three T'ang stories, which are close in time, can be considered as synchronic variations as well as diachronic changes in spite of their common source.

Third, from the structural point of view, the prototypal *Yang Lin* anecdote, though containing all the necessary elements, is but a plot skeleton which can be considered morphologically the root of a word; the three later versions include the derivational and inflectional affixes added to it. Or put in terms of transformational grammar, *Yang Lin* serves as the deep structure of the cycle, from which are generated three surface structures through stylistic, cognitive, and connotative transformations. This is like the case of the Oedipal myth which "has only reached us under late forms and through literary transmutations concerned more with esthetic and moral preoccupations than with religious or ritual ones, whatever these may have been."[6]

The above three reasons justify a comparative study of the *Yang Lin* cycle. Such a study has another instructive purpose: It serves as a touchstone to test the applicability of the formalist-structuralist operation of plot simplification which can be extended to other stories, thus arriving at a structurally oriented typology of T'ang *ch'uan-ch'i*.

Our analysis involves two reverse but complementary procedures. The first one sets out to distinguish the *fabula* from the *sjuzhet,* by reducing the stories, especially the more elaborate T'ang versions, to minimum units, and separating the constant from the variable, the dynamic from the static, the functional from the indicial elements after the manner of Propp, Tomashevsky, and Barthes.[7] The final aim is to restore the basic structure of the stories. Such a procedure amounts to Barthes' two steps of structuralist activity, namely, *découpage,* decomposing individual tales into elements and *agencement,* recomposing the elements into a deep structure.[8] The second procedure assumes a reverse order. We shall start from the *Yang Lin* plot skeleton to examine how the "affixes" are added to the "root"; "how little sentences grow into big ones";[9] and how the "deep structure" of *Yang Lin,* so to speak, is transformed into "surface" ones. Such a homology of the macro-structure (text) and microstructure (sentence) has been a much advocated (and sometimes abused) structuralist hypothesis. The Dutch critic Teun A. van Dijk postulates: "The whole textural deep-

---

[4] John Lyons, *Introduction to Theoretical Linguistics* (London & New York: Cambridge Univ. Press, 1968), p. 49. A "state" or "point" is some limited period of time.

[5] Ibid., p. 50.

[6] Lévi-Strauss, p. 213.

[7] Boris Tomashevsky, "Thematics," in *Russian Formalist Criticism,* trans. & ed. Lee T. Lemon & Marion J. Reis (Lincoln: Univ. of Nebraska Press, 1965). Roland Barthes, "Introduction a l'analyse structurale des récits," *Communications,* 8 (1966).

[8] Roland Barthes, "L'Activité structuraliste," *Éssais critiques* (Paris: Seuil, 1964), p. 216.

[9] This is the title of Kellogg W. Hunt's article on transformational grammar.

structure can be considered as analogous to the deep-structure of a complex sentence, which is a result of a number of embeddings, transformations, etc. of 'simpler' construction [sentences] of the deep-structure."[10] Or as Barthes puts it in a different context, "le récit est une grande phrase, comme toute phrase constative est, d'une certaine manière, l'ébauche d'un petit récit."[11] As a matter of fact, the whole approach of Todorov is a syntactic one, which he rigorously demonstrates in "Narrative Transformation" and many other works.[12]

The reductive operation will enable us not only to isolate the constituent elements, but also to obtain a basic narrative syntagm which reflects human beings' conceptual mode. And the generative operation will show how the affixed or embedded elements, once integrated into the structural and semantic hierarchy, result in various levels of meaning, especially such as based on cultural, historical, and aesthetic considerations.

I

Before running into *découpage* and *agencement,* we shall first trudge into an excursion, summarizing the stories and comparing some of their important elements in a traditional way. The heroes' experiences in the four stories are almost identical: A young man has something ungratified in this world; through a spiritual guide he has a dream in which his wishes of marriage and official rank are fulfilled; after the dream he gains some knowledge of life. The original *Yang Lin* anecdote of this trite theme "Life is a dream" is brief enough for complete citation:

> During the Liu Sung Dynasty, in a temple at Chiao Hu there was a jade pillow with a crack on it. One day Yang Lin, a merchant of Shan Fu, went to the temple to pray. The temple priest asked him, "Would you like to have a good marriage?" Lin answered, "Very much so!" The priest conducted him to the pillow, whereupon Lin crawled into the crack. There he found painted halls and gem-studded chambers and met the Minister of War Chao, who gave Lin his daughter in marriage. Six sons were born to him and they all became scribes in the imperial secretariat. For several decades he lived there and had no thought of returning. Then he suddenly woke up and found himself by the pillow as before. He was greatly moved by his experience.[13]

宋世焦湖廟有一柏枕，或云玉枕，枕有小坼。時單父縣人楊林爲賈客，至廟祈求。廟巫謂曰：「君欲好婚否？」林曰：「幸甚。」巫卽遣林近枕邊，因入坼中。遂見朱樓瓊室，有趙太尉在其中。卽嫁女與林，生六子，皆爲祕書郎。歷數十年，並無思歸之志。忽如夢覺，猶在枕旁。林愴然久之。

---

[10] Teun A. van Dijk, "Some Problems of Generative Poetics," *Poetics* 2 (1971), 20-21.
[11] Barthes, "Introduction," 4.
[12] Tzvetan Todorov, *The Poetics of Prose,* trans. Richard Howard (Ithaca & New York: Cornell Univ. Press, 1977).
[13] *T'ai p'ing kuang-chi* 太平廣記 (T'an-k'ai 談愷 print), *chüan* 283. All the quotations of the stories are from this edition, except those of *Chen-chung chi,* which follow Wang Kuo-yüan's 汪國垣 anthology.

This brief narration reads so much like the synopsis of a longer work that one can hardly find any aesthetic value. However, it has the necessary ingredients of narrative: definite setting, characters, and action. Furthermore, the story involves two worlds which are presented in a frame structure. In the world of reality (not in the Platonic sense), the time-span covers no more than one day (one day in the Sung Dynasty); the locale is the temple at Chiao Hu; the characters are the hero and the priest; the action includes praying and dreaming. It is interesting to note that in the frame the fictional time is close to the real time. In the world of dream or the story within the story, the time-span is several decades; the locale begins with "painted halls and gem-studded chambers," the rest of it is unidentified; characters involved are the hero, Minister Chao, the hero's wife and six sons; the main action is marriage. The incident of marriage links the two worlds as well as the frame and the story within: the hero's wish of marriage in reality is fulfilled in dream.

In addition to the wish of marriage, there are two other elements which serve to link reality and dream: One is the person who leads him to dream (the priest); the other is the transition between the two worlds, the "crack" on the pillow, through which the hero enters the dream world. These two important elements are preserved in all the three T'ang stories, only they are made more complicated. Let us compare the two images in them:

> *Yang Lin*: The priest conducted him to the pillow, whereupon he crawled into the crack.
>
> *Chen-chung chi*: The old man Lü Weng reached into his bag and took out a pillow and gave it to Lu Sheng . . . . The pillow was made of green porcelain and had an opening at each end. Lu Sheng bent his head toward it and as he did so the opening grew large and bright, so that he was able to crawl into it.
>
> (*Kuang-chi*, *chüan* 82)
>
> *Nan-k'e t'ai-shou chuan*: Ch'un-yü took off his hat and lay on the pillow. He felt drowsy as if in a dream and saw two messengers dressed in purple . . . . He followed them to the door . . . . Coming out of the house, they headed for the hole under the old locust tree. The messengers drove into the hole . . . and came to a big city with towered walls . . . . Suddenly the gate was opened. Ch'un-yü dismounted from the carriage and entered the gate.
>
> (*Kuang-chi*, *chüan* 475)
>
> *Ying-t'ao ch'ing-i*: As soon as he seated himself in the lecture room where the monk was expounding sutras . . . Lu Tzu began to feel tired and fell asleep. In his dream, he came out of the temple gate and saw a maid dressed in green, sitting with a basket of cherries at the threshold . . . . Lu Tzu followed her across Tienchin Bridge and into the quarter to the south of the river. They stopped in front of a mansion with a tall gate. The maid entered the gate and let Lu Tzu wait outside. A while later,

>   four young men came out to greet him . . . . Then he
>   was led to the northern hall.
>
>   (*Kuang-chi, chüan* 281)

「楊林」：巫卽遣林近枕邊，因入坼中。

「枕中記」：翁乃探囊中枕以授之⋯。其枕青甆，而竅其兩端。生俛首就之，見竅漸大，明朗。乃舉身而入。

「南柯太守傳」：生解巾就枕，昏然忽忽，髣髴若夢。見二紫衣使者⋯隨二使至門⋯出大戶，指古槐穴而去。使者卽驅入穴中⋯又入大城，朱門重樓⋯。俄見一門洞開，生降車而入。

「櫻桃青衣」：見一精舍中有僧開講⋯盧子方詣講筵，倦寢。夢至精舍門，見一青衣攜一籃櫻桃在下坐。⋯盧子便隨之過天津橋，入水南一坊。有一宅，門甚高大。盧子立門下，青衣先入。少頃，有四人出門，與盧子相見⋯。斯須，引入北堂。

The images of guide and entrance in *Yang Lin* are the simplest: the priest and the crack on the pillow. In *Chen-chung chi* the entrance is the same as that in *Yang Lin*; but the description of the situation and the characterization of the guide are more detailed. But compared with *Nan-k'e* and *Ying-t'ao*, the first two stories have a more straight-forward description of the hero's entrance into the dream world. In *Nan-k'e*, the guide is first played by the two messengers who lead the hero out of the house. They head for and pass through the hole. After that we have a minute description of the alien landscape resembling T'ao Ch'ien's 陶潛 T'ao-hua-yüan 桃花源. Having passed through the palace gate, Ch'un Yü is greeted by a minister who, replacing the two messengers as the guide, leads him through another door and into the inner court. In *Ying-t'ao*, the role of guide has undergone several transformations, from the monk in reality to the maid of cherries and the four young men at the threshold in dream. Although the experience of passing from reality to dream is only a matter of seconds, in the latter two stories, however, the heroes' action of reaching their destinations is apparently slowed down.

To show the process from simplicity to complexity of the four stories, we can further compare their endings, that is, the heroes' experience of returning from dream to reality, from the story within to the frame. Again, the ending in *Yang Lin* is the simplest: "Then he suddenly woke up and found himself by the pillow as before. He was greatly moved by his experience." No moral lesson is given here. In *Chen-chung chi,* we find the hero who

>   woke up with a start and found himself lying as before in the
>   roadside inn, with Lü Weng sitting by his side and the millet
>   that his host was cooking still not yet done. Everything was
>   as it had been before he dozed off. "Could it be that I have
>   been dreaming all this while?" he said, rising to his feet. "Life
>   as you would have it is but like that," said Lü Weng. For a
>   long while the young man reflected in silence, then he said,
>   "I now know at last the way of honor and disgrace and the
>   meaning of poverty and fortune, the reciprocity of gain and
>   loss and the mystery of life and death, and I owe all this
>   knowledge to you. That's why you have tried to restrain my

desire. How dare I not take your advice?" With this he bowed his thanks and went away.

盧生欠伸而悟，見其身方偃於邸舍，呂翁坐其傍，主人蒸黍未熟，觸類如故。生蹶然而興，曰：「豈其夢寐也？」翁謂生曰：「人生之適，亦如是矣。」生憮然良久，謝曰：「夫寵辱之道，窮達之運，得喪之理，死生之情，盡知之矣。此先生所以窒吾欲也。敢不受教。」稽首再拜而去。

The passage is strongly didactic in purpose, but didacticism is diluted by the author's use of dialogue and realistic description of external events (e.g., the cooking of millet) and thus becomes more convincing.

Toward the end of the episodic *Nan-k'e,* "Ch'un-yü woke up and found the servants were sweeping the yard, his two friends were washing their feet on the couch, the setting sun was still above the West wall, and the dregs in the jar on the East window were still damp. He came to realize that a whole life in dream was but a moment in reality. Ch'un-yü was deeply moved and heaved sighs, and told his friends about the experience." The story does not end here. Ch'un-yü and his friends would go so far as to excavate the locust hole. The author makes use of explicit allegorical method to establish a one-to-one relationship between the ant hill and the fairy kingdom in order to satirize the vanity of human wishes. At the end of his narration, the author goes even farther to append an epilogue to prove the truth of the story and to state his moral and didactic intention. All these show that *Nan-k'e* is an artificial work, deliberately emphasizing artistic and moral value.

The ending of *Ying-t'ao,* though similar to that of *Chen-chung chi,* produces a more ironical effect; the irony is two-fold, both of situation and of life. The hero in dream (in the story within) has attained high rank and inspected the temple which he visited before sleep (in the frame). This time he listens to the monk's expounding sutras as the prime minister waited upon by entourage. This is in sharp contrast with his first visit here when he was down in luck. Most ironically, Lu Tzu

mounted the temple to worship the Buddha. Suddenly he swooned, lying unconscious for a long time. He heard the monk addressing him: "Danapati, why don't you awake?" At this he suddenly woke up and found himself in the same white robe as usual and all the attendants disappeared. Confused and disturbed, he walked out slowly. Outside, he saw his young servant standing at the doorway, holding his hat and donkey. The servant asked him: "What has kept you so long? The donkey and I are both hungry." Lu asked him what time it was. The servant replied, "It's almost mid-day." Lu Tzu in a daze heaved a sigh: "Honor, wealth, glory, obscurity, poverty—all these are only natural in life. From now on, I will not search for official glory." With this knowledge, he started searching for the Taoist divines and was not heard from this world hereafter.

升殿禮佛，忽然昏醉，良久不起；耳中聞講僧唱云：「檀越何久不起？」忽然夢覺。乃見著白衫服飾如故。前後官吏，一人亦無。迴遑

> 迷惑，徐徐出門。乃見小豎捉驢執帽，在門外立，謂盧曰：「人驢並
> 餒，郎君何久不出？」盧訪其時，奴曰：「日向午矣。」盧子悯然歎
> 曰：「人世榮華窮達，富貴貧賤，亦當然也。而今而後，不更求官達
> 矣。」遂尋仙訪道，絕跡人世矣。

Awakened from his dream of glory, the hero has returned to the cruel reality where both men and the donkey are hungry. Decades in dream last less than a day in life. This is indeed the irony of life. The story does not have an external force like Lü Weng in *Chen-chung chi,* which presides over the hero's fate. The function of the monk is not obvious; the hero's acquisition of knowledge is through the process of self-realization. Therefore, the reader does not feel that the author is moralizing, not explicitly at least. Furthermore, the author's art of realism is successful. His description of Lu Tzu walking out of the temple is vivid. There is a sharp contrast between the world outside where the young servant holds the donkey and the world inside where he is attended by entourage. All these show that the author is more realistic in description than the authors of *Chen-chung chi* and *Yang Lin*. And his restraint from authorial intrusion renders the story less didactic and more convincing.

The above situations show that the four stories, though the earlier ones not of necessity influential on the later, have undergone a process of complication and elaboration. According to the chronology, *Yang Lin* was written by Liu (403-444) during the Six Dynasties, *Chen-chung chi* in 780, the year before Shen Chi-chi's death, *Nan-k'e* supposedly in 843, and *Ying-t'ao,* if the author can be ascertained, between 841 to 846. The style of *Nan-k'e* is highly elevated, embellished by poetry and four-word and six-word antitheses. The story is appended with a *tsan* 贊, in which the author reinforces his moral didacticism. All these stylistic features and moral considerations indicate that the story was written to win the favor of the examiners in the civil service examination. These stylistic features are not found in *Ying-t'ao,* but the technique of writing is rather mature. It is probably one of "the late works," as Professor Yeh Ch'ing-ping 葉慶炳 observes, "which have no insertions of poetry, no moral arguments, apparently no longer under the influences of Buddhist translations and the convention of *Wen Chüan* 溫卷 in order to pass the examination, and become therefore fiction of purely artistic creation."[14]

The evolution from simplicity to complexity is partially a consequence of the insertion of non-literary elements such as historical and political ones. One example can bear this out. In the prototypal *Yang Lin,* the hero's identity, a variable element and a static motif, is a merchant; what he seeks for is marriage, not official rank—both marriage and official rank are variable and static. The reader is not told of Yang Lin's political ambition. Therefore, that his six sons become scribes in the imperial secretariat is irrelevant to his wish-fulfillment. But in *Chen-chung chi* and *Ying-t'ao,* the hero's identity is transformed from a merchant to an obscure young scholar aspiring to political fame. Such a wish is fulfilled in his dream through marrying a high-ranking officer's daughter. This clearly reflects the political structure based on civil service examination and the social structure based on the marriage between aspiring scholars of humble origin and daughters of noble families during the middle T'ang

---

[14] Yeh Ch'ing-pin, *Chung-kuo wen-hsüeh shih* 中國文學史 (Taipei: Hung Tao, 1974), pp. 274-75.

Dynasty. In *Nan-k'e,* the hero becomes a frustrated knight errant who becomes in dream the magistrate of a prefecture. Ch'un-yü's gratification of suppressed desire reflects the political phenomenon of the sovereign powers of contending feudal lords 藩鎭 during the later period of the T'ang Dynasty. Since the present study does not intend to interpret the four stories in terms of historical and cultural contexts, we shall respectfully leave the aforesaid to traditional scholars.

II

Now we may venture to undertake the "structuralist activity": decomposing the stories into elements and recomposing the elements into a deep structure. The first step as Barthes suggests is to reduce the works into constituent elements homologously as we reduce a sentence into grammatical elements. For instance, the prototypal *Yang Lin* can be dissected into the following constituents: the hero, the priest, the crack, entrance, marriage, exploits, return. Here we find the reductive operations of Propp, Tomashevsky, Greimas, and Barthes most effective. All these reductions have one common feature, namely, the elements are reduced into binary pairs. Thus we find constant elements versus variable elements; bound motifs versus free motifs (Propp);[15] dynamic motifs versus static motifs (Tomashevsky);[16] dynamic predicates or functions versus static predicates or qualifications (Greimas);[17] indices versus functions (Barthes),[18] etc. Take *Yang Lin* for example. The two major functions "entering" and "marrying" are constant elements, dynamic motifs or predicates, whereas the personages and the locales are variable elements, static motifs; their attributes are static predicates, qualifications, informants, or indices. While the guide as *actant* (*adjuvant* here) has a constant function of guiding, the *actant's* manifest identities, i.e., the priest, the monk, the messengers as *acteurs* are variables. It follows that Greimas' three sets of *actants* in binary opposition are constants; their embodied *acteurs* with different attributes and identities are variables.[19] Furthermore, the two major functions in *Yang Lin* which change the hero's situation are dynamic motifs; all the remaining elements are static. For instance, the "ungratified" quality of the hero is an index; his passing "through a gate" is a catalysis to the cardinal function (nucleus) of "entering," etc.

Having thus reduced the stories into elements, we may further examine their relationships. We find all of them are in binary opposition. Not only are the constants opposed to the variables, the dynamic motifs to the static ones, functions to indices, but each category shows opposition in itself. We can put aside Greimas' actantial model which is rooted on his essentially binary semantic universe. If we examine the other elements, we find an equally interesting opposition. A few examples can bear this out. The index "ungratified" is opposed later by the index "gratified"; the function "return" can be dispensed with since it is a negative of the function "enter"; the world of reality is opposed by the world of dream; the hero's illusion is negated by his disillusionment. This binary opposition of the constituents, when distributed on

---

[15] Propp, p. 20.
[16] Tomashevsky, pp. 68-70.
[17] A. J. Greimas, "Structural Semantics," trans. Harjeet Singh Gill, *Pakha Sanjam,* 6 (1973), 232-315.
[18] Barthes, "Introduction," 8-11.
[19] A. J. Greimas, *Du sens* (Paris: Seuil, 1970), p. 209f.; "Structural Semantics," 273.

various levels and integrated into a narrative hierarchy, helps to form the narrative syntagm of the four stories and accounts for the frame-story structure.

In the following, we shall actually reduce the *Yang Lin* story series in the manner of Propp, Tomashevsky, and Barthes. First we should have an abstract of *Yang Lin* as a kernel sentence: "The ungratified hero led by a guide passes through a gate and enters another world where he marries a noble lady and gains fame and returns to the world with some knowledge of life." From this summary we find the variable elements or the static motifs which are subject to transformation are: 1) the hero, 2) the guide (the priest), 3) the entrance (the crack), and 4) the adventures in dream (e.g., marriage, begetting sons, etc.). The constant elements or dynamic motifs which form the action are: 1) the encounter with the guide (sender or dispatcher, provider or helper), 2) the entering into the dream or mysterious world, 3) the fulfillment of wishes (marriage, political aspiration, etc.), 4) the return from the dream world, and 5) the hero's reaction to the dream experience.

The dynamic motifs in *Yang Lin* and the other three stories are rather limited. There are approximately D^1: the hero's encounter with the guide, D^2: the hero's entering the dream world, D^3: the hero's marrying the daughter of a noble family, D^4: the hero's acquisition of official rank (this is not found in *Yang Lin*, but is in the other three stories), D^5: the hero's being slandered by villains and thus put into prison by the emperor (in *Chen-chung chi*), D^6: the hero's reconciliation with the emperor (only in *Chen-chung chi* and *Nan-k'e*), D^7: the hero's searching for his father in dream (in *Nan-k'e*), D^8: the hero's return, D^9: the hero's acquisition of knowledge. D^1 and D^9 as the beginning and the end take place in the real world and in the frame; D^2 and D^8 at the threshold between the two worlds, and are therefore the points where the frame and the story within intersect; the other functions take place in dream and the story within the story. Such an action pattern corresponds to Joseph Campbell's monomyth of the hero's departure and return and Greimas's disjunctional syntagm. Thus the whole plot, with one dynamic motif after another in chronological order,[20] as in most Chinese narratives, forms a complete circle and produces, as Todorov would put it, a sense of equilibrium.[21]

---

[20] Critics like Lévi-Strauss (1960), Doležel (1972), and Fokkema (1976) might question my application of Propp's chronological model on the following grounds. First, Propp deals with folklore texts, not literary texts, the former being sometimes oral narration. Second, Propp does not and need not distinguish *fabula* (story) from *sjuzhet* (plot) because in folktale, which is almost exclusively chronological, the two always overlap. Third, the study of invariants does not amount to the structural analysis of narrative. My answer is very simple: The four stories under discussion, not to mention the other Chinese stories, are chronological in time sequence. The authors' artistic idiosyncracy of deforming the *fabula* does not lie in time sequence but in something else. For these criticisms of Propp, see Claude Lévi-Strauss, "La structure et la forme: Réflexions sur un ouvrage de Vladimir Propp," *Cahiers de l'Institut de Science Economique Appliquée*, No. 99 (1960), 3-37. Lubomir Doležel, "From Motifemes to Motifs," *Poetics* 4 (1972), 55-91; D. W. Fokkema, "Continuity and Change in Russian Formalism, Czech Structuralism, and Soviet Semiotics," *PTL* 1 (1976), 153-96. For the Propp-Lévi-Strauss controversy and Propp's response, see Serge Shishkoff, "The Structure of Fairytales: Propp vs. Lévi-Strauss," *Dispositio*, 1 (1973), 271-76 and Vladimir Propp, "Study of the Folktale: Structure and History," in the same issue of *Dispositio*, 277-92.

[21] "The minimal complete plot consists in the passage from one equilibrium to another. An 'ideal' narrative begins with a stable situation which is disturbed by some power or force. There results a state of disequilibrium; by the action of a force directed in the opposite direction, the equilibrium is re-established; the second equilibrium is similar to the first, but the two are never identical." *The Poetics of Prose*, p. 111.

However, such an outline sketch of plot does not in the least account for the artifice of the three elaborate stories. Elaborations result from transformations of variable elements, static motifs, and insertions of indices and catalyses to functions. For the sake of comparison, we have now to decompose the three T'ang stories, put side by side corresponding elements, and finally examine how aesthetic and semantic elements are added to the original prototype. In the following chart we shall use the letter S to stand for the static motifs.

Motif	Chen-chung chi	Nan-k'e	Ying-t'ao
S^1 (time)	the seventh year of K'ai Yüan (719 A.D.)	the seventh year of Chen Yüan (791 A.D.)	the earlier years of T'ien Pao (c. 750)
S^2 (guide) dispatcher helper	the T'aoist priest Lü Weng	two friends ⟶ two messengers ⟶ prime minister	the monk ⟶ the cherry-maid ⟶ four cousins
S^3 (hero) subject	scholar Lu Sheng	knight errant Ch'un-yü	scholar Lu Tzu
S^4 (entrance)	the crack on the pillow	locust hole ⟶ the gate of the palace	the door of the temple ⟶ the door of the house
S^{5a} (object^1 = wife) sought-for-person	the daughter of the Tsui family of Ch'ingho	Princess Golden Bough	the daughter of the Cheng family
S^{5b} (object^2 = official rank)	civil service examination ⟶ imperial scribe ⟶ military officer ⟶ imperial censor ⟶ prime minister	Magistrate of the Southern Branch	civil service exam ⟶ military officer ⟶ imperial censor ⟶ prime minister
S^{5c} (object^3 = sought-for-person)	The Emperor Hsüan	The Emperor of Huai An (locust)	the Emperor Hsüan

These are approximately the replaceable but necessary elements of the three tales. Other static motifs include the hero's adventures and ordeals which can be found to different extents in the stories. For instance, in *Ying-t'ao* the hero does not undergo any ordeals; the hero in *Nan-k'e* has more adventures because of the story's episodicity. Furthermore, one character may play more than one role (e.g., Lü Weng in *Chen-chung chi* serves at once as the donor, the helper, and the dispatcher); or one role may employ several characters (e.g., the guide may be multiple, as we have shown above; in *Ying-t'ao* Lu Tzu's aunt plays the roles of helper as well as the sought-for-person). There are to be sure other static elements which are subordinate to the above mentioned motifs. These qualificative elements, though not absolutely necessary, produce the aesthetic and semantic significance of the stories. Suppose we use the letter Q to stand for them, the following shows the descriptions of the heroes, and the sought-for-person:

Qualificative S^3Q (hero)	Yang Lin	Chen-chung chi	Nan-k'e	Ying-t'ao
	a merchant of Shan Fu (No descriptive elements)	wore a plain, short coat and rode a black colt; looking at his [own] shabby clothes	taken to drinking and ill-tempered; did not behave himself; recalcitrated his commander and was fired; became dissipated and indulged in drinking	had taken the civil service exams for years without success and become poverty-stricken

		"I have devoted myself to study and have enriched myself with travel . . . but now at the prime of life I still have to labor in the fields."		
S⁵ᵃQ (sought-for-person)	Chao gave his daughter to Lin (no descriptive elements)	the girl was very beautiful	she was about 14 or 15, as beautiful as a fairy	his wife was at the age of 14 or 15, as beautiful as a fairy

These descriptive elements added to the narrative elements make the story more elaborate.

III

However, to trace the corresponding elements is one thing; to see how they are respectively integrated in the stories is another. To probe into the stylistic and structural evolution of the stories, we may resort to a variety of formalist-structuralist theories of narrative, such as: 1) Émile Benveniste's distinction between the two linguistic systems, *histoire* (narrative) and *discours* (discourse), a concept most popular among French structuralists; 2) the theory of digression as postulated by Shklovsky, Genette, and Todorov; 3) rules of narrative transformation, particularly those suggested by Propp and Todorov; 4) the Prague School's theory of the *dominant*. Some of these theories have limitations in application since they are based on linguistic models other than Chinese. For instance, hitherto we have little knowledge, if any, about the syntactics and discourse linguistics of the T'ang language and therefore find it difficult to apply Todorov's and Benveniste's approaches to an indisputable extent.

Furthermore, some of the aforesaid theories are not mutually exclusive, but are related to one another. Propp's "expansion" of an element[22] corresponds to Todorov's "embedding."[23] Shklovsky's *ostranenie*, defamiliarization of the reader's automatic perception by laying bare some devices[24] can be understood in light of Jakobson's concept of shifting the *dominant*[25] or Mukařovský's "foregrounding" of the utterance.[26]

To apply all these theories exhaustively to our analysis of the four stories would be too ambitious an undertaking. We shall therefore facilitate our task by restricting ourselves to the theory of digression of Shklovsky and others while occasionally excursioning into the other related ideas.

Shklovsky's concept of "making strange" originally refers to the poet's use of techniques to impede perception which has become habitual and automatic.[27] Later

---

[22] Vladimir Propp, "Fairytale Transformation," in *Readings in Russian Poetics*, trans. and ed. Ladislav Matejka & Krystyna Pomorska (Cambridge, Mass. and London: The M.I.T. Press, 1971), p. 103.

[23] Todorov, *The Poetics of Prose*, p. 70.

[24] Victor Shklovsky, "Art as Technique," in Lemon and Reis, p. 12.

[25] Roman Jakobson, "The Dominant," in Matejka and Pomorska, p. 83.

[26] Jan Mukařovský, "Standard Language and Poetic Language," in *A Prague School Reader on Esthetics, Literary Structure, and Style*, trans. and ed. Paul R. Garvin (Washington, D.C.: Georgetown Univ. Press, 1964), pp. 17-30.

[27] Shklovsky, p. 12.

he extends this concept to other literary genres, narrative for one. A famous example he gives is Tolstoy's "Kholstomer" whose narrator is a horse. The horse-narrator makes comment on human sense of property and thus makes a familiar content strange.[28] This technique of shifting focus to achieve new perception of something familiar is adopted by Shen Chi-chi. As has been said above, the theme of *Yang Lin* is a trite one and the anecdote itself has been popular and widely circulated before artistic elaborations come into being. The introduction of any new element would shift the reader's perception and make the familiar incident novel. A comparison of the descriptions of the guides in *Yang Lin* and *Chen-chung chi* shows how in the latter the author's focus is shifted and a new perception is achieved.

Yang Lin opens with a presentation of the locale, an element which Barthes would call an informant. Then the author introduces the hero to the temple where he meets the priest. The priest asks him if he wishes for good marriage and conducts him to the pillow. Although the priest directs the hero's adventure, no description is given to him. The story focuses apparently on Yang Lin. Compare this with Shen Chi-chi's *Chen-chung chi*. The story opens with a brief exposition of the priest:

> In the seventh year of K'ai Yüan a Taoist priest by the name of Lü Weng, who had acquired the magic of the immortals, was traveling on the road to Hantan. He stopped at an inn, took off his hat and loosened his belt. He was sitting and resting with his back against his bag when he was joined in a very genial conversation by a young man named Lu Sheng.
>
> 開元七年，道士有呂翁者，得神仙術，行邯鄲道中，息邸舍，攝帽弛帶，隱囊而坐。俄見旅中少年，乃盧生也。

This passage shows that the author's focus is on the priest rather than on Lu Sheng though it shifts to the hero in the story within the story. Whatever the author's purpose is, this relative emphasis on the importance of the guide is a novel viewpoint in comparison with the original episode in *Yang Lin*. The guide is actually the person who manipulates the hero's fate. The hero himself is only a passive figure. Although the active and manipulating function of the guide is true of Yang Lin as well as of Lu Sheng, yet Shen Chi-chi's shift of focus from the hero to the guide in the opening scene not only makes new the popular opening in *Yang Lin* which is familiar to most readers, but also is artistically successful. Shen's device of defamiliarization, to use a metaphor of transformational grammar, is, as it were, the application of the rule of passive transformation through which the actant is transformed into a patient.

One way of defamiliarizing plot elements is Shklovsky's concept of *unrolling* (*razvertivanie*) of the subject. It consists of "disproportionately extended description of individual parts of the plot which result in their being felt by the reader to be digressions although they still constitute a main link in the narrative sequence of a story."[29] Compare again the conversation between the guide and the hero in both *Yang Lin* and *Chen-chung chi*. In the first story there is only an exchange of a few words: "The temple priest asked him, 'Would you like to have a good marriage?' Lin answered,

---

[28] Ibid., p. 14.
[29] Tzvetan Todorov, "Some Approaches to Russian Formalism," in *Russian Formalism*, ed. S. Bann and J. E. Bowlt (New York: Barnes and Noble, 1973), p. 13.

'Very much so!'" We know nothing about the characters since they are not motivated. But in the second story the dialogue is extended, "unrolled" into a much longer one so as to expose the hero's past history and reveal his motivation:

> After a while Lu Sheng suddenly sighed and said, looking at his shabby clothes, "It is because fate is against me that I have been such a failure in life!" "Why do you say that in the midst of such a pleasant conversation?" Lü Weng said, "For as far as I can see, you suffer from nothing and appear to enjoy the best of health." "This is mere existence," Lu Sheng said. "I do not call this life." "What then do you call life?" asked the priest, whereupon the young man answered, "A man ought to achieve great things and make a name for himself; he should be a general at the head of an expedition or a great minister at court, preside over sumptuous banquets and order the orchestra to play what he likes, and cause his clan to prosper and his own family to wax rich—these things make what I call life. I have devoted myself to study and have enriched myself with travel; I used to think that rank and title were mine for the picking, but now at the prime of life I still have to labor in the fields. What do you call this if not failure?"
>
> 久之，盧生顧其衣裝敝褻，乃長歎息曰：「大丈夫生世不諧，困如是也！」翁曰：「觀子形體，無苦無恙，談諧方適，而歎其困者，何也？」生曰：「吾此苟生耳。何適之謂？」翁曰：「此不謂適，而何謂適？」答曰：「士之生世，當建功樹名，出將入相，列鼎而食，選聲而聽，使族益昌而家益肥，然後可以言適乎。吾嘗志於學，富於游藝，自惟當年青紫可拾。今已適壯，猶勤畎畝，非困而何？」

Lu Sheng's exposition of his ambition in life, structurally speaking, is not a digression but an organic part. But compared with Yang Lin's wish for marriage, it is undoubtedly extended, since between the two dynamic motifs or functions of *encountering* and *dreaming*, it is an inserted static motif which serves only the purpose of index or informant.

The unrollment of plot elements can be achieved by the insertion not only of indices and informants but also of catalyses between two nuclei. We may compare the passages between D^2 (the hero's entering the dream world) and D^3 (the hero's marrying the daughter of a noble family) in *Yang Lin, Chen-chung chi,* and *Ying-t'ao ch'ing-i.* In *Yang Lin* the hero, conducted by the priest, 1) *crawls* into the crack (D^2); 2) *finds* painted halls and gem-studded chambers; 3) *meets* Minister Chao; and 4) *marries* his daughter (D^3). Between the two dynamic motifs, the two main functions (nuclei) 1 and 4, we have two static motifs 2 and 3. But 2 serves as an index to the "good marriage" by indicating the family's wealth; 3 serves both as an index which indicates the family background of his future wife and a catalysis which, in Barthes' words, is "parasitic" on D^3 because only after meeting the Minister can Yang Lin fulfill his wish of a good marriage. The relation of 3 to 4 is precisely that of a catalysis to a nucleus.

The corresponding passage in *Chen-chung chi* is as follows: (We have put down a number before each motif for the convenience of discussion.)

> After he finished speaking 1) he felt a sudden drowsiness. 2) The innkeeper was steaming some millet at the time. 3) Lü Weng reached into his bag and 4) took out a pillow and 5) gave it to Lu Sheng, 6) saying, "Rest your head on this pillow; it will enable you to fulfill your wishes." 7) The pillow was made of green porcelain and had an opening at each end. 8) Lu Sheng bent his head toward it and as he did so 9) the opening grew large and bright, 10) so that he was able to crawl into it (D^2). 11) He found himself back home. 12) A few months later he married the daughter of the Ts'ui family of Ch'ingho (D^3) . . . .
>
> 言訖，而目昏思寐。時主人方蒸黍。翁乃探囊中枕以授之，曰：「子枕吾枕，當令子榮適如志。」其枕青甆，而竅其兩端。生俛首就之，見其竅漸大，明朗。乃舉身而入，遂至其家。數月，娶清河崔氏女。

The two major dynamic motifs are 10 and 12. They are the nuclei with which catalyses can be saturated. To 10 are subordinate 1, 3, 4, 5, 6, 8, and 9. 2 is an index which serves as an objective correlative to show at the end of the story the brevity of external time during the hero's sleep. 7 is relatively a non-functional and purely descriptive informant. These are the *unrollment* before the appearance of D^2 and can be therefore disposed of. It is clear that between D^2 and D^3 no descriptive and catalytical elements are inserted.

Much more elaborate than the above two examples is the corresponding part between D^2 and D^3 in *Ying-t'ao ch'ing-i*.

> 1) As soon as he seated himself in the lecture room where the monk was expounding sutras, 2) Lu Tzu began to feel tired and 3) fell asleep. 4) In his dream he came out of the temple gate and 5) saw a maid dressed in green, sitting with a basket of cherries at the threshold. 6) Lu Tzu asked where she came from and 7) sat beside her and 8) ate cherries together. 9) The maid in green said, "My mistress's maiden name is Lu; she is married to the Ts'ui family. She is now widowed and lives in the city." 10) Lu Tzu asked about her relations and 11) discovered that the widow was his aunt. 12) The maid in green said, "How could you not pay her a visit since you both are in the same city?"
>
> 13) Lu Tzu followed her across Tienchin Bridge and into the quarter to the south of the river. 14) They stopped in front of a mansion with a tall gate. 15) The maid entered the gate and 16) let Lu Tzu wait outside. 17) A while later, four young men came out to greet him. 18) They were the sons of his aunt and ranking officials: one served as the *Lang Chung* in the Ministry of Finance, another was the former Minister of War in Cheng Chou; another the *Kung Ts'ao*

in Honan, the last one a *T'ai-ch'ang Po-shih* in charge of the imperial rituals. 19) Two of them were dressed in red; the other two in green. 20) They all had good countenance and figure. 21) Lu Tzu and his four cousins greeted one another and 22) talked delightedly.

23) After a while, Lu Tzu was led into the northern hall to call on his aunt. 24) The aunt was clothed in purple color, about the age of sixty, sonorous in voice, dignified and awe-inspiring in demeanor. 25) Lu Tzu was frightened and 26) dared not raise his eyes. 27) The aunt ordered him to sit, asked after his family and relations, and then 28) asked Lu Tzu whether he was married or not. 29) Lu Tzu replied, "Not yet." 30) The aunt said, "I have a niece whose maiden name is Cheng. Her parents died early and she was brought up by my sister. She is beautiful and virtuous. I can arrange the marriage for you." 31) Lu Tzu rose to his feet and accepted with thanks.

32) The aunt then sent for her sister and niece. 33) Before long, the whole family arrived on lofty and costly carriages. 34) They consulted the calendar to select a good day for marriage and found the day after the next day was auspicious. The day was then set and Lu thanked his aunt. 35) The aunt said, "You don't have to worry about the presents for betrothal, the invitation cards, and the wedding banquet. I have arranged for everything. If you have relations in the city, just submit their names and residences." The next day, invitations were sent to thirty families as well as to the officials at the state, provincial, prefecture, and county levels. 37) That same evening the wedding was held. Everything was gorgeous and splendid as if not of this world. 38) The day after, the banquet was held to treat all the relatives in the Capital. 39) After the banquet, Lu Tzu was led into a chamber which was decorated with screens, tapestries, and bed, all extremely rare and precious. 40) His wife was at the age of 14 or 15, and as beautiful as a fairy.

盧子方詣講筵，倦寢。夢至精舍門，見一青衣攜一籃櫻桃在下坐。盧子訪其誰家，因與青衣同殷櫻桃。青衣云：「娘子姓盧，嫁崔家。今孀居在城。」因訪近屬，即盧子再從姑也。青衣曰：「豈有阿姑同在一都，郎君不往起居？」盧子便隨之。過天津橋，入水南一坊。有一宅，門甚高大。盧子立於門下，青衣先入。少頃，有四人出門，與盧子相見，皆姑之子也：一任戶部郎中；一前任鄭州司馬；一任河南功曹；一任太常博士。二人衣緋；二人衣綠。形貌甚美。相見言敍，頗極歡暢。斯須，引入北堂拜姑。姑衣紫衣，年可六十許，言詞高朗，威嚴甚肅。盧子畏懼，莫敢仰視。令坐。悉訪內外，備諳氏族。遂訪兒婚姻未？盧子曰：「未。」姑曰：「吾有一外甥女子姓鄭，早孤，遣吾妹鞠養，甚有容質，頗有令淑，當為兒平章，計必允遂。」盧子遽卽拜謝。乃遣迎鄭氏妹。有頃，一家並到，車馬甚盛。遂檢歷擇日,云後日大吉,因爲盧子定。謝。姑云:「聘財函信禮席,兒並莫憂,吾悉與處置。兒有在城何親故,並抄名姓,幷具家第。」凡三十餘家,並在臺省及府縣官。明日下函,其夕成結。事事華盛,殆非人間。明日拜席,大會都城觀表。拜席畢,遂入一院。院中屏帷牀席,皆極珍異。其妻年可十四五,容色美麗,宛若神仙。

The above quotation covers almost half of the whole story, but with the *Yang Lin* story as basis of intertextuality, there are only two nuclei or major dynamic motifs; the other motifs are centered upon them. On account of the elaborate extension and long duration of the passage between the hero's falling asleep to the consummation with his wife, it is probably difficult to decide the definite points on which these two nuclei fall. Under this condition, we have to examine the text in closer detail. Suppose the hero's falling asleep is the dividing line between reality and dream, between the frame and the story within, his entrance into the mysterious world should begin in 3, but its process is prolonged and not completed until 23, the time when he is led into the mansion, which paves the way for the next dynamic motif of marriage.

The image of entrance (or the nucleus of entering), unlike that in *Yang Lin* and *Chen-chung chi* which is no other than a crack on the pillow, manifests itself in the shape of several doors. The first one is the temple gate. Since the hero falls asleep in the conscious (rational) world of the temple (and later awakened to life in the temple), his exit from the temple door in 4 marks paradoxically the starting point of entering the unconscious mysterious world. If we take his entering into the mansion in 23 as the completion of the process, then all the motifs before then are either indices or catalyses supporting the nucleus of entering. Thus 5, 6, 7, 8, 10, 11, 12, 13, 14, 15, 16, 17, 21, and 22 are catalyses which lead to the next nucleus; 9 is an index informing him of the identity of his aunt; 18, 19, and 20 are indices showing the wealth and high status of the family and foreshadowing the hero's future prosperity. After passing one more door in 23, the dynamic motif of entering (D^2) is consummated.

The same motif 23 serves as a transition between entering (D^2) and marriage (D^3), where his aunt replaces the maid in the role of guide who leads him to D^3. 24 is an index describing the aunt; 25, 26, 27 are catalyses which lead to the final important question about marriage in 28. Therefore D^2 is the actual beginning of D^3 which lasts until 40 when the wedding has been held. The duration between 28 and 40 is again inserted with a couple of indices, such as 37 and 39, and a dozen catalyses, all of which are arranged in a chronological and consecutive order.

It is apparent at this point that the basic dynamic motifs or nuclei in the three stories remain constant while the static motifs or indices and catalyses are variable. The only thing that makes *Ying-t'ao ch'ing-i* differ from *Yang Lin* and *Chen-chung chi* is the "unrollment" through the insertion of descriptive, informative, and catalytical elements between D^2 (entering) and D^3 (marrying) although it is these elements that contribute to the artistic effect. This is like the rules of transformational grammar which extend the noun phrase and verb phrase and thereby render the deep structure into a surface one. The following diagrams will show how the structure between D^2 and D^3 is different from that of the other two simpler stories only in number of indices and catalyses. For the sake of clarity, we shall replace the Tomashevskyan dynamic motif (D) with the Barthesian nucleus (N) (i.e., N^2 = entering and N^3 = marrying) and use *D* instead to stand for the moment when the whole action is completed, that is, when a whole nucleus is fully constructed. We shall use the letter

I for the index, the letter C for the catalysis, and the parenthetical numbers will refer to those we have used for motifs in our above quotations.

I. *Yang Lin*:
$$N^2 \longrightarrow N^3$$
$$D^2 (1) \longrightarrow I (2) \longrightarrow C (3) \longrightarrow D^3 (4)$$

II. *Chen-chung chi*:
$$N^2 \longrightarrow N^3$$
$$C^1 (1) \longrightarrow I^1 (2) \longrightarrow C^{2\text{-}5} (3\text{-}6) \longrightarrow I^2 (7) \longrightarrow C^{6\text{-}7} (8\text{-}9) \longrightarrow D^2 (10\text{-}11) \longrightarrow D^3 (12)$$

III. *Ying-t'ao ch'ing-i*:
$$N^2 \longrightarrow N^3$$
$$C^{1\text{-}8} (1\text{-}8) \longrightarrow I^1 (9) \longrightarrow C^{9\text{-}16} (10\text{-}17) \longrightarrow I^6 (30) \longrightarrow C^{25\text{-}30} (31\text{-}36)$$
$$I^{2\text{-}4} (18\text{-}20) \longrightarrow C^{17\text{ }19} (21\text{-}23) \qquad \uparrow I^7 (37) \longrightarrow CC^{31\text{-}32} (38\text{-}39) \longrightarrow D^3 (40)$$
$$\searrow \text{(Transition)}$$
$$I^5 (24) \longrightarrow C^{20\text{-}24} (25\text{-}29)$$

Shklovsky's concept of unrollment is later elaborated by Genette. Genette argues that there are three structurally distinctive types of digression or amplification. He borrows the Aristotelian term *"diégèse"* (narrative) which constitutes the main theme inside a story and adds to it three distinct sorts of digression.[30] The first kind of digression is *intradiégétiques*, the second *metadiégétiques*, and the third *extradiégétiques*.

Intradiegetic digressions usually correspond to cases classified by Shklovsky as examples of unrollment. They consist of "swelling the story from within by making use of its lacunae, spreading out its subject-matter and generally multiplying the diverse detail and incident in the plot." Thus an action that is supposed to last for a short while can be described in even minute detail so that it gives rise to "a work of major proportions."[31] This kind of digression has been shown above by the passage between the two functions of entering and marrying in *Ying-t'ao ch'ing-i*. More examples can be found in *Nan-k'e t'ai-shou chuan*, owing to the episodicity of the dream experience. One notable example is Ch'un-yü Fen's encounter with the flirtatious fairies before his marriage, which, seemingly a digression, serves at once as an index pointing to the fantastic and Taoist nature of his experience and as a catalysis leading to his consummation with the Princess of the Golden Bough. Another digressive incident is the reference to the hero's missing father, a motif not well motivated but justified by the second type of digression.

The second type of digression is metadiegetic amplifications. They correspond to stories within stories. Genette argues, "Second-hand narration is constituted wherever a narrative agent (or general representational factor) conducts the story inside the primary narration."[32] This kind of amplification reminds us of Todorov's "embedding" in his essay "Narrative Man." According to Todorov, whenever a new character is introduced, the reader can be made aware that a new story might be told. He argues that "the appearance of a new character invariably involves the interruption of the preceding story, so that a new story, the one which explains the 'Now I am here' of

---

[30] Gerard Genette, "Frontières du récit," *Communication* 8 (1966), 152. "Pour Aristotle, le récit (*diègèsis*) est un des deux modes de l'imitation poétique (*mimèsis*), l'autre étant la representation directe des événements par des acteurs parlant et agissant devant le public."

[31] Gerard Genette, *Figures II* (Paris: Seuil, 1969), p. 196.

[32] Ibid., p. 202.

the new character, may be told to us. A second story is enclosed within the first; this device is called embedding."³³ Since we are in "the realm of narrative men," the more characters are involved, the more embeddings are likely to happen.

In *Ying-t'ao ch'ing-i* the cherry maid's appearance leads to a long passage (Motifs 5-16), including informants and indices concerning herself, the hero, and the aunt. Her mission as messenger accomplished, the maid disappears. She is replaced by four new characters who have to account for themselves and thus a new episode is produced (Motifs 17-22). The encounter with the aunt is likewise an embedding, a story of the aunt's, which catalyzes the second major function of marriage (Motifs 23-40). Thus every character is protactic to a new one (the four cousins act as one character), and a new story is embedded in the action. This is also true of *Nan-k'e* which has more "narrative men" (and women) and therefore more embeddings. The extended *Nan-k'e* is precisely a result of embeddings or metadiegetic amplifications.

The third type of digression is called the extradiegetic amplifications. They occur whenever the absent narrator (i.e., the author himself) conducts his own digressions, usually consisting of moral reflections on his characters or their actions but not representing the opinions of any one figure in the work. Put in terms of Benveniste's distinction between two sign systems, this is the insertion of discourse, the speech-act of the author, into narrative which represents external action.³⁴ Among the four stories, the one that apparently uses this type of digression is *Nan-k'e* where the author, instead of intervening every now and then during the course of narration (except once towards the end), summarizes the story with a moral lesson. Although didacticism also characterizes the outcome of *Chen-chung chi,* the author does not "intrude" to moralize. On the contrary, he assumes the consciousness of Lü Weng and makes comment through the mouth of this presiding character. This is not the case of *Nan-k'e*. Before the story closes with the hero's death, there are three incidents after his awakening from dream: his excavation of the ant hole, his visit to the two friends whom he saw in dream, and his resignation to Taoism. We have an authorial intrusion after the first incident: "Alas, one cannot hope to understand fully the intelligence of ants, let alone the mutability of such great things as mountains and trees!" Such an exclamation by no means evokes an external reality, but reveals the speaker's speech-act and his intention to influence his listener.³⁵ The author has obviously confused discourse whose temporal reference is to the moment of speech with narrative whose temporal reference is to the moment of event.³⁶

At the end of his narration, the author even goes so far as to add to it an epilogue, showing his moral intention:

> In the August of the eighteenth year of Chen Yüan, I stopped over at Huaip'u on my way from Wu to Lo. There I met Ch'un-yü Fen by chance. I asked him about the story, paid a visit to the remnants of the ant hole, and found everything proved to be true. Therefore I recorded the above story for those who are interested. Although it deals with mysteriousness

---

³³ Todorov, *The Poetics of Prose,* p. 70.
³⁴ Ibid., p. 25.
³⁵ Ibid., pp. 25-26.
³⁶ Émile Benveniste, *Problèmes de linguistique générale,* p. 244. Quoted in Jonathan Culler, *Structuralist Poetics* (Ithaca and New York: Cornell Univ. Press, 1975), p. 197.

and uncanniness and is aberrant to orthodox views, it is a fair admonition against the will to power. You gentlemen of later generations, listen to the moral of *Nan-k'e* and do not be proud of your rank and fame. The former officer Li Chao of Hua Chou sums up: "The highest official ranks, the power that subverts a kingdom—these are no other than an ant-hill in the wise men's eyes!"

公佐貞元十八年秋八月，自吳之洛，暫泊淮浦，偶覯淳于生夢，詢訪遺跡，翻覆再三，事皆摭實，輒編錄成傳，以資好事。雖稽神語怪，事涉非經，而竊位著生，冀將爲戒。後之君子，幸以南柯爲偶然，無以名位驕於天壤間云。前華州參軍李肇贊曰：「貴極祿位，權傾國都，達人視此，蟻聚何殊。」

Here the subject "I" of discourse is identified with the subject of narrative, the impersonal "poetic personality," as Todorov puts it.[37] Some people would argue that the shift of point of view is intentional, and that, with the epilogue put aside, the story itself is narrated from the third person omniscient point of view. But how can they explain the aforementioned exclamation? And what is the significance of "*I recorded the above story for those who are interested*" from a *third person* point of view? And what is the third person point of view if the hero Ch'un-yü Fen himself told *his* own story? Judging from this, *Nan-k'e's* digression largely results from the author's fusing discourse or meta-discourse with or into narrative. This renders *Nan-k'e* more personal than the other three "a-personal" narratives (*récits a-personnels*).[38]

The above principles of digression can help us understand how the four stories have undergone a process of transformation from simplicity to complexity. We can further apply the semiological and semantic methods of Barthes and Greimas to analyzing the stories within their cultural contexts, by reducing them to semes[39] or lexias[40] distributed on levels of code and then examining how the data of each level are integrated to produce different meanings. Such an attempt would show, as far as the cultural referential code goes, that the three T'ang elaborations have respective focuses. For instance, *Chen-chung chi* deals with a farm boy's illusion of political fame, therefore static motifs (i.e., exposition of the hero's wish) are related to the dynamic motif of encounter in the opening scene and the function of the guide becomes more explicit than those in the other two stories. On the other hand, *Ying-t'ao ch'ing-i* shows the political organization established on the foundation of scholar-clan marriages, therefore a lengthy passage is devoted to the transition between D^2 and D^3, and the function of the monk is replaced by the cherry maid and the hero's aunt. Finally, *Nan-k'e t'ai-shou chuan* reflects the military disturbance of the late T'ang period and the political situation of frontier feudalism; the identity of the hero (a static motif) is thus changed from a scholar to a knight-errant and more static elements (indices and catalyses) are given to his ordeals and adventures. However, an investigation of these thematic aspects based on the variations and extensions of static motifs would lead us astray from the original path of structural analysis.

---

[37] Todorov, *The Poetics of Prose*, p. 27.
[38] Barthes, "Introduction," 20.
[39] Greimas, *Du sens*, p. 189.
[40] Roland Barthes, *S/Z*, trans. Richard Miller (New York: Hill and Wang, 1974), p. 13.

IV

Earlier in this paper we have mentioned Greimas's actantial model based on the binary opposition of human conceptual mode. The model consists of three sets of oppositional actants whose relationships, along with the functional predicates, will generate narrative sequence. The six actants in three sets, subject/object; sender/receiver; helper/opponent, as derived and reduced from Propp's seven spheres of action, may be joined together syntactically to form narratives. For instance, in the stories of quest, the hero is the subject and the sought-for-person, i.e., the princess, is the object. With the six actants or their manifest acteurs as nominal groups, Greimas envisages three basic narrative syntagms: contractual syntagms, performative syntagms, and disjunctional syntagms. The contractual syntagm involves the situation of establishing and breaking of contract; the performative syntagm involves trials, struggles, and the performance of tasks; the disjunctional syntagm involves such movements as departures and returns.[41]

When cast in Greimas' syntagmatic models, the *Yang Lin* series as stories of quest and initiation fits most obviously into the disjunctional syntagm. The hero departs from the world of reality to the world of dream and returns from dream to reality. The actant-sender manifests in such acteurs as the priest, the cherry maid, the monk, the messengers, etc., whereas the hero himself is the receiver. But we find also in the four stories, though to a minor extent, variations of the other two syntagms, performative and contractual.

The performative syntagm is seen in the hero's experience of quest, especially for the illusory fame and the archetypal woman. In *Chen-chung chi,* for instance, Lu Sheng's various adventures in dream can be regarded as ordeals and exploits in the course of quest.

> As the Governor of Shensi, he built a canal eighty *li* in length, which brought so many benefits to the people of the region that they commemorated his achievement upon stone.
>
> 自陝西鑿河八十里，以濟不通。邦人利之，刻石紀德。

Later, serving the Emperor as the Associate Director of the Censorate and Governor General of the Hosi Circuit,

> Lu Sheng routed the barbarians, killing seven thousand men. He conquered nine hundred *li* of territory and built three cities to guard the frontier. The people of the frontier region built a monument on the Chüyen Mountain to commemorate his exploits, and when he returned to court he was received with triumphal honors. . . . No name carried so much prestige as his and he had the universal acclaim of popular sentiment . . . .
>
> 大破戎虜，斬首七千級。開地九百里，築三大城以遮要害，邊人立石於居延山以頌之。歸朝冊勳，恩禮極盛⋯時望清重，羣情翕習。

---

[41] Greimas, *Du sens,* p. 191.

In this context the hero serves as the subject; official rank, worldly fame, and a noble wife become the object (*objet-valeur*). At the same time, the hero is also the receiver whose sender is again the priest, etc.

The contractual syntagm is more complicated since it shows different levels in the stories. To begin with, there is a contract established between the priest as contractor (sender) and the hero as contractee (receiver). Then there is one between the hero and the other characters, such as the king, the aunt, the Princess of the Golden Bough, etc. Finally there is an abstract contract between the hero and the reality to which he should conform. The hero is not contented with his reality and seeks for illusion. Therefore, he has violated the interdiction (Propp's functions 2 and 3) and broken the moral or ethical contract. Accordingly, a new contract is established between the sender-contractor (the priest) and the receiver-contractee (the young man) in order to test the hero. Thus begin his disjunction and performance, initiation and quest. This contract is fulfilled when the hero returns, with performance accomplished and his illusion shattered.

To analyze the four stories in terms of the Greimasian actantial and syntagmatic models is most rewarding, but it is also beyond the scope of this short paper. Let us content ourselves with the following conclusion. Once when the quest is performed, the journey finished, and the contract observed, the hero returns to the starting point with some new knowledge of life. The structure becomes thus a circle like the one provided by Campbell,[42] which I modify as follows:

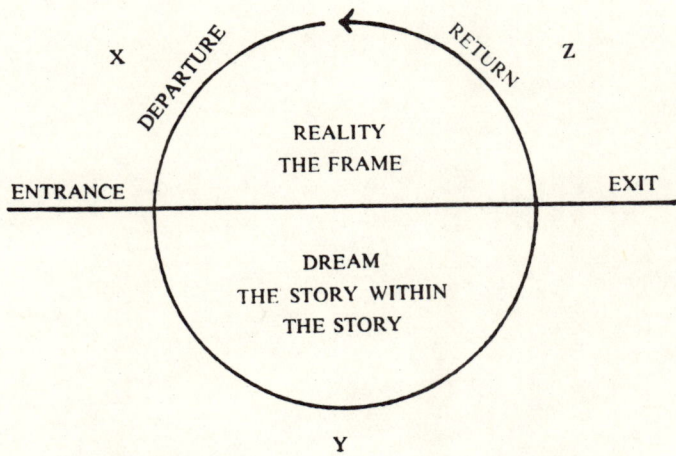

The meeting of the points of departure and return is significant in two senses. For one thing, it marks the structural pattern of complete cycle of these stories. For another, a sense of equilibrium, as Todorov suggests, is achieved, not only by the reader, but also by the hero himself. This is related to the hero's shift of perception from an erroneous one to a correct one. In other words, the importance of the events is not so important as the hero's (or the reader's) perception of the events or the degree of knowledge that the hero or the reader has about them. The first type of narrative, which mainly stresses the succession of events, Todorov terms *mytholo-*

---

[42] Joseph Campbell, *The Hero with a Thousand Faces* (Princeton: Princeton Univ. Press, 1968), p. 30.

gical narrative; the second type of narrative which deals more with the character's perception, he terms *gnoseological* narrative.[43] We may roughly equate the first type to the popular plot story, the second to the psychological or character story. The *Yang Lin* series, dealing primarily with the hero's *rites de passage* from ignorance to knowledge, from adolescence to adulthood, from illusion to reality, is precisely a gnoseological narrative characteristic of the initiation story.

---

[43] Tzvetan Todorov, "The Two Principles of Narrative," *Diacritics*, 1 (Fall 1971), 40.

Cross-cultural Currents in the Theatre: China and the West

Clara Yü Cuadrado

Since the middle of this century, many excellent comparative studies on Chinese and Western drama have appeared. Nevertheless, these often deal with specific periods, such as *Elizabethan and Yüan: A Brief Comparison of Some Conventions in Poetic Drama* by James J. Y. Liu 劉若愚; single dramatic works, such as "The Original Chinese Orphan" by Liu Wu-chi 柳無忌; or individual authors, such as *Ts'ao Yü: The Reluctant Disciple of Chekhov and O'Neill* by Joseph S. M. Lau 劉紹銘 and the recent works on Brecht's indebtedness to Chinese dramaturgy, including Renata Berg-Pan's dissertation, "The Chinese Influence on the Dramaturgy of Bertolt Brecht," and Kenneth D. Weisinger's "Brecht and Chinese Theater." The present paper differs from these works in that it is not confined to one single period, work or author. Rather, it surveys the theatre development in these two traditions and outlines the impact they have made on each other at various times, from one type of theatre to another, from one individual to another, with the purpose of demonstrating the extent of the exchanges of theatrical heritage between China and the West, and illustrating the trend towards a convergence as a result of these exchanges.

I

In the last decade of the seventeenth century, Sir William Temple declared in his *Essay upon the Ancient and Modern Learning* that, while science and arts had run their circles in the several parts of the world, "They are generally agreed to have held their course from East to West."[1] But the Western world had only seen the beginning of the influx of Eastern arts and learning, for it was the eighteenth century that witnessed Europe's unprecedented orientalomania in which Cathay featured so prominently.

The trend was perhaps natural. Reports about Cathay had trickled in during the

---

[1] Cited in Earl Miner, *The Japanese Tradition in British and American Literature* (Princeton: Princeton Univ. Press, 1966), p. 9.

preceding centuries to warrant a genuine interest in that mysterious Eastern land of riches and ancient civilization. In the Age of Reason, China became in many European minds a perfect state realized—a culmination of the expressed yearnings from Plato's *Republic* to More's *Utopia* and Bacon's *New Atlantis.* Confucius, the Chinese sage noted for his practical moral philosophy, appealed strongly to the *bon sens* of the Enlightenment. And the image of the "Sage of the East" was transformed into a literary archetype, i.e., an oriental witness of European follies and vices, such as Goldsmith's Lien Chi Altangi in *The Citizen of the World.*

In the theatre, as the Baroque passion for grandeur and luxury continued, lavish spectacles and magical stage devices found a new pretext for theatrical extravaganza in the exotic East, and Europe reveled in the "Chinese" masques and balls, in the comic operas with "Chinese" harlequins—often fully decked out in Turkish costume, executing a droll *pas* choreographed by French ballet experts, to the music of Italian opera masters.

Very little was known of the Chinese theatrical conventions, but it did not matter. Exoticism is at its best with blessed ignorance and imaginative creation. The important fact is that eighteenth-century Europe had become accustomed to the Italian opera and *commedia dell'arte,* the French *ballet de cour* and *opéra comique,* as well as the English masque and opera—in short, it was familiar with theatrical features shared by the classical Chinese theatre: singing, music, dance, and mime. Thus, despite their ignorance of the stylization, music and poetry of the Chinese theatre, the Europeans could actually create their own version of the "Chinese" theatre without violating the conscience of an age characterized by its love not only for the exotic, but for Reason and Knowledge as well.

On January 7, 1700, the fashionable courtiers and ladies attending Louis XIV's ball awaited with great expectation the exciting moment. Then, the "King of China," seated on a genuine palanquin, was carried in by thirty musicians, all dressed in splendid Chinese costume. Music and dance broke out, the entire court luxuriated in the novel "divertissement," and the celebration of the advent of the new century reached its climax. How fitting it was to mark the beginning of a century so much under the spell of Cathay with this little piece entitled *Le Roi de la Chine*!

While "Chinese" masquerades and balls flourished as court pastime, the public theatre also took to plays set in China or dealing with Chinese motifs. In 1723 Parisians had the pleasure of seeing a musical comedy entitled *Arlequin, Barbet, Pagode et Médecin.* Its scene was set in the exterior of the Imperial Palace of Peking, reportedly bearing much likeness to the real palace. At the end of this extravaganza, the "King of China" pardons his children with these French-Chinese phrases: "Pardonaon, levaon, divertissaon, dansaon." The children obey and dance, and the curtain falls.[2]

Research shows that the Chinese vogue was wide-spread in eighteenth-century European theatres. The second half of the century was especially flooded with theatrical productions such as the following: *L'Eroe cinese* (1752), *La Shiava cinese* (1752), *Ces Chinois* (1753), *Il Cinese Rimpatriato, divertimento scenico, da rapresentarsi in Parigi, nel Teatro dell'Opera* (1753), *Le Chinois de Retour* (1753), *Les Fêtes chinoises* (1754), *Le Chinois poli en France* (1754), *L'Orphelin de la Chine* (1755),

---

[2] Adolf Reichwein, *China and Europe: Intellectual and Artistic Contacts in the Eighteenth Century,* tr. J. C. Powell (New York: Alfred A. Knopf, 1925), p. 68.

Proteus, or Harlequin in China (1755), *Le Ballet chinois et turc* (1755), *Les Tartares* (1755, a ballet), *The Orphan of China* (1759), *Turandot* (1761), *La Matrone chinoise* (1765), *La Fête chinoise* (1778, a ballet), *L'idolo cinese* (1779), and *The Mandarin, or Harlequin Widower* (1789). As late as the nineteenth century, plays such as *The Clown of China* (1812) and *Harlequin and Fortunio, or Shing-Moo and Thun-Ton* (1815) were still popular in England. Most of these works are pseudo-Chinese musical comedies, spectacles, ballets, or satirical skits ridiculing European fashions and institutions from the viewpoint of a Chinese citizen, following the tradition of the "Chinese letters."

An interesting episode in theatre history involves the unfortunate enterprise entered into by David Garrick, by far the most celebrated English actor-manager of the eighteenth century, and Jean Georges Noverre, the equally reputed French ballet master and choreographer. For the Drury Lane Theatre's 1754-55 winter season, Noverre, as Thomas Davies reports, "composed that accumulation of multifarious figures, called the Chinese Festival; a spectacle, in which the dresses and customs of the Chinese were exhibited, in almost innumerable shapes and characters."[3] But the frontier conflict in America ignited the hostility between England and France, and the London public became indignant at Garrick's employment of such a large number of Frenchmen for Drury Lane. The first night of the ill-fated "Festival" turned into a riot. Amidst fist fights, Garrick had to be escorted out of the theatre under police protection.

The Garrick-Noverre venture is but one indication of the European theatre's high esteem for the Chinese vogue. Mlle. Clairon, one of the most acclaimed actresses in France, starred in a "Chinese" play, *L'Orphelin de la Chine,* which was authored by none other than Voltaire. Pietro Metastasio, perhaps the most popular Italian playwright of his time, also wrote a court drama on the same story.

Although the extent of the influence of theatrical chinoiserie has yet to be determined by further research, the deluge of Chinese harlequinades, musical comedies and satirical plays had doubtlessly left an impact on the European theatre. Adolf Reichwein, an expert on the intellectual relationship between China and Europe, once remarked that the Eastern influence on the initial development of the lyrical stage of Europe is difficult to overrate.[4] But, looking beyond the vogue of chinoiserie, one is likely to ask the question: "Were there any genuine Chinese plays staged in Europe at the time?" The true answer is, "Yes, and no."

Four plays dealing with the theme of a Chinese orphan were written in the eighteenth century: *L'Eroe cinese, L'Orphelin de la Chine, The Orphan of China,* and a fourth by the name of *The Chinese Orphan: A Historical Tragedy* which, unlike the others, never saw a stage production. All these plays have one thing in common: they are more or less "authentic," deriving their origin from the translation of a Chinese drama. And this fact sets them apart from all the fictitious fabrications of chinoiserie.

This Chinese play, *Chao-shih ku-erh* 趙氏孤兒 [The Orphan of Chao], was the first play ever translated into European languages, and the first Chinese drama to inspire Western imitation. A detailed account of the original Chinese play as well as of the various European versions has been given in Liu Wu-chi's excellent article,

---

[3] Cited in Margot Berthold, *A History of World Theatre* (New York: Frederick Ungar, 1972), p. 491.

[4] Reichwein, p. 68.

"The Original Chinese Orphan,"[5] here we are only concerned with the textual and productional transformations of the Chinese drama that are relevant to the present study.

The Orphan of Chao was written in the thirteenth century by Chi Chün-hsiang 紀君祥, a minor dramatist of the Yüan Dynasty. In 1731, the Jesuit priest Joseph Henri Prémare translated the play into French as *L'Orphelin de la Maison de Tchao*. Later the translation was included in the third volume of Jean Baptiste Du Halde's *Description géographique, historique, chronologique, politique, et physique de l'empire de la Chine et de la tartarie chinoise* (1735). In his translation, Prémare omitted the songs in the original, merely indicating, in their place, that a character now "sings" or "recites some verse." One does not have to look far for the reason for these omissions. Du Halde volunteered a good explanation in his advertisement for the Chinese play: "There are plays the songs of which are difficult to be understood, because they are full of Allusions to things unknown to us, and Figures of Speech very difficult for us to observe."[6] Aside from this technical difficulty, Prémare might not have found the songs particularly worth translating. The fact that he chose a minor dramatic work for translation indicates that Prémare was not preoccupied with the introduction of excellent Chinese drama. The Jesuit priest was probably more interested in the play's theme of loyalty and self-sacrifice, and intended to recommend these Chinese virtues to his European readers.

If indeed this was Father Prémare's intention, he was by no means disappointed. Europe responded enthusiastically to this first sample of Chinese drama, not for its dramatic or theatrical excellence, but for its luminous moral content. During the eighteenth century at least four adaptations and three English translations were made of Prémare's French version of the Chinese play, yet none of these showed any attempt to restore the missing songs. What Europe witnessed at the time, therefore, was not an authentic Chinese drama, but various versions made of a mere synopsis of the drama, an empty frame from which all its poetry, music, as well as theatricality had been removed. A Westerner could perhaps imagine the result if he tries to envision an Italian opera stripped of everything but its libretto.

Strange as it may seem, despite the vogue of theatrical chinoiserie, eighteenth-century Europe never felt the urge to explore the formal features of the Chinese theatre. This may be explained, in part, by the attitude of Voltaire and his contemporaries toward the Chinese theatre: while its subject matter was interesting and its morals commendable, its dramaturgy was too barbarous to be presented in the European theatre without major revision.

In his dedication of *L'Orphelin de la Chine* to the Duke of Richelieu, Voltaire exalted Chinese drama, maintaining that it had developed for about three thousand years before the Greeks invented their drama, that it renders vivid portraits of human action, and that it establishes moral instruction.[7] However, to the French savant who had an unmistakable taste for classical propriety, the long history and moral excellence of the Chinese drama were not matched by its form. Voltaire remarked tersely:

---

[5] "The Original Chinese Orphan," *Comparative Literature*, 5 (Summer 1953), 193-212.

[6] Du Halde, *The General History of China* (London: J. Watts, 1786), III, 196.

[7] Voltaire, *The Works of Voltaire*, tr. William F. Fleming (Paris: DuMont, 1901), XV, 176.

> One can only compare the "Orphan of Tchao" to the English and Spanish tragedies of the sixteenth century, which still please beyond sea, and on the other side of the Pyrenees. The action lasts five and twenty years, as in some of the monstrous farces of Shakespeare and Lope de Vega, which are called tragedies, though they are nothing but a heap of incredible stories.[8]

To improve this Chinese piece in which "there is no unity of time or action, no picture of the manners, no sentiment, eloquence, reason or passion,"[9] Voltaire modified the structure of the original, making his *L'Orphelin* "a Confucian moral of five acts"; introduced a love theme between his hero, the Tartar conqueror Genghis Khan, and the beautiful yet incorruptible Idamé; and eliminated the theme of revenge, a sign of barbarism.

Voltaire was not the only one that felt compelled to remold the Chinese drama. In the other adaptations of the play, the unities of time, place and action were also observed, and the authors also altered the plot at will to suit their own purposes. Just as Voltaire's play was designed to show the natural superiority of reason and civilization over barbaric force, so was William Hatchett's *The Chinese Orphan: a Historical Tragedy* to serve as a political attack on Sir Robert Walpole. Metastasio turned the original play into a light-hearted court comedy in *L'Eroe cinese,* and *The Orphan of China* became a sensational melodrama in the hands of Arthur Murphy.

The neoclassic demand for dramatic unities did not seem to contradict the urge for verisimilitude in theatrical productions at a time when crude stage realism was emerging. One recalls that Diderot is usually credited as the first to propose the "fourth-wall" stage practice in his famous "De la poésie dramatique":

> Whether you are writing or acting, think no more about the audience than if it did not exist. Imagine a big wall across the front of the stage, separating you from the audience. Act as if the curtain had not risen.[10]

In the same work Diderot praised Mlle. Clairon for her courage to defy custom and fashion. "Trust your taste and your genius," he urged her: "Show us nature and truth."[11] The play in which Mlle. Clairon appeared in an oriental costume—*sans paniers*—and so shocked the audience that Diderot was obliged to come to her support was none other than *L'Orphelin de la Chine.* For the Comédie Française's production of his play in 1755, Voltaire demanded accurate oriental costume as well as new, custom-made oriental settings. After the initial uncertainty, the public received the innovations favorably, and actors and actresses of the French theatre began to dress each role in proper costumes thereafter. The significance of the Chinese drama in eighteenth-century Europe thus exceeded the realm of mere theatrical chinoiserie. Besides providing exotic spectacles and serving as an instrument for moral instruction, it also marked an important turning point in the attitude toward realistic staging, thus

---

[8] Ibid., 178.
[9] Ibid., 179.
[10] Denis Diderot, *Oeuvres Esthétiques* (Paris: Garnier Frères, 1965), p. 231. The translation is mine.
[11] Ibid., p. 268.

touching the core of the dichotomy of realism and conventionalism. It is ironic, however, that the strictly non-realistic theatre of China should have been transformed into a propelling force for stage realism in Europe, while its real formal features remained unrecognized.

In the seventeenth and eighteenth centuries, the Jesuits served as the intellectual link between Europe and the Far East. When the Jesuit influence diminished in late eighteenth century, commercial interests began to dominate European minds as far as China was concerned. As contacts became more frequent, unfavorable reports about the Chinese nation and its people also increased. The most earthy aspects of Chinese life were now captured and transmitted to Europe by the visitors from the West. The streets of glistening gold that Europeans were wont to envision were now revealed to be dusty dirt roads; the glamorous silk and embroidered garments were replaced by dull-colored coarse cotton robes; the reported moral excellence of the mandarins gave way to the image of the indolent opium smokers, ghastly in their death-like lethargy. As the visionary Cathay gradually declined into a backward kingdom of barbarism, the chinoiserie myth began to dissolve, and with it the taste for "Chinese" spectacles, musical operas and ballets.

II

Well into the third decade of the twentieth century, Sheldon Cheney gave the following evaluation of the classical Chinese theatre in his encyclopaedic work, *The Theatre: Three Thousand Years of Drama, Acting and Stagecraft*:

> Truth to tell, dramatic literature in China never reached the importance a Sophocles or a Shakespeare endowed it with in the West. The Chinese themselves make no claims for it; and even allowing for the lack of language-embroidery values possibly lost in translation, the Western reader may agree that Chinese plays are little more than melodrama or hack journalistic plays—or grand opera *libretti*. The situations are pretty well standardized, the characters run to obvious types, the "effects" are neither deeply dramatic nor cumulatively emotional. All that the Western mind craves in tragedy is overlooked or dissipated: taut dramatic structure, suspense, psychologic truth. The casual nature of the plot, indeed, explains the apparently shattering confusion in the auditorium, the constant going and coming of spectators, the tea-drinking, the conversations and eating and even games while the actors are going through a particularly important passage. There is no continuity of mood, no built-up tension. The performance probably lasts from late afternoon till after midnight; but the programme includes several plays. As the actors from one go out of the exit door the players of the next enter by the other, so that action is continuous. And so is the music that sounds so squeaky and clangy to Western ears.[12]

---

[12] *The Theatre: Three Thousand Years of Drama, Acting and Stagecraft* (London: Longmans, Green and Co., 1929), pp. 119-20.

Compared to the eighteenth century men of letters who were entirely ignorant of the Chinese dramaturgy, Cheney was well-informed. Yet his opinion of the Chinese theatre reveals a discrepancy in standards even an expert in theatre arts could not breach. A Western realist whose definition of good drama is tight structure, breath-taking suspense and sweeping emotion could not very well appreciate the conventional theatrical form of an alien culture on its own terms.

In order to achieve a better understanding, we have to, first of all, clarify certain terminologies before applying them to the Chinese theatre. To begin with, the two terms equally frequently applied to the Chinese theatre, "opera" and "drama," are both misleading to some degree. Although singing and music are its integral parts, the Chinese "opera" should not be perceived as similar to that form which rose in Italy towards the last years of the sixteenth century and later spread to most parts of Europe.

The European opera was born and nurtured in all the scenic grandeur and extravagance, all the magical effects of stage transformation of the Baroque and Renaissance. The Chinese "opera," on the other hand, depends almost exclusively on the actor's personal resources for artistic expression, with virtually no reliance upon outer assistance, such as scenery or special effects.

With the exception of such forms as the English "Ballad Opera," the music of Western opera is specially composed for each work and is the opera's primary artistic expression. Not so in the Chinese opera. While the voice technique and expression of the actor's singing is of utmost significance, the music is rarely original. The arias are usually taken out of an existing repertory of popular tunes, and are shared by works of the same category.

When Cheney compares the text of the Chinese drama to "grand opera libretti," he obviously means to belittle its literary quality. But here, too, he stumbles into a pitfall. For, while few Western opera libretti are read separately as literature, the texts of classical Chinese dramatic works, especially those of the Yüan and Ming Dynasties, have enjoyed no less prestige as poetic literature in China than Shakespeare in the West.

Here we should point out that Cheney's history of world theatre, like many other works of broad scope, makes no distinction between the classical Chinese drama of different periods, nor does it specify which style is chosen as representative in its discussions. To avoid confusion, unless otherwise indicated, the term "classical Chinese theatre" used in the present study will subsequently refer to the most well-known of the "modern" styles, namely, *Ching-hsi* 京戲 (or *Ching-chü* 京劇), better known in the West as "Peking Opera."

To a person trained in the orthodox Western literary theories, it is perhaps natural that all literature should fit in one of the three slots: the "epic," the "lyric," and the "dramatic." And under the "dramatic" there are the polar divisions of "tragedy" and "comedy." Unfortunately this system does not quite apply to *all* literature. The Chinese "dramatic" literature, for one, happens to partake much of the "epic" and "lyric" elements: the songs are written in verse, and, in a Yüan or Ming drama, they are often poetry of the highest quality; narratives are used to set the dramatic situation, describe scenery, explain events, and express emotion; the action flows through various locales and often spans a considerable length of time. The Chinese drama also refuses to lend itself to the arbitrary division of the "tragic" and the "comic."

Much ink has been spilt over the controversy about "Chinese tragedy." Those who believe that such a thing does not exist often equate that fact with a verdict of inferiority of the Chinese drama. The opponents, desperate in their attempt to battle such prejudice, often resort to the argument that certain Chinese plays do indeed fit the notion of the "tragic" or that there is much "tragic sense" in the Chinese drama in general. There is a prevalent reluctance to deny the importance of being tragic, perhaps because "tragedy" has been endowed with the sacred glow of excellence in Western literary tradition. However, if one judges the classical Chinese drama on its own terms, one easily realizes that a dramatic tradition fostered by the trinity of Confucianism-Buddhism-Taoism, preaching personal virtue, social order, universal harmony, and demanding unmistakable poetic justice cannot produce works that are truly "tragic" in the Greek sense.

Besides not being quite "operatic," not being exclusively "dramatic," the classical Chinese theatre possesses another basic feature: not being "realistic" at all. The qualities that Cheney looks for—taut structure, psychological portrait, cumulative emotional effects, mood, built-up tension—are not to be found in the classical Chinese theatre. The audience of this theatre is, one may say, deprived of the peephole thrills so enjoyed by the spectators of a realistic drama, for the walled-in illusion of reality does not exist in this theatre. Nearly always, the dramatic action is derived from a familiar story told and retold through ages, and if that is not enough, the characters will take it upon themselves to describe and explain the situation time and again, so that no one misses the point. Characters come in set types, each possessing its strict conventions for voice techniques, gestures, movements, costume, and make-up. Color-and-design-coded face-painting is employed for certain character types to indicate their temperament and personality. Actors recite, declaim, sing, pose, and move about in stylized gaits, always displaying themselves in the most conspicuous manner. The small orchestra is placed on stage for all to see. Stage-hands move the few pieces of functional property—usually a table and two chairs—in full view of the audience, and these serve to indicate an unlimited variety of locales whenever they are demanded by the dramatic action.

One may say that the classical Chinese theatre represents the utmost sophistication of a stylized, conventional, non-realistic theatre. From the viewpoint of the realist, however, it can also be described as extraordinarily primitive and naive. The difference in opinion is a result of different evolutions in theatre history.

At first, an actor was not distinguishable from a dancer, singer, or a general performer of physical feats, his only resources being those of his own person—his voice, expression, movement. Then, a mask and/or costume was invented, and the actor began to mimic, or "act" in his disguised self, usually on a raised platform to command attention. Later, some platform stages were given a roof, a surrounding, and the open pit was sometimes made into an enclosure. But the concept of this stage is nevertheless a defined "acting area," and life in this area is only represented by tokens and symbols, frequently dictated by convention. Lacking a better name, this kind of theatre has been termed the "conventional" theatre. In some parts of the world, this theatre has proven quite sufficient through all ages. In other parts, however, the theatre took another direction in its development. There was demand for a more convincing, or "real," environment. Painted scenery began to be used to define the setting of the dramatic action, then it was replaced by the box-set, complete with real furniture and all the bric-a-brac of real life. The actor was now supposed to *be* his character—inwardly as well as outwardly. Finally, an imaginary one-way mirror was installed across stage front, and there we have a slice of life neatly wrapped up on stage. The audience laughs, sighs, weeps, and squirms in its files of seats, in the darkened auditorium. This theatre has been designated as the theatre of "realism," in the broad sense of the word.

In his admirable survey of the development of world theatre, *The Seven Ages of the Theatre,* Richard Southern points out that, in the cases where external resources are added to the personal resources of the player, although the show is made more complex and more organized, there is nothing to show that one performance is made any better or more significant.[13] "It may be called evolution if you please," Southern concludes, "yet it is evolution in a spiral sense round a centre rather than evolution along a straight path from something imperfect to some eventual perfection."[14]

In the West, the theatre has taken precisely such a spiral course. The Attic style, with its masks, chorus, and *skene*—a permanent façade, was primarily "conventional." As much as Shakespeare aspired for realistic staging, his theatre relied heavily upon the imagination of the spectator. Verbal décor, asides and soliloquies, free-flowing scenes, and the telescoping of time and space are but a few of the practices that made the Elizabethan theatre an outstanding example of conventionalism. The Renaissance saw the invention of painted perspectives, indoor lighting and elaborate stage machinery, thus taking a stride in the direction of realistic techniques. The classicism of the eighteenth century, carrying out the Aristotelian principles and beyond, nevertheless had its claim to verisimilitude by using "accurate" costumes and settings, often in the name of the exotic. With the well-made play of Scribe and Sardou, the decline of the repertory system, the replacement of wings and backcloths by box-sets and building-sets, the employment of lime and electric lighting, the nineteenth century witnessed the peak of drawing-room realism. In the last decades of the nineteenth century, criticism of this middle-class drama led to the rise of European naturalism, a representational style that aimed at the removal of artificiality in playwriting as well as in stage practice, so as to achieve a natural, exact reproduction of life on stage, exposing the "human animal" as a product of his milieu.

As soon as naturalism rose to eminence, however, other dramatic schools mushroomed in its opposition: symbolism, expressionism, theatricalism, constructivism, surrealism . . . , all striving to break away from the representational style. After all, argued the anti-naturalists, there is more to "reality" than an outer appearance. The mind itself needs expression, and naturalism is incapable of projecting subjective reality. In place of the illusion of actuality, the anti-naturalists proposed total production, emphasizing the harmonious integration of all the resources of the theatre: music, lighting, stage design, and, perhaps most important of all, the actor's physical expression. Rhythm, music, gesture, dance, and stylization were reintroduced into his act, drawing the cycle of the "spiral evolution" closer to its completion. It was in such an environment that the West's interest in the Chinese theatre resurfaced, and it was in such a context that the Chinese influence played a significant role in the modern Western theatre.

---

[13] *The Seven Ages of the Theatre* (New York: Hill and Wang, 1961), p. 31.
[14] Ibid., p. 32.

III

What has happened in modern Western theatre? The question cannot be answered without consideration of what has happened in the modern Western world.

The modern world witnessed man's greatest material achievements. Time and space diminished in the machine age, and man was no longer confined within national or cultural boundaries. He became affected by events occurring thousands of miles away as well as at home. The telescoping of our vast world into a close neighborhood stimulated communication and exchange in different civilizations, but it also sharpened the rivalry among nations. The two devastating world wars demonstrated how little control man had over himself and the world surrounding him, while technology continued threatening to turn his society into a dehumanization camp. Disillusioned and bewildered, the Western man became thoughtful. With the increase of his knowledge of the Eastern world, he found a haven in the traditional Oriental philosophy of self-recognition and self-cultivation. The Taoist doctrine of non-action and the Buddhist practice of inner tranquility rescued him from the bustle and rush of his mechanical world. On the other hand, the anxiety and frustration arising from the failure of Western liberalism led the more radical to a new assessment of the politico-economic structure of their society, and a subsequent sympathy for socialism. For them, modern China served as living emblem of the struggle of an emerging socialist state.

The different appeals of the Orient for modern Western man are reflected in a variety of literary works. Oriental mysticism permeated Hermann Hesse's novels about the spiritual quest of an artist-dreamer; classical Chinese poetry kindled Ezra Pound's creative imagination and propelled the entire movement of Imagism; Eisenstein hailed the junction of kabuki and sound film; *La condition humaine* and *Der kaukasische Kreidekreis* exemplified the political commitment of André Malraux and Bertolt Brecht. Regardless of their philosophy or political belief, regardless of their attitude toward art, many of the greatest literary minds of the modern age have turned to the East for inspiration, and this phenomenon is most pronounced in the field of theatre.

To begin with, the realistic theatre is incapable of dealing with the complex inner world of the individual. Of this perhaps none said it better than John Gassner in *The Theatre in Our Time*:

> For plumbing the depths of the individual psyche, realism was of little avail because the realistic technique, with its "fourth-wall" convention and its absence of poetic dialogue and soliloquy, could present our experience and feeling on only one plane: it could let audiences see only the surfaces that any outsider sees. Realistic drama is preeminently logical, but the inner self is not logical.[15]

And what of the social, economic and political realities intertwined with events happening around the world, the class conflicts and international imbroglios? How efficient is realistic theatre in treating these subjects? Gassner continued:

> How can the realistic playwright, who often lays claim to importance precisely on the grounds of giving us a grip on reality,

---

[15] *The Theatre in Our Time* (New York: Crown, 1966), p. 16.

> cope with such a whirlgig of facts and relationships? . . . The alternative to showing everything, is to show next to nothing. He will tend to content himself with a miniscule situation which may arouse our sympathies but will demonstrate little more than the immediate throb of the moment in a living room.[16]

To escape from the narrowness of realism, twentieth-century dramatists and theatre artists have explored other possibilities. Anouilh, Cocteau, Giraudoux and Eliot wrote modern myths modeled on Greek tragedy, others have taken their ideas from Shakespeare, but an even more popular trend has been to experiment with Eastern theatrical styles, including the classical Chinese theatre.

Nineteenth-century Europe could boast of the knowledge of but a handful of Chinese plays translated into various English, French, or German versions, such as *Han-kung ch'iu* 漢宮秋 [The Sorrow of Han], *Hui-lan chi* 灰闌記 [The Chalk Circle], and *Hsi-hsiang chi* 西廂記 [The West Chamber]. Although the number of translations of Chinese drama increased in early twentieth century, it was not until the mid-1920s that serious scholarship began to emerge. In such outstanding works as A. E. Zucker's *The Chinese Theatre* (1925), L. C. Arlington's *The Chinese Drama* (1930), Cecilia S. L. Zung's *Secrets of the Chinese Drama* (1937), and Arlington and Harold Acton's *Famous Chinese Plays* (1937), the reader could now find a fairly detailed and accurate description of the art of classical Chinese theatre. In the meantime, authentic examples of the Chinese theatre also became available. *Lady Precious Stream* (王寶川, *Wang Pao-ch'uan*), a popular Peking Opera translated into English by Hsiung Shih-i 熊式一, won immense success in London, New York, as well as in various other cities on the European Continent in the mid-1930s. The visits of Mei Lan-fang 梅蘭芳 to America in 1930 and to Russia in 1935 not only brought the excellent acting techniques of the Peking Opera to the general public of these countries, but also fascinated some very important spectators, among them Belasco, Stark Young, Eisenstein, Stanislavsky, Meyerhold, Vakhtangov, and Brecht.

One should also point out that not everyone had to wait for the Chinese theatre to come to the West. Paul Claudel, for instance, lived more than a decade in China as a diplomat; Thornton Wilder spent his early years in Shanghai and Hong Kong with his parents, and Vsevolod Meyerhold employed a Mongolian expert to assist him in the instruction of "biomechanics." The Chinese influence, however, manifested itself in quite different aspects of their works. Claudel's poetic drama pertains to a special lyrical, musical quality much akin to that in the classical Chinese theatre. Wilder, dissatisfied with what he called "the obtrusive bric-a-brac" of the realistic stage, was especially interested in the imaginary décor of the Chinese theatre. On his stage, as in the Chinese tradition, a few chairs suffice for all "settings." Meyerhold, however, saw in the Chinese actor the quality of a gymnast-acrobat, capable of expressing himself through a physical language, and therefore particularly suited for his constructivist stage.

Claudel, Wilder and Meyerhold are by no means the only names that are related to the Chinese theatre. Any student of modern Western theatre knows the significance of the ritualistic frenzy of Artaud, the avant-garde experiments of Cocteau and

---

[16] Ibid., p. 17.

Barrault, the festive magic of Reinhardt, the candid theatricality of Vakhtangov, the popular theatre of Tennessee Williams, the grotesque drama of Genet, the collective improvisation of the Living Theatre, the strictly player-oriented "poor theatre" of Jerzy Grotowsky, and of course, the "epic theatre" of Bertolt Brecht. Collectively, these forms and styles have made contemporary Western theatre what it is today, yet it is little known that all the above-mentioned theatre artists, theorists and playwrights have been influenced by the classical Chinese theatre.

It is easier to pinpoint this Chinese influence on the dramaturgy or stage-craft of certain individuals and styles than others. But when one steps back to look at the whole picture of contemporary Western theatre, one easily realizes that many of its features are directly linked with the characteristics of the traditional Chinese theatre. To name a few: the predominant open dramatic structure and free-flowing scenes; candid theatricality in demonstrative acting, symbolic gesture, and suggestive setting; re-introduction of narration, music and songs into the "word drama"; the use of rhythmic movements bordering on dance; the employment of exaggerated costume, mask, or face-painting; the invitation—and sometimes provocation—of audience participation.

Of all those who have received the Chinese influence, Bertolt Brecht commands the most attention. This is not only because he is one of the most brilliant poet-dramatists of our time; not only because his "epic theatre" has inspired such prominent playwrights as W. H. Auden, Friedrich Dürrenmatt, Max Frisch, John Osborne and Robert Bolt; but also because, through open acknowledgement of his debt to the Chinese dramaturgy, he demonstrated how a synthesis of the theatrics of the East and the West can be achieved. Furthermore, in many aspects, Brecht's "epic theatre" bears a close resemblance to what has been known as the "revolutionary model drama" developed in China in the past fifteen years. This resemblance suggests that there exists a comradeship in contemporary theatre East and West, resulting from mutual respect and emulation.

The impact of Chinese philosophy, poetry and theatre upon Brecht's works has drawn much scholastic attention. We have learned that he was interested in the teachings of Confucius, Lao-tzu 老子, Chuang-tzu 莊子, Mo-tzu 墨子 as well as those of Mao Tse-tung 毛澤東; that he was fascinated by the poetry of Li Po 李白 and Po Chü-i 白居易; that many of his works have a Chinese setting or deal with "Chinese" themes. These include two of his most acclaimed plays, *Der kaukasische Kreidekreis* and *Der gute Mensch von Sezuan,* as well as minor works such as *Turandot oder der Kongress der Weisswäscher, Leben des Konfutse, Me Ti. Buch der Wendungen,* and *Der Tui-Roman.* But by far the most significant affinity lies between Brecht's dramaturgy and the classical Chinese theatre.

Although critics—and Brecht himself—have felt the inadequacy of the term "epic theatre," it nevertheless serves to describe some of the features of the Brechtian theatre. As the term suggests, Brecht's theatre proposes to depart from the Aristotelian doctrine of the dramatic. The advantage of the epic over tragedy is made quite clear by Aristotle himself:

> For the purpose of extending its length, epic poetry has a very great capacity that is specifically its own, since it is not possible in tragedy to imitate many simultaneous lines of action but only that performed by the actors on the stage. But because of

> the narrative quality of epic it is possible to depict many simultaneous lines of action that, if appropriate, become the means of increasing the poem's scope. This has an advantage in regard to the elegance of the poem and in regard to varying the interest of the audience and for constructing a diverse sequence of episodes.[17]

In his "epic theatre," Brecht not only broadened the realm of the "dramatic" by introducing narration and montage techniques, but, because he was such a distinguished poet, incorporated the "lyric" element as well. Since the integration of the "epic," the "dramatic," and the "lyric" is also a basic feature of the classical Chinese theatre, it is not surprising that Brecht should find the classical theatre of China fascinatingly close to his own, and be able to adopt the conventions of the Chinese theatre effectively.

The technical aspects in Brecht's theatre are tightly linked with its political function. Since Brecht's Marxist world view is inseparable from his concept of the theatre, his "epic" approach of theatre aims at the presentation of the dialectics of human affairs, relating man's private drama to the world that causes or conditions it. Brecht would like his spectator to reflect on the problems demonstrated in his theatre, to associate the stage presentation with the socio-economic conditions in real life, and to take such actions as will contribute to the change of the society.

For this reason, Brecht's stage is a platform rather than a locale. His spectator is expected to judge the situation presented rather than to identify with it. His actor is to report and demonstrate, rather than to transform himself into a character. To achieve these goals, he abandoned illusory staging for candid theatricality, exposing lighting instruments, musicians, and scene-changes. He inserted songs, narrations, and comments to break up the coherence of the plot. Instead of *Einfühlung*, or "feeling into" one's role, he demanded the actor to practise the art of *Verfremdung* ("alienation"), setting a distance between himself, his role, and the audience.

The term "alienation effect" first appeared in the English translation of an essay written by Brecht, published in *Life and Letters* (London, 1936). The essay later became one of Brecht's best-known theoretical pieces, under the title "Verfremdungseffekte in der chinesischen Schauspielkunst" (Alienation effects in Chinese dramatic art). On his manuscript Brecht wrote the following note in pencil: "This essay arose out of a performance by Mei Lan-fang's company in Moscow in Spring, 1935."[18] In this essay, Brecht briefly referred to some of the conventional symbols used in the classical Chinese theatre: a general's rank is indicated by the little pennants on his costume, poverty is revealed through "mended" robes with silk patches of different colors, the articles of "furniture" are carried in during the action of a play, actors perform with the aid of face-painting. But what attracted Brecht most was the acting techniques of the Chinese theatre.

Apparently, in addition to the public performance given by the Peking Opera troupe in Moscow, Brecht also attended a discussion session held for a select group, during which Mei Lan-fang, "without special lighting and wearing a dinner jacket, in

---

[17] *Aristotle's Poetics,* tr. Leon Golden (Englewood Cliffs, N.J.: Prentice-Hall, 1968). pp. 43-44.

[18] John Willett, ed. and tr., *Brecht on Theatre* (New York: Hill and Wang, 1964), p. 97.

an ordinary room full of specialists,"[19] demonstrated the elements of Chinese acting. Brecht was profoundly impressed by Mei's ability to "exhibit" his act, without disguising his awareness of being watched by an audience. "The Chinese actor never acts as if there were a fourth wall," observed Brecht.[20] Instead, he displays himself, shows himself off, solicits judgment from the audience, observes his own act, and uses his countenance "as a blank sheet, to be inscribed by the gest of the body."[21] The Chinese artist's performance often strikes the Westerner as cold, Brecht remarked, because, instead of trying to bring his spectator into the closest proximity to the events and the character he portrays, the Chinese actor holds himself remote from the character portrayed and deliberately prevents the sensations from reaching the spectator: "He acts in such a way that nearly every sentence could be followed by a verdict of the audience and practically every gesture is submitted for the public's approval."[22] These artistic acts of self-alienation, according to Brecht, prevent the audience from identifying itself with the characters in the play, and provoke thoughtful judgment on the dramatic actions presented.

Brecht's observations are keen. There is doubtlessly an element of remoteness in Chinese acting that may be described as an "alienation effect." However, he overshoots the mark when he interprets traditional Chinese acting as a kind of doubt or judgment cast by the actor towards the action, for the "coldness" in Chinese acting is a result of rigid stylization in an age-old, conventional theatre, and the actor's attitude is a purely aesthetic one. He does not, as Brecht expects him to, "discover, specify, imply what he is not doing," or "allow the other possibilities to be inferred,"[23] for he is not concerned with the ideological content of the play, but concentrates on the art of acting itself. It is true that there is a constant contact between the actor and his spectators; the actor does look to the audience for approval during his performance. Yet, the question he poses is not the Brechtian "Should I do this?" or "Is this the correct attitude?" Instead, he asks, "Am I doing a good job?" or "Isn't this gesture beautifully executed?" Furthermore, his actions and words are never suspected or judged by the audience on their meaning, because the meaning has already been made extremely clear. Virtue is to be rewarded and vice punished. The characters are clear-cut heroes and villains. The story of the play is usually a familiar legend with a well-learned moral lesson. The acting itself is not thought-provoking, but provides enjoyment. In fact, since the spectator's primary reason for going to the theatre lies in his enjoyment of excellent acting and singing, the classical Chinese theatre is rather "culinary," and not at all revolutionary.

Regardless of whether Brecht's understanding of the classical Chinese theatre is entirely correct, numerous modern Western directors and dramatists have profited from his theory of the "A-effect," and the stylization of Chinese acting has won great acclaim in the West. Ironically, in modern China, the classical acting techniques have not been perceived in the same light. During the "literary revolution" in the early twentieth century, the traditional theatre came under severe attack precisely because of its "coldness" and its indifference to realistic representation of life. Ch'ien Hsüan-

---

[19] Ibid., p. 94.
[20] Ibid., p. 91.
[21] Ibid., p. 92.
[22] Ibid., p. 95.
[23] Ibid., p. 137.

t'ung 錢玄同, a leading member of the New Literature Movement, voiced the following complaint:

> The Peking opera of today possesses neither ideal nor literary value.... The old theatre concentrates exclusively on singing techniques, while its listeners pay no attention to the content of the songs. Furthermore, the preposterous face-painting and the naive stage devices offer nothing that is capable of arousing emotion. Acting should aim at a close resemblance to real people and real-life situations.... What fails the resemblance violates the definition of play-acting. Why is it that our actors of today do not pay the slightest attention to this problem?[24]

If the above criticism recalls Sheldon Cheney's opinion of Chinese theatre, it is because its author belonged to an age characterized by the Western influence it so eagerly embraced. The communist regime of China was no less critical of the traditional theatre. Since 1949, reform projects have been launched to remove various classical conventions and to introduce new, contemporary elements into the theatre, including the acting techniques and stagecraft of realism.

IV

For centuries China remained indifferent to her Western suitors. While Europe indulged in the increasing craze of Sinomania, China was quite unaffected by European ways. But the situation had changed by mid-nineteenth century. Her door was literally stormed by the Western powers, and her citizens suffered humiliation and disillusion as she yielded to the material superiority of the West.

The history of early twentieth-century China is molded by the nation's reaction to the West. On the one hand, the West represented the hated and dreaded enemy that encroached on her national rights and territory, exploited her wealth, and shattered her age-old complacency. On the other hand, however, the West's demonstration of power and affluence convinced young Chinese intellectuals that Westernization was the only route to their country's resurrection. Thus, the Boxer uprising occurred side by side with the Ch'ing government's reform efforts to "self-strengthen" by relatively democratic means; the May Fourth Movement kindled by student protests against international injustice went hand in hand with the "literary revolution" that called for total abolition of traditional literature and advocated all-out imitation of Western models. It was in such an atmosphere that the Western realistic drama was introduced to China; and there it thrived in the fertile soil of political turmoil and social unrest, of protests and revolts. Zola's thundering proclamation that the experimental and scientific spirit

---

[24] *Chung-kuo hsin-wen-hsüeh ta-hsi* 中國新文學大系 (Hong Kong: Hsiang-kang wen-hsüeh yen-chiu-she, 1963), I, 79-80. The translation is mine. The original passage is as follows: 若今之京調戲，理想既無，文章又極惡劣不通，固不可因其為戲劇之故，遂謂有文學之價值也。又中國舊戲，專重唱工，所唱之文句，聽者本不求甚解，而戲子打臉之離奇，舞台設備之幼稚，無一足動人感情。夫戲中扮演，本期肖實人實事，即觀向來「優孟衣冠」一語，可知戲子扮演古人，當如優孟之像孫叔敖。苟其不肖，即與演戲之義不合，顧何以今日之戲子，絕不注意此點乎？

should dominate the modern stage found a loud echo in the midst of calls to abolish the classical theatre and to establish a new "speech drama" capable of dealing with social realities.

In February, 1907, the Spring Willow Society 春柳社, an amateur dramatic organization of Chinese students in Japan, presented its first Western-style dialogue play in Tokyo. The play was Ch'a-hua-nü 茶花女, an adaptation of La dame aux camélias by Dumas fils. The choice of the play was interesting in itself. Since the Chinese intellectuals were primarily looking for representational techniques, the fine division between European realism and naturalism was unheeded. The French play, with its irresistible emotional sweep and its well-made structure, spelled ideal theatre for the young enthusiasts of China. In addition, the French original employed prose dialogue instead of the poetic dialogue prevalent at its time, and therefore was especially attractive to the advocates of the speech drama.

In June of the same year, the Spring Willow Society staged its second play, Hei-nu yü-t'ien lu 黑奴籲天錄, the script of which was based on Harriet Beecher Stowe's novel, Uncle Tom's Cabin. The theme of revolt against racial oppression appealed strongly to the patriotic feelings of the young Chinese. To suit their purpose, the students radically changed the material of the original novel. For instance, the play ended with the victory of the negroes after killing the slave traders and pursuing troops. Ou-yang Yü-ch'ien 歐陽予倩, member of the Society and pioneer in the new theatre movement, called this ending "a permissible change in order to stir the audience."[25] It is worth noting that in their alteration of the plot, the Chinese students betrayed their indebtedness to the classical drama, which demands an ending fulfilling poetic justice, yet they were motivated by the same eagerness to "arouse emotion" as expressed by Ch'ien Hsüan-t'ung, who denounced the classical drama.

In the autumn of 1907, Hei-nu yü-t'ien lu was produced in Shanghai, marking the first performance of the Western-style speech drama in China. Other experimental productions of this nature followed, dramatic societies rose one after another, and literary magazines vied to publish translations and discussions of Western plays for their avid Chinese readers. The social commitment of this new experimental theatre naturally led it to emulate the social dramas of Western playwrights. Ibsen, Shaw, Chekhov, Gorky, Turgenev, Galsworthy, Synge, Wilde, Strindberg, Hauptmann, Kaiser, and Schnitzler all became familiar names, their works frequently quoted and discussed. As a result, when playwrights of the speech drama began to emerge in China, their works were stamped with the predominant traits of their Western models.

One good example of this apprenticeship would be Lei yü 雷雨, written by Ts'ao Yü 曹禺, one of the most famous playwrights of the speech drama. The complicated plot of this play deals with the conflict between the capitalist and the worker, as well as the struggle between the individual and the society. Adultery, incest, madness and deaths are carefully woven into a dramatic action which develops within twenty-four hours. Divided into four acts, the play begins at a late point in the story and proceeds to unfold itself under the threat of an imminent thunderstorm, which sets the tone. Ts'ao Yü relentlessly exploits the suspense in the plot, and dictates "true-to-life" acting by giving detailed directions for the movement, gesture, tone of voice, as well as facial expression of his characters. The play turned out to be a huge success. Realism won

---

[25] Ou-yang Yü-ch'ien, "The Modern Chinese Theatre and the Dramatic Tradition," *Chinese Literature*, No. 11 (1959), p. 103.

the heart of the urban theatre-goers as they wept and sighed over the fate of the lovers who are destined to commit incest and die. *Lei yü* demonstrated a "well-made" type of theatricality, and, as A. C. Scott perceptively observed, "For the first time it provided middle-class Chinese audiences with a theatrical experience within this genre [speech drama] which touched deep response."[26]

This preeminently realistic theatre, fostered by the revolt against classical theatre, the newly discovered effectiveness of illusory staging, and the conviction that theatre should bear resemblance and relevance to life, was essentially a genre borrowed from the West by young intellectuals, and its place was won in the universities and urban areas. In the meantime the classical theatre still dominated most of the rural areas, where the populace, brought up in the classical tradition, could not and would not identify with this foreign import. Thus, a dilemma began to manifest itself: China was faced with two forms of theatre, one realistic in nature, capable of treating contemporary subjects and serving the needs of the modern age, but little understood or enjoyed by the masses; the other, the old theatre, with its historical figures, feudal morals, and remote conventions, quite detached from contemporary life, yet loved by the vast majority of the Chinese people. This dilemma had to be resolved for the theatre to continue to be a vital and functional part of Chinese life. Viewed from another angle, this dilemma can also be described as a strife between the conventional theatre and the realistic theatre. In this struggle we find the common grounds of modern theatre in China and in the West.

The founding of the People's Republic of China marked the beginning of another epoch in the evolution of modern Chinese theatre. By 1949 there were two separate forms of theatre co-existing in China: the classical theatre with its four hundred regional styles of "operatic" drama on the one hand, and the modern speech drama with its dialogue form and stage realism on the other. After 1949, the two forms continued to co-exist in Taiwan, Hong Kong, and other Chinese communities in Asia, but in mainland China the situation changed. With the establishment of the new regime, the theatre became more than ever a political weapon, and, to make this weapon effective, the authorities gradually eliminated the feudal content of the classical theatre and replaced it with new morals of the proletarian revolution and socialist construction of China. In formal aspects, there appeared a merger of the popular conventions of classical theatre and the techniques of realism. Even Western ballet and symphonic music have become an integral part of some recent products of the Chinese theatre.

As early as 1942, Mao Tse-tung had unequivocally pointed out the comradeship between politics and art:

> In the world today all culture, all literature and art belong to definite classes and are geared to definite political lines. There is in fact no such thing as art for art's sake, art that stands above classes or art that is detached from or independent of politics.[27]

To ensure that "literature and art fit well into the whole revolutionary machine as a

---

[26] A. C. Scott, *The Theatre in Asia* (New York: Macmillan, 1973), p. 169.

[27] Mao Tse-tung, *Talks at the Yenan Forum on Literature and Art* (Peking: Foreign Languages Press, 1967), p. 25.

component part,"[28] a series of activities were launched as part of the "drama reform." Committee meetings, conferences and political orientation classes were held for theatre workers; encyclopaedic works of dramatic material were published; specific criteria for play proscription and revision were publicized and numerous classical plays were subsequently banned; theatres all over the nation were re-organized to coordinate with local bureaus of cultural affairs; exchanges between regional styles were encouraged. By 1964, the theatre was ready to move to its next phase. In that year, a "National Festival of Peking Opera of Contemporary Themes" was held in Peking, involving twenty-nine troupes from eighteen provinces and municipalities. Thirty-five modern Peking operas were staged for approximately two hundred thousand spectators. This was a pilot program to be followed by similar "festivals" all over the nation. The authorities explained the purpose of this experiment with admirable clarity:

> The reform of the art of Peking opera is a demand of the time and the masses. At the same time, it also reflects need in the growth of the art itself. Any art that fails to fit in with the demands of the advancing times inevitably loses its vitality and is headed for extinction. There is no lack of example in history. . . . For this reason, only by constant renovation can Peking opera art fit itself to portray our present-day life, only so can it open a broad avenue of advance for itself.[29]

Out of the Festival came the first four "models" directed by Chiang Ch'ing 江青, who was to emerge as a virtual dictator in the Chinese theatre from the Cultural Revolution to the early 1970s. Regardless of her recent political fall, Chiang Ch'ing's personal influence over the Chinese theatre in the past fifteen years cannot be dismissed. Her former acting career in the Western-style drama and status as spouse and devout follower of Chairman Mao largely shaped the formal and ideological mode of the new genre, *ke-ming yang-pan-hsi* 革命樣板戲 (revolutionary model drama).

The "model drama," rising at a time of bitter political rivalry between the Maoist faction and the "revisionists," is strictly didactic in content. In subject matter, it deals with the struggle of the peasants, workers and soldiers against landlords, capitalists and foreign invaders. The ideological significance is underscored by beginning each script and production with quotations from Chairman Mao, and the typical ending of a play is a choral song by the victorious revolutionary heroes, reiterating the lesson learned through the dramatic action, and eulogizing the new society. A similar framework, one recalls, is used in Brecht's *Der kaukasische Kreidekreis*.

Supported by the new theory of "revolutionary realism and revolutionary romanticism combined," the model drama idealizes revolutionary heroes at the expense of convincing characterization. To make certain that the audience gets the correct message, the villain, who used to be portrayed as cunning and resourceful, is now depicted as utterly stupid and uninteresting, whereas the proletarian hero stands out radiant with courage and wisdom. As a result, the model drama has a certain characteristic flatness such as found in Michael's accounts of the future world in the last books of *Paradise Lost*.

---

[28] Ibid., p. 2.
[29] *Peking Review*, 12 June 1964.

In acting techniques, the model drama shows a mixture of conventional and realistic elements, following Mao's dictum, *ku wei chin yung, yang wei chung yung* 古為今用，洋為中用 (let the ancient serve the modern, let the foreign serve the Chinese). The general principle in the selection of techniques is a utilitarian one: if the conventions of the traditional theatre are capable of depicting the contemporary themes effectively, they are retained; if not, they are replaced by the realistic style. By and large, the rigid conventions of the classical theatre have been relaxed. For instance, the fixed role types, together with their respective voice techniques, gestures and movements, have been abandoned. Voice training is no longer restricted to the high-pitched falsetto, but includes the broader, deeper tenor similar to that in an Italian opera. Ordinarily, the realistic supersedes the suggestive in acting. Dialogues of everyday speech take the place of declamation and elocution. Stage movements and gestures are also carried out in the naturalistic fashion. Highly emotional scenes and dramatic climaxes, however, are intensified by traditional techniques. Thus, exaggerated and stylized acting is employed to arrest the attention of the spectators and to underscore the action, not unlike Brecht's principle of alienation.

Just as "armed struggle" is a predominant theme in the model drama, so physical prowess is one of the revolutionary hero's major traits. An area of concentration in the new drama, therefore, is the creation of exciting scenes with abundant action. This is where the traditional feats of acrobatics are most effective. In fact, acrobatic techniques are so popular that special plot situations have to be created in which hand-to-hand combats are demanded, or physical confinement has to be overcome, for only in such situations can the acrobatic skills be fully exploited. Traditional weapons such as spears and swords are now replaced by rifles and pitch forks. In addition to indigenous techniques, the model drama also makes use of ballet and symphonic music to enhance the revolutionary passion and to highlight the mood of heroism.

The orchestra has expanded considerably both in size and in the variety of instruments. Instruments of different regional opera styles are mixed in use. Western instruments such as piano, violin, brass and woodwinds are also included. However, in scenes where specific arias require specific traditional instruments, these remain the sovereign of the stage. In highly emotional scenes, the staccato clapper still punctuates the rhythmic movements, exaggerated gestures, as well as intense facial expressions of the actor, for the effect of "close-up" and "tableau." In stage-design and scenery, elaborate sets are used, concrete objects have taken the place of the symbolic or imaginary ones. Lighting and sound effects are employed as in a realistic drama.

Costume and make-up are true to life only in so far as they create positive images of the proletarian masses. For instance, even in the most difficult dramatic situations, the uniform of the revolutionary army is never tattered or soiled. Instead, it is covered with neat patches similar to those on the beggar's costume in the traditional theatre. Although symbolic designs and colors of the conventional face-painting are now abolished, the revolutionary protagonist is portrayed with extraordinarily red cheeks and dark eyebrows to emphasize his heroic temperament. On the other hand, the face of the villain is shadowed, either by makeup or lighting, with a sinister, greenish hue. Here, as in many other aspects of the model drama, "revolutionary romanticism" supercedes efforts of stage realism.

In short, the model drama is characterized by its rigid ideology as much as by its extremely flexible utilization of theatrical means. The authors of the model drama may use a combination of narration, soliloquy, song, as well as dialogue to develop the dramatic action. The directors may utilize all the means available to the modern stage in addition to the effective conventions in the old theatre. Kenneth Rea, who recently visited China to observe its new theatre, pointed out another aspect of this new theatre: one of the secrets of its success lies in "the sheer depth of involvement on the part of all concerned."[30] The theatre artists go out to the workers, peasants and soldiers to learn from them the true spirit of good revolutionaries; in turn, the audience goes to the theatre to see its own image, to "feel proud" for being portrayed as the hero of the stage. The contact between the actor and the spectator thus extends beyond the confines of the theatre, to the core of life itself. This, we recall, is also the professed goal of some recent experimental theatres in the West—such as the Living Theatre and the Bread and Puppet Theatre.

Twenty years ago Faubion Bower provided us with some food for thought in his *Theatre in the East:*

> Part of China moved from the ox-cart to the airplane directly without the intermediate phase of railway trains ever appearing. It is possible, too, that China will avoid the conventional industrial revolution by going straight from an agrarian civilization into an atomic one. Perhaps there is a parallel with the theatre to be drawn from all this.[31]

Indeed, we may now say, there has been a parallel. For centuries, two different theatrical traditions developed in opposite directions: from Renaissance to late nineteenth century, the Western theatre grew consistently narrower in domain. As it evolved more and more toward realistic presentation, opera, ballet, and mime all came to be separated from the "legitimate drama." On the other side of the globe, the Chinese remained contented with their conventional theatre from the Sung and Yüan dynasties down to late Ch'ing. Like Chinese painting of the "splashing ink" style, the classical Chinese theatre showed little regard for perspective or actual details, but was able to capture the essence of its object with an aesthetic depth all its own. There was a conspicuous absence of interest in stage-design, scenery, lighting, and, in general, the illusion of actuality. Then, in the twentieth century, the trend was reversed. In both traditions a revolt sprang up, and the two theatres began marching toward each other. The modern West started its effort to break the shackles of the realistic tradition, the Chinese also began to feel the insufficiency of their conventional stage art. The West, seeking to reintegrate the various theatrical elements into a synthetic whole, found a living example of the fusion of action, music, dance and mime in the traditional Chinese theatre. The Chinese, on the other hand, found themselves fascinated by the emotional sweep and entrancing effects of the realism imported from the West.

Cross-cultural currents have their own intriguing ways. Despite the progress in world communication, exoticism still plays an important role in man's imagination

---

[30] Kenneth Rea, "New Theatre in China," *The Drama Review,* 21 (March 1977), 18.
[31] *Theatre in the East: a Survey of Asian Dance and Drama* (New York: Grove, 1960), p. 302.

and aesthetic judgment. As it were, when Ts'ao Yü's imitations of Ibsen and Chekhov took the Chinese urban theatres by storm, Mei Lan-fang's foreign tours were inspiring the avant-garde theatre artists of Europe and America with the artistic virtuosity of the classical drama. When Brecht exalted the "alienation effect" in the coldness of classical Chinese acting, the Chinese actors of the new speech drama were training to project "inner reality" into their roles.

Despite the curious process of these theatrical exchanges, they have contributed much to the mutual appreciation of Chinese and Western theatre arts. Without having deliberately set out to "meet" each other half-way, the East and the West have each produced a theatre that can be described as a "world theatre." Today, a symbolic gesture may be appreciated in Shanghai as well as in New York, an "opera"—whatever form it may be—can be enjoyed in Bayreuth as well as in Peking. John Gassner once said that, since a reconciliation of the polarities of realism and theatricalism is inherent in the nature of dramatic art, "the future of our stage depends greatly upon the possibility of turning the present chaotic coexistence of realism and non-realistic stylization into an active and secure partnership."[32] From all indications, the future of world theatre looks brighter than ever.[33]

---

[32] *Form and Idea in the Modern Theatre* (New York: Dryden, 1956), p. viii.

[33] The material of this article is based upon my dissertation, "Chinese and Western Theatre: Contrasts, Cross-currents, and Convergences," University of Illinois at Urbana-Champaign, 1978.

The Nature and Limitations of Shakespeare Translation*

Simon S. C. Chau

Since the first Chinese translation of Shakespeare appeared in 1903,[1] the task of rendering Shakespeare into Chinese has been followed up by no less than forty translators, many of whom are distinguished poets, writers, scholars and dramatists in their own rights.[2] When Professor Liang Shih-ch'iu 梁實秋 published the first Chinese complete works of Shakespeare in 1969, most of the plays had been translated three times, some as many as six or even nine times.[3] While this is an honor not bestowed on any other Western writer, the phenomenon is hardly surprising. After all, Shakespeare's plays are among the most widely translated literary works in the world, ranking possibly only after the Bible.

The completion of Liang's translation did attract a lot of attention and criticism. Many compared his work with the other existing versions, especially the popular Chu Sheng-hao 朱生豪 version.[4] While many of these articles can be dismissed as superficial or trivial, the more serious and influential ones, such as those by Ch'en Tsu-wen 陳祖文 and Yeh Shan 葉珊,[5] focused their attention on several aspects (such as the

---

* This paper is adapted from Chapter 2 of the author's book *A Critical Study of the Chinese Translations of Hamlet* 漢譯哈姆雷特研究, which will be published in Chinese by the Comparative Literature and Translation Centre of the Chinese University of Hong Kong in 1978.

[1] *Hai-wai ch'i-t'an* 海外奇談 (Strange Tales from Overseas), translator unknown, published by Ta-wen she 達文社 in 1903. It was a collection of ten stories from *Lamb's Tales from Shakespeare*.

[2] Including Lin Shu 林紓 (1904), T'ien Han 田漢 (1921), Hsü Chih-mo 徐志摩 (1932), Liu Wu-chi 柳無忌 (1944), Ts'ao Yü 曹禺 (1944) and Pien Chih-lin 卞之琳 (1956), to name but a few.

[3] For a detailed account of Chinese translation of Shakespeare, see my article "Sha-chü Han-i ch'i-shih n'ien" 莎劇漢譯七十年, *Shu-p'ing shu-mu* 書評書目, No. 53 (1977), 52-63.

[4] Chu completed the translation of thirty-one plays before his death in 1944. These were reprinted by no less than twenty publishers in Taiwan, Mainland China and Hong Kong in the fifties and sixties. Cf. *A Critical Study of the Chinese Translations of Hamlet*, Ch. 1.

[5] Ch'en Tzu-wen, "Li-erh wang i-tuan-hsi ti san-chung chung-i" 李爾王一段戲的三種中譯, *Ch'un-wen-hsüeh* 純文學, No. 22 (1969). Yeh Shan (Wang Ching-hsien 王靖獻), "Liang-i Sha-chü ti yin-hsiang" 梁譯莎劇的印象, *Ch'un-wen-hsüeh*, No. 19 (1968).

translators' scholarship and style) and ignored other equally important and certainly more basic ones. Many of these discussions are somewhat off the mark because they have treated the translations as translations of literary works (like poetry or fiction), but not as *plays* which Shakespeare had meant them to be.

In this paper the Chinese translation of Shakespeare is used as an example to illustrate the nature and limitations of dramatic translation, that is, to show what exactly one is doing when one translates a play, what are the difficulties one has to face, and which of these are often beyond one's power. The paper begins by discussing the characteristics which are common to all human communicative processes (Part I), then narrows down step by step to those which are unique to the translation of drama—and for that matter, Shakespeare's plays (Parts II and III). The last part briefly describes the history of Shakespeare production in China, and, by analyzing the elements which are beyond the translator's control, shows why Shakespeare, always so popular in many other parts of the world, has not been readily accepted by the Chinese audience.

I. The Nature and Limitations of Translation as a Process of Communication

It is common for the discussions of translation theories to begin with the question: Is translation possible? And it is equally common for critics to conclude by admitting that perfect translation is impossible. But translation is obviously possible, as we do have before us so many good examples—surrounded by a larger number of less desirable ones, though. Then a more sensible question seems to be: Why not the best? In other words, why is perfect translation impossible? And if so, where is the limit? What can a good translator not do?

When talking about the nature of "translation," it is often very helpful to distinguish between two different senses of this word. The first and broader sense comes from the Latin root *translatio*—to transfer or to change to another form. The second and narrower sense refers to the rendering of a text into another language.[6] Before analyzing the difficulties imposed by language, it should be pointed out that all communicative acts involve "translation" in the broader sense, notably the coding and decoding of the message into and from the medium.

Strictly speaking, human communicative acts, verbal or otherwise, are seldom perfect. (For the present purpose, a "perfect" act of communication implies simply that the communicant receives the message exactly as the communicator intended it to be, no distortion, no more, no less.) In "translating" his message into the medium, the communicator too often fails to make it clear and exact. At the other end of the line, the communicant, when decoding the message, receives possibly little more than those parts which happen to coincide with his past experiences. Moreover, there are so many different kinds of forces at work to hinder the transmission process, not the least of which are the communicant's subjective views and prejudices. No two persons experience things in the same way. In his attempt to decode and to re-create the message, the communicant inevitably sees things from his own standpoint, which is more often than not different from that of the communicator. Inexactness is, after all, a dominant feature of human communication.

---

[6] See the entry "Translation" in *Webster's Third New International Dictionary*.

When it comes to human language, there is one important feature which is basic to one's understanding of the possibilities and limitations of translation. As Werner Winter has noted: "Languages are systems of arbitrarily selected, but conventionalized signs which serve to convey arbitrarily selected, but conventionalized meanings," so that "sign and meaning cannot be dissociated from each other," and "no sign and no meaning exists by itself, but only as part of a system."[7] No two languages or parts of two languages are identical. A language is not only a system of signs and their form of construction, but also a unique system of ideas and mode of thought. Thus, "there is no completely exact translation. If our interpretation of reality as formulated in Language A does not exist in any isolation, but only part of the system total of this language, then its correlative in Language B cannot be isolated from the overall system of B, which must be different from A."[8] Furthermore, every language is integrated with the culture in which it operates. A word in any language is nothing but a cluster of connotative as well as denotative meanings which it has accumulated down the centuries since its birth. Being part of a cultural system, it is impossible to retain its meaning while replacing it by another sign belonging to another system. These, at least, are the limitations one must accept when translating from one language to another.

II. The Nature and Limitation of Literary Translation

As a form of communication, literature is unique at least in two ways. First, it is a form of art. Like any other form of art, the artist expresses in a subjective way his subjective insights and feelings. Second, the medium employed is the human language, or, to be more precise, human language as recorded in written form. At the same time, a piece of literary work is a historical being, itself a finite entity. It is a world by itself. These characteristics are, again, some of the roots of the limitations of literary translation.

Strictly speaking, every act of communication is unique. A most simple statement made a second time by the same speaker is no longer the same one. The external conditions could not have remained identical, nor the mood of the speaker and listener and their relations. Thus the impact is different. Also, on hearing the same statement for the second time, one's reaction cannot be identical with the first. It is even less realistic to expect that two persons will react in an identical way to the same speech. Again, just like any other form of communication, one's understanding and impression of any work of art is the sum total of many subjective as well as objective factors. If no two persons can react in the same way to the same piece of literary work, and if no one can react in the same way in two different readings of the same piece, a "thorough" or "standard" comprehension of any utterance is not possible. And even if it is, there is no objective method to verify it. This being the case, how can one interpret a text properly in order to re-create it?

---

[7] Werner Winter, "Impossibilities of Translation," in *The Craft and Context of Translation*, ed. William Arrowsmith and Roger Shattuck (Austin: The Univ. of Texas Press, 1961), pp. 68-69.

[8] Ibid., p. 69.

Then there are the various kinds of textual problems which can very often be quite serious with classical literature. The editing of a classical work is by itself an enormous task of criticism in which the editor (who might even be the author himself) cannot but interpret the text subjectively. In choosing the text to be based on, the translator is again going through a process of subjective elimination. Until an "authorized" version of the particular literary work appears, the translator cannot possibly exempt himself from this painstaking job.

Yet it is after the final choice of the text that one of the greatest challenges awaits the translator. Before he puts down the first word, he has to interpret the text. Apart from the very basic hermeneutical problems mentioned above, the interpretation and criticism of a literary text involve a lot more. The translator will inevitably face a paradox: as a re-creator, he cannot possibly approach the text as the author did—for he does not know all the things the author knew. On the other hand, the translator does know considerably more than the author, for the translator is surrounded by an ever increasing amount of exegeses, textual notes, criticism, etc., from which the author is denied. Nor can the translator react to the text just like any other reader, ancient or contemporary, who is coming across the text for the very first time. The translator knows the text "too well." It sounds paradoxical to say that criticism and exegeses hinder the task of translation. But the truth is that the more that has been said about any particular piece of work, the more difficult it is for any reader, of whom the translator is one, to confront the text in a fresh and original manner. After Samuel Coleridge and A. C. Bradley, Shakespeare was no longer the same old swan of Avon. Translation is possible only to the degree that legitimate interpretation is possible. With the above picture in mind, one has to admit that translation at its best, like interpretation, can be no more than a mixture of approximations and compromises.

There is another important but difficult choice the translator has to make, if the literary work to be translated happens to be an ancient one. What should he aim at: the author's intended response from his contemporary readers, or the response of the modern readers who read the text in the original? Or, to be more specific, when translating Shakespeare into another language, should one reproduce the impact the Globe audience had (if that is at all possible), or to reproduce that of the modern English-speaking audience? For example, should one imitate Shakespeare's fresh and imaginative language use that was so typical of the Renaissance period, or should one emphasize the archaic flavor which is experienced by so many English-speaking readers today? Who, after all, are Shakespeare's audience? If the translator feels guilty in reproducing merely the response of the twentieth-century readers of which he himself is one, how can he assess the impact a Shakespearean production had on the Globe audience, who was anything but homogeneous?

The last, but by no means the least, paradox a literary translator has to face is that which exists between creation and re-creation. Artistic expression is by definition subjective and personal. When one creates, one cannot but make use of one's own talents, every bit of which betrays one's personality. When translating, one re-creates what has been created. Re-creation is also a form of creation. Then the problem is: how can one make use of one's own personality, yet at the same time forsakes it in order to serve and imitate another? As long as the original is a creative kind of writing, this paradox haunts the translator, adding to the difficulties of literary translation.

III. The Nature and Limitations of Dramatic Translation

A dramatic work exists at least in two forms: the printed script, and its realization on the stage. As an art form expressed through written words, drama is quite similar to the other literary genres such as prose and poetry. But a drama translator who knows his business understands that there is a lot more involved when a dramatic work is re-created in another language. Except for the comparatively rare dramatic works which are intended to be read rather than performed, the translation of drama is not from a script written in Language A to another written in Language B, but the transformation of an event, or a "happening," from one theatre to another. Drama exists primarily in the theatre. The script is no more than a tool of secondary importance.

This is especially true as far as Shakespeare is concerned. The bard did not write for the armchair reader. He was a man of the theatre, and had never intended to publish his plays as immortal literary monuments to be worshipped and analyzed by generations and generations of scholars and readers all over the world. As the producer, he revised and cut his own plays from time to time. For him and his audience, it is what will be shown on stage in the following afternoon alone that matters. Before going on to discuss the problems of translating Shakespeare, it will be helpful to analyze the nature of translating dramatic works first.

Unlike the other literary genres, the process of communication in drama is far more complicated, involving many more parties. For poetry, prose, novel, etc., the process is an "author-text-reader" one, as shown in the table below:

Table 1 The communication process of literary works in general

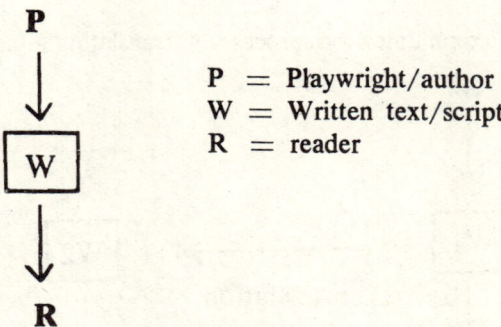

P = Playwright/author
W = Written text/script
R = reader

But in drama, the parties involved are the playwright, the script, the director and the audience, and there is also the process of translating from the written text to the spoken language:

Table 2 The communication process of a dramatic work

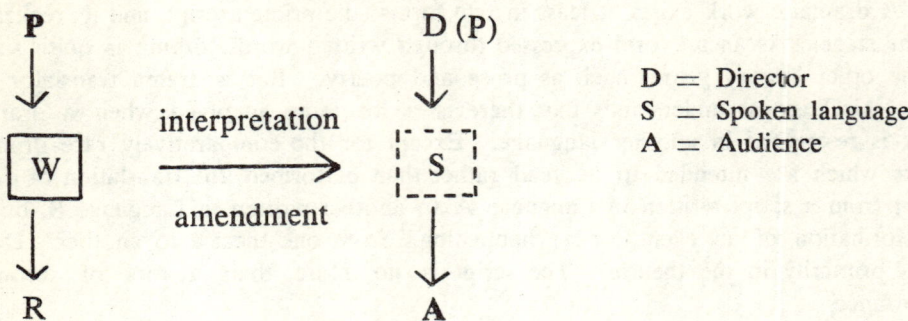

Note that the box for "spoken language" in the above table is drawn in dotted lines because, unlike the written text which is comparatively stable, the words to be spoken on stage often vary from performance to performance, depending on the amendment of the director. Also, unlike prose, poetry or fiction which are presented in printed form and suffer less possible distortion in the hands of the editor and the book designer, the play has to be realized by the director, the actors and the whole production crew, and thereby is affected by many elements which may all work for as well as against the playwright. So the playwright, when compared to the poet and the novelist, has far less control over the final outcome and the impact of his work on the audience.

When a piece of literary work is translated into another language, the translator re-creates the work of art by employing the very same medium (written language) used by the writer:

Table 3 The communication process in translating literary works in general

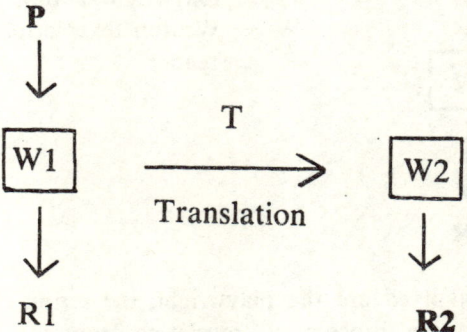

This is a comparatively simple process. For one thing, the translator is himself one of the communicants of the original (R1). He comes into direct contact with the original medium of communication (the text). Moreover, he can put the original (W1) and his own re-creation (W2) side by side in order to compare the effects. He can be his own critic before showing the translation to others. Thus he comes into direct contact with his own re-creation. In this way, the translator can at the same time be the translator (T), the original reader (R1), and the prospective reader of the translation (R2), and has the privilege of comparing the impacts of the two texts.

This is not true of drama translation. With Table 2 in mind, one will be able to see the special difficulties involved in such a process. What actually happens is that the drama translator comes into contact merely through the script (W1) which is itself a very inadequate way to represent the total effect of the "original performance," including the actual words spoken (S1), and has to re-create that effect by employing the written medium (S2) which has to be re-translated into the spoken words on stage (W2). In other words, the translator re-creates by reconstructing in his mind something which has never existed in standard form, and by imagining some future effects he desires but ultimately has little control over:

Table 4 The communication process of drama translation

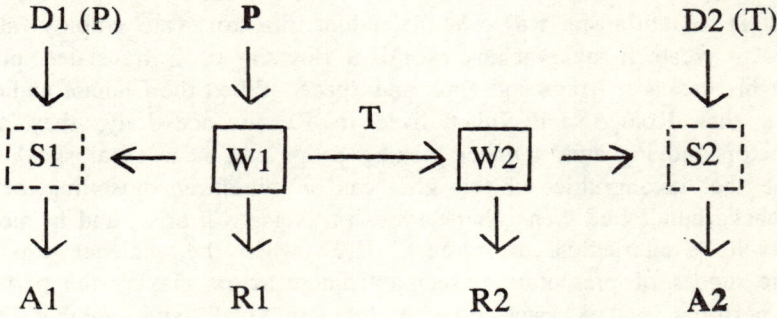

The above relation is still true even if the play happens to be written and produced by a contemporary playwright, for the translator can witness no more than a few of the innumerable performances produced by the playwright himself. As mentioned earlier, the effect of each performance differs, and there is no "standard" performance for any play.

Thus one can see that the drama translator has to face quite a lot of problems which are unknown to the translator of other literary genres. Unless the playwright is a contemporary one, the translator can only guess at the effect of the original performances (which are supposed to be the "norm"), basing on the script and whatever background information available. Then he has to use the written language (W2) to represent the expected spoken language (S2) in the theatre to imitate the spoken language in the original playhouse (S1) as represented by the written language in the script (W1). Unlike the translator of poetry or fiction, the words put down by the drama translator (S2) are far from being the final means to communicate with his audience. The printed medium is not an end by itself. (For the same reason, the criticism of drama translation, especially when it is based on the printed script alone, becomes all the more risky if not far-fetched at times.) The drama translator is only responsible for a part of the translation process. Like the playwright, he has comparatively little control over the final outcome of the creation. Again, unlike the translator of poetry or fiction, the drama translator cannot "feel" the impact of his work in advance. The manuscript in hand is but the very beginning of a long process. Furthermore, the target of drama translation is to make the audience of the translation (A2) respond to the translation in the same way the original audience (A1) did to the original. But such a statement is very vague, if not misleading, for it presupposes that the original response is a homogeneous one, which was seldom the case, as every Shakespearean scholar knows so well. So there is simply no bull's eye for the translator to aim at.

The cultural element is always a very real obstacle in translation. In drama, any cultural gap between the two audiences is inevitably exaggerated when a play is performed on stage (see discussion below). As a form of art, drama is far more "concrete" and "physical" than other literary genres. The audience does not merely re-create the scene in their minds. Compared to music or fiction, they have much less room for imagination, as they are supposed to re-live the experience through sight and sound in person in the theatre. A novelist or a poet can take his reader to any part of the world in any age at will. His imagination is only bounded by his writing skill and the creative power of his readers. The playwright hardly enjoys the same kind of liberty, for he is obliged to represent his ideas on the stage, though not necessarily in a naturalistic way. While a film director can employ all kinds of techniques to create a make-believe world, a director of a translated play is quite limited in his means to transcend time and space. When the Chinese audience are led to believe that Romeo and Juliet lived in Renaissance Italy, they actually *see* Chinese actors moving amidst queer looking props and hear them speaking Chinese. (It is true that incongruities of this kind can be minimized by setting the plot in the Chinese background, but then other serious problems will arise, and in most cases the audience will be puzzled all the more.) Even when the audience can accept less naturalistic modes of presentation, seeing Chinese actors playing the parts of foreign dramatis personae makes spectators feel far less "real" and credible than reading their story in print and letting the heroes act on the imaginary stage.

For drama, after all, is the product of a particular age and culture, as well as a part of the way of living of a particular society. When divorced from its tradition and background, it loses much of its impact and "meaning." If it requires tremendous effort and imagination to reproduce poetry in a different verse form in another language, the task of reproducing a play on a stage with a different tradition is all the more challenging. The drama translator does not merely experiment with language, he may have to change the stage tradition and re-orientate the prospective play troupe as well as the audience. The task of re-orientating an audience can turn out to be far more prohibiting than translating prose or fiction, for the playgoers are by and large more conservative and less imaginative than the average reader of fiction, prose and poetry. Other things being equal, the average playgoer is less literate than the literary reader. The playgoers come from a more diversified background, and their tastes and expectations from the play are also more varied. An anthology of poetry, prose or fiction in translation, catering for a much more specific group of readers, can exist in print with comparatively less production cost. A play in translation, on the other hand, will be doomed unless the box office of the first nights is promising. By its very nature, drama has to be more audience-oriented. This is a very realistic problem which the translator has to face.

There are other risks which are quite unique to the process of drama translation. Like music, drama is a temporal form of art. Also like music, the creator and the audience communicate through interpreters. This implies that the creator's ideas have to be realized through the imagination and professional skills of the producer, the director, the actors, the set-designer and many others who are involved in the production. It is only too common for some of them to misinterpret or twist the intention of the playwright. Their "intervention" is certainly more influential than the editors and the designers who produce a book, and their incompetence more disastrous than the careless typesetter and proofreader. This threat is often aggravated by the fact that drama is a temporal art. Should a reader raise doubts about the meaning of a sentence in a novel, he can always pause and think. Should he miss a line or two, he can always turn back and check later. But when an actor fails to speak a line clearly and accurately, or when the playgoer fails to understand it or misses it altogether for whatever reason, there will be little chance for remedy. The playgoer can neither freeze the action nor resort to footnotes. Furthermore, the playgoer does not react to a play by himself. The impact comes as much from the actions on stage as from the reaction of the audience who, in turn, is influenced by innumerable factors well beyond the control or even expectation of the playwright and the producer. No matter how well the play is translated and produced, its success hinges on factors like the weather, the set-up of the theatre, and the mood of the particular group of playgoers who comes for the occasion. These factors which are peculiar to playwriting make the translation of drama considerably different from that of other literary genres.[9]

IV. The Basic Difficulties of Staging Shakespeare in Chinese

"A 'perfect' act of translation would be one of total synonymity. It would presume an interpretation so precisely exhaustive as to leave no single unit in the source-text—phonetic, grammatical, semantic, contextual—out of complete account, and yet so calibrated as to have added nothing in the way of paraphrase, explication or variant."[10] Even if that is possible, and the producer is blessed with a copy of "perfect" Chinese translation of a Shakespearean play, he will still find it impossible to achieve the ultimate goal, namely, to give the Chinese audience the "correct" impact and impression—those received by the Globe audience. The forces that are working against him are analyzed below.

Students of English and Chinese dramas have discovered a lot of striking similarities between the two dramatic traditions. The theatre, the props and costumes, organization and nature of the troupe, the tastes and components of the audience, the nature and elements of the performances, and the technique of acting and the treatment of the plots of the Elizabethan and the traditional Chinese drama are found to share a great deal in common.[11] While it is true that the similiarities between Elizabethan

---

[9] The fact that Shakespeare's plays are written primarily in poetic forms with a tradition of its own certainly further complicates the matter. While the classic controversy on the translatability of poetry is too complicated to be dealt with in the present discussion, it should be pointed out that this is another great obstacle faced by the Shakespeare translator, especially when poetic forms are alien to the Spoken Drama form into which Shakespeare is translated and performed. If the earlier translators of foreign plays had found it difficult to write fluent and comprehensible prose passages for delivery on stage, presenting the speeches in poetic form is apparently out of the question. This problem, together with the consequent loss of dramatic effect, is discussed in detail in Chapter 4 of *A Critical Study of the Chinese Translations of Hamlet*.

[10] George Steiner, *After Babel: Aspects of Language and Translation* (London: Oxford Univ. Press, 1975), p. 407.

[11] See, for example, James Liu, *Elizabethan and Yüan: A Brief Comparison of Some Conventions in Poetic Drama* (London: China Society, 1955).

and traditional Chinese dramas are greater than those between Elizabethan and modern Western dramas, one must also remember that the traditional Chinese drama had for some time ceased to be the dominant form. While it is meaningful and interesting to attempt to translate Shakespeare into traditional Chinese dramatic forms, it is hardly practical to stage such translations.[12] Nearly all the theatres in China today have adopted the framed stage, and plays are usually performed in the modern Western fashion. (They are called the "New Drama" 新劇 or "Spoken Drama" 話劇.) Thus the fact that Shakespeare's dramatic tradition resembles that of the traditional Chinese one is almost irrelevant. Moreover, there are vital differences too—not the least the emphasis on singing in traditional Chinese drama.

Since its advent at the turn of the century, the New Drama had gradually been replacing the Old Drama as the most popular form of dramatic expression in China. The Chinese, especially those who lived in the more Westernized coastal cities like Shanghai and Hong Kong where Shakespeare was studied in colleges and performed in public, were by and large ready to accept novel Western concepts and artistic expressions. Many of the intellectuals as well as the not-so-educated mass had the curiosity and appetite to learn more about the West, as witnessed by the unprecedented popularity of the Western novel in translation during the first two decades of this century. Translations of Shakespeare's plays were equally popular—T'ien Han's 田漢 *Hamlet* 哈孟雷特, among the first of its kind, came out in seven impressions in ten years.[13] Then, it is only logical to expect that Western plays would be equally successful on the Chinese stage. Unfortunately, this was not the case.

The New Drama did have a good start between 1907 and 1912, when adaptations of Western plays and novels like Harriet Beecher Stowe's *Uncle Tom's Cabin* and Alexandre Dumas fils' *La Dame aux Camelias* were staged in Chinese. But those performances were confined to narrow circles. As soon as the dramatists attempted to reach a wider audience, they found it impracticable. The Chinese audience did not welcome translated plays, so much so that the professional New Drama troupes had to stop staging them. As Teng Sui-ning 鄧綏甯 pointed out in *Chung-kuo hsi-chü shih* 中國戲劇史: "[After the May Fourth Movement in 1919] even though a great number of Western plays had been translated, most of them do not quite fit the Chinese background. It is all right for reading, but when it comes to staging them, the difficulty is tremendous."[14] Fu Szu-nien 傅斯年 also said, "The Western plays are made of materials taken from the Western society which is quite alien to the Chinese audience. If you stage a literal translation before the Chinese audience, they will not be able to understand the play. That will be disastrous."[15] It is only natural that the Chinese audience, like their counterpart in the West, like to see on the stage heroes and stories they had been acquainted with since childhood. Just as Shakespeare

---

[12] A serious attempt can be found in Chang Ch'ang-hsin 張常信, "Shakespeare in China," M.A. Thesis Birmingham 1951.

[13] See Appendix 2 of *A Critical Study of the Chinese Translations of Hamlet*. According to T'ien Ch'in 田禽, Shakespeare ranks first among the most often translated playwrights between 1908 and 1938 (seconded by Chekov and Shaw). See *Chung-kuo hsi-chü yün-tung* 中國戲劇運動 (Shanghai: Shang-wu, 1946), p. 107.

[14] (Taipei: Chung-hua wen-hua, 1956), p. 140.

[15] Quoted by Hung Shen 洪深 in his introduction to the ninth volume of *Chung-kuo hsin-wen-hsüeh ta-hsi* 中國新文學大系, ed. Chao Chia-pi 趙家璧 (1936; rpt. Hong Kong: Wen-hsüeh yen-chiu, 1962).

did not invent the heroes and plots in most of his plays, the heroes and plots one finds in a Chinese play had mostly been dramatized in different forms in the past hundreds of years. Historical figures like Ts'ao Ts'ao 曹操, legendary figures like Monkey and Pigsy, and romances like the Butterfly Lovers had appeared on the Chinese stage for centuries with local variations. So when the enthusiastic "New" dramatists staged Shaw's *Mrs. Warren's Profession* in Shanghai in 1921, the audience walked out in the middle of the first performance, and the production turned out to be a great failure.[16] Even though Shakespeare is of all ages, it takes quite some time before the great English dramatist can be accepted by an audience in a totally different culture such as China.

As if to make matters worse, Shakespeare was not introduced into China at the most favorable time. In the nineteenth century, the interest of the Chinese in the West lay in technology and other "practical" subjects such as economics and political science. It was only after 1900 that the Chinese came to realize that Western literature could be interesting too. Yet in the first three decades most of the translated plays staged, like the most popular translated novels, were those concerning social issues with progressive spirits such as the works of Shaw, Dickens and Ibsen. That explains why only one play of Shakespeare's, and none other than *The Merchant of Venice*, was known to have been performed in public in China before 1940.[17] The other romances, histories and comedies were ignored and seldom translated, simply because they did not suit the taste and need of the time. Thus Shakespearean productions failed to appeal to the Chinese audience in the developing stage of the New Drama. And no sooner had the New Drama replaced the Old Drama as the most popular form around 1930, than China had to prepare herself to resist the Japanese invasion. The New Drama became a very effective means of arousing patriotism and anti-Japanese feelings. From that time onwards until after the Second World War, nearly all the plays were morale-boosters (*kuo-fang hsi-chü* 國防戲劇). There was no place for Shakespeare.[18]

Shakespeare was rarely performed in Mainland China after the establishment of the Communist regime in 1949, as the nature and the themes of his plays do not quite fit the party line of the time.[19] Several performances were staged in Taiwan in the past thirty years, with varying degrees of success.[20] In Hong Kong where Shakespeare was performed fairly regularly in English by local as well as visiting companies, productions in Chinese were rare until very recently.[21]

---

[16] Ibid., pp. 36-37.

[17] In 1912 (in an adapted form) and in 1930 (based on the translation of Ku Chung-i 顧仲彝).

[18] Other known public performances before 1949 are Liang Shih-ch'iu's productions of *Hamlet* and *Othello* in Chungking in 1942. See B. Atkinson, "*Hamlet,* at the Kuo T'ai Theatre in Chungking, Is Not Yet Quite Ready for Broadway," *The New York Times,* December 18, 1942.

[19] The only exception, perhaps, is the staging of *Romeo and Juliet* in 1956 in Peking. See "Shakespeare in China: *Romeo and Juliet* Performed in Peking," *The Illustrated London News,* October 13, 1956, p. 615.

[20] See Liang Shih-ch'iu, "Sha-shih-pi-ya tsai Chung-kuo" 莎士比亞在中國, *Central Daily News* 中央日報, April 25, 1964.

[21] Cantonese productions of *Taming of the Shrew* (1975) and *Hamlet* (1978) by local companies aroused a lot of enthusiasm. In both cases the scripts were translated by the production crew especially for the occasion. *Macbeth* will be staged in 1979.

When all these have been said, it should be pointed out that the difficulties mentioned in Part IV are temporal factors which may change with time (as opposed to those far more permanent ones discussed in Parts I, II and III). As time goes by, cultural gaps are bridged, and one might look forward to the day when the Chinese audience will be perfectly at home with the Elizabethan-style apron stage, and be as familiar with Hamlet, Lear and Falstaff as was the Globe audience. Then, naturally, the problem of acceptance which barred the Chinese audience from Shakespearean productions in the past generations will cease to exist, and arguments like Fu Szu-nien's quoted above will no longer be valid. Even so, the nature of languages and drama as a literary form will not change that much, and the limitations of translation, as analyzed in Parts I, II and III, will somehow always remain to challenge the drama translator.

Tou O yüan as Tragedy

Ping-cheung Cheung

Whether there is tragedy in traditional Chinese drama is a moot question. Some say there is, and some say there is not. As might be expected, opinions are split in the case of *Tou O yüan* 竇娥冤, a drama by the well-known Yüan playwright Kuan Han-ch'ing 關漢卿 (c. 1220-c. 1300), which is probably the most widely discussed Chinese play today.[1] This disagreement reflects the wide divergence of modern critical views on tragedy. In this essay, which is in part another attempt to define tragedy, I shall try to keep to the facts in the works that I shall discuss or refer to, and try not to do theorizing about tragedy without their support. Apart from this goal, I shall argue, from the conclusions in my discussion of tragedy, that *Tou O yüan* is a tragic play.

I

The word "tragedy" in Greek literally means a goatsong. How it came to become the name for the dramatic performances at the spring festival of Dionysus at Athens

---

[1] Ch'ien Chung-shu's 錢鍾書 "Tragedy in Old Chinese Drama," *T'ien Hsia Monthly,* 1 (Aug. 1935), 37-46, is a vigorous argument that the Chinese did not produce tragedy; see also Gilbert Murray, *Aeschylus: The Creator of Tragedy* (Oxford: Oxford Univ. Press, 1940), p. 5; and Henry W. Wells, *The Classical Drama of the Orient* (New York: Asia Publishing House, 1965), pp. 52-69. Wang Kuo-wei's 王國維 *Sung Yuan hsi-ch'ü k'ao* 宋元戲曲考, in *Wang Kuo-wei hsi-ch'ü lun-wen chi* 王國維戲曲論文集 (Peking: Chung-kuo hsi-chü ch'u-pan-she, 1957), p. 106, is probably the first, though brief, assertion that there are tragedies in traditional Chinese drama. Some of the more recent efforts concerning particular plays are: John Y. H. Hu, "*The Lute Song*: An Aristotelian Tragedy in Confucian Dress," *Tamkang Review,* 2, No. 2 & 3, No. 1 (1971-72), 345-58, and "*The Lute Song* Reconsidered: a Confucian Tragedy in Aristotelian Dress," *Tamkang Review,* 6, No. 2 & 7, No. 1 (1975-76), 449-64; Cyril Birch, "Tragedy and Melodrama in Early *Ch'uan-ch'i* Plays: 'Lute Song' and 'Thorn Hairpin' Compared," *Bulletin of the School of Oriental and African Studies,* 36, Pt. 2 (1973), 228-49. Articles devoted to *Tou O yüan* are: Chang Han-liang 張漢良, "Kuan Han-ch'ing ti Tou O yüan: i ko t'ung-su chü" 關漢卿的竇娥冤：一個通俗劇, *Chung-wai Literary Monthly,* 4, No. 8 (1976), 128-41; Ku T'ien-hung 古添洪, "Pei-chü: Kan t'ien tung ti Tou O yüan" 悲劇：感天動地竇娥冤, *Chung-wai Literary Monthly,* 4, No. 8 (1976), 112-26; and Chang Shu-hsiang 張淑香, "Ts'ung hsi-chü ti chu-t'i chieh-kou t'an Tou O ti yüan" 從戲劇的主題結構談竇娥的冤, *Chung-wai Literary Monthly,* 5, No. 2 (1976), 174-216.

is a question in the history of classical drama.[2] Greek tragedy, as we know it today, consists of the works of Aeschylus, Sophocles, and Euripides, who are generally regarded also as its greatest writers. In the *Poetics* it is treated basically as a literary art rather than as a theatrical event. Without depreciating the importance of the latter in our experience of tragedy, I shall, following Aristotle's example, concentrate here on the literary aspects of tragedy although my approach to the subject may not be Aristotelian.

The Greeks created at least two kinds of tragedy, each revealing a structure distinct from that of the other, as a result of the difference in their visions of reality. The first kind of tragedy can be represented by *Oedipus the King,* where man is presented as a doer, engaging in actions that will lead to his fall. The other can be represented by *The Trojan Women,* where man is presented as a passive sufferer, enduring afflictions imposed upon him by agents other than himself. These dramatic patterns, reflecting different accounts of human suffering, also serve to distinguish two kinds of drama. Indeed, man as a victim of external circumstances is the stable formula of hundreds of melodramas flourishing in the nineteenth century. They manifest the same view of life and exhibit the same dramatic structure with *The Trojan Women*. As far as this is true, we may call the kind of tragedy exemplified by *The Trojan Women* melodrama and preserve the name "tragedy" for the kind of plays exemplified by *Oedipus the King*.[3]

At this point, I should caution that "tragedy" and "melodrama" are employed here strictly as generic terms, detached from their respective honorific and pejorative implications that one often encounters in modern criticism. So tragedy is not superior drama, nor melodrama inferior drama. It is not difficult to see that both the reverent use of tragedy and the abusive use of melodrama are confusing the generic with the evaluative. And it is a matter of clarity that these terms should be conceived as neutral designations of two species of dramatic works.[4] Thus *Oedipus the King, Oresteia, Antigone,* and *Bacchae* are tragedies; *The Trojan Women, Philoctetes, Oedipus at Colonus,* and *Andromache* melodramas. It stands to reason that if a work is thought to be tragic, it makes sense only if it is tragic in the way that the above tragedies are tragic.

---

[2] Gerald F. Else, *The Origin and Early Form of Greek Tragedy* (Camb., Mass.: Harvard Univ. Press, 1965), pp. 9-31. The author discusses the literal meaning of the word "tragedy" in the context of the early development of Greek tragic drama.

[3] James L. Smith, *Melodrama* (London: Methuen, 1973) is a study of melodrama which discusses works by Aeschylus, Sophocles, Euripides, Shakespeare, Ibsen and others as well as the nineteenth-century melodramas. Other studies that have influenced my view of melodrama are Eric Bentley, *The Life of the Drama* (New York: Atheneum, 1974) and Robert Bechtold Heilman, *Tragedy and Melodrama*: *Versions of Experience* (Seattle: Univ. of Washington Press, 1968). I am indebted to Professors Bentley and Heilman for the idea that tragedy and melodrama are separate genres each informed by a different sense of reality, although my concept of tragedy is different from theirs.

[4] On the honorific and abusive uses of the words "tragedy" and "melodrama" James L. Rosenberg writes: "But why must generic classification necessarily degenerate into a game of hierarchies? Is it not enough to perceive that there are various modes of perception—the tragic, the comic, the melodramatic, the farcical. . . . Can we not be satisfied with saying that tragedy and comedy and melodrama and farce are different modes of perception, each with its own validity, none necessarily better than the others?" See "Melodrama," in *The Context and Craft of Drama*: *Critical Essays on the Nature of Drama and Theatre,* ed. Robert W. Corrigan and James L. Rosenberg (Scranton, Penn.: Chandler, 1964), p. 172.

The idea that tragedy portrays man himself as a cause of his grief is hinted at in Aristotle's description of his ideal tragic hero as "a man who is not eminently good and just, yet whose misfortune is brought about not by vice or depravity, but by some error or frailty."[5] Modifying Aristotle, Northrop Frye remarks:

> The particular thing called tragedy that happens to the tragic hero does not depend on his moral status. If it is causally related to something he has done, as it generally is, the tragedy is in the inevitability of the consequences of the act, not in its moral significance as an act.[6]

This is apparent in Oedipus, Orestes, Antigone, and Pentheus. A. C. Bradley observes that the Shakespearean tragic hero "always contributes in some measure to the disaster in which he perishes."[7] Such an impression is amply confirmed by Richard III, Brutus, Antony, Othello, Lear, Macbeth, and Coriolanus. The Racinian tragic figure, like Athalie, Oreste, Pyrrhus, Néron, Titus, and Bérénice, does not always perish, but always suffers for his deeds. In Ibsen the tragic people, such as Mrs. Alving, Rebekka West, Hedda Gabler, Halvard Solness, always help to ruin themselves. The tragic, therefore, is the sense that man has responsibility in his suffering in terms of the things he does, as opposed to the melodramatic that sees man as a victim of external forces.

To this concept of the tragic, *Hamlet,* so-called "the tragedy of inaction," appears to be a serious challenge. Yet is the hero of the play tragic, in the sense that Oedipus, Macbeth, and Lear are? The contrast between him and them is obvious: he is as much a man of inaction as they are men of action. Like Antigone, he has to accept a plight not caused by himself. But while Antigone acts toward a single purpose and dies because of it, his death is the result of a trick played upon him by the king and Laertes. Or like the Orestes of Aeschylus, he has a father to avenge. But while Orestes does his duty and suffers, he keeps putting it off. Then, when he at last kills the king, it is almost an accidental act, not his express intention of accepting the king's invitation to the sword-match with Laertes. Besides, for a considerable part of the play his mind is tormented, not because of something he has done, but because of his inability to realize an obligation. This image of Hamlet is brought into further focus by the role of Laertes, who, with Fortinbras, is set up by Shakespeare as a foil to him. Nothing, not even damnation, would prevent Laertes from avenging his father. He conspires with the king, accomplishes his goal, and dies by the envenomed sword with which he kills Hamlet. He is tragic.

To endure the murder of his father, the incestuous marriage of his mother, and the abrupt apathy of Ophelia, Hamlet is the victim of circumstances. But his inability to act is a reproach for which he can blame only himself. Indeed he is keenly aware of his inertia and constantly rebukes himself on account of it. Whatever its cause, his being unable to take revenge makes up a good part of his anguish, which

---

[5] S. H. Butcher, *Aristotle's Theory of Poetry and Fine Art, with a Critical Text and Translation of "The Poetics,"* with a prefatory essay "Aristotelian Literary Criticism" by John Gassner, 4th ed. (1907; rpt. New York: Dover, 1957), ch. 13, p. 45. Hereafter cited as the *Poetics.*

[6] *Anatomy of Criticism*: *Four Essays* (Princeton: Princeton Univ. Press, 1957), p. 38.

[7] *Shakespearean Tragedy*: *Lectures on Hamlet, Othello, King Lear, Macbeth* (1904; rpt. London: Macmillan, 1950), p. 12.

is not melodramatic because it is not afflicted on him from without, nor tragic because it is not derived from any deed by him. This work of Shakespeare is simply not to be classified; one should respect the integrity of the play and leave it as it is. But the point is that it does not help nor disprove our concept of the tragic.

I may mention as well that, like *Hamlet*, *Phèdre* is neither a tragedy nor a melodrama. The source of Phèdre's agony is not anything she has done, but her secret illicit passion for Hippolyte, the son of her husband Thésée. Although the struggles within her mind may be spoken of as "internal actions," they are not exactly actions, which are things men do and have an external existence.[8] Moreover, her confession of love to Hippolyte is too late in the play to contribute to her pain significantly, for prior to it she has already suffered beyond measure. Her torturous passion as dramatized by Racine is neither tragic nor melodramatic. Probably there are other plays of suffering than *Hamlet* and *Phèdre* that do not fit in with our descriptions of the tragic and the melodramatic. However, the great number of works that fit attests to the validity of these concepts, which are, after all, derived from the works themselves.

So the tragic man is first of all a man of action through which he will injure himself and very often those around him. Oedipus, Medea, Lear, and Macbeth are such doers par excellence. In its non-moral sense evil means what is painful. The tragic vision sees that man is in one way or another a plague to himself. Rather than suggesting that man is masochistic, it stresses man as a creature actively asserting his self in a manner that he must suffer or add to his suffering. The tragic concerns man as a cause of evil no less than man as a sufferer. However, the tragic consequence of an act is not to be confused with poetic justice, which awards the good and punishes the bad. In tragedy the virtuous and the wicked suffer alike. Nor should the notion of responsibility suggest that the tragic man deserves his fate. Macbeth merits his while Cordelia does not. And Lear can say that "I am a man / More sinned against than sinning."[9] The question of desert is simply impertinent to tragedy.

Tragedy can also be appreciated in terms of the irony of human existence. All men strive to attain happiness and to stay away from evil, some through admirable means while others through nefarious methods. For some mysterious reason many come to the opposite of their pursuits by their own doing. Tragedy delineates man who works against himself blindly or knowingly. In his tragic fate he may, like Oedipus, manifest the greatness of human spirit, or he may, like Hedda Gabler, show how repugnant and sterile man can be. In whatever manner he meets with his suffering, the tragic man makes his mark on his destiny. "For it is the perpetual tragic

---

[8] The concept of internal action used here is from Francis Fergusson's definition that *"action (praxis) does not mean deeds, events, or physical activity: it means, rather, the motivation from which deeds spring"* (Introd., *Aristotle's "Poetics,"* trans. S. H. Butcher, New York: Hill and Wang, 1961, p. 8). This definition, which reduces the physical aspect of action to insignificance, cannot explain the working of any tragedy. In *Oedipus the King,* it is not the hero's noble motives, but his deeds that bring about his tragedy. So is it with Deianira (*The Women of Trachis*). They never motivate the crimes they commit. Although Macbeth already suffers in his conscience because of his intention to murder Duncan, it is the real deed that plunges him into a no-return course of fall, making the tragic character he is, not otherwise. The tragic act is always a physical act. Intention alone may produce suffering, but not tragedy.

[9] *King Lear* III. ii. 58-59. Subsequent references to Shakespeare's works are to *The Complete Signet Classic Shakespeare* (New York: Harcourt Brace Jovanovich, 1963).

irony of the Tragedy of Life," says F. L. Lucas, "that again and again men do thus laboriously contrive their own annihilation, or kill the thing they love."[10] Hence the tragic may be expressed in the circular relationship of actor, act and suffering: an actor is tragic only if he suffers for his action; an act is tragic only if it entails pain to the actor; a suffering is tragic only if it is causally related to the sufferer's act.

The tragic that has been so defined is proposed here as the quintessence of tragedy. It may be taken as an attitude toward life, but our interest is more in how it works in a tragedy. Let us use for our example *Oedipus the King,* which critics since Aristotle have employed to illustrate their theories of tragedy.

The events of the play can be arbitrarily divided into two kinds: the past and the present. Though the present is directly witnessed by the audience, its final significance is entirely determined by the past, which is made known through the recollections and reports of the personages. First, the murder of the late king, an event from the past, gives definite direction to the present action, which begins with Oedipus' search for the culprit, and leads to his conflicts with Teiresias, the blind seer, and with Creon. Then Jocasta provides the turning point of the action when she tells how Apollo's oracle—that Laius' son should kill his father—did not come true. This story from the past gives Oedipus the first crucial clue to who he really is and starts him on the quest of his true identity again, which he undertook once. Finally when the old Herdsman from Corinth tells the part of the past he knows, the present action comes to its conclusion, that is, both of Oedipus' quests are successful—he has found out who he is and who Laius' murderer is. Oedipus' parricide and his incestuous marriage make up his past, but these deeds are tragic only because they destroy him and his family now. Therefore, in the play the tragic appears to be a structural principle by which the protagonist, his actions, and his sufferings are not arbitrarily but causally related.

Now, the tragic as such obviously does not explain everything in the play, nor can it account for all of Oedipus' sufferings. It leaves entirely out of its picture the hero's universe, which includes above all the gods and their oracles. "A tragic action or purpose," observes Oscar Mandel, "taken out of its world, its context, never carries in itself the cause of the actor's grief."[11] Doomed to disasters, Oedipus is a victim of the higher powers inhabiting his universe. This is the melodramatic aspect of Sophocles' tragedy.

As mentioned earlier, the melodramatic vision sees man as the victim of the forces surrounding him. They operate in a variety of forms: villains, enemies, natural disasters, chance, accidents, fate, gods, etc. *The Trojan Women* portrays victims of war. Romeo and Juliet are victims of ancestral hatred and of a malignant fate; Pericles a victim of hostile nature and of evil, ungrateful people; Andronicus of revengeful villains. *A Doll's House* exposes how a woman has been dehumanized by the egoism of those closest to her. *The Wild Duck* shows how one family have been exploited by an unscrupulous man and then led into unretrievable disaster by that man's son who preaches the gospel of idealism but is ignorant of man's limited capacity to bear reality. They are all melodramas where man's responsibility in his fate is neither questioned nor stressed.

---

[10] *Tragedy: Serious Drama in Relation to Aristotle's "Poetics,"* rev. ed. (New York: Collier, 1957), p. 97.

[11] *A Definition of Tragedy* (New York: New York Univ. Press, 1961), p. 33.

As formulations of human suffering, the tragic and the melodramatic each have their sources in life. Neither paints a more inclusive picture of reality than the other; they are complementary visions of that reality. Indeed, as human suffering is inconceivable apart from the universe where man lives, so is a pure tragedy where the melodramatic is totally absent. The tragic, however, goes beyond the melodramatic. It sees man's responsibility as this: he himself is a cause of his woe. Therefore a drama of human suffering is a melodrama if it presents man *chiefly* as a victim of his circumstances, and a tragedy if it presents man not merely as a victim, but *substantially* as a doer who acts and suffers as a result.[12] This will become manifest if we compare *Oedipus the King* with another play of Sophocles, *Oedipus at Colonus*.

That Oedipus has committed terrible things against his parents and suffered accordingly is given as a fact in the latter work. Nevertheless, the emphasis is not on what he has done and then suffered, but on how he has been treated. Now old and feeble, though as imperious and compelling in his bearing as in the former play, the protagonist, led by Antigone, his daughter, has left Thebes and traveled to Colonus. Embittered by years of hard life as an exile, he appeals to the sympathy of the Athenians, telling how he was banished ungratefully by the Thebans, and even deserted by his two sons. He claims innocence in his notorious deeds: he is just a victim of the gods. Now the Thebans, having learned from an oracle that Oedipus will bring blessing to the place of his death, want him back. Even so, they will not allow him to dwell within their city because he is unclean to them, but they will let him live on its outskirts so that they can reap the benefits of his death. For this purpose they send Creon to Colonus. Having met with Oedipus' resistance and the Athenians' interference, he accuses, in front of Theseus, king of Athens, and his people, Oedipus of parricide and incest. This provokes Oedipus to a vigorous and lengthy defense of his innocence, to the effect that he cannot be responsible for those acts simply because he is doomed to do them.

> The bloody deaths, the incest, the calamities
> You speak so glibly of: I suffered them,
> By fate, against my will! It was God's pleasure,
> And perhaps our race had angered him long ago.
> In me myself you could not find such evil
> As would have made sin against my own.
> And tell me this: if there were prophecies
> Repeated by the oracles of the gods,
> That father's death should come through his own son,
> How could you justly blame it upon me?
> On me, who was yet unborn, yet unconceived,
> Not yet existent for my father and mother?
> If then I came into the world—as I did come—
> In wretchedness, and met my father in fight,
> And knocked him down, not knowing that I killed him
> Nor whom I killed—again, how could you find
> Guilt in that unmeditated act?
> As for my mother—damn you, you have no shame,

---

[12] Cf. Heilman, p. 90.

> Though you are her own brother, in forcing me,
> To speak of that unspeakable marriage;
> But I shall speak, I'll not be silent now
> After you've let your foul talk go so far!
> Yes, she gave me birth—incredible fate!—
> But neither of us knew the truth; and she
> Bore my children also—and then her shame.[13]

It is not just Oedipus' own feeling that he is a prey of fate, of the gods, of circumstances, of the Thebans, his own sons, and Creon; but this is what the play presents him to be. In *Oedipus the King*, though he is made wretched by the gods, he is a resolute doer to bring sorrows upon himself and his family. The difference is one between tragedy and melodrama. On the other hand, the mere hint of the tragic in a play is not enough to make it a tragedy. *Oedipus at Colonus* has a hint of it as a fact in the background, not in the focus, of the play. Romeo and Andronicus are also tragic to a slight degree; yet in Shakespeare's plays they appear principally as victims, not self-inflicted sufferers. A play of suffering, though always melodramatic in some measure, is a tragedy when its main action is tragic in structure.

Nevertheless, another question arises: how is a play decided where both the tragic and the melodramatic are working actively? In fact, *Oedipus the King* is such a case, where both fate and human action play important roles in the fall of the hero. The crucial point is that although tragedy means to present human action and suffering in a cause and consequence pattern that conveys a truth not perceived by the melodramatic vision, it does not exclude melodrama, but presupposes and transcends it. Eric Bentley describes the relationship of the two genres in this way:

> It is hard to draw a line between melodrama and tragedy. Rather than separate blocks, the reality seems to be a continuous scale with the crudest melodrama at one end and the highest tragedy at the other. . . . Yet the idea of such a scale is misleading if it suggests that tragedy is distinct from melodrama. There is a melodrama in every tragedy, just as there is a child in every adult.[14]

That the tragic vision stresses human responsibility makes it the vision of the adult in the sense that the grown-up can be charged with responsibility while the child cannot be. (Of course, this use of the word "adult" is metaphorical, without hinting at artistic superiority.) As far as it presents man as a victim of fate, *Oedipus the King* is a melodrama. However, it stands to reason that the play should be recognized for what it has grown and developed into, namely, a tragedy. The same can be said of other great tragedies, too.

It is clear that my approach to tragedy is first to derive a meaning of the tragic from tragic drama and then to find out how it functions with other elements in its original dramatic context. This procedure indicates two things. First, my notion

---

[13] *Oedipus at Colonus,* trans. Robert Fitzgerald, in *The Complete Greek Tragedies,* ed. David Grene and Richard Lattimore (Chicago: Univ. of Chicago Press, 1957), II, vv. 962-84. Further references to Sophocles' plays are to this edition.

[14] *The Life of the Drama,* pp. 217-18.

of the tragic is not based on a philosophical idea or system that exists outside the tragedies I have referred to in support of my argument. Rather than attempting a theory of the tragic, I am proposing that the tragic as has been defined is the primary denominator of all tragedies. Second, the tragic, essential as it is, is not in itself an adequate statement nor a sufficient cause of tragic drama, as is already implied in our discussion of its relationship with the melodramatic. It means that we have to find out the other conditions that make a work a tragedy.

So far the tragic has been defined in reference to the relationship between the actor and his action and his suffering, but the nature of these things themselves has not been looked into. Clearly, the action cannot be inconsequential, the suffering slight, and the actor trivial. If a person suffers slightly for what he has done, he has no tragedy although his experience can be said to contain tragic implications. Tragedy does not always present death, but it does always deal with great sufferings. And the serious nature of the tragic act is evident in the happiness or damage it can bring to the doer and the people around him. The greater the happiness and damage are involved, the more serious the act is.[15] Then the seriousness of the tragic act suggests the necessary condition of the tragic man. In Aristotle's ethical theory a man's character is shaped by what he does.[16] In the same way, the tragic man, being not only a doer but also a doer of serious action, is a person who has the power to do great good or harm to himself and others. He may be good or evil, but he is never negligible in the sense that his action has no grave influence upon the lives of other people. Barabas (*The Jew of Malta*), Richard III, and Hedda Gabler may be ridiculous and despicable, but since they are not only vicious but also able to do things, they are dangerous and destructive.

And the serious nature of the tragic act is more an objective fact in the circumstances of the play than a judgment of the audience. To some people the burial of Polyneices is probably not so important a matter that life should be risked for it. For example, it does not appear so to Antigone's sister, Ismene. Yet Sophocles makes it very clear that in the conditions of his play Antigone's success or failure to perform the burial rite is a matter of great happiness or sorrow to the heroine. Thus the seriousness of her undertaking is established within its dramatic context, and the audience is invited to take this standpoint while viewing the action.

Still, a play on a tragic and serious action does not become a tragedy automatically. The strife that involves the four citizen lovers of Athens in *A Midsummer Night's Dream* seems to be stuff for tragedy, but the play is a comedy even where things become most bitter to Helena, in whose ordeal there are strong tragic suggestions. One reason is Shakespeare's treatment of his dramatic material. And that the "most cruel death of Pyramus and Thisby" is a "most lamentable comedy"[17] is in part because of the ridiculous manner the "death" is performed before Theseus's court by Bottom and his company. In *A Midsummer Night's Dream* Shakespeare demonstrates how painful experience can be presented in such a way that mirth and relaxation, instead of graveness and pathos, are the fundamental mode of the audience's response. That is to say, the action of tragedy not only reflects a certain way of

---

[15] Elder Olson, *Tragedy and the Theory of Drama* (Detroit: Wayne State Univ. Press, 1961), pp. 161-62.

[16] Gerald Else, *Aristotle's Poetics: The Argument* (Cambridge: Harvard Univ. Press, 1963), pp. 70-71.

[17] *A Midsummer Night's Dream* I. ii. 11-13.

ordering reality, but also involves a presentation that elicits serious reaction. (And vice versa, that *A Midsummer Night's Dream* is a comedy is not only a matter of presentation, but also a matter of perception from the comic point of view.) Although it must be recognized that Shakespearean tragedy seldom fails to incorporate the humorous with the somber, it remains essentially an experience where graveness and pathos prevail. And while melodrama also causes serious response, it is distinguished from tragedy in its perception and ordering of reality.

Tragedy, then, is a form of literature that presents in a serious manner a serious action in which man suffers severely not only because of external circumstances but to a considerable degree because of his doing. This definition is not meant nor required to be an adequate description of any individual tragedy. It does not concern the artistic merit of the work, nor the aspects that make for the special and unique character of the work as it is. It is only a statement of all the necessary conditions that a work needs in order to be a tragedy.

There are other views of tragedy, it may be noticed, that have not been taken into account. For example, it is thought that the tragic man must be guilty of some fault, suffer a divided mind, and come to a recognition like self-knowledge or insight into the human condition through his suffering.[18] Since they are some of the most prevalent ideas about tragedy in modern criticism, I would like to consider them briefly before I turn to the other part of my discussion.

Guilt, whether it is a fault or a serious crime, is not a requisite of the tragic man. As a person, Antigone may be a saint to some or an egocentric to others, but as a tragic figure she is blameless. In other words, her tragic act—the burial of Polyneices, her brother—is not presented as a transgression in Sophocles' tragedy. The Hegelian view, that *Antigone* dramatizes the conflict between the claims of the family and the state and that Antigone, though right from the viewpoint of the family, is wrong from the viewpoint of the state, is not borne out by the play. First, although Creon is king, he is not shown to represent the opinion of the state, that is, the people, in his decree to expose Polyneices' corpse. It is his own decision, not the decision of the state.[19] It is this impious and inhuman edict that Antigone challenges. But more significantly, the Thebans' general approval of her as reported by Haemon, Teiresias' condemnation of Creon's actions, the advice of the Chorus (who used to support him but now change their position) to him that he should free Antigone and bury the dead, and finally Creon's attempts to undo what he has done, all these facts indicate unequivocally the attitude of the play with regard to Antigone and Creon. Plainly, Antigone is shown to be right whereas Creon is wrong. It is possible that a tragedy on the clash of two valid claims can be made out of the same story, but that is not what Sophocles did in *Antigone*.[20]

Nevertheless, it is said that Antigone, a young girl, should be subject to the

---

[18] In *Tragedy and Melodrama* Professor Heilman expounds his concept of the tragic man chiefly in terms of guilt, inner conflict, and self-knowledge. Others who advocate one or more of these ideas are, for example: Bradley, *Shakespearean Tragedy*, p. 18; Francis Fergusson, *The Idea of a Theater: a Study of Ten Plays: the Art of Drama in Changing Perspective* (Princeton: Princeton Univ. Press, 1949), pp. 18-19; Richard Benson Sewall, *The Vision of Tragedy* (New Haven: Yale Univ. Press, 1959), pp. 47, 72; Bentley, *The Life of the Drama*, pp. 261, 265-66.

[19] Brian Vickers, *Towards Greek Tragedy: Drama, Myth, Society* (London: Longman, 1973), pp. 528-30, 535-36, 538, 544-45.

[20] G. H. Gellie, *Sophocles: a Reading* (South Australia: Melbourne Univ. Press, 1973), p. 49.

authority of her uncle Creon by the fact that her parents are dead. Also, in the eye of the Athenian audience, Antigone, being a woman, is guilty of not submitting to the rule of man. In short, "the people approve of what she did, but they do not approve of the fact that *she* did it."[21] In support of this view, Ismene is quoted as saying to Antigone:

> We must remember that we two are women
> so not to fight with men.
> And that since we are subject to strong power
> we must hear these orders, or any that may be worse.[22]

Granted that Ismene expresses the general Greek view on the roles of man and woman, she may not be taken as speaking for the play. For the attitude of the play is clearly conveyed by Teiresias and by the common people, who, as Haemon tells Creon, give their support to Antigone unanimously.

> But in dark corners I have heard them say
> how the whole town is grieving for this girl,
> unjustly doomed, if ever woman was,
> to die in shame for glorious action done.
> She would not leave her fallen, slaughtered brother
> there, as he lay, unburied, for the birds
> and hungry dogs to make an end of him.
> Isn't her real desert a golden prize?
>
> (vv. 692-700)

The people like what she has done. They do not find her guilty of the fact that she is young and a woman. Instead, they admire her. Haemon is young, too. When his advice is rejected by Creon on account of his youth, he says: "I urge no wrong. I'm young, but you should watch / my actions, not my years, to judge of me" (vv. 728-29). Despite his young age, his conflict with Creon is not presented as a fault. If his break with Creon does not become him as a son, it does not at all invalidate what he has said to him. But Creon appears entirely wrong in that scene, for all his age and his authority as the father and the king. When Haemon tells him that the citizens think Antigone is right, he retorts, "Is the town to tell me how I ought to rule?" (v. 734) It should be noted that he does not doubt the truth in Haemon's statement but accepts it as a fact challenging his power. The state's attitude toward Antigone and Creon is the play's and therefore Sophocles'. I do not suggest that this is how Sophocles looks at man and woman in general, but that this is how he regards Antigone and Creon. We are concerned with his play, not his view of man and woman, nor his contemporaries'.

To the theory of the guilty tragic hero, Antigone is certainly an important, but by no means the only, exception. Iphigenia appears at first as the victim of the goddess

---

[21] It is a statement by Wilamowitz, quoted in John Ferguson, *A Companion to Greek Tragedy* (Austin: Univ. of Texas, 1972), p. 178. But it is Ferguson's views on Antigone I am opposed to.

[22] *Antigone*, trans. Elizabeth Wyckoff, in *The Complete Greek Tragedies*, II, vv. 61-64. All further references to this play appear in the text.

Artemis and of the Greeks' passion for military glory (*Iphigenia in Aulis*). Yet later on she resolves her predicament with dignity, courage, and understanding. Now she is no longer forced but goes voluntarily to Artemis' altar to be sacrificed. Her tragic act consists purely in the exertion of a noble will. For a tragic heroine she has more feminine charms than Antigone and is equally blameless. In Racine's *Bérénice*, Titus is guilty of self-deception in his conflict between honor and love.[23] But Bérénice suffers simply because she loves Titus, who must choose between her and the throne of Rome, and also because she chooses to live on, enduring her despair rather than to die. The decision reveals her tragic strength which she imparts to Antiochus, who bears an unrequited love for her. And in *The Wild Duck*, Hedvig chooses to shoot herself, not the crippled bird, in testimony to her love for Hjalmar as well as for the bird. She is both tragic and innocent.

It is true that the tragic act as a flaw is evident in many a tragic figure in Greek tragedy, Racine, and Ibsen. And I suspect that those who must find the tragic man blameworthy are under the influence of Shakespeare, whose tragic hero is always guilty one way or another. Nonetheless the fact is that tragedy does not always depend on the so-called "tragic flaw." Therefore a critic remarks: that "a criminal as well as a saint can be the protagonist of a tragedy illustrates the flexibility of the genre."[24]

Like guilt, inner conflict is not a trait of the tragic man. The only place Antigone may be said to show it is when she is being led off to the tomb. Now she mourns her fate—young, unmarried, and doomed to a living death. Whereas how much inner conflict is allowed to be seen in her lament is uncertain, one thing is perfectly clear: she never regrets her actions. The last words she speaks are: "Look what I suffer, at whose command, / because I respected the right" (vv. 942-43). Macbeth suffers a violent rift in his mind before and after his murder of Duncan. By contrast, Antigone is marked for her singleness of purpose in her decision and deeds. Does she ever hesitate in her commitment at the thought of death? It is only human that she does, but this aspect of her mind is not shown in the play. The point is that we are not dealing with such a situation in real life but with tragedy as literature. Any formulation of tragedy should be based on what is given, and on how things are represented, in the work, not on what is merely probable and possible in the fictional situation of a tragic drama. In the present case, Sophocles does not allow Antigone to wail over her misfortune until the moment her tragedy has almost run its full course. Whatever significance there is in her self-mourning, it has little bearing on her tragedy.

And even when inner conflict appears central in the suffering of a tragic figure, its relationship to his tragedy can remain peripheral. The storm in Lear's soul, heightened by the external one in nature, is a powerful representation of a mind besieged by contradictions within itself and in the reality outside. Although the inner view of Lear's tortured soul gives depth to his suffering and is crucial to our appreciation of the play, it is not an inherent factor of his tragedy. For he is tragic, with or without a revelation of his afflicted mind, as long as he is suffering for having given away his kingdom in the fashion he did.

The issue of recognition is more complicated. Aristotle defines it as "a change

---

[23] Titus has been aware that his love for Bérénice will some day be in conflict with his responsibility to Rome (*Bérénice*, IV. v.). But he ignores this premonition, living in self-delusion that it may not happen. Thus he brings himself and Bérénice into a most painful experience of unfulfilled love.

[24] Mandel, p. 138.

from ignorance to knowledge." But in chapter 11 (where this meaning is given) and chapter 14 of the *Poetics,* where he expounds the function of recognition in tragedy with examples, he seems to mean by it the sudden discovery of two persons of their blood relationship at the moment one is about to do a fatal act to the other. Recognition is conceived chiefly as a highly effective plot technique, especially when it is accompanied by a reversal, to generate the emotions of pity and fear in the spectator. In other words, Aristotle's concern is not the philosophical implications of recognition.[25]

Nevertheless, what Aristotle does not explore is amply made up by modern critics. Some maintain that recognition as self-knowledge is inherent in the tragic man's experience. Yet in *Agamemnon,* the hero comes home from his campaign against Troy and is welcomed into his house, that is, into death, without being given any chance for enlightenment. In *The Eumenides,* Orestes goes free at the end without seeming to know himself better. Self-knowledge does not occur to Antigone, nor to the Hippolytus of Euripides. Brutus is utterly incapable of understanding the mistakes he has made about Caesar. Cordelia is more seasoned in her reunion and reconciliation with Lear, but it is questionable whether she has consciously gained deeper knowledge about herself.

Although some do not require the tragic man to attain self-knowledge, they insist that his suffering should be capable of indicating some kind of significance to those around him, including both the dramatic personages and the audience.[26] As might be expected, what that significance is varies according to different critics. Thus it means a number of things: the discovery of the identity of a person or thing, the knowledge of self, the realization of human nobility, the understanding of man's fundamental nature or condition, the exploration of the metaphysical and existential question, "What is man?" etc.

The fact is that recognition of a philosophical dimension is not the particular property of tragedy, but of all forms of literature. This is a plain truth to Aristotle, who raises the question why men take delight in works of art.

> Poetry in general seems to have sprung from two causes, each of them lying deep in our nature. First, the instinct of imitation is implanted in man from childhood . . . and no less universal is the pleasure felt in things imitated. We have evidence of this in the facts of experience. Objects which in themselves we view with pain, we delight to contemplate when reproduced with minute fidelity: such as the forms of the most ignoble animals and of dead bodies. The cause of this again is, that to learn gives the liveliest pleasure not only to philosophers but to men in general. . . . Thus the reason why men enjoy seeing a likeness is, that in contemplating it they find themselves learning or inferring, and saying perhaps, "Ah, that is he."[27]

---

[25] Walter Kaufmann, *Tragedy and Philosophy* (New York: Anchor, 1968), p. 68.
[26] Dorothea Krook, *Elements of Tragedy* (New Haven: Yale Univ. Press, 1969), pp. 8, 12, 47; Sewall, p. 48.
[27] *Poetics,* ch. 4, p. 15.

According to Gerald Else, Aristotle does not mean here the "recognition that 'this person is that person,' but that he is 'that *kind* of creature.' "[28] So the aesthetic experience of a work of art is accompanied by a recognition of truth. This recognition, admittedly unlike what he conceives as a technical device in the tragic plot, comes close to the modern sense of the word. But, as Aristotle points out, recognition of this sort is a quality of art in general, not unique to tragedy.

Perhaps there is something peculiar to the recognition yielded by tragedy, as different from what is given, for instance, by melodrama. It cannot be self-knowledge, nor the nobility of man, nor even assertions about the human condition. Each of these plays, *The Trojan Women, Oedipus at Colonus,* and *Romeo and Juliet,* has some particular things to say about human existence. Contemplating man in relation to the power governing his universe, they can be considered as different postures of putting forward this question: is man just the prey of the wanton gods? Yet they are melodramas. The recognition peculiar to tragedy, if there must be, is this: man suffers for what he does.

The fact that tragedy has been written in different languages and in different ages proves the universality and the continuous appeal of the tragic vision. It is not suggested, however, that the tragic writers consciously see things from the tragic point of view. The reality seems to be that when the fate of man is contemplated and conceived in terms of his purpose, aspiration, and ability, the creative mind tends to construct events in the mode of the tragic. *Tou O yüan,* which we shall attend to presently, is about a young woman who lives and dies for a purpose.

II

A word is needed about the text of *Tou O yüan* before the discussion of the play itself. Like all other Yüan *tsa-chü* 雜劇 plays, *Tou O yüan* has not survived to us in its original form. Today it is found in three separate collections of plays printed in the Ming dynasty (1368-1644): *Ku ming-chia tsa-chü* 古名家雜劇, compiled by Yü-yang Hsien Shih 玉陽仙史, style of Wang Chi-te 王驥德 and published in the Wan-li period (1573-1620); *Yüan ch'ü hsüan* 元曲選, edited by Tsang Mao-hsün 臧懋循 in 1616; and *Ku-chin ming-chü ho hsüan* 古今名劇合選, edited by Meng Ch'eng-shun 孟稱舜 in 1633.[29] They provide three variant texts of *Tou O yüan,* which will be referred to as the Wang text, the Tsang text, and the Meng text. Cheng Ch'ien 鄭騫 in his article, "Kuan Han-ch'ing Tou O yüan tsa-chü i-pen pi-chiao" 關漢卿竇娥冤雜劇異本比較, shows that the Meng text follows the Tsang text in most respects. Therefore the comparison of these texts is mainly that between the Tsang and the Wang texts. According to Professor Cheng, Wang's text is on the whole closer to the

---

[28] *Aristotle's Poetics*, p. 132.

[29] *Ku ming-chia tsa-chü* and *Ku-chin ming-chü ho hsüan* are not available to me, but I have access to their texts of *Tou O yüan* which are reprinted in vols. 16 and 111 of *Ku pen hsi-ch'ü ts'ung k'an* 古本戲曲叢刊, 4th series (Shanghai: Shang-wu, 1958). The bibliographical information about these two collections of plays given in the text is from Cheng Ch'ien, *Yüan Ming ch'ao-k'e-pen yüan-jen tsa-chü chiu-chang t'i-yao* 元明鈔刻本元人雜劇九種提要, in his *Ching-wu ts'ung pien* 景午叢編 (Taipei: Chung-hua, 1972), I, 422-32. The *Yüan ch'ü hsüan* I use is a four-volume modern edition (Peking: Chung-hua, 1958). *Tou O yüan* is in vol. 4.

original than Tsang's.[30]

As to Cheng's reasons given in support of this conclusion, some are convincing while others have to be regarded with reservations. For example, Tsang's text is apparently guilty of alterations in the matter of Tou O's age.[31] But it is doubtful that it can be accused of the same fault in the question of the relationship between Old Woman Ts'ai 蔡婆婆 and Old Chang 張老. In the Wang text, Old Chang says in Act II that he has married Ts'ai. In the Tsang text, he says that his desire to marry Ts'ai has been thwarted by Tou O's objection. And on no other ground than this difference does Professor Cheng decide that Tsang's version is a change on the part of the editor. His reason is: if Ts'ai has not married Old Chang, the charge that Tou O poisons her "father-in-law" cannot be established.[32] In fact, this charge could never have been imposed successfully upon Tou O if she had not chosen to save Ts'ai, her mother-in-law. But in order to spare Ts'ai, Tou O would submit to any charge against her, namely, not only the murder of Old Chang, but the murder of him as her father-in-law. Obviously, neither the charge itself nor Tou O's confession of her "crime" can be taken as what has actually happened. So her conviction cannot be used as a supporting evidence for the authenticity of the Wang text in the question of Ts'ai's relationship with Old Chang. And the question itself cannot be solved by the surviving versions of the play themselves.

In the preface of *Yüan ch'ü hsüan* Tsang states that he works from several editions of plays to produce the texts of his own edition. Granted that he incorporates his own work into those texts, evidently not all the things that are found only in his edition are his fabrications. Some of them could have been preserved from the original texts. And the Tsang text gives us a *Tou O yüan* much fuller in detail than the Wang text. Hence I shall use the Tsang text for this discussion but consult the Wang text where it seems to me the latter is unquestionably more genuine. Fortunately there is no difference of detail between them such as would seriously affect one's consideration whether the play is a tragedy.

There is a lapse of thirteen years between the Prologue of *Tou O yüan,* where the protagonist is a seven-year-old, and Act I, where she is a grown person of twenty. (I follow the Wang text in the matter of her age.) In Act I, by way of introducing herself to the audience, she tells the sad story of her life: at three her mother died, at seven her father left her with (actually sold her to) Old Woman Ts'ai to seek his fortune at the imperial court; at seventeen she was married to Ts'ai's son, who died soon after the marriage, and at present she still wears mourning clothes. As it is told, her life is nothing but sorrow. For it will not be long before she will have to die owing to the contrivance of a villain and the evil practice of a wicked prefect. If this were the total image of Tou O, that is, a complete victim submissively and

---

[30] The article is included in *Ching-wu ts'ung pien,* I, 433-445 (see n. 29 above). Although Cheng is the first to discuss the differences between the extant texts of *Tou O yüan,* a collated edition of the play with the text of *Ku ming-chia tsa-chü* as the primary text has been prepared in *Kuan Han-ch'ing hsi-ch'ü chi* 關漢卿戲曲集, ed. Wu Hsiao-ling 吳曉鈴 et al. (Peking: Chung-kuo hsi-chü ch'u-pan-she, 1958).

[31] In the Tsang text, Tou O should be twenty-two years old according to what Old Woman Ts'ai says of her in Act I, but in the same act Tou O says she is twenty. The Wang text has no inconsistent information about Tou O's age. In it she says she is twenty: see Cheng, I, 436.

[32] Ibid., 439.

relentlessly afflicted at every important turn of her life, the play would be a melodrama (which is not to say that it would be an inferior work). But Tou O is far from being a mere victim.

It has been pointed out that Tou O's death is the result of a voluntary act, which she does to save her mother-in-law.[33] It is a deed in the mode of the tragic rather than of the melodramatic. On the other hand, if it were a sudden upsurge of heroic compassion that compelled her to die for Ts'ai, it would be an unexpected act on her part. In that case her death, still noble and tragic, would not give much tragic quality to the central action of the play. The fact is that Tou O's self-sacrifice is the culmination of a purpose which she has pursued in her life. We need to look into the play closely.

In the first act where she is contemplating her past life, Tou O is acutely aware that it consists of nothing but calamities, which inevitably lead up to the question, "Why me?" She looks for an answer in order to find sense in an apparently absurd reality. "Is it my fate, to be unhappy all my life?" 莫不是八字兒該載着一世憂 she starts to surmise.[34] This fatalism she renounces immediately because it leaves her as unenlightened as before. So she must find the answer in another direction.

> Is it because I did not burn enough incense in my last life,
> That in this life I have to suffer?
> I urge people to do good deeds to cultivate a better next life.
> I serve my mother-in-law and mourn for my husband:
> My words must be fulfilled.
>
> 莫不是前世裏燒香不到頭？今也波生招禍尤。勸今人早將來世修，我將這婆侍養，我將這服孝守，我言詞須應口。
>
> (Act I, "T'ien-hsia lo" 天下樂)

Thus, through the secularized Buddhist belief of retribution, she sees the existence of an intelligible moral order. And on that basis she sets up goals for her present life, with a view to obtaining a better next life.

This discovery of or identification with a meaning in her hitherto extremely frustrated life is a point of departure in the development of Tou O. Up to that moment she has been oppressed by events that are not only catastrophic but also inexplicable to her young mind. So she does not know how to cope with them. She has been forced into a position where she has been used to being acted upon. Now she finds a ground on which she can commit herself to a course of meaningful action, to a purpose. However conventional her moral outlook is, it expresses the urgent need of a rational soul that has to find order in an orderless world so as to live and remain sane.

This reorganization of Tou O's universe is the key to the meaning of the play. For presently we shall see that external circumstances are pressing on her, threatening to destroy her scheme of life. Now her mother-in-law brings home two scoundrels, Donkey Chang 張驢兒 and his father. They have rescued her from being strangled by

---

[33] Wang Kuo-wei, p. 106.

[34] *Tou O yüan*, in *Yüan ch'ü hsüan*, Act I, "Yu hu-lu." The English translation is from *Injustice to Tou O ("Tou O yüan"): a Study and Translation*, trans. Chung-wen Shih (Cambridge: Cambridge Univ. Press, 1972). All subsequent quotations are from this edition.

Doctor Lu 賽盧醫, her debtor. But in their turn, they have forced a promise of double-marriage from her: she shall marry Old Chang and Tou O shall marry Donkey Chang. Needless to say, their proposals are to be rejected by Tou O. On the one hand, her marrying Donkey Chang when she still mourns her husband is an express violation of morals in her society, not to mention her emotional commitment to the mourning and her strong repulsion toward Chang. On the other, Ts'ai's acquiescent attitude toward the Changs and their demands provoke Tou O's moral indignation, which is not exactly in line with her earlier decision to serve Ts'ai well. At any rate, the Changs will stay in the house. In this predicament it is difficult for Tou O to observe mourning. She is conscious that the presence of these strangers will contaminate her reputation (Tou O's first speech in Act II). Moreover, the licentious Donkey Chang is ever a menace to her chastity. And the pressure upon her to comply is not only from the strangers, but also from her mother-in-law. This is why her moral stance becomes increasingly conservative, so much so that she declares, "One horse cannot wear two saddles" 我一馬難將兩鞍鞴 (Act II, "Ke-wei" 隔尾), meaning that she would be faithful to her deceased husband and not marry again. The statement exceeds her original intention to mourn, obviously due to the sudden intrusion into her life of two evil men.

Still, to withstand Donkey Chang is relatively simple as compared with her now somewhat altered relationship with Ts'ai. She has been effective in the first task because she knows that she is dealing with a vicious enemy and that she should fight him without pity. But Ts'ai, who time and again urges her to give in to Donkey Chang, does not deserve her respect but contempt, and yet she is her mother-in-law, whom she has just vowed to please. In this dilemma, Tou O attempts to keep her esteem for Ts'ai while trying to make her become sensitive to moral commonsense. But Ts'ai is not to be enlightened. Therefore, as is pointed out by Chang Shu-hsiang,[35] there is a discernible toughening up of tone in her dialogues with Ts'ai, a tendency in which her tenderness toward her is giving way to satirical scorn. What has to be stressed here is that despite her discontent with Ts'ai, Tou O is struggling hard to hold fast to her early intention. But a more severe trial is awaiting her.

Now, in Act II, the scene of conflict is moved from Tou O's home to the court, where she is being forced with torture to admit the crime of murdering Old Chang. The injustice of the court is in effect shattering the moral universe she has found not long ago.

> They beat me till pieces of my flesh fly about,
> And I am dripping with blood.
> Who knows the bitterness in my heart?
> Where could I, this insignificant woman, have secured poison?
> Oh Heaven, why don't the sun's rays
> Ever reach underneath an overturned tub?
> (Act II, "Ts'ai-ch'a ko" 採茶歌)

打的我肉都飛，血淋漓，腹中冤枉有誰知？則我這小婦人毒藥來從何處也？天那，怎麼的覆盆不照太陽暉？

The "overturned tub" is a vivid image of the dark court, where Tou O is being

---

[35] Pp. 189-91 (see n. 1 above).

tortured.³⁶ The last question she raises is to ask what is obvious, but the sense implied is: "Why should Heaven allow this injustice to happen to me?" So she has discovered a discrepancy between her moral universe and reality. She has believed in a just Heaven, as suggested by her belief of retribution. This Heaven, however, seems indifferent to the injustice being done to her. Now she is back to where she was, suffering and bewildered. To give vent to her sore disillusion, she will have to scold Heaven and Earth, and she is seen to do just that in Act III.

At that moment of spiritual crisis, she suffers without the help of any religious conviction. Her survival through the ordeal depends entirely on the obstinacy of a will refusing to surrender, like that of Prometheus. But there is a difference: whereas Prometheus draws strength to endure from the fact that he is holding back a secret fatal to Zeus, Tou O has only a will not to yield. As a result, this trial brings out what is most characteristic of Tou O's person, namely, her enormous capacity of will power.

Now, the protagonist has lost her faith in Heaven. Why does she die for Ts'ai, who has brought her into this plight, and whose lack of moral concern makes her unworthy of reverence? She does it probably for the reasons that have been offered by Chang Shu-hsiang. First, it is an act of compassion. She has just been beaten. From that experience she knows that her old mother-in-law would not survive it. Second, the act is expiatory like the one in which she was sold to pay her father's debt when she was a child. There is some kind of psychological link between the two events, the difference being that while she was a victim before, now she does it out of free will.³⁷ What I want to add to these insights is that the heroine's choice is a brave moral act out of a sense of responsibility. In her present frustration with Heaven, her hope of a reward in the next life on the basis of how she lives in this life is much undermined. In other words, to save Ts'ai, she is just doing what she considers to be right at that moment, much less motivated by the hope of gaining a reward in an unknown, remote future. It is true that immediately after her confession of guilt she appeals to Heaven and Earth again. This is psychologically understandable: in view of the fact that she is not only to die but to die as a criminal, she has a desperate desire to justify herself and would cry out for help to anybody.

Eventually Tou O will restore her faith. I shall return to this question later. At present we need to dwell on her self-sacrifice as a tragic act. It is not, in the light of what has been said, unrelated to her previous actions. On the contrary, it has grown out of what she consistently has aimed at and strived toward. Her motivation has undergone discernible modification, from a desire for a better next life toward a more purified recognition of moral responsibility. So her death is the ultimate realization of what she has taken to be the meaning of her life and at the same time an assertion of her courageous moral will. She is able not only to accept a value just for its own sake but also to commit her life to it.

In fact, as a tragic figure Tou O is in many respects like the Antigone of Sophocles. The life of the Greek heroine is full of family disasters: as a child she saw the death of her mother as well as the ruin of her father, and just now her two brothers have taken each other's life in the battle-field. Even then, she would choose death to perform an obligation to a dead brother. But the similarities between her

---

³⁶ Shih's annotation in *Injustice to Tou O*, 181, the note to 11. 683-4.
³⁷ Chang Shu-hsiang, pp. 200-03.

and Tou O are not limited to external circumstances only. Antigone believes in a moral universe where the gods, comparable to Tou O's Heaven and Earth, uphold what she does. All the same, she feels deserted by the gods:

> What divine justice have I disobeyed?
> Why, in my misery, look to the gods for help?
> Can I call any of them my ally?
> I stand convicted of impiety,
> the evidence my pious duty done.
>
> (vv. 921-25)

And just before being led away to the tomb, she wails:

> O town of my fathers in Thebes' land,
> O gods of our house.
> I am led away at last.
> Look, leaders of Thebes,
> I am last of your royal line.
> Look what I suffer, at whose command,
> because I respected the right.
>
> (vv. 937-43)

Her belief in the gods, her frustrations with them, her final despairing appeal to them, and her firm belief in the righteousness of her deed and of her innocence are states of mind strongly reminiscent of Tou O's. More parallels can be drawn, but what has been said should justify the juxtaposition of the two heroines. One more resemblance, however, needs to be pointed out, that is, they both possess an indomitable will. Although all tragic personages must exercise their will, will is especially important to Antigone and Tou O because it is the only weapon they can fall back on.

The presence of the melodramatic is conspicuous in the ordeal of Antigone. When the play begins, all her pains are due to the fact that she happens to have been born into the house of Oedipus. As far as this is true, she is a victim of fate. On the other hand, that which marks her most prominently as an individual and a tragic figure is the unswerving exertion of her will toward a purpose. Tou O is conventional in her moral outlook, yet not more so than Antigone who is just doing what is right according to the gods. But what is radical about Tou O and also about Antigone is their courage and persistence to do what they think is right. Like Antigone, Tou O is for the most part of her life a melodramatic victim, but like her also she achieves a tragic stature by her commitment to a purpose, which composes the main action of *Tou O yüan*.

In this connection the title character of *Iphigénie en Aulide* is interesting as a contrast to Tou O and Antigone. In Racine's play, Agamemnon is tragic, who suffers extremely because of his decision to sacrifice Iphigénie, his daughter, in order to achieve military glory in Troy. Also tragic is Eriphile, who, led by a passion for Achille, follows Iphigenie to Aulide, where she is found out to be the daughter of Thésée and Hélène, originally also called Iphigénie, and therefore the Iphigénie as the demanded sacrifice to the goddess Diane. Notwithstanding, the play is above all the play of Iphigénie, whose lot is the chief emotional concern of the audience.

She is summoned out from home to Aulide by Agamemnon with the false reason that she will marry Achille. Soon after her arrival she learns that she has been deceived, that she will be sacrificed to Diane, and that her joy to be Achille's bride is a delusion. Now she must die in obedience to her father's wish, to spare him from the wrath of the Greeks, to whom he has promised to offer her as the sacrifice required by the gods.

> Ma vie est votre bien. Vous voulez le reprendre:
> Vos ordres sans détour pouvaient se faire entendre.
> D'un oeil aussi content, d'un coeur aussi soumis
> Que j'acceptais l'époux que vous m'aviez promis,
> Je saurai, s'il le faut, victime obéissante,
> Tendre au fer de Calchas une tête innocente.[38]

These words, which she says to Agamemnon when she finds out why she has to come to Aulide, form an image which is typical of her in the play: a passive, enduring, and innocent sufferer. Prior to the exposure of Eriphile's true identity, like Tou O, she has to die to fulfill a filial obligation, but the contrast between them is important. She never makes her own decision; her will is entirely submitted to Agamemnon's. To subject her to further grief, Agamemnon bids her to hate Achille, who has defied his authority on her account. Now, she has to treat her betrothed as an enemy or to disobey her father's command. The dilemma is beyond her capacity of endurance.

> Ah, sentence! ah, rigueur inouïe !
> Dieux plus doux, vous n'avez demandé que ma vie !
> Mourons, obéissons. Mais qu'est-ce que je voi ?
> Dieux ! Achille ?[39]

Achille enters. He threatens that he will kill Agamemnon and make a bloodshed at the altar if she offers herself there to be sacrificed. So she is crushed in the collision of two very proud men. Her suffering, entirely inflicted upon her from without, is melodramatic. Her role is one of submissive endurance, providing us with a foil to Tou O, who, like Iphigenia, Iphigénie's tragic prototype, seals her fate with an act of self-assertion. As a passing note, it can be mentioned that in Iphigénie we see how a character can experience the anguish of inner conflict without being tragic.

In the foregoing discussion, I hope I have shown that Tou O is tragic in a sufficient sense without playing down the melodramatic aspect of her story. At this point, perhaps I should consider the opposite view that Tou O is merely a melodramatic victim, as given by Chang Han-liang in his essay, "Kuan Han-ch'ing ti Tou O yüan: i ko t'ung-su chü" ["Kuan Han-ch'ing's *Tou O yüan*: a Melodrama," see note 1].

Mr. Chang's argument consists of two parts: the first gives the definitions of the tragic hero and the melodramatic man; the second attempts to prove that Tou O is one and is not the other. The tragic hero, according to him, possesses a number of

---

[38] *Oeuvres complètes* (Paris: Gallimard, 1950), I, Act IV, Scene iv. For a translation of *Iphigénie en Aulide*, see *The Complete Plays of Jean Racine*, trans. into English verse and with a Biographical Appreciation by Samuel Solomon, 2 vols. (New York: Random House, 1967).

[39] *Iphigénie en Aulide*, V. i.

qualities. In the first place, he has a flaw, which is usually *hybris*, namely, pride as expressed in the undaunted spirit of Greek humanism, but the tragic flaw can also be moral defects of the hero. In his *hybris* the tragic hero will trespass the moral universe in which moderation, the golden mean, is the rule. The conflict is not only external but also internal within the hero's soul. Moreover, the tragic hero needs to pass from the stage of ignorance to that of understanding, which is recognition, or in Chang's words, "acquisition of knowledge."[40]

In addition to the points as paraphrased above, Chang offers this definition:

> The tragic hero should be a solid, round, and three-dimensional character, but is not a personification of morality nor morality itself. Neither is his opponent the personification of evil. A perfect tragic hero is one of blood and flesh, capable of feelings and desires, of character development, and possessing psychological depth. On the contrary, the people in melodrama and farce are either good or bad, flat, conceptualized, and stereotyped.
>
> 悲劇英雄應當是一個三度空間的，立體的圓形人物。他既非道德的化身，更非道德本身；與他衝突的人亦非邪惡的化身。完美的悲劇人物造型有血有肉，有感覺有情慾，性格有變化，心理有深度。相反的，概念化的、類型固定的、忠奸判然的扁平人物便是通俗悲（或喜）劇人物。[41]

First of all, *hybris*, which is never mentioned in the *Poetics*, does not mean pride as defined by Chang. Rather it means "wanton disregard for the rights of others."[42] As to the issues of inner conflict, recognition, and guilt of whatever kind, I have already shown that whereas they are found in individual tragic heroes, they are not the necessary conditions of the tragic man.

At the same time, Chang's uses of the terms "tragedy" and "melodrama" are respectively honorific and abusive. Such uses, as have been commented upon, confuse the "type" with the "quality" of a literary work. The kind of melodrama he refers to was first brought to its conventional form and made popular by René Charles Guilbert de Pixerécourt (1773-1844), known in dramatic history as the father of melodrama, on the "boulevard du Temple" in Paris in the nineteenth century.[43] Rapidly it became also the prevalent dramatic event in England and America, and has survived in today's movies and television plays. Admittedly this drama is crude, and its char-

---

[40] Chang Han-liang, p. 135. Chang's views of tragedy which I summarized are expressed chiefly on pp. 130-31 of his article.

[41] Ibid., p. 132.

[42] H. J. Rose, *Religion in Greece and Rome* (New York: Harper, 1959), p. 29. Rose's description of *hybris* is quoted by Kaufmann in his discussion of the meaning of the word in Greek tragedy (*Tragedy and Philosophy*, pp. 73-79).

[43] The most comprehensive treatment of the nineteenth-century melodrama is Frank Rahill, *The World of Melodrama* (Univ. Park: Pennsylvania State Univ. Press, 1967). For studies on Pixerécourt, see Jules Marsan, "Le mélodrame et Guilbert de Pixerécourt," *Revue d'histoire littéraire de la France,* 7 (1900), 196-220; Willie Gustav Hartog, *Guilbert de Pixerécourt: sa vie, son mélodrame, sa technique et son influence* (Paris: H. Champion, 1913); and Alexander Lacey, *Pixerécourt and the French Romantic Drama* (Toronto: Univ. of Toronto Press, 1928).

acters are, as Chang has noticed, flat and stereotyped. But what many critics, including Mr. Chang, do not recognize is that the controlling vision of reality implicit in this vulgar form of melodrama is also, as has been pointed out earlier, the basic structural principle of much accomplished drama. Therefore, melodrama was not actually invented by Pixerécourt. It existed before him and has always been a major mode of literature.

I have tried to give a fair account of Mr. Chang's concepts of tragedy and melodrama in order to show where I disagree with him. But my disagreement is not only with his theoretical formulations but also with his treatment of the play *Tou O yüan*. According to Chang, Tou O, a mouthpiece of morality, is accusing Ts'ai of seducing Donkey Chang in these words: [44]

> Now your knot of hair is as white as snow,
> How can you wear the colorful silk veil?
> No wonder people say,
> You cannot keep a grown girl at home.
> Now you are about sixty years of age,
> Isn't it said that "when middle age arrives, all is over"?
> With one stroke, you mark off the memories of former love;
> Now you and this man act like newlyweds.
> To no purpose you make people split their mouths with laughter.
>
> 梳着箇霜雪般白鬏髻，怎將這雲霞般錦帕兜？怪不的女大不中留。你如今六旬左右。可不道到中年萬事休，舊恩愛一筆勾，新夫妻兩意投，枉把人笑破口。
>
> (Act I, "Hou t'ing hua" 後庭花)

Here, doubtless Tou O is a bit caustic; she is telling her mother-in-law that she, a sixty-year-old, would be a butt of the people's laughter to be a bride now and that what she has meant to do seems to convince her (Tou O) that a grown girl cannot be kept at home and that people would forget old love in their middle age. This is said immediately after Ts'ai reports that she has contracted herself and Tou O respectively to Old Chang and Donkey Chang in marriage. Given due consideration of its context and the speaker's satirical tone, the dramatic import of this passage is not to be missed. The question of seduction is not raised.

Or concerning the lyric "Liang-chou ti ch'i" 梁州第七 in Act II, Mr. Chang takes it also as a piece of pure moral preaching.[45] In it Tou O makes her points by referring to some historical and legendary stories, under the slanderous circumstance that Ts'ai has already taken home the Changs to stay with them as though they were members of the family. Again, she is satirical. She uses the story of Cho Wen-chün 卓文君 working lovingly with her husband as a barmaid in their tavern, and the story of the affectionate couple Meng Kuang 孟光 and Liang Hung 梁鴻 to compare with what is going on between Ts'ai and Old Chang. Then, in the "soup scene" that quickly follows the singing of this lyric by Tou O, the audience is allowed to understand her meaning. In there Ts'ai and Old Chang are showing affection for each other. Seeing them,

---

[44] Chang Han-liang, p. 133.
[45] Ibid., p. 134.

Tou O is so disgusted that she has to relieve her resentment in another lyric "Ho hsinlang" 賀新郎. And her later allusions to women of great courage and integrity in "Liang-chou ti ch'i" are only natural; she conjures them up as contrasts to Ts'ai and as models for her own emulation. This lyric is closely related to its context and reveals the tensions in Tou O's mind. Mr. Chang does not appear to see its dramatic significance nor the different functions of the first and second sets of allusions in the lyric. If Tou O were doing what Chang thought she did in the play, she would be merely a spokesman of morality. But the dramatic life in Tou O has obviously evaded his attention.

Tou O is tragic, but is *Tou O yüan* a tragedy? The question turns us back to our discussion of the play, which has already covered Act II. Act III begins with the scene in which Tou O is on her way to the place of execution. She scolds Heaven and Earth because of their failure to administer justice in this world. Even so, it is worth noting that up to this moment she has taken her grievance mainly as a single, isolated event, as indicated by her last words to Ts'ai:

Oh mother, do not cry or fret or complain to high Heaven.
It is I, Tou O, who has no luck,
And who has to suffer in confusion such great injustice.

婆婆也，再也不要啼啼哭哭，煩煩惱惱，怨氣衝天。這都是我做竇娥
的沒時運，不明不闇，負屈含冤。

(Act III, "Pao lao erh" 鮑老兒)

What she thinks of is clearly her own fate. Then, all of a sudden, she requests the executioner to hang a twelve-foot long piece of white silk on a flagpole, her reason being that when her head is cut off the blood will fly up to the silk-piece without one drop of it falling on the ground, as a sign that she has been unjustly convicted. Then she adds that her innocence will be vindicated by two more preternatural occurrences: first, there will be a heavy snowfall when she dies despite the fact that it is the hottest time of summer, and second, there will be a three-year drought in the Ch'u-chou District. From the lyrics she sings in that scene we learn that she has some specific persons in mind when she is making those wishes. In "Shua hai-erh" 耍孩兒 she refers to Ch'ang Hung 萇弘, whose blood, after he is unjustly killed as an official of the Chou 周 dynasty, turns into a green jade; to Tsou Yen 鄒衍 in "Erh sha" 二煞, for whom Heaven sends down frost even in the fifth month in the summer season when he is imprisoned in spite of his loyalty to King Hui 惠 of the state of Yen 燕; and to the filial woman of Tung-hai 東海, who is executed on a false charge of murdering her mother-in-law and whose death is followed by a three-year drought in the prefecture.[46] The poetic significance of these allusions is obvious: in the heroine's

---

[46] The stories of Ch'ang Hung, Tsou Yen, and the filial woman of Tung-hai can be found respectively in Wang Chia 王嘉, *Shih i chi* 拾遺記 (in *Han Wei ts'ung shu* 漢魏叢書), 3.6a-7a; *T'ai-p'ing yü lan* 太平御覽, comp. Li Fang 李昉 et al. (984; rpt. Peking: Chung-hua, 1960), 14 (I, 69): and Kan Pao 干寶, *Sou shen chi* 搜神記 (Shanghai: Sao yeh shan fang, 1922), 11.4b. The story of the filial woman of Tung-hai as recorded by Kan Pao is probably an expanded version of the same story in Pan Ku 班固, *Han shu* 漢書 (Peking: Chung-hua, 1962), 71 (pp. 3041-3042). Kuan Han-ch'ing seems to have based his play on the expanded later version. In *Injustice to Tou O* (pp. 4, 5, 215, 217), Professor Shih retold or translated all these stories, with references to their sources.

mind she now knows that she does not stand alone in suffering injustice. She takes the blood-turned jade, the summer frost, and the three-year drought as indications of Heaven's displeasure regarding those three victims of injustice. Now from these precedents she understands that Heaven does care, and that it is only the corrupt officials who answer for the pains of the people (Act II, "I sha" 一煞). Her mind is enlightened. No more does she confuse Heaven with these officials. As a result, she regains her faith and knows that her grievance is a part of the universal suffering of generations of people.[47]

It must be noted, however, that this is the melodramatic aspect of Tou O's story, which presents her as a victim. The tragic theme has not faded out of sight. It recurs with the appearance of Ts'ai who comes to see Tou O off to the execution court. Emotionally as well as morally the young woman is the stronger of the two. In this farewell scene, as she always does with Ts'ai, she plays the role of the protector. Now, the situation has altered; it is no longer one where the old woman needs moral admonition. So instead of blame, she gives her consolation. While mildly reminding her mother-in-law that she is involved in this tribulation for her sake, she urges her not to grieve anymore. This brief scene emphasizes again that the protagonist's death is a heroic consummation of a goal that she has made for her life. As in all other tragedies, the tragic in *Tou O yüan* co-exists with the melodramatic. They do not exclude but supplement each other, giving a more inclusive and balanced view of human suffering.

The fourth and last act of the play, because of its comical aspects, seems most detrimental to the claim of *Tou O yüan* as a tragedy. There is no denying that it raises a good deal of laughter. But so does Act II, in which the seriousness of the action does not seem to be nullified by the ridiculous judge. In this last act, the judge is Tou T'ien-chang 竇天章, Tou O's father, who seems to be a very funny person. Perhaps we should see how funny he really is.

At the beginning of the play he appears as a poor scholar who can only live in debt, unable to make a more secure survival for his daughter and himself. And worse, he sells her to Ts'ai, who then changes her name from Tou Tuan-yün 竇端雲 to Tou O (that is why he does not know who she is when he examines the court record of her case years later). In so doing, he pays his debt to Ts'ai and also obtains some money from her so that he can go to the capital for the imperial examination, the normal step taken by a scholar to enter into government service. Now he returns as the Imperial Surveillance Commissioner whose duty it is to discover and correct evil practices of government officials. It is in this capacity that his personality is further exposed to the audience.

Now, he is reviewing files of past cases. The first one he comes upon is Tou O's. It is commonsense that the more serious the case is, the more carefully it should be examined. But despite his recognition of the seriousness in Tou O's case, his attitude toward it betrays his shallow egotism: he is annoyed by the mere fact that the convict could have the same last name as his. So on the ground that it is a concluded case, he puts the file away, feels weary and falls asleep. Then he is wakened by Tou O's ghost. He holds up his sword and strikes the desk with it. (Characteris-

---

[47] Cf. Chang Shu-hsiang's views on Tou O's restoration of her faith, pp. 207-11. I am afraid that Miss Chang's interpretation is not wholly supported by the play.

tically, he does not attack the ghost.) He brags about his title and threatens to kill her. Soon his outward show gives way to his fear; he is entirely out of his wits.

But no sooner does he recognize who the ghost is than he starts a long, grandiloquent speech in the manner of a self-inflated judge and patriarch. It only displays his pompous moralism and his sheer ignorance that he should demand so much from Tou O for the name of their family and yet be utterly unaware how little he has done for her. In the trial on the following day, his incompetence is completely revealed in his dealing with Donkey Chang, who makes him sound like a fool. At his wits' end, he cries, "My wrongly slain child, this is an important court case. If you do not come to defend yourself, how can things be made clear?" 我那屈死的兒嗦，這一節是要緊的公案，你不自來折辯，怎得一個明白？ (Act IV, "court scene.")

Surely the author does not take such pains to portray him just for making him look funny. He is perhaps more humorous than the earlier judge, but certainly not more efficient. His ability comes far short of what the duties of his position require of him. He would never have vindicated Tou O if her ghost had not compelled him to pay attention to her. In a world where injustices abound, how can people be rendered justice by such a Surveillance Commissioner? He is the dramatist's image of the incompetent judge. That he is made to say the last word for the play signifies clearly that he is the kind of official whom people will look to for justice. And one wonders how much help he will be able to offer. On the surface he is an amusing character, but at a deeper level he is a cause of disappointment. In short he is ridiculous and sad.

Besides, the return of Tou O as a disquiet ghost should qualify the view that Act IV is a comical end tagged on to a melancholy drama. It is true that compared with Act III, it seems to be more on the humorous side. But in this act Tou O is, as she has always been, the focus of the dramatic action. That is to say, her mood is an important index to the tone of the act, and her ghost should inspire the audience with a sense of ruth and irrecoverable loss. Suffering as a central fact of the play is kept within view and not taken over by the comic. So Act IV is not exactly a happy conclusion of the play. Justice is done, but it is not what is called poetic justice. Although the wicked are punished and Tou O is vindicated, her death remains irremediable. If this ending is still considered to be too happy for a tragedy, I need only cite the example of *The Eumenides,* the last part of Aeschylus' tragic trilogy *Oresteia,* whose ending is not only happy but optimistic about the propects of human affairs. In comparison *Tou O yüan* finishes with a much less cheerful note; justice will not fare much better in the hands of such people as Tou T'ien-chang.

However, it is said that Tou O's return as a ghost to avenge and vindicate herself makes the play un-tragic and melodramatic.[48] This is a rather superficial view of the play. Again in *Oresteia,* the ghost of Clytemnestra returns to take revenge on her son, and has for this purpose the help of the horrible Furies, the goddesses of night and the underworld. Needless to say, this does not render Clytemnestra or the trilogy un-tragic. Nor does it make them melodramatic. In itself, it does not prove one or the other. On the other hand, there is a structural significance in the fact that Tou O comes back as a ghost in Act IV. Since the play is centered on Tou O, she gives meaning to all the incidents and, as it were, weaves them into the tragic story of her heroic commitment to a purpose. It is correct to say that she links Act IV

---

[48] Chang Han-liang, pp. 136-37.

with the previous acts, but it is more apt to say that she carries the action from Act III over to the last act. Her somber presence is a vivid reminder of what has just happened in Acts II and III. In this regard, the return of Tou T'ien-chang, who makes a short appearance in the Prologue and is absent until the last act, gives a sense of completion to the action, too.[49]

In my discussion of *Tou O yüan,* I have tried to give an objective analysis of the work. I hope I have been speaking for the play instead of making it speak for my concept of tragedy. In other words, I have argued that *Tou O yüan* is a tragedy in its own right; it has all the elements of a tragedy, which need only be recognized. It is my contention that tragedy was created not only by the Greeks, but has also existed outside Western culture. The tragic in Chinese literature is yet to be discovered and explored. Besides *Tou O yüan,* there are other Yüan plays that are rich in tragic implications, such as *Hu-tieh meng* 蝴蝶夢, *Han-kung ch'iu* 漢宮秋, *Huang-liang meng* 黃粱夢, *Ch'ü-chiang ch'ih* 曲江池, *Huan lao mo* 還牢末, *Ho han-shan* 合汗衫, *Cheng pao-en* 爭報恩, *Chao-shih ku-erh* 趙氏孤兒, *Pao chuang ho* 抱粧盒. Whether they are tragedies is a challenge to students of Chinese drama. I believe that a study of these and other Chinese plays may lead to a sound and solid view of Chinese tragedy, to which this discussion is meant to be a preliminary effort.

---

[49] Chang Shu-hsiang, p. 213.

Peasant Dialectics:
Reflections on Brecht's Sketch of a Dilemma

Antony Tatlow

天下莫柔弱於水而攻堅強者莫之能勝[1]

In a work famous for the power of its suggestion and the beauty of its language, this must surely be one of the most intriguing passages. It is a fascinating and classic expression of a peasant dialectic, for it fuses the sharp observation of natural particularity with the social hopes of a class of survivors. In rejecting the "virtues" required of them in a feudal society, the Taoists here align their concept of social cohesion with the direction of natural process.

The matter of subsequent and traditional attitudes to the *Tao Te Ching* does not here directly concern us. The question of a culture's self-understanding depends upon the degree of that culture's sense of homogeneity, upon the extent of any agreement about the determinants of that culture and about the evaluation of the products of those determinants. With the vast social changes that have occurred in this century, that concensus has now disappeared.

The later variants of that mechanistic theory which sees cultural forms, works of art and literature, simply as direct reflections of social relationships has been discredited. The connection between economic base and cultural superstructure cannot be accounted for so simply since it is mediated by many interposing factors. Certain areas of the superstructure can without question be more directly related to the economic base—the law and property relations, for example—but this cannot be maintained for other areas except in a much more general sense, though it is true that they often reflect unconsciously and can certainly be consciously used as ideological weapons for the preservation or alteration of the relations of production. If works of literature are in some sense the products of historically determinable factors, they also have the power

---

[1] *Tao Te Ching*, Ch. 78. In D. C. Lau's translation: "In the world there is nothing so submissive and weak as water. Yet for attacking that which is hard and strong nothing can surpass it." Lao Tzu, *Tao Te Ching* (Middlesex: Penguin, 1963), p. 140.

which can be adopted as an act of will by the intellectual élite who can alone secure the necessary social transformations:

> Apart from Dostoievsky, no mind in the last ten years has made so strong an impact as Lao Tse's on the young students of Germany who have been so disturbed by the war. That this movement is taking place in a fairly small minority in no way detracts from its importance; the minority that has been effected is precisely the one that matters: the most gifted, most conscious, most responsible section of student youth.[6]

Brecht's response stands against this background.

During his exile in Denmark in the thirties Brecht began to gather anecdotes in which he embodied and refracted the problems of his times and which he entitled: *Me-ti, Buch der Wendungen*.[7] He possessed and carefully read the German sinologist Alfred Forke's translation of Mo-tse 墨子. Brecht's observation of the dialectical quality in the writing and of the concern with practicality and his appreciation of the anecdotal style in some sections of the work all help to explain his own title. Among the papers in the Brecht Archives there is an unpublished note which suggests another reason for the title:

> Exiled in a half-fascist country Bertolt Brecht wrote a "Book of Experiences" from which the following story derives. To disguise the authorship it is written as if it derived from an old Chinese historian.[8]

Brecht's caution was in all probability not solely in response to the fascist threat for he criticized Stalinist shibboleths as well.

Although most of the book is devoted to an analysis of European events in a Chinese disguise, Brecht's *Me-ti* contains many fascinating refractions of Chinese thought. As an example of Brecht's delineation of a peasant dialectic we may consider:

> *Wei and Yen's inability to keep discipline*
>
> Winter, the worst season, surprised the enemy in a land almost deprived of food. The laziness of the peasants, caused by the cruelty of the landowners, was responsible, and the peasants were sufficiently self-seeking to remove and hide all their own provisions. The enemy army grew extremely hungry.
> The inconsiderate and unscrupulous people of Hao who

---

[6] Hermann Hesse, *Gesammelte Werke* (Frankfurt: Suhrkamp, 1970), XII, 27.

[7] We may describe it as a book of practical dialectics. The title is a pun on the usual German translation of *I Ching* which is *Buch der Wandlungen*. "Wendung" means "turn," as in "turn of phrase" or "(unexpected) turn of events"; it can also mean "change." "Wandlung" can only mean "change."

[8] Bertolt Brecht Archiv, 1334/145.

had been educated to observe all the military virtues seized the landowners and slaughtered most of them, for they could produce no food. But then their army disintegrated in the terrible famine and fled to the border. The mass of the people of Hao perished in those border regions which they had laid waste.

In the spring the peasants crawled out of their huts again and, as Yen had hoped, their old weakness, selfishness, appeared again to an astonishing degree. The landowners had been killed by the enemy or were cowed and defenceless and the peasants, sure of being able to bring home their own harvest, began to sow like men possessed. Wei prospered.

When the good ruler Yen died, it could be truthfully said that he had won a great war without military victories, simply through the cowardice of his subjects, and that without government decrees or warnings he had transformed the land of Wei into a garden.[9]

This anecdote fascinates for several reasons. Before tracing the characteristic twists of Brecht's dialectic, we recall how the strife between states is a primary topic in Mo-tse. That work also distinguished deprived though indolent peasants and their grasping superiors.

Brecht suggests specific causes for this indolence and implies certain remedies. The good ruler Yen finally achieves his aim through a policy of non-intervention which in some sense relates to the Taoist principle of *"wu wei"* 無為. Yen places his faith in the natural egoism and in the saving pusillanimity of the people. Yet this Taoist ending to the anecdote is surely not the point of the story, for the good ruler Yen could never have achieved his aim without the unwelcome assistance from the martial people of Hao who have no qualms whatsoever about killing the alien landowners, tolerated by the people of Wei under the good ruler Yen's benevolence.

We can see, therefore, that Wei's prosperity was inhibited by its system of land tenure and that the people of Wei themselves actively accomplished nothing which could be regarded as the direct cause of the alteration of that system. The anecdote shows how one set of hard men destroys another and that the non-combattant victims of both survive and eventually prosper. This anecdote therefore presents a dilemma and, in terms of Brecht's work and of a transferral of this peasant dialectic beyond its own framework, a criticism of the efficacy of such an ethic, whilst at the same time demonstrating its manifest success on this occasion.

There are in Brecht's work of the late thirties and early forties, those times of "confusion and disorder," three topics which relate to the Taoist peasant dialectic: the critique of virtues, the strategy of survival and the problem of natural process.

It is plain enough that there can be no question, in any Marxist context, of a consistent principle of non-contention, whether it be Taoist or Tolstoian in character. On the other hand it would be patently dogmatic and undialectical to insist that non-contention never solves anything. Tolstoy was particularly interested in the Taoist principle of *"le non-agir"* which he had encountered through a French translation

---

[9] Bertolt Brecht, *Gesammelte Werke* (werkausgabe) (Frankfurt: Suhrkamp, 1967), XII, 544.

and ultimately inefficacious peasant dialectic which no serious Marxist could ever think of applying to modern problems. Or we can say that they illustrate utopian hope, open to similar objections. Or we can consider whether there is not contained in such a dialectic a core of valuable experience which may offer something more substantial than a sense of nostalgia for an agrarian past or an inaccessible future.

For some years now a new sensibility about man's relationship to the natural world has slowly begun to question the wisdom of a life of piracy. Some social groups are more acutely conscious than others of the scale and inevitable consequences of such steady depredation. As the epitome of economic and social pillage, imperialism still thrives in ecological terms. Whilst the protest against the values of such exploitive strategies has taken often dramatic but always more obvious shape in the ideological "West," there is also in the advanced industrial societies of Eastern Europe a strong sense of discomfort which, because of the greater role played by theoretical questions in public life, immediately effects discussion of philosophical principles and of the forms of social organization which allow such exploitive strategies to unfold. In Eastern Europe we can discern what I have heard called "a certain absence of theory," a sense of the inadequacy of established dogma. We may be witnessing the beginning of the end of that tenacious, essentially nineteenth century mechanical materialism in favor of a more truly dialectical form. The new subjectivism in poetry is a signal of this sense of change. The problems of ecology simply remind us that natural and social philosophy are ultimately inseparable—something which was well understood in China.

The philosophy adequate to the demands of natural and social ecology might be termed radical organicism.[20] And here, no matter how provocative such an assertion must appear, something may be learnt from the Taoist peasant dialectic. The deep peasant suspicion of outsiders derived from the observation that such intruders merely deprived the peasant producers of the means of subsistence. *Mo-tse* and the *Tao Te Ching* both have much to say about such institutionalized robbery. The Chinese peasant text envisages a time when there will be no such intruders and the egalitarian peasant cooperative would eliminate the impediments to democracy. What distinguishes Taoist thinking is the quality of its perception of the relationship between such values and natural process.

In the West organicism has invariably connoted political conservatism, but organic naturalism in China involved no such connotations although the Neo-Confucianists undoubtedly later integrated it with a hierarchical social system. The Tao, the order of Nature, does not govern by force but by "a kind of natural curvature in space and time."[21] The sage must work as the Tao, not as the ideal Confucian ruler from above, but from within and from behind. The water symbol, so important for Taoism as an image of process, expresses the ideal of a feminine yieldingness which Needham has

---

[20] The mechanical materialism of earlier days has been totally discredited by modern science. However, its political consequence, the Stalinist revolution from above, administered through an ubiquitous bureaucracy, is still about us. A properly understood "dialectical materialism" might serve as another term for what I mean by radical organicism. Briefly, such dialectical materialism implies the interpenetration and inseparability of the "material" and the "spiritual"; it also implies individual involvement in and the nuturing of a recognition of the reality of individual responsibility for forms of social organization.

[21] Joseph Needham, *Science and Civilisation in China* (Cambridge: Cambridge Univ. Press, 1962), II, 37.

called "the poetical expression of a cooperative collectivist society."[22] What this can mean in political terms may be deduced from the following passage in *Chuang Tse*:

> The hundred parts of the body . . . are all complete in their places. Which should one prefer? Do you like them all equally? . . . Are they all servants? Are these servants unable to control one another and need another as ruler? Or do they become rulers and servants in turn? Is there any true ruler other than themselves?[23]

We have seen how Brecht made use of the Taoist image of process which, unlike its Heracleitan counterpart, was linked with a social prediction. There is also evidence in Brecht's *Me-ti* and elsewhere of speculation strikingly akin to Taoist attitudes:

Occupation with Morality

> There are few occupations, said Me-ti, which so damage a man's morality than the occupation with morality. I hear people say: One must love truth, one must keep one's promises, one must fight for the Good. But the trees do not say: one must be green, one must drop the fruit vertically to earth, one must rustle the leaves when the wind passes.[24]

This may remind us of another Chinese assumption: that morality is more a matter of that good government which, attuned to natural process, allows men to develop their potential. The problem lies in establishing the necessary constraints.

Whilst all modern culture depends upon an immensely complex process of differentiation, and hence a return to any peasant cooperative would be a denial of all that has been enabled by transcending it, this very process of differentiation has also produced social behavior that now forces us to acknowledge natural constraints and limitations. We must now learn to live with nature, and not against it, in a natural-social continuum which is not at war with itself. It is first of all a matter of consciousness. Perhaps a radical organicism might both achieve and develop from a sudden shift of consciousness, like the blow from a Zen monk, which would enable us to overcome that debilitating sense of alienation from nature which Marx also deplored but which the administrators of his nineteenth century testament have yet to dispel.[25] It will, however, need more than a blow from a monk to translate any such recognition into social praxis.

---

[22] Ibid., II, 59.
[23] Ibid., II, 52.
[24] *Werke*, XII, 504.
[25] Marx is full of surprises. For example: "Atheism, as a denial of this non-essentiality (of nature and of man) no longer makes sense, for atheism is a negation of God and through this negation posits the existence of man; but socialism as socialism no longer needs any such mediation; it begins with the theoretical and practical sensual consciousness of man and of nature as essence." *MEGA*, III, 125.

> . . . Underlying this application are the tacit assumptions that comparable features and qualities exist between Chinese and Western literatures and that comparable standards are applicable to both. Deferring consideration of the question whether these assumptions are true or not, we may take note of three beneficial effects that the comparative approach has had: first, it has brought fresh insights to Chinese literature; second, it has placed Chinese literature in a wider perspective, thus helping avoid cultural chauvinism or parochialism; third, it has made Chinese literature more accessible to non-specialists. To enlarge on the last point: it is due to the efforts of comparativist students of Chinese literature that scholars in Western literature and comparative literature have recently become more aware of—and interested in—Chinese literature. . . . On the other hand, the application of Western critical approaches to Chinese literature raises some serious questions. How far are critical methods and standards derived solely from Western literature valid when applied to Chinese literature, given the widely divergent cultural environments in which the two literatures have been produced? Should we totally ignore traditional Chinese critical concepts and standards, dismiss them lightly as being too vague or outmoded? And if not, how far are they intelligible and acceptable to us? Are there universal qualities and features of literature, universally applicable criteria for the evaluation of literary works? Should we be content with historical and cultural relativism; or should we aspire to be trans-historical and trans-cultural? . . . Furthermore, it would be desirable to attempt a synthesis of Chinese and Western theories of literature and of critical concepts and methods, so as to provide the study of Chinese literature with both a theoretical basis and a practical methodology (28-29 passim).

The three most important journals (in reverse chronological order) for promoting studies of literary relations between China and the rest of the world are numbers 12, 9, and 2 listed earlier. These journals, especially 12 and 9, endeavor to attract relevant articles, so that this focusing of materials can help to minimize the time-consuming search in periodicals not specifically comparative as well as communicate such research more economically.

The serious student of East-West literary relations will certainly peruse the three above-mentioned journals on a regular basis. A special feature of these journals is to promote conferences on Oriental-Western literary relations and to publish the proceedings. Although uneven in quality, these published proceedings have the advantage of concentrating a wide variety of scholarly views on Oriental-Western relations. These and other proceedings are listed below in chronological order:

a) Indiana University Conference.
[*Proceedings of the First Conference on*] *Oriental-Western Literary Relations*, ed. Horst Frenz and G. L. Anderson. University of North Carolina

Studies in Comparative Literature, No. 13. Chapel Hill: Univ. of North Carolina Press, 1955.

This conference took place in 1954 and was the first of a series helping Western scholars to become better informed about the largely neglected area of Asia's cultural heritage. The essays are divided into four sections: Poetics; Modern Oriental Literature; Issues and Ideas; and Discussion of Oriental-Western Cultural Relations, Translation Problems, and the Teaching of Oriental Literature.

b) Indiana University Conference.
Asia and the Humanities: Papers Presented at the Second Conference on Oriental-Western Literary and Cultural Relations, ed. Horst Frenz. Bloomington, Ind.: Comparative Literature Committee, Indiana Univ., 1959.

This conference took place in 1958 and emphasized cultural understanding (as opposed to political considerations) as a basis for all future relations between East and West. Papers are divided into four sections: Literature, Philosophy, the Arts, Cultural Values, Cultural Understanding, and Miscellaneous Discussions.

c) Indiana University Conference.
[Proceedings of the] Third Conference on Oriental-Western Literary and Cultural Relations, ed. Horst Frenz. *Yearbook of Comparative and General Literature,* 11 (1962), 119-236.

Meeting in June of 1962, this conference devoted itself primarily to the discussion of drama and theatre, fiction, poetry, literary criticism, and folklore, with a special emphasis on the cultural interrelations between the Far East and the West. Issued as a supplement to *YCGL*.

d) Indiana University Conference.
[Proceedings of the] Fourth Conference on Oriental-Western Literary and Cultural Relations, ed. Horst Frenz. *YCGL,* 15 (1966), 157-224.

This conference, held in 1966, concentrated on East-West cultural interchanges, particularly in the visual arts, literary criticism, poetry, and drama. Issued as a supplement to *YCGL*.

e) Tamkang College of Arts and Sciences.
Proceedings from International Comparative Literature Conference [On Chinese-Western Relations], ed. Yen Yuan-shu. Taipei: Western Literature Research Institute, Tamkang College of Arts & Sciences, 1972.

Published in a double issue (525 pp.) of the *Tamkang Review* 2, No. 2 (1971) and 3, No. 1 (1972). This First Conference held in Taiwan in 1971 is described by A. Owen Aldridge, one of the participants, in *YCGL,* 21 (1972), 65-70.

f) Indiana University Conference.
"Islam in World Literature." *[Symposium held During the] Fifth Conference on Oriental-Western Literary and Cultural Relations,* ed. Horst Frenz. *YCGL,* 20 (1971), 57-88.

This symposium was held in 1970 and the Islamic topics seem to have been the only material published from the conference.

Literary Relations," 295
"Problems in the Study of Literature," 4
Proceedings from International Comparative Literature Conference, 297
Proceedings from the Second International Comparative Literature Conference, 298
Propp, Vladimir, 122, 195, 196, 202-3, 205, 214, 215
Proteus, 219
Proust, Marcel, 173
Průšek, Jaroslav, 292
Psychology of Tragedy, the. 97
Pulleyblank, E. G., 86
Pushkin, A. S., 3

R

Racine, Jean, 253, 254, 261, 268-9
Raleigh, Sir Walter, 73
Rank, Otto, 195
"Rapids by the Luans," 155
Rapport sur le "Dictionnaire International des Termes Littéraires," 291-2
Rea, Kenneth, 236
"Rebirth of the Monk Poet Han Shan, the," 92
"Reciting Alone in the Mountain," 78
Reeve, Clara, 165
Reichwein, Adolf, 219
Reimann, 283
Reinhardt, Max, 228
Remak, Henry, 47
Republic, 218
Richardson, Samuel, 165
Rise of the Novel, the, 166
Robbe-Grillet, Alain, 163
Roger, Jacques, 54
Romantic Generation of Modern Chinese Writers, the, 300
Romeo and Juliet, 263
Rose, Ernst, 54
Rosenbaum, Peter, 140-1
Rousseau, Jean Jacques, 172
Rousset, Jean, 50
Ryder, Japhy, 90

S

Said, Edward, 300
San-kuo yen-i, 168, 169, 171, 172

Sardou, Victorien, 225
Sawyer, Albert, 103
Schlegel brothers, the, 175
Schnitzler, Arthur, 232
Schweyk in the Second World War, 282
Scott, A. C., 233
Scribe, Eugene, 225
"Second Thoughts on Currents and Periods," 45
Secrets of the Chinese Drama, 227
Sesar, Carl Gordon, 300
Seven Ages of the Theatre, the, 225
"Shadowy, Luxuriant," 109
Shakespeare, William, 40, 85, 132, 183, 223, 225, 227, 239-50, 253-4, 257, 258-9, 261; in China, 247-50
Shaw, George Bernard, 232, 249
Shen Chi-chi, 195, 206
Shen Te-fu, 175
Shih Ching (The Book of Songs), 71, 72, 75, 78, 181
Shih-p'in, 37
Shih Te, 87, 91
Shing-Moo, 219
Shklovskij, Viktor, 3, 4, 195, 205-8, 211
Shui-hu chuan, 169, 171, 172, 179
Shulman, Frank Joseph, 301
"Singing Aloud," 78
"Sir Patrick Spence," 121, 122
Sixth Conference on Oriental-Western Literary and Cultural Relations, 298
Snyder, Gary, 85, 89-91
Sophocles, 252, 254-7, 258, 259-61, 267-9
"Sophora Walk," 154
Sorrow of Han, the, 227
"South of the River," 123, 124
Southern, Richard, 225
Spenser, Edmund, 69, 71, 72-6
Spring Willow Society, the, 232
Ssu-k'ung T'u, 26, 28, 30
Ssu-ma Hsiang-ju, 56
Ssu-pu pei-yao, 133
St. John of the Cross, 25
St. Teresa, 25
Staël, Madame de, 175
Staiger, Emil, 2
Stallknecht, Newton P., 295, 299
Stanislavsky, Konstantin, 227
Sterne, Laurence, 163, 170, 173

Stowe, Harriet Beecher, 232, 248
Strindberg, August, 232
"Study of Chinese Literature in the West: Recent Developments, Current Trends, Future Prospects, the," 295-6
"Study of Han Shan, a," 86
"Study of Poetry, the," 39
Su Hsüeh-lin, 62-3
Su Shun-ch'in (Su Tzu-mei), 36
Su Tung-p'o, 20-1, 26, 28; Su Shih, 38, 58
"Substantive Level, the," 127-9
Sui-yüan shih-hua, 37-8, 39, 41
"Summer near the River," 78-83
Sun K'ai-ti, 178
"Sun on the Silk,: Ezra Pound and Confucianism, the," 301
Sung Ch'i, 61
Sung Yü, 55
Syllabus of Comparative Literature, 290
"Symposium on Periods," 45
Synge, John Millington, 232
Szili, Joseph, 59

T

T'ai-ho cheng-yin p'u, 36
Taine, Hippolyte, 1
Tale of Genji, 176
T'an Cheng-pi, 63
T'ang I-ch'iao, 100
T'ang-shih san-pai-shou, 129, 137
T'ao Ch'ien, 58, 199
Tao Te Ching, 277, 279, 282, 284
Tay, William, 295, 301
Teele, Roy E., 293
Temple, Sir William, 217
Teng Sui-ning, 248
Theatre in Our Time, the, 226
Theatre in the East, 236
Theatre: Three Thousand Years of Drama, Acting and Stagecraft, the, 222-3
Theories of Literature in the Twentieth Century, 292
Third Conference on Oriental-Western Literary and Cultural Relations, 297
Thun-Ton, 219
T'ien Han, 248
"To P'ei Ti from the Cottage on the Wang River," 160-1

Todorov, Tzvetan, 195, 197, 203, 205, 211-2, 215-6
Tolstoy, Leo, 3, 4, 206, 281-2
Tomashevsky, Boris, 3, 195, 196, 202-3, 210-1
Tou O yüan, 251, 263-75
"Touchstones," 33, 38-41
Toulmin, Stephen, 11
Trojan Woman, the, 252, 255, 263
Tsang Mao-hsün, 263-4
Ts'ao Chih, 58, 65
Ts'ao Hsüeh-ch'in, 57
Ts'ao Pi, 43
Ts'ao Yü, 232-3, 237
Ts'ao Yü: The Reluctant Disciple of Chekhov and O'Neill, 217, 300
Tso-chuan, 55
Tu Fu, 34, 35, 56, 58, 63, 65, 92, 96, 141-2, 148, 149
Tu Kuang-t'ing, 87
Tu Mu, 63, 142-3
"Tui-yü pien-hsieh chung-kuo wen-hsüeh shih ti chi-tien i-chen," 64-5
"Tune of the K'ung-hou Harp, the," 112-4, 124
Turandot, 219
Turandot oder der Kongress der Wiesswäscher, 228
Turgenev, Ivan, 232
"Twenty Poems on the Wang River, the," 142
"Twenty-seven Poems by Han Shan," 89
Tynjanov, Jurij, 4
Tz'u-p'in, 41
Tzu-ssu, 55
"Tzu-yeh Songs," 78, 79, 82

U

Uncle Tom's Cabin, 232, 248
Upton, John, 74
Utopia, 218

V

Vakhtangov, Eugene, 227, 228
"Valediction, Forbidding Mourning, A," 82
Van Dijk, Teun A., 196-7
"Verfremdungseffekte in der Chinesischen Schauspielkunst" ("Alienation Effects in

THE LIBRARY
ST. MARY'S COLLEGE OF MARYLAND
ST. MARY'S CITY, MARYLAND 20686